A HISTORY OF POLITICAL PHILOSOPHY

THE OLD KING, by Georges Rouault

A History of
POLITICAL PHILOSOPHY

HENRY J. SCHMANDT

Associate Professor of Political Science
University of Wisconsin — Milwaukee

THE BRUCE PUBLISHING COMPANY | *Milwaukee*

Library of Congress Catalog Card Number: 60–10556

© 1960 The Bruce Publishing Company
MADE IN THE UNITED STATES OF AMERICA

PREFACE

THE subject of politics involves more than the administration of public affairs, more than the structure and organization of governments, more than the periodic and colorful election campaigns. It embraces human aspirations, ideals, beliefs, and values. It deals with theory as well as practice, philosophy as well as technical skills. Politics is dynamic and pervasive; its hand can be observed in all the social strivings of mankind. Behind governmental institutions and processes lie tradition, theory, and philosophy which provide deep and sophisticated insight into political reality. From Plato's academy to the great universities and colleges of today, the study of political philosophy — of the ideas that helped to shape our social heritage — has received warm and appreciative reception.

The present volume is primarily an historical treatment and analysis of political philosophy as it has found expression in the writings of major theorists. The works chosen for discussion are those that have been influential in developing the political thought of the western world. They range from the social speculations of the ancient Greeks to the modern efforts to formulate a political theory based wholly on empirical research. They include the ethics of Aristotle and the amoralism of Machiavelli, the constitutionalism of Cicero and the totalitarianism of Stalin, the natural law of Thomas Aquinas and the economic determinism of Marx, the democracy of Attlee and the dictatorship of Hitler.

Selection and emphasis in a survey that covers almost 2500 years in time inevitably give rise to difficult decisions. Personal predilection cannot fail but influence the author's judgment and choice. Some of the material that he includes, others would omit as of little consequence; some that he neglects, others would feel indispensable to the subject. The area of discretion is large, the opportunity for error great. Regardless of individual choice, a survey of this nature must give an integrated and meaningful picture of the field if it is to serve its purpose. Efforts have therefore been made in this volume to concentrate on those aspects of political thinking that are (1) fundamental to an understanding of the state and man's relation to it; and (2) relevant to contemporary political life. An attempt has also been made to set the entire work within a common

v

frame of reference so that comparison and evaluation of the various theories can be more readily made.

The author makes no pretense to originality of interpretation or profundity of analysis. A HISTORY OF POLITICAL PHILOSOPHY is intended principally as a text for the college student, although it is hoped that the general reader who is interested in political fundamentals will find it of value. The book is designed for either a one or two semester course in the political science, history, or general social science curriculum. If used in a two semester course, more extensive assignments can be made in the original works. For this purpose references to pertinent selections from the originals are included in the Appendix. These materials supplement the text and provide an excellent means for acquainting the reader with the great theorists themselves. No treatment or commentary, regardless of its adequacy, can take the place of original sources. Fortunately, there is now available a growing list of inexpensive paper-bound editions of important political treatises that make supplemental reading of original materials more feasible and convenient for classroom use. A partial list of these is also contained in the Appendix.

The author wishes to thank his former colleagues in the Department of Government at St. Louis University who contributed valuable suggestions, advice, and criticism for this volume. He also wishes to acknowledge his indebtedness to the many scholars who have dealt extensively with specific phases of the total field of political theory and from whom he has borrowed heavily. Others, including the students in his political science classes, have aided in one way or another in the preparation of this manuscript. Appreciation is due to all of them for their kindness, patience, and assistance.

HENRY J. SCHMANDT

CONTENTS

PART ONE | INTRODUCTION

Chapter I

POLITICAL PHILOSOPHY: ITS MEANING AND SIGNIFICANCE

"Give instruction to a wise man and he will be yet wiser" (*Prov.* 9:9).

FROM the time that speculation about the nature of the social, as distinguished from the physical, universe first began over 2500 years ago, political theory has attracted the great minds of all ages. No field of human knowledge and culture has been left untouched by the passion for political speculation. Included in the imposing list of those who have sought to probe into the nature of political phenomena are theologians, such as St. Augustine, Maimonides, St. Thomas Aquinas, and Calvin; philosophers, including Plato, Aristotle, Kant, Hegel, and Maritain; poets as famous as Dante and Coleridge; novelists as different as Dostoevski, Hawthorne, and Orwell; scientists of the eminence of Priestley and Huxley; mathematicians as noted as Einstein; and statesmen of the caliber of Cicero, Burke, Calhoun, and Wilson. This deep interest and concern is hardly surprising since man is, as Aristotle described him, a political animal. Wherever he is found, he exists in a political society of some sort. So intimately is his whole life woven into the complex fabric of this society that it would indeed be strange if he did not seek to explore beneath the surface of social realities.

Men have always asked questions about themselves, their environment, their role in the universe, and the purpose and end of their existence. It is as though they have been led by an innate and impelling necessity to seek the answers to these fundamental queries. And from this never ending but persistent quest for truth, a treasury of thought has emerged — challenging, provocative, stimulating, and enlightening — that has broadened the vista of human knowledge and understanding. Occupying a pivotal

3

position in this process has been the speculation about man as a political animal, a member of civil society.

THE MEANING OF POLITICAL THEORY

The term "political theory" is used in various senses. It may mean a set of hypotheses about governmental processes or institutions, or it may refer to the moral principles and norms that regulate political behavior. In either case, it denotes an organized set of ideas which seek to explain reality. Political theory, moreover, may be used for different objectives. It may simply seek a better understanding of governmental functions; it may attempt to provide the policy makers with principles that will aid them in coping with specific sociopolitical problems; or it may endeavor to provide a set of norms for judging what is ethically good in political life.

As originally understood, the study of political theory was an attempt to acquire genuine knowledge about political fundamentals. These fundamentals included, as professor Leo Strauss has observed, two groups of subject matter: (1) the nature of political institutions and forces such as governmental organizations, laws, programs, interest groups, power, and social custom; and (2) the morally proper or just political order.[1] In modern times there has been a tendency to regard these two aspects of political theory as completely separate fields of inquiry. The first has come to be referred to as political science (or causal theory as one writer recently called it[2]); the second as political philosophy.

In terms of the above distinction, we are in the realm of political philosophy as soon as we begin to ask the question, "what is the common good or the good society." This type of theory examines the moral premises and postulates that underlie the political and social system. It is concerned with ends and goals that ought to be pursued by political society. It seeks to answer questions dealing with the purpose of the state, the moral justification of political power, and the dividing line between governmental authority and human freedom. It inquires into the manner in which political power ought to be used and the moral limitations that should be placed upon it. Since these are questions that deal primarily with ends or final values, the answers to them cannot be empirically

---

[1] "On Classical Political Philosophy," Social Research, Feb., 1945, p. 98.
[2] See David Easton, The Political System (New York: Knopf and Co., 1953), p. 52.

verified; they can only be presented in the light of man's nature and his place in the universe. Catlin describes political theory of this kind as part of the "seamless robe of philosophy, philosophy speaking with a social emphasis."[3]

Used in the causal sense, political theory refers to a set of concepts about political facts and the relations among them. Its objective is to bring order and meaning to a mass of data that would otherwise remain disconnected and purposeless. It pursues its task by constructing certain hypotheses about the processes of government from empirical investigations (by observation and experience) into political phenomena. Robert Michels' "iron law of oligarchy" is an illustration of theoretical formulation in the political sphere just as the law of diminishing returns is in the field of economics. From a study of political parties and social groups, Michels concludes that all organizations tend to concentrate power into the hands of a small group of elite.[4] His so-called law is a theory since it seeks to explain the phenomenon of power in all organized groups and not merely in those which he actually investigated.

While it is helpful in the interests of clarity and orderly research to distinguish between political philosophy and causal theory, it is also important to keep in mind that each is a facet of political science in the broad sense of the term. All thinking about ends and moral norms takes place within an historical context while all political behavior has ethical implications. Classical thought regards the relationship between political science and political philosophy not as that between one field of inquiry and another but as between the way and the goal. Any comprehensive political theory, in the traditional meaning, must consist of a set of logically related propositions about what is and what ought to be the case in civic matters. The political philosopher as well as the political scientist is interested in knowing whether selected means will accomplish given ends. Causal theory is necessary to show the connection between the means used and the end to be pursued. What procedures, for example, or what institutional devices will best assure that political power will be used for the common good and not for the selfish interests of a few? The political philosopher may hold that the ultimate goal of the state is the creation of a social and cultural environment in which each indi-

---

[3] George Catlin, "Political Theory: What Is It?" *Political Science Quarterly*, Mar., 1957, p. 23.

[4] *Political Parties: A Sociological Study of the Oligarchical Tendencies of Modern Democracy* (Glencoe: Free Press, 1949).

vidual has the material and educational means to maximize his inherent potentialities. But how are the means to be selected for attaining this objective? Here we must turn to causal theory or political science (as narrowly defined) for guidance.

Legitimate inquiry into political morality cannot take place in a vacuum. Such investigation requires knowledge about the phenomena of political life; it can be explored only in relation to factual conditions. No worthwhile theory was ever derived from an analysis of human nature considered apart from its particularization in a changing time and space context. However, since political philosophy deals with the moral ideals embodied in political institutions, and political science with the operations and effects of these institutions, it is possible to orient a treatment of political theory toward one or the other. The present text is weighted on the side of political philosophy. It is interested in penetrating (through the speculations of the great thinkers) into the ideas and purposes that social institutions embody and the ethical values they represent. In this way, it seeks to obtain a "comprehensive picture of political life that relates our living together in a common political entity with our private and general ends and our final aims."[5]

It has been charged that political theory as an academic discipline has been intellectually sterile because of its historical preoccupation with the ethical study of politics. Although there is a measure of truth in this criticism, the analysis of the crucial moral questions of political society can never become outdated. Unlike the subject matter of the physical disciplines, the subject matter of political science has moral dimensions that cannot be disregarded by the investigator. Moreover, an approach which stresses political philosophy need not avoid involvement with causal theory. On the contrary, it can endeavor to relate such theory to the matter of ultimate ends and goals. There is no incompatibility between the idea of man as a free moral agent and the existence of regularities in political life that are capable of formulation as empirical laws.

It is true that most of the basic problems posed by the masters of political thought have been ethical in nature. Yet questions pertaining to the effects of environmental factors on government, the balancing or separation of political power, the role of parties and interest groups, the factors which generate social unrest and revolution, and the influence

---

[5] David G. Smith, "Political Science and Political Theory," *American Political Science Review*, Sept., 1957, p. 746.

of economics on the political process have figured prominently in their writings. Modern society owes a heavy debt to the classical theorists not only for their formulation of basic political issues and concepts, but also for their penetrating insights into matters of political science proper.

AN APPROACH TO THE STUDY OF POLITICAL PHILOSOPHY

Political philosophy is not an historical discipline, even though it cannot exclude the historical dimension. It is more than a mere recital of the ideas of social and political thinkers or a survey of ideas concerning public morality. The question as to the nature of political reality cannot be mistaken for the question of how this or that writer discussed or answered the problems involved. What these men thought is important to the student of political philosophy only in so far as it leads to a better understanding of political life, its nature, its goals, and its right guidance. Historical perspective, for example, can often suggest important hypotheses about social phenomena that might be overlooked by those busily engrossed with current events.[6]

The social philosopher must do more than record the political theories of the past, important as they have been in forming the mentality of modern civilization. He must seek in them logical evidence for answering the great questions of man and the state. He must measure and compare them in the light of his own philosophical and religious predispositions, and he must endeavor to ascertain their relevancy to contemporary political circumstances. In the process, he may find added support and justification for his own views; he may discover solutions to problems which have baffled him; he may clarify and sharpen his own thinking; or he may be led to modify his original beliefs and assumptions. To immerse oneself in the thought of the masters is a great intellectual experience, but the student of politics cannot be content to stop at this point.

The present text endeavors to set forth a framework for analyzing and evaluating the basic ideas of the various writers. These ideas are considered in the light of their fidelity to a suggested standard or set of criteria. The model proposed is one which, in the opinion of the author, constitutes a pattern of critically tenable concepts or a rationally acceptable political philosophy. It is based on the classical Greek-Christian

---

[6] See in this connection, Leo Strauss, "Political Philosophy and History," *Journal of the History of Ideas*, Jan., 1949, p. 30 ff.

tradition as it has found expression in western thought and in western institutions. The standard should prove of some use as a frame of reference even to the reader who does not regard it as valid, or who does not fully agree with the description of it as given.

The classical tradition is primarily concerned with ends and final values, with political philosophy; yet it does not neglect political science or causal theory as evidenced by its interest in the institutions and operations of government. Traditional theory does not overlook the fact that the body politic functions in an historical environment. It consequently offers many significant insights into the processes of government — insights that are important to the systematic study of political phenomena.

THE CLASSICAL TRADITION

In the long course of western political thought certain basic concepts have played a dominant role. Not all of these ideas have been consistent with one another; some of them have varied only in their accidental attributes, others have been diametrically opposed. Nevertheless, in the maze of political speculation to which the West has fallen heir, it is possible to discern a common thread running through the checkered pattern. This thread is what many have chosen to call the classical or Christian tradition.

The classical tradition is not a static, reactionary transmission of the past. It is a growing, dynamic, and vigorous body of law, custom, and ideas that has helped to shape the course of western civilization. It is akin to the western genius which has been described as "not simply a finished product, consisting of intellectual achievements and institutions which can be handed down unchanged from generation to generation," but "a design or blueprint, which possesses an organic, continuous life, and which must be ever freshly realized according to the changing conditions of each new era."[7] Classical tradition embodies in it Greek and Hebraic as well as Christian thought and culture, although Christianity has been the chief instrumentality for transmitting this heritage to the modern world. As Professor Foster has noted, "through all the countless channels by which it has exercised its pervading and penetrating influence, Christianity has been the means of bringing to bear in the shaping of

---

[7] Josef Pieper, "The Christian West," *Commonweal*, Mar. 15, 1957, p. 608.

the minds of modern men not only the civilization of the Hebrews but the Greek and Roman elements which Christianity absorbed."[8]

The major premises of the classical tradition as applicable to the development of western political philosophy can be reduced to six in number: (1) the rational, moral, and religious character of man; (2) the existence of a natural moral law; (3) the organic nature of the state; (4) the necessity of constitutional government; (5) the desirability of subsidiarity as an operative principle of government; and (6) the validity of democratic rule. Although this list does not exhaust the conceptual ideas that have helped to shape western political thought, it does include those (either expressly or by implication) which have been most vital to the development of the Christian political tradition.

Not all of these premises were present full-bodied from the beginning. Some of them gradually emerged or became more clearly formulated as the pattern of western thought developed. Their acceptance, moreover, has not been unanimous. Some of the prominent thinkers of the West have challenged one or more of them. Yet in the main, these characteristics have demonstrated an enduring vitality and a continuing capacity to win wide acceptance.

The Rational Nature of Man

The history of political thought amply illustrates the intimate connection between an individual's concept of the nature of man and his political philosophy. It is trite but none the less important to note that every social and political order must ultimately rest upon a philosophy containing certain basic assumptions and beliefs about man. So also must every political treatise be set in some conception of the nature of the universe. Since the political community is designed to further the ends of man, it becomes important to learn what these ends are. If we know what man is, we can then determine how he should act and what objectives he should pursue. And if we possess this knowledge, we are in a position to ascertain the role that the state should play and the goals it should seek. Political philosophy, therefore, must start with man. The theoretical structure which any thinker designs will, in final analysis, be determined by his concept of man's nature and end.

Lying at the center of the western tradition is the conception of man

---

[8] M. B. Foster, *Masters of Political Thought* (London: Harrap and Co., 1942), p. 26.

as a rational creature with a free and self-determinative will, and with an ultimate destiny that transcends the political and social processes in which he is involved. As a moral being endowed with reason and will, and living in a world at the center of which is a Divine Reason holding and directing all, the human individual aspires to truth and happiness. By following the paths marked out for him by the dictates of his reason, he acquires human dignity, finds his true freedom, and fulfills his personality. The task of perfection is not an easy one since man is also influenced in his behavior by prejudice and passion. But in western thought, reasoning man, complemented by faith in God, is capable of making at least substantial strides toward his natural end.

Natural Law

For more than 2000 years the concept of natural law has played a prominent role in political and social thought. The idea that the political order must be based on a moral code which transcends the vagaries of time and place furnishes the key to an understanding of the Christian tradition. For at the basis of this tradition is the firm conviction that morals, in the sense of the choice of right means to rationally determined ends, constitutes the foundation of politics.

If man is to have a standard for measuring the ultimate legitimacy of social institutions and the propriety of political behavior, he must seek that standard either in some objective order which is not subject to human tampering or he must look to himself as the source and creator of it. By accepting the latter position, he rejects the existence of an objective basis for upholding the validity of his moral views. Ethical norms in such a context become nothing more than individual or group preferences. All that can then be said about a particular view is that it represents or deviates from the predominant preference of the controlling group at any given time. A study of political philosophy within such a framework could be little more than an historical description of past moral ideas rather than a constructive search for an objective pattern of human values.

The theory that social and political values are but the reaction of human preferences to social and political facts did not come into prominence until the nineteenth century. This new view, with its moral relativism, ran counter to the overwhelming espousal of natural law in prior thinking and belief. As such, it constituted a direct repudiation of the Greek-Christian position with its normative foundation.

Since various meanings have become attached to the term "natural law," it is important when speaking of it to distinguish the particular meaning that is intended. As it was universally understood throughout the Christian era until the seventeenth century, natural law is what John Wild describes as the "authentic doctrine of natural law," a universal pattern of action applicable to all men everywhere, required by human nature itself for its completion.[9] So conceived, the principal characteristics of this law are:

1. Its essential prescriptions are embedded in the very nature, the ontological structure, of things and are discoverable by observation. Maritain refers to it as "the normality of functioning proper to a given nature." Each individual entity is marked by an essential nature which it shares in common with other members of its species. There is a certain order of inclinations in each being which moves it toward its end, the fulfillment of its specific nature. From the observation of this internal source of motion and these innate tendencies, a system of law emerges which must be followed if the nature of the particular being is to be fully realized. So far as these tendencies are directed toward their natural fulfillment, the entity is healthy and good; so far as they are perverted or obstructed, it is unhealthy and evil.

Animate being, other than man, has its intrinsic principles of motion and rest (the physical laws of nature) which move it automatically toward its end. Man, in addition to these tendencies, is capable by virtue of his rationality not only of apprehending the end, as other being is not, but also of acting on his own choice to realize or frustrate this end. Thus while the physical laws apply to the necessary and automatic, to agents incapable of choosing between alternative courses of action, the natural moral laws apply to the contingent, to acts performed by free agents capable of deliberation and choice.

2. Its normative pattern is not made by man as a legislative assembly enacts law, but is discoverable in human nature. Through knowing what he is, man obtains knowledge of what he ought to do. By studying his

---

[9] *Plato's Modern Enemies and the Theory of Natural Law* (Chicago: University of Chicago Press, 1953), p. 64.

nature and the world about him, he is able to form judgments concerning human actions. In this way he realizes that certain acts tend to make him more perfect while others degrade him. By doing the former he moves toward the fulfillment of his being; by committing the latter he acts in a manner unbefitting his character as a rational creature.

The investigation of natural law calls for the study of man historically and psychologically. It involves an examination of individual good in the context of the common good, and it entails a painstaking examination of the practical workings of society. As understood in this traditional sense, the moral law furnishes an objective standard that is not found in the heavens ("a brooding omnipresence in the sky" as Justice Holmes called it) but in the nature and structure of man.

3. It is not a code rolled up in the mind of man which perfectly equips him with a complete set of rules covering every phase of human life. Exponents of the classical theory of natural law do not claim the existence of an ideal body of specific rules tailored in detail to fit particular situations. They do contend that there are certain fundamental principles of justice and morality governing all human conduct. While they hold that the general course which must be followed for human development is found in the factual structure of man's nature, they are fully aware that men exist in a changing historical environment. They recognize that individuals are confronted with many varied factors and circumstances in any given situation, and that it is in these concrete and particular instances that decisions must be made.

As conceived by the traditionalists, the natural law can provide man only with the general and universal principles that he must follow in his quest for perfection. The application of these broad precepts to individual cases is more than an intellectual exercise. It demands experience, prudence, and practical judgment. The classical thinkers stressed the vital importance of natural law to the political life of man because of its broad normative structure. They were convinced that practical acts and policies could be formulated within this framework to meet the demands of the historical environment in such a way as to promote the fulfillment of human nature. They felt that in the absence of an objective moral law there could be little assurance that human society would not ultimately be committed to the Greek sophists' position, that morality is simply social convention while justice is nothing else than the interest of the stronger.

The Organic Nature of the State

Most theories concerning the nature of the state fall into two major categories: organic and mechanistic. The works of Plato, Aristotle, and Burke are typical representations of the former; those of the social contract theorists, of the latter. Of the two, the organic theory has prevailed throughout most of the history of western thought. According to this view, the state is an ethical institution with a moral end. It is a human society, a community of persons, united in a co-operative effort to attain mutual ends. Its members interact with one another with a common perception of their goals and purposes, although disagreement over the means of attaining them may at times give rise to group conflict.

The organic theory holds that the unity of the body politic is derived from the innate predisposition in man which impels him toward association with his fellow creatures. As rational beings men realize that it is the state which makes life possible and productive for them. A social or moral unity results from their collective will to join together and function as members of a community. It is this unity which gives political society its organic character.

The mechanistic theory tends to ignore the social character of man by viewing the state as an artificial institution based on the claims of individuals. It regards the state merely as a tool or machine which arises as a result of agreement among individuals who are bent on satisfying their particular desires and who are not concerned with any shared ends involving other members of the group. At the base of this theory is a conception of the universe as a mechanism operating in accordance with certain fixed laws which automatically bring about a natural harmony of interests. Thus, each individual in pursuing his own interests best serves those of the community.

Like natural law, the organic theory has acquired many meanings over the course of time. Political thinkers with such diverse ideas about the state and society as Aristotle and Hegel have been referred to as supporters of the organic view. The difficulty is more semantic than substantive. Since basically different concepts have been labeled "organic," it is necessary to determine what each writer means when he uses the term. It is misleading to place in the same category all theories which are today referred to as "organic." Some writers, for example, have gone so far as to depict the state as a biological organism or a distinct and superior entity in which the individual is totally subordinated to the political body as a mere cell to the physical body. This conception, sometimes called "organic," is patently at odds with the meaning of the term in classical thought.[10]

The main stream of traditional thought regards the state as a consciously organized group whose members propose a common end. The good of the whole group is dependent on the proper functioning of the members, and these in turn profit from the existence of the social whole. The latter, however, has no existence independent from that of the members who compose it. These members, on the other hand, have an end of their own separate and distinct from the social whole of which they are a part. Each member performs his separate function under an order that is directed toward the good of the whole. The function of politics is the direction of this common life.

Constitutional Government

Implicit in the idea of constitutional government or constitutionalism is a theory of limitations upon the sphere of public authority. The belief that governmental acts should be subject to certain restrictions and not left wholly to the discretion and whims of those who hold political power has been one of the most notable and persistent features of western political history. In the eyes of the ancient Greeks, the political constitution was analogous to that of the human body: it consisted of the operative principles inherent in and regulating the civic community. Aristotle referred to it variously as "a community of interests" which the citizens of a state have, and as "the common way of living" which a people has chosen. Viewed in this light a constitution includes the whole matrix and scheme of living of the state. Just as the physician must observe the nature and composition of the human body in treating it, so must the ruler follow the constitution of the body politic in governing it.

During the middle ages, the concept of constitutionalism became closely linked to that of natural law. There was explicit recognition in theory that the king was limited by the natural law and by the customs of

---

[10] In order to distinguish between the two uses of the term, some writers designate as "organismic" those theories which regard the state as a biological or metaphysical entity. See, for example, F. W. Coker, *Organismic Theories of the State* (New York: Columbia University Press, 1910).

the realm even though he was subject to no legal restraints. The sovereign was said to be above positive law, but beneath the law of God and nature. A medieval ruler may have been an autocrat *de jure*, but he was not a despot. The expression "what the king has willed has the force of law" was theoretically applicable only when the king's will was expressed in a manner that recognized the limitations on his power.

Constitutionalism also reflects a facet of man's nature as disclosed in Hebraic and Christian doctrine. Due to sin, man's nature is no longer unpolluted and unvitiated. It is a fallen nature, one thwarted and damaged by original sin. Man lives in an orderly universe of God's creation but it is a world that has been disturbed by the primal alienation from God. A philosophy of politics "based on a view that sees man and the world still in the primal harmony of an unmarred creation is quite obviously going to prove inadequate when it comes face to face with the realities of human existence and social life."[11] In the light of this concept of man's nature, the Christian tradition holds that it would be unwise to entrust any individual or group of individuals with unlimited and arbitrary power over the community.

The Principle of Subsidiarity

Subsidiarity has much in common with the modern idea of a pluralistic society in which variant groups and cultures are permitted to exist side by side and to enjoy a large measure of freedom. The concept received recognition at an early date although the doctrine of subsidiarity itself was not formally expressed as an operative standard until recent times. The principle rests on the assumption that the end of the state is the common good, and that the extent to which government should intervene in the social and economic order to insure this good is a matter of prudential determination. Subsidiarity seeks to provide a standard that may be employed in making this determination and in outlining the role of government in concrete historical situations.

Expressed in somewhat different terms, subsidiarity is the principle by which societies of various kinds and at various levels are set up. These societies are established to carry out functions which individuals are incapable of handling satisfactorily or in the common interest. Traditional theory regards all organized social groupings, from the family to the

---

[11] Will Herberg, "The Presuppositions of Democracy," *Commonweal*, June 3, 1955, p. 236.

political community, solely as aids to man. It looks upon the state as necessary because these lesser forms of associations are unable to meet the full demands of human needs. It also embodies the conviction that man's entire life is not coterminous with the state and that in every society there should be lesser units of government and numerous voluntary associations in which the individual can participate.

The principle of subsidiarity specifies that the lowest unit of society which is capable of accomplishing a needed function in an adequate manner and within the framework of the general welfare should be permitted to do so. Thus, if a task essential to man's well-being cannot be performed by individual or family effort, it should be undertaken through private groups such as labor unions, trade organizations, cooperatives, or neighborhood improvement associations. If these lesser societies are unable to cope with the matter effectively, the task should be assigned to the lowest level of public administration with sufficient means and capabilities. Depending on the complexity and magnitude of the problem, this will in some instances be local or provincial authorities, in other cases the national or even an international government.

The concept of subsidiarity springs from the reality of human nature. The end of man is the fulfillment of his nature, and individual initiative is a means of helping him attain this objective. Just as a man's body cannot be developed physically by letting others perform the calisthenics, neither can his moral and intellectual faculties be enlarged when all decisions pertaining to his social and economic life are made for him by higher authorities. As one writer has said, "the individual's self fulfillment is radically foiled if his social impulse is restricted to an ignoble, passive, subservient role and is deprived of any active and constructive part in shaping the life of the community, political as well as industrial."[12]

The object of political government is not to absorb or destroy the members of the social body but to make it possible for society to function properly in the interest of the common good. The role of government is thus subsidiary in the sense of providing help and direction to individuals and lesser communities. Whenever government assumes tasks which private initiative is willing and capable of handling, it deviates from its subsidiary character and diminishes the opportunity for personal growth.

Contained in the notion of subsidiarity is a conception of the natural

---

[12] Johannes Messmer, "Freedom as a Principle of Social Order," *Modern Schoolman,* Jan., 1951, p. 103.

character of private or voluntary associations. The consciousness of the individual's own insufficiency leads him to form various societies in order to achieve certain ends. Similarity of occupation or profession, of social and political views, or of other like interests provides the basis for such organizations. By enabling individuals to unite in the performance of tasks which singly they could not accomplish, these associations relieve the political government of a vast burden. And by helping to maintain a pluralistic society in which private groups are permitted a certain degree of autonomy within given spheres, they prevent undue centralization and total dependence on state action. In fact, the existence of such organizations may be said to be a necessary condition of democracy. "A state where no voluntary organizations exist cannot be democratic, for it is impossible to conceive of a society of free individuals without combination of like-minded individuals. Out of freedom to combine arises organized opposition which is an essential characteristic of political democracy."[13]

The history of political thought is replete with theories pertaining to the role of the state. These theories range from the advocacy of complete *laissez faire* to the insistence on full collectivism. Midway between these extremes stands the classical tradition. Recognizing that the common good is best obtained by leaving to each person a large area of freedom for his development, it also demands that this area remain at all times commensurate with the general welfare. While it emphasizes individual initiative as a means of self-perfection, it is fully aware that many social and economic problems have passed beyond the capabilities of private means. For as society organically expands and increases in complexity, the number and character of socioeconomic interactions and relationships multiply beyond man's individual ability to cope with them.

Democratic Government

To advance the concept of democratic government as an essential part of the western tradition may seem strange since popular rule was virtually unknown during the long period from the days of the city-state to the modern era. But tradition, like history, does not stand still; it develops and modifies itself to meet the needs and aspirations of a

---

[13] V. L. Allen, *Power in Trade Unions* (London: Longmans Green & Co., 1954), pp. 9–10.

growing and expanding civilization. The seeds of democratic government were sown in ancient Greece; they began to sprout during the medieval era even though monarchy prevailed. As the premises of democracy became more explicit in the thought of the middle ages, awareness of the desirability of self-rule grew. This tendency was strengthened by the beliefs — well grounded in the theory of the period — that political authority has its ultimate source in God, that no man or special group of men possesses the inherent right to command others, and that the rulers hold power only as representatives of the people and with their consent. From these premises, it was only a step to the "conviction that the normal state toward which human societies must tend is a state in which the people act as an adult person or one come of age in the political life."[14] In such a society, the human person is called upon to participate in political life regardless of his race or social condition. The realization of this goal was made possible in the West as educational opportunities expanded and technological developments brought more leisure time to the average individual.

Some theorists have justified popular rule on the basis of the collective judgment of the people; others have looked upon it as a device to prevent the abuse of political power. But beyond these grounds, valid as they may be, lies the more fundamental reason implicit in Western thought: the compatibility of democratic government with the nature of man. The human creature finds his natural perfectibility through social living. As a being endowed with an intellect, a free will, and the capacity to make judgments, it is unbefitting for him to sit passively by while all of the community's decisions are made by rulers over whom he exercises no direction or control. The ancient Greeks pointed out that active participation in the things that make up a civilized existence — society and state — is an indispensable part of each man's personal happiness and dignity. To deny him the opportunity of taking part in the governmental process is to impede him in the development of an important facet of his nature.

THEORY OF KNOWLEDGE

A study of political theory is not a study of epistemology, or the nature, limits, and validity of knowledge. However, since the problem of

---

[14] Jacques Maritain, "Christianity and Democracy," *Commonweal*, June 11, 1954, p. 240.

knowledge is basic to all philosophy, political and otherwise, and since it constantly reappears in the works of political theorists, the student must at least be aware of its presence and its significance. To what extent, for example, can the moral assumptions or postulates which lie at the root of the various political theories be rationally justified? Is it possible to know these premises as true or untrue, or is a true knowledge of ends and values impossible?[15]

If we start from the premise that truth can be established solely by empirical observation, we can have no ultimate demonstration of the truth or falsity of a moral proposition since such a proposition is not scientifically verifiable. Whether the state is acting justly or not, or whether human rights are being violated by government would have to be determined on the basis of what is expedient, workable, or pleasant and not on the basis of any universal norm of justice and rightness (since this theory of knowledge would not permit the establishment of such standards). Reason, in this view, would have an instrumental function only. It could tell us what means would most likely be effective for achieving whatever ends we might desire, but it could not determine whether these ends were proper, and whether they ought to be sought by man.

At the other extreme is the theory, often referred to as "rationalism," which holds that it is possible to establish truths by the a priori insight of reason independently of sense experience. Under this theory, categorical answers can be given to all the problems of government by abstract reasoning without reference to sense experience or the historical context out of which problems arise. This type of thinking is illustrated by Descartes and his followers.

A third theory of knowledge stands midway between the extreme forms of rationalism and empiricism. Formulated by Aristotle and developed by later thinkers, it disputes the doctrine that abstract reasoning divorced from the totality of experience can establish truths about reality. With equal force it rejects the view that valid knowledge must be limited to sense knowledge. Striking a middle position, it holds that the intellect and reason give us knowledge of the essences and properties of things which are more than the mere enumeration or collection of relations that

---

[15] The importance of epistemology to the study of political philosophy is discussed by A. R. M. Murray, *An Introduction to Political Philosophy* (New York: Philosophical Library, 1953), Chap. 1.

we have sensorially experienced. This realistic theory of knowledge is basic to the classical tradition. It assumes that there is a meaningful political reality whose existence does not depend on our knowledge of it and that we are endowed with the faculty to grasp in some measure its true meaning. Hence it is possible for society to discover moral objectives and ends in reality itself and to answer the question of what ought to be in the political sphere.[16]

SUMMARY

A history of political philosophy is a study of ideas and institutions as they have developed during the course of time. It seeks to impart an understanding of the way in which men of all ages have formulated and implemented their political and social aspirations. But political philosophy is also something more than an analysis of past political theories. It seeks to discover universal principles which underlie political phenomena under all historical circumstances. In so doing, it attempts to achieve a better understanding of contemporary politics both from an ethical and causal standpoint.

The study of politics is not confined to a description and analysis of existing institutions and the manner in which they function. Behind these institutions are the values and purposes which they embody and the ends for which they are designed. Politics, like ethics, is basically a science of the order in which human nature aspires to its maximal perfection. Political philosophy, or the investigation of political behavior and phenomena in an ethical framework, is an integral part of the study of politics. All of the great social thinkers have recognized this close interrelationship. They have not hesitated to ask metaphysical questions about the nature of man and the values that a society ought to pursue simply because such questions cannot be answered by the techniques of the physical sciences.

The material in the present chapter suggests a number of questions that might aid the reader in evaluating the work of the various political thinkers.

1. Is the writer concerned with the moral aspects of politics or does he avoid these altogether?
2. What is his concept of man's nature?
3. What view does he hold as to the nature and objectives of the state?
4. Does he accept or deny the existence of natural law, and what meaning does he attach to the term?
5. How large and what kind of a role does he advocate for political government?
6. Does he believe in constitutional rule?

---

[16] For a detailed treatment of the various theories of knowledge, see W. P. Montague, *The Ways of Knowing: Or the Methods of Philosophy* (New York: Macmillan Co., 1928).

7. What form of government does he support?
8. What is his attitude toward the common man?
9. Is he interested in causal theory as well as political philosophy?
10. What theory of knowledge does he espouse?

BIBLIOGRAPHY

Apter, David, E., "Theory and the Study of Politics," *American Political Science Review*, September, 1957.
Braybrooke, David, "The Relevance of Norms to Political Description," *American Political Science Review*, December, 1958.
Carritt, Edgar F., *Morals and Politics* (Oxford: Clarendon Press, 1935).
Catlin, George, "Political Theory: What Is It?" *Political Science Quarterly*, March, 1957.
Cobban, Alfred, "The Decline of Political Theory," *Political Science Quarterly*, September, 1953.
Easton, David, *The Political System* (New York: Knopf, 1953).
Eckstein, Harry, "Political Theory and the Study of Politics," *American Political Science Review*, June, 1956.
Glaser, William A., "The Types and Uses of Political Theory," *Social Research*, Autumn, 1955.
Griffith, Ernest S., "Research in Political Science," *American Political Science Review*, August, 1944.
Hacker, Andrew, "Capital and Carbuncles; The Great Books Reappraised," *American Political Science Review*, September, 1944.
Hermens, F. A., "Politics and Ethics," *Thought*, Spring, 1954.
Jacobson, Norman, "The Unity of Political Theory: Science, Morals and Politics," in *Approaches to the Study of Politics*, Young, Roland, ed. (Evanston: Northwestern University Press, 1958).
Jenkins, Thomas P., *The Study of Political Theory* (New York: Doubleday, 1955).
Kaufman, Arnold S., "The Nature and Function of Political Theory," *Journal of Philosophy*, January, 1954.
Kaufmann, Felix, "The Issue of Ethical Neutrality in Political Science," *Social Research*, September, 1949.
Land, P., and Klubertanz, G., "Practical Reason, Social Fact and the Vocational Order," *Modern Schoolman*, May, 1951.
McCloskey, R. G., "American Political Theory and the Study of Politics," *American Political Science Review*, March, 1957.
Morgenthau, Hans, "Power as a Political Concept," *Review of Politics*, October, 1955.
Mure, G. R. G., "The Organic State," *Philosophy*, July, 1949.
Murray, John M., "The Moral Foundations of Democracy," *Fortnightly*, September, 1947.
Pennock, J. Roland, "Political Science and Political Philosophy," *American Political Science Review*, December, 1951.
Rapoport, Anatol, "Various Meanings of Theory," *American Political Science Review*, December, 1958.

Rees, J. C., "The Limitations of Political Theory," *Political Studies*, October, 1954.

Rommen, Heinrich A., *The Natural Law* (St. Louis: Herder, 1947).

Simon, Yves R., *Philosophy of Democratic Government* (Chicago: University of Chicago Press, 1951).

Smith, David G., "Political Science and Political Theory," *American Political Science Review*, September, 1957.

Stearns, R. P., "A Plea for Political History," *Review of Politics*, October, 1955.

Strauss, Leo, "The Origin of the Idea of Natural Right," *Social Research*, March, 1952.

Taubes, Jacob, "Theology and Political Theory," *Social Research*, Spring, 1955.

Voegelin, Eric, *The New Science of Politics: An Introduction* (Chicago: University of Chicago Press, 1952).

Watkins, Frederick, *The Political Tradition of the West: A Study of the Development of Modern Liberalism* (Cambridge: Harvard University Press, 1948).

Wormuth, F. D., *The Origins of Modern Constitutionalism* (New York: Harper, 1949).

PART TWO | **THE POLITICAL PHILOSOPHY OF THE ANCIENTS**

PRE-POLITICAL SPECULATION

The first philosophical thinking of any consequence took place in Greece during the sixth century B.C. Prior to this time, the speculation which occurred was so immersed in mythology and religion that the great questions of life received little rational scrutiny. Beginning with scholars like Thales (600–550 B.C.), the Greek thinkers became interested in the natural sciences, and directed their efforts toward investigating the nature and structure of the physical universe. In the century or so that followed, they occupied themselves primarily with the problem of matter, seeking assiduously to discover a permanent substratum underneath all of nature's appearances and changes. What is the fundamental "stuff," they asked, of which everything is made? Where is the unity which lies behind variety and change to be found?

It was not until the middle of the fifth century B.C. that the accent switched from cosmological to anthropological or humanistic speculation. Greek philosophy at that time reached an apparently insoluble impasse between the conflicting schools of the cosmologists as represented by Heraclitus and Parmenides. The former taught that everything is in a constant state of flux and that the only reality is change or becoming. "Nothing ever is, everything is becoming." One cannot step into the same river twice or feel the same flame a second time. Yet the process of existence continues on with nothing remaining static.

Parmenides, on the other hand, held that nothing changes. All things are one; the universe is a single, continuous object. Change and motion are merely illusions of the senses. The paradox of Achilles and the tortoise illustrates this. No matter how swift he may be, Achilles can never catch up with the turtle that he is pursuing. To do so he must first reach the point where the turtle started, but by this time his quarry will have moved on. By the time Achilles makes up this additional distance, the object of pursuit will have moved a little more, and so on ad infinitum. For Heraclitus, science would be a virtual impossibility since nothing is certain and necessary, while for Parmenides there could be only one science, that of being.

Faced with this dilemma, the Greek philosophers began to shift their primary attention to the study of man as an ethical, social, and political animal. Thus, from the riddle of the physical universe, they turned to the riddle of the smaller cosmos — the state — and to the problems of the human individuals who compose it. Socrates expressed the new trend when he exclaimed that the noblest of all investigations is the study of what man should be and what he should pursue.

The city-state was the unit of Greek political life throughout the classical period. Not only was it the chief subject of concern for Plato and Aristotle, but its institutions and processes have found reflection in many of the political practices of the West. Because of the major importance of the classical Greek thinkers to subsequent political thought, an examination of the focal point of their speculation — the city-state — is a necessary part of the history of political philosophy.

THE CITY-STATE: ATHENS

Greek democracy reached its highest stage of development in Athens during the fifth century B.C., a period known as the "Golden Age of Pericles." The standard governmental unit at this time was the polis or city-state. This form of political organization, alien to an age of great powers and national states, finds no modern counterpart. There were several hundred Greek city-states of various sizes and forms of government, and of different levels of civilization. The most influential of these in the development of western political thought was Athens. It was here that Greek intellectual life attained its highest expression and that learning began to have political and social power.

Population-wise, Athens was no larger than a medium size American city such as Rochester, New York, or Birmingham, Alabama. In territorial extent it could be compared to a large American county. The typical polis, unlike the modern city, combined both town and country and both industry and agriculture. There was an urban area surrounded by walls and a rural fringe lying immediately outside with its vineyards, pastures, and fields. Athens and the other city-states differed from the modern municipality in a more significant sense than size or physical characteristics. They were sovereign political entities legally independent of any superior governmental power. They had their own constitutions, made their own laws, and conducted their own foreign relations. In fact, for the Greeks, state and polis remained convertible terms to the end of the classical period. Their philosophers knew no state that was not a polis.

Because of its small size and sovereign powers, the city-state constituted an intimate and intense form of political society. And because the whole citizen body played a direct and comprehensive role in the governance of this microcosmic commonwealth, the individual had a strong sense of belonging to the city, of being a partner rather than a subject of it. The Greeks were in general agreement that a truly civilized life could be lived only in connection with a polis. For it was the city that was the heart and inspiration of their great achievements in the field of literature, art, philosophy, and in the development of the good life.

Social Classes

The city-state of Athens had a population estimated to be somewhere between 300,000 to 400,000. Of this number, approximately half lived in the central town and the other half in the surrounding rural area. The population was divided into three major social classes, each with a distinct legal and political status: the citizens, the metics or resident foreigners, and the slaves.

Men over eighteen years of age of Athenian parentage were enrolled in the citizen class. This class numbered about 40,000, or together with wives and children, 160,000. Citizenship could be acquired only by birth, not by any process of naturalization. The chief advantage of citizenship lay in the political privileges it conferred on the holder, namely the right to take part in the governance of his city and in the management of its public affairs. There were no particular social privileges that accompanied the status of citizen. The class was open to all of Athenian stock, noble and commoner alike. It included men in the lower economic brackets as well as the wealthy, the artisan and farmer as well as the shopkeeper and the professional man. But there was one important omission, the Athenian woman. Like modern Switzerland, classical Greece felt that woman's place was in the home, not at the polls, or on jury service, or in public office. Since the Greeks could not conceive of citizenship apart from the right to participate actively in government, they logically excluded women from the category of citizens.

The second class, the metics, consisted of free aliens who were permanently domiciled in the city. With their families they numbered close to 100,000. Athens welcomed immigration as the words of Xenophon recall: "We throw open our city to the world and never pass decrees to exclude foreigners."[1] This liberal policy toward aliens was not inspired altogether by humanitarian motives. Athens needed workers, particularly artisans and craftsmen, not only to supply her domestic needs but also to produce goods for her expanding foreign trade. The majority of the metics were therefore found in the ranks of the craftsmen and the small traders.

Aside from the denial of political privileges and the right to own land, the resident alien's status was not an unhappy one. He enjoyed a large measure of social equality with the citizen class, he was not discriminated against except in political matters, and his economic position was generally "middle-class." The failure to provide a legal process for acquiring citizenship was the only facet of Athenian policy toward the foreigner that could be termed illiberal by modern standards.

At the bottom of the social scale were the slaves, most of whom had been kidnaped or taken as war prisoners in Asia Minor and the adjacent territory. There were between 80,000 and 100,000 slaves in Athens, or about one fourth the city's total population. Apart from those who were used in the public silver mines, the lot of the Athenian slave was generally good. He was protected by legislation against physical abuse and was normally assigned to jobs commensurate with his capabilities and talents. He could be found working side by side with the citizen and metic in all kinds of work from menial tasks to the trades and even the professions. Some of the slaves were skilled craftsmen and others were employed in the city service in such positions as clerk, policeman, and inspector. In dress and appearance, the slaves were indistinguishable from the ordinary citizen. Many of them, moreover, were paid for their work, and by saving their earnings they could in time buy their freedom and become assimilated to the free alien population.

The distinctions in class and the existence of slavery, even though well established and universally accepted customs of the time, obviously detract from the democratic character of Athenian institutions. Yet, what is most significant about this period is that the smallness of the city-state and its life within common walls drew men together in a natural intimacy despite the drawbacks of status. Men of all social walks of life — slave, metic, and citizen — could be found associating in the market square on a basis of equality. The city-state may not have abolished the

---

[1] *Memorabilia*, ii, 3, 3.

prestige of wealth and culture but it did establish a tradition of easy intercourse among all classes.[2] It was this civic intimacy that gave Athens her distinctive flavor in the history of democratic institutions.

Government of Athens

Pericles, in his famous Funeral Oration, declared that the government of Athens is called a democracy because its administration is in the hands of the many. Similarly, the great dramatist Aeschylus proudly observed that there is no government in Athens for the people is the government. Although a measure of poetic license is evident in these expressions, the citizen class in Athens actually did participate in government to a degree unknown in the modern democratic state. Accustomed as we are to government by representatives, it is difficult for us to visualize a society in which every citizen shares directly in the formulation of public policy and, to a considerable extent, in its execution. At any given time, at least one out of every four or five Athenian citizens could be found performing some public service — either legislative, administrative, or judicial. Those entitled to so participate were the male citizens who had reached the required age. This group, it must be remembered, constituted only a small fraction of the people, certainly not more than twenty-five per cent of the adult population.

For administrative purposes, Athens was divided into 100 demes or local governmental areas which were equivalent in many respects to present-day counties. Through an assembly of the citizens and an elected mayor, the demes managed the local affairs of the neighborhood, collected certain taxes for the central government, recorded real estate transactions, conducted judicial proceedings in minor matters, and kept the register of citizenship. They also served as electoral units for nominating candidates for the Council, and judges or jurymen to serve on the courts.

The Assembly: There were three principal organs of government at the central level: the Assembly, the Council, and the Courts. These correspond roughly to the modern legislative, executive, and judicial branches. The supreme lawmaking power was vested in the Assembly (*ekklesia*), the outstanding historical example of direct or primary democracy in action. Each of the 40,000 Athenian citizens was entitled to attend its meetings and to participate in its deliberations — not through

---

[2] E. Barker, *Greek Political Theory, Plato and His Predecessors* (London: Methuen and Co., 1947), 3rd ed., p. 19.

representatives, but in person. Basic to Greek democracy was the belief that the collective judgment of the people is superior to the judgment of experts. Because of this conviction, the Greeks were reluctant to surrender any important decision to representatives. Government at the local and provincial levels in a number of modern democracies retain some vestiges of this notion. The referral of many decisions to popular vote, such as the issuance of bonds for capital expenditures or proposals for changes in constitutions and charters, are examples of this same tendency.

It is clear that not all Athenian citizens attended the Assembly meetings, no more so than all eligible voters in the United States go to the polls on election day. In fact, if all citizens had turned up, the Assembly would have been hopelessly unwieldy and unmanageable. Attendance often entailed a sacrifice which many Athenian citizens were not in a position to make. Some of them who were engaged in farming lived a day's journey or more from the central town where the meetings were held, and they could ill afford to be absent from their fields for any prolonged interval.[3] The only occasion for which attendance figures at an Assembly meeting are extant reveals that 3616 members were present. Whether this number is typical or not is a matter of pure conjecture. Meetings of the Assembly were held at least ten times a year, always during the day and always in the open air. Lawmaking in Athenian style can still be witnessed today in several of the smaller Swiss cantons.

Unfortunately none of the stirring debates which took place on "Parliament Hill" in Athens have been recorded for posterity. Certainly the meetings of the Assembly were great popular occasions, and certainly they gave the citizen an intimate feeling of directly sharing in the responsibility of making public policy. If the meetings were at all similar to those of the modern Swiss canton, they were orderly and dignified, and the citizen body was collectively conscious of the great significance of the task for which it had gathered. As one modern observer has noted, it is impossible to attend a cantonal meeting without deep emotion. From all over Switzerland fathers bring their children to witness a sight that is unique in present-day democracies, and unequaled as an inspiring lesson of civic responsibility and of devotion to the commonweal.[4]

---

[3] For an account of this period see J. O. Larsen, *Representative Government in Greek and Roman History* (Berkeley: University of California Press, 1955).

[4] Wm. E. Rappard, *The Government of Switzerland* (New York: Van Nostrand, 1936), p. 36.

It would, however, be naïve to believe that four or five thousand people, no matter how well trained in the art of good citizenship, could actually transact the intricate business of lawmaking by mass action. Even in the modern day parliaments of four or five hundred members, the real lawmaking power has become concentrated more and more in the hands of cabinets and committees. The same could be said of ancient Athens and the Assembly. The actual task of preparing the laws and of mapping out public policy was entrusted to a smaller organ of government known as the Council. Yet it was in the Assembly — in the people themselves — that the sovereign power of the state resided since this body retained the ultimate authority to accept, reject, or modify the work of the Council.

The Council: The Council (*boule*) was a representative organ of government consisting of 500 members chosen by lot from a list of candidates elected by the demes. Any citizen, thirty or more years of age, was qualified to stand for election in his district provided he had not already served two terms on the Council. This limitation was intended to give a larger portion of the citizen body an opportunity to serve. Since 500 was still too large a number for the effective transaction of business, the Council was divided on a tribal basis into ten subcommittees of fifty members each. Each of these committees in turn assumed the day-to-day control over all Council business for a tenth part of the year. From among the fifty, a presiding official called the president was chosen by lot each day. Again for the purpose of assuring a wide rotation of offices, no Athenian was eligible to hold this honor as titular head of state for more than one day in his entire life.

The Council was the mainspring of the governmental machinery. It had a twofold purpose, serving as a steering committee for the Assembly and as the principal administrative arm of the state. In its legislative capacity, it prepared the agenda for the Assembly meetings and drafted and introduced the bills to be acted upon. While the Assembly could amend the bills so proposed, it did not itself have the power of initiation. This system does not differ essentially from the practice in modern parliamentary governments, such as Great Britain, where the lawmaking body is limited almost wholly to action on bills introduced by the ministry.

There must be some permanent central authority in every political unit to direct and supervise the course of public affairs. The Council served this purpose in Athens. It sat daily to transact business; it was responsible for national defense and the conduct of foreign affairs; it managed the city's finances, prepared the budget, and assessed and levied taxes; it handled the public property and watched over the administrative duties performed by the lesser officials. This last function was of peculiar importance since Athens had no permanent civil service except in the lower ranks. Practically all of the administrative offices were filled annually by lot without the privilege of reappointment. This practice was based on the theory (later to find re-expression in Jacksonian democracy) that every citizen is competent to discharge the ordinary duties of governmental administration and equally entitled to a share in it. Even the minor officials, such as the director of public works and the commissioner of health, were selected in this manner. Only in those instances where the position required highly specialized and expert knowledge was the office filled by show of hands in the Assembly.

The Courts: The administration of justice in Athens deviated strangely from modern practices. In keeping with the belief that all phases of government should be entrusted to the citizen body, no provision was made for professional judges. All cases were decided by juries of the people without the assistance or instruction of a trained jurist. Individual juries were chosen by lot, as the need arose, from a panel of 6000 jurymen elected by the demes.[5] The average jury consisted of 501 members, all of whom had to be citizens over thirty years of age. Both civil and criminal cases were heard. Parties to the litigation had to plead their own cause, and in criminal matters a private citizen acted as prosecutor. The decision of the jury was by majority vote. There was no provision for appeal since under Athenian theory an act of the court was an act of the whole people. The chief reason for the large size jury was to eliminate the danger of bribery or intimidation. It was also felt that the collective judgment of the many is better than that of the few.

The Generals: In addition to the above three agencies, there was a fourth public instrumentality of major political importance — the offices of General, of which there were ten. The position of the Generals was unique in the Athenian organizational scheme since they were the only officials elected annually by direct popular election and subject to no

---

[5] Aristophanes, in his *Wasps*, depicts the jurors, many of whom resided in the rural areas, carrying their lanterns as they trudged along the roads to the city before daybreak in order to be on hand when the courts opened.

restriction as to re-election. In theory, the Generals were purely military officials, but in practice (as might be expected in an office popularly elected on a national basis) they were able to exert great influence over the Council and Assembly. Not only did they command the army and the navy, but they exercised many of the functions performed in a modern state by the ministry. It was not as a political official but as a General that Pericles was able to direct Athenian policy for over thirty years. Yet his power to do so was dependent on his ability to win and maintain the support of the Assembly. His position in this respect was similar to that of a prime minister who must keep the confidence of a majority in parliament in order to remain in office.

Ostracism: To serve as a safeguard against overly ambitious political leaders, the Athenians instituted a curious expedient called ostracism. Once a year at an Assembly meeting, the question was put to the citizens whether there was need for ostracism. No specific names as targets for banishment had to be mentioned. If the motion carried, a special election was held two months later. The voter could write any name he wanted on the ballot (which was a broken piece of pottery). A minimum of 6000 votes had to be cast. The man with the greatest plurality was then exiled from the country for a period of ten years. After that time, he was free to return and regain all his civil, political, and property rights.

THE CITY-STATE: SPARTA

The polis of Athens is of prime importance in the development of western political thought and institutions. However, a second Greek city-state also exerted considerable influence on Hellenic thinking. Sparta, the champion of reaction, represented the virtual antithesis of Athens. While the latter was developing her democratic institutions, the former was devoting her energies to the systematic suppression of subordinate groups and preparing herself for the leadership of the Greek peninsula.

The population of Sparta fell into three major social classes: spartans, perioeci (dwellers-around), and helots. The first group was of Dorian lineage, and although it constituted less than five per cent of the total population, it exercised absolute control over all public affairs. Admission to this exclusive class was by birth only. The Spartan's whole life centered around the public service. No career in business or commerce was permitted him. At the age of seven, he was taken from his parents and placed in boarding schools operated by the state. Through vigorous and severe training in gymnastics and military drill, he was brought to a high degree of physical perfection. The education which the Athenians so highly esteemed — reading, rhetoric, the arts, and music — was looked upon with scorn. The sole aim of the Spartan educational system was to provide good soldiers wholly devoted to the state. Most of the student's time was spent in learning how to be submissive to discipline, indifferent to pain, and superior in combat. As part of his training, he was taught to steal; and if caught he would be punished — not for stealing but for not learning his lesson well enough.

The Spartan was occupied chiefly with military affairs during the greater part of his life. Only in his later years was he eligible to share in the tasks of civil administration. He was permitted to marry, but until he reached the age of thirty he had to live in barracks apart from his wife. It was the practice of the state that no Spartan should be either destitute or wealthy. None was allowed to own gold or silver. Each was given a small plot of land and was expected to live on its produce. The land was cultivated by a helot who also received a share of the produce.

Since the Spartans devoted all of their time and energy in the service of the state, the burden of supplying the material needs of the community fell to the other two classes. The perioeci consisted mainly of imported workers who were assigned to the tasks of commerce, trade, and the handicrafts. They enjoyed a large measure of civil rights but their social position was definitely inferior to that of the Spartans, and they were excluded from all share in the government of the city. The helots, who comprised almost two thirds of the population, were simply slaves or serfs. They were engaged almost exclusively in tilling the soil and in supplying the food needs of the whole population. Possessed of no rights, either civil or political, and subject to rigid supervision and at times ruthless suppression, their lot was not a happy one.

The government of Sparta was highly centralized in fact, although complex in form. It consisted of four principal branches: the Kings, Ephorate, Council, and Assembly. At the head of the state were two hereditary kings whose position gradually became that of mere figureheads as the real power was transferred to other organs, particularly to the Ephorate. The latter agency was an annually elected board of five members which supervised the training of the youths, presided over the Council and Assembly, heard nearly all civil suits, exercised complete and dictatorial power over the helots, and carried on foreign affairs. The Council or Senate was composed of twenty-eight elders past the age of sixty years who were elected for life by the whole citizen body. The Council considered measures to be presented to the Assembly and exercised certain judicial functions, such as hearing all important criminal cases in which citizens were involved. The Assembly was open to all citizens over thirty years of age. Its function was limited to that of voting on measures submitted to it by the Council; it had no authority to debate. For various reasons, the Spartan Assembly came to have little significance, meeting only occasionally to register its approval of some important measure advocated by the ephors.

The highly regimented life in Sparta with its asceticism and enforced discipline, the rigid suppression of all nonconformist ideas, the practice of political absolutism, and the ruthless marshaling of all the state's human and material resources, enabled her to become the dominant power in Hellas. In contrast to the many other Greek city-states that were plagued by revolutions, Sparta was able to maintain stable government over a long period of time. Her ability to do so aroused the admiration of many Hellenic thinkers, including Plato. Yet Sparta's contribution to the western tradition was almost wholly of a negative character. She may have succeeded in creating a race of invincible warriors and maintaining a system of oligarchical institutions, but she played no part in the development of that which has made ancient Greece famous: culture and civilization.

THE FALL OF ATHENS

Even at the time that Athens was reaching the full development of her democratic institutions, events were taking place which boded ill for her future. After defeating the invading Persians at the great naval battle of Salamis in 480 b.c., Athens became the acknowledged leader of a large section of Hellas and the head of the newly formed Delian League of city-states. In this new position of power, she directed her foreign policy toward the expansion of her commerce and industry and the domination of the Aegean Sea. Athens, in strange contrast to the humane and liberal practices which prevailed in domestic matters, exploited her confederates in a rather selfish, shameful, and undemocratic manner, extracting tribute from them and going so far on several occasions as to use force in order to prevent the secession of a League member. This last action was explained away on the ground that it was necessary to preserve a united front of Greek city-states in the face of the continued Persian threat.

The Melian dialogue, as related by Thucydides, illustrates the manner in which Athens dealt with reluctant allies or neutrals. When the island of Melos sought to remain neutral in the war between Athens and Lacedaemonia, Athens demanded submission. The Melians inquired as to why they could not be neutral, "friends instead of enemies, but allies of neither side." Rejecting the offer of neutrality, the Athenian envoys declared that the safety of their empire would not permit the existence of Melos as an independent state. "Besides extending our empire, we should gain in security by your subjection." In answer to the Melian complaint of injustice in this attitude, the Athenians replied, "You know as well as we do that right, as the world goes, is only in question between equals in power, while the strong do what they can and the weak suffer what they must."[6] These are words that have a distinctly familiar and modern tone.

The expansionist policies of Athens threw many of the other important city-states, such as Corinth, into the Spartan orbit, and eventually led to the Peloponnesian War. For twenty-seven years (431–405 B.C.), the Athenian bloc was locked in a struggle with the Spartan confederacy. When the conflict was over, not only had Athens fallen but all of Hellas was weakened and drained of her strength by this internecine strife. As a result, Greece became an easy prey in the following century for the Macedonian king and adventurer, Phillip II (382–336 B.C.). It is significant to note in this connection that Plato and Aristotle wrote after Athens had been defeated by Sparta and during the days of her subsequent decline. It is perhaps for this reason that they became severe although sympathetic critics of the political institutions that had failed to withstand the crises of their day.

SUMMARY

The social and political thinking of classical Greece is generally recognized as a vital force in the development of western thought. Since Greek speculation revolved largely around the city-state, an understanding of its institutions

---

[6] *Thucydides*, Modern Library Edition (New York: Random House, 1934), pp. 330–337.

and practices is a necessary prelude to the study of political philosophy. Much of Plato and Aristotle, for example, would not be intelligible without such knowledge. And without a basic understanding of these two major theorists, much of the subsequent development of western political thinking would be difficult to analyze.

But the city-state is of more than historical or background importance; it has in itself meaning and significance for modern political science. It has demonstrated in the concrete the importance of active participation in public affairs to the full development of human personality. It has revealed many of the tangible and intangible benefits that accrue to the individual and his community from such participation. It has illustrated how the smaller social units, because of their intimacy and close association, can awaken a more acute sense of voluntary co-operation in solving common problems and a deeper feeling of pride in civic accomplishments. It has also shown the weaknesses and dangers that are connected with the small political unit. Finally, it has provided a significant example of the ways in which men have been organized for political purposes.

BIBLIOGRAPHY

Agard, Walter, What Democracy Meant to the Greeks (Chapel Hill: University of North Carolina Press, 1942).

Barker, Ernest, "Elections in the Ancient World," Diogenes, Autumn, 1954.

Bonner, R. J., Aspects of Athenian Democracy (Berkeley: University of California Press, 1933).

Burn, A. R., Pericles and Athens (New York: Macmillan, 1949).

Chroust, A. H., "Treason and Patriotism in Ancient Greece," Journal of the History of Ideas, April, 1954.

Constanzo, J. F., "The Graeco-Roman Politeia — The City of Man," Fordham Law Review, June, 1951.

Cornford, F. M., Before and After Socrates (Cambridge: Cambridge University Press, 1932).

Fowler, Wm. W., The City-State of the Greeks and Romans (New York: Macmillan, 1904).

Freeman, Kathleen, Greek City-States (London: Macdonald, 1950).

Fustel de Coulanges, N. D., The Ancient City: A Study of the Religion, Laws, and Institutions of Greece and Rome, trans. by Wm. Small (New York: Doubleday, 1956).

Glotz, Gustave, The Greek City State and Its Institutions, trans. by N. Mallinson (London: Kegan Paul, 1929).

Glover, T. R., Springs of Hellas (New York: Macmillan, 1946).

——— Democracy in the Ancient World (New York: Macmillan, 1927).

Gulick, Charles B., The Life of the Ancient Greeks (New York: D. Appleton, 1902).

Halliday, Wm. R., The Growth of the City State (London: Hodder and Stoughton, 1923).

Hammond, Mason, *City State and World State in Greek and Roman Political Theory Until Augustus* (Cambridge: Harvard University Press, 1951).

Harper, Geo. M., Jr., "Democracy at Athens," in *The Greek Political Experience: Studies in Honor of William Kelly Prentice* (Princeton: Princeton University Press, 1941).

Hignett, Charles, *A History of the Athenian Constitution* (Oxford: Clarendon Press, 1952).

Jones, A. H. M., "The Social Structure of Athens in the Fourth Century, B.C.," *Economic History Review*, December, 1955.

Larsen, J. A. O., *Representative Government in Greek and Roman History* (Berkeley: University of California Press, 1955).

Livingstone, R. W. (ed.), *The Legacy of Greece* (Oxford: Oxford University Press, 1921).

Meiggs, Russell, "Athenian Democracy," *Parliamentary Affairs*, Spring, 1949.

Myres, J. L., *The Political Ideas of the Greeks* (New York: Abingdon, 1947).

Vlachos, N. P., *Hellas and Hellenism: A Social and Cultural History of Ancient Greece* (New York: Ginn and Co., 1936).

Wheeler, M., "Self-sufficiency and the Greek City," *Journal of the History of Ideas*, June, 1955.

Zimmern, Alfred, *The Greek Commonwealth: Politics and Economics in Fifth Century Athens*, 5th ed. (Oxford: Oxford University Press, 1931).

Chapter III

PLATO: THE SCIENCE OF ROYAL RULE

"Neither cities nor states nor individuals will ever attain perfection until the small class of philosophers . . . are providentially compelled, whether they will or not, to take care of the State, and until a like necessity be laid on the state to obey them" (Plato, *Republic*, VI, 499).

THE history of systematic political theory begins with Plato. This time-honored philosopher was born in 427 B.C., four years after the Peloponnesian War had begun. He was twenty-three when he saw Athens fall at the hands of Sparta, an event that convinced him of the weakness of democratic rule. He died in 347 B.C. at the age of eighty, just ten years before Philip of Macedon brought the Greek world under his sway. Plato came from a distinguished family. On his mother's side he was related to Solon, the noted Athenian lawgiver; and from his father, he inherited a venerable and aristocratic lineage.

During his youth, Plato was attracted by the prospect of an active political life. As he wrote, "in my youth I had the same idea of many others; I thought that as soon as I attained my majority, I would take part in the affairs of my country."[1] The opportunity for such participation arose shortly after the close of the Peloponnesian War when the government of Athens passed into the hands of a committee of thirty prominent citizens. Plato accepted the invitation to join this group because, in his words, "I thought that their aim was to turn the city from its life of injustice to the way of justice and so govern it."[2] It was not long, however, before the excesses of the new rulers so thoroughly disillusioned him that he withdrew from all activity in public affairs. His interest was later rekindled when the democrats returned to power, only to be ex-

---

[1] *Letters* VII.
[2] *Ibid.*

40

tinguished when the new government put his friend and teacher, Socrates, to death. Thereafter, Plato never again took an active part in the political life of Athens. After an extended trip abroad, he returned to the city of his birth and in 388 B.C. founded his famous Academy, or school of philosophy, in an olive grove outside the city. Although established primarily for the pursuit of pure knowledge and not for practical training, the Academy sent forth many of its students to occupy high political offices in the various Greek city-states.

THE SOCRATIC INFLUENCE

Some knowledge of Socrates (470–399 B.C.) is necessary as a preface to Plato's political theory because of the deep influence that the master had upon his disciple. Socrates, the son of an Athenian sculptor, dedicated himself early in life to combating the skepticism of the Sophists.[3] His brilliant mind, his dry humor, and his gift of repartee attracted a circle of admiring young pupils about him. The most faithful and discriminating member of this group was Plato. Socrates unfortunately committed nothing to writing; what knowledge we have of his doctrines is derived from the accounts given by others, particularly Plato, Xenophon, and Aristotle.

Socrates made no direct contribution to the development of political theory. He was interested mainly in the individual, and only incidentally in the state as a political institution. Indirectly, however, his legacy to the philosophy of government is threefold: the establishment of the inductive method of examining reality; the formulation of the doctrine that virtue is knowledge; and the teaching that there is an intellectual and moral order which can be discovered by man.

Socrates devoted considerable attention to the development of a methodology or mode of procedure for attaining truth. His efforts culminated in the establishment of a method of definition or dialectic, in the sense of critically examining into the truth of an opinion. By a process of successive questions and answers, he would seek to penetrate to the essence or nature of a subject, such as justice or freedom, in order to

---

[3] The Sophists were itinerant teachers who made their livelihood by offering instruction to young men. They formed no separate school of philosophy, usually teaching whatever their students were willing to pay for. Most of them were skeptics who denied the existence of any universal norms of human conduct. They openly boasted that through their technique "the worse course could be made to appear the better."

arrive at a universal definition. He would first elicit a superficial definition of the term from his listeners, and then through cross examination lead them to see its shortcomings. His questions always steered them slowly and imperceptibly toward the region where he believed that truth lay. Every step on the way was subjected to the critical inspection of reason. Socrates referred to this method as "maieutic," from the Greek *maieutikos* meaning midwife; hence the art of intellectual midwifery which seeks to deliver the slumbering thought from the mind and aid the intellect in arriving at the essence of a thing. The dialogues of Plato illustrate the Socratic method at its best.

According to Socrates, virtue is knowledge. The virtuous man is one who knows while the sinner is merely ignorant. Right knowing leads always of itself to right action; evil-doing results from deficient insight. It was inconceivable to Socrates that a man who knows the nature of goodness and truth would behave in an evil manner. For no man sins wittingly; only knowledge is needed to make him perfectly virtuous. The task, therefore, is to teach men to grasp and understand the great truths of life so that, knowing them, they will act virtuously and thereby remedy the defects of human society. A thorough and disciplined training of the mind is necessary if this objective is to be achieved.

Basic to his other contributions, Socrates taught that there are certain unchanging and universal principles of morality lying beneath the varying laws and customs found in the world. He insisted that such norms of truth exist independent of and paramount to individual opinion. When the Sophists argued that laws were but conventions established for the sake of expediency and that truth was simply what each individual thought it to be,[4] Socrates replied that there is a suprahuman realm of nature whose ordinances are binding on all men. This idea was not new (Sophocles' Antigone, for example, had appealed from certain edicts of King Creon arguing that they conflicted with a higher law which was "everywhere and eternally valid") but the belief that a higher law existed was based largely on mythology and religion. With Socrates, who predicated the presence of such a law on reason, the concept became formally incorporated into philosophical speculation.

Although Socrates criticized such Athenian practices as selection by

---

[4] Or as the Sophist Thrasymachus answered when asked to define justice, "everywhere there is one principle of justice, which is the interest of the stronger" (*Republic*, I, 339). Excerpts from the *Republic* are taken from the Modern Library edition, trans. by B. Jowett (New York: Random House).

lot and expressed doubt over the popular composition of the Assembly, he spent little time theorizing about the state and its institutions. It was with his pupil, Plato, that the first attempts at systematic political speculation began.

THEORY OF KNOWLEDGE

The introductory chapter emphasized the importance of the logical foundations or theory of knowledge that are implicit in all political thinking. Plato provides an excellent case study in this connection since his political theory cannot be fully grasped without first understanding his concept of knowledge. The Socratic doctrine that virtue is knowledge is basic to his speculations about the state. When we turn to this premise, we are immediately compelled to ask what he means by knowledge. Of what kind of knowledge is he speaking and how is it obtained — through the senses, by a *priori* thinking, or in some other fashion? Until we have an answer to these questions, the equating of virtue and knowledge can have little more than superficial significance.

Plato, like Parmenides and Heraclitus, was troubled by the problem of change and permanency, of the one and the many. He saw the world in a constant state of flux, but he felt that there was something permanently inherent in that which was changing. To answer this problem, he formulated his doctrine of Ideas, which is essentially a theory of knowledge. The knowledge which man obtains through the senses is a knowledge of the impermanent and changing. Perception brings into consciousness the world of changing appearances, of things that come and go. But there is another kind of knowledge, that of ideas as conceived by reason, or intuitively grasped independent of sense experience. This is the knowledge of true reality, of the essence of objects, of the universal and permanent. There are thus two worlds: the world of ideas which is and never becomes, and the world of sense perception which becomes but never is.

Plato's ideas are not mere thoughts, for thoughts are fleeting and transitory. His ideas, while incorporeal, have real existence separate and apart from the corporeal objects in which they appear. Hence the idea of man is different from any particular man, or the idea of the state different from any existing political institution. Corporeal man and corporeal state are merely reflections or shadows of the ideas man and state.

The objects which men perceive are not true reality since reality, the permanent and unchanging, cannot be seen but only thought. Nor do the objects of sense perception include the idea; they are but shadows or copies of it. The ordinary world of the senses may be a passing Heraclitean stream or flame, but the forms of river and fire exist in timeless and changeless perfection. These forms or ideas are the objects of true knowledge.

In the last book of the *Republic*, Plato explains that whenever individual objects have a common name, they also have a common form. To state this concept more simply, there is only one idea or form of a table even though there are many tables in the world. Just as the reflection of a table in a mirror is only apparent and not real, so are the individual tables unreal. They are only copies of the idea, the real table made by God — the "One who is the maker of all the works of all other workmen."[5] Of this one real table there can be true knowledge while of the many such articles made by cabinetmakers there can be only opinion. The philosopher is principally interested in the idea or form of desk, not in the many found in the sensible world.

The famous allegory of the prisoners in the cave which appears in the fourth book of the *Republic* is also helpful in understanding Plato's meaning of "idea." The prisoners, representing individuals who are destitute of philosophy, are chained in their underground cell so that they can look only to the front. In back of them is a blazing fire, and between the fire and the prisoners is a track with a parapet built along it. Behind this parapet are "persons carrying along various artificial objects, including figures of men and animals in wood or stone or other materials" which project above the barrier. The captives cannot see the objects being carried but only their shadows (the knowledge obtained by the senses) which are reflected before them on the wall of the cave. Even if a prisoner managed to turn and examine the objects, he would see that they were artificial and "not so real" as what he had thought them to be.

The path to true knowledge is tortuous and difficult. Only a select few, those who have learned to contemplate, are able to master it. Plato cautions that the facility for contemplation is limited to those whom nature has endowed with innate capacity for this task; and even for these, the ability is not acquired automatically but only by effort and

---

[5] *Republic*, X, 596.

training. He points out that if a prisoner in the cave is released and brought into the light of the upper world, the glare will so distress him that he will be unable to see "a single one of the things that he was now told were real." Only by a slow and painful process of forcing himself to turn toward the light will he gradually be able to see and understand.

> . . . just as the eye was unable to turn from darkness to light without the whole body, so too the instrument of knowledge can only by the movement of the whole soul be turned from the world of becoming into that of being, and learn by degrees to endure the sight of being, and of the brightest and best of being, or in other words of the good.[6]

The soul that reaches this stage will have successfully ascended into the intellectual sphere away from the changing world of shadows and artificial objects — it will have attained the beatific vision of the Good.

What role does sense knowledge play in the process? Plato answers that the senses make man curious and spur him on in his efforts to know reality. The soul, before its entrance into earthly existence, has gazed upon the world of ideas. It therefore recalls them when it sees their copy in the sense world. What training and discipline will best accustom the mind to grasp reality? Plato prescribes mathematics since it compels "the soul to reason about abstract number" and to rebel "against the introduction of visible or tangible objects into the argument." It teaches man "to raise out of the sea of change and lay hold of true being."[7] Do all men have equal capacity to attain true knowledge? Plato answers in the negative, since men are basically unequal in talent and potentiality. Even if all men possessed the same inherent capacity, few would be able to discipline and train themselves to the point where reason becomes supreme master over the passions and appetites; and only when reason dominates absolutely is the soul able to grasp reality.

To sum up Plato's theory of knowledge, sensible objects of the world cannot be known with any certitude since they are in a continual state of flux.[8] Particular things, in other words, are not real; they are inter-

---

[6] *Ibid.*, VII, 518.

[7] *Ibid.*, VII, 525.

[8] Aristotle's lucid résumé of Plato's epistemology should be noted. "Socrates . . . fixed thought for the first time on definitions; Plato accepted his teaching, but held that the problem applied not to sensible things but to entities of another kind — for this reason, that the common definition could not be a definition of any sensible thing, as they were always changing. Things of this sort, then, he called Ideas, and sensible things, he said, were all named after these, and in virtue of a relation to these; for

mediate between being and not-being. But there is another genus of being separate from matter and movement, called ideas, of which the sensible objects are only reflections. These ideas or forms are true reality, and since they are permanent and unchanging, they can be grasped and understood by the human intellect. The objects of the senses are true and good only to the extent that they correspond to their ideal prototype. Virtue therefore has its real existence in the same way that it exists in the mind, that is, immaterially and universally. We attain it by knowing it. Thus the man who knows what temperance or justice is will by that very fact be a temperate and just man.

THE PREMISES OF PLATO'S POLITICAL THOUGHT

Plato's literary style takes the form of a dialogue in which Socrates is the principal conversationalist.[9] Three of these dialogues contain substantially all of his political ideas, the Republic, Statesman, and Laws. The first is his masterpiece, one of the great works of all time. It is not an easy book to read with its wide range of subject matter, its treatment of all facets of the author's philosophy, and its poetic imagery and symbolism. Commentators cannot seem to agree as to whether it is a treatise primarily on justice, politics, or education. It has been characterized as a work which defies classification, belonging neither to politics, ethics, economics, or psychology, though it includes all these and more.[10] Despite these difficulties, it is possible to find a clear and unified pattern in those portions of the Republic which deal with political theory.

There are four fundamental concepts that lie at the basis of Plato's political philosophy: virtue is knowledge; men are unequal in talent, aptitude, and capability; the state is a natural institution; and the end of political society is the common good.

---

the many existed by participation in the Ideas that have the same name as they" (Metaphysics, I, 897).

[9] Professor Foster has noted that the dialogues were probably intended as memorials to Socrates but actually became vehicles for Plato's own development of his master's thought. As a result, it is now impossible to know with certainty when Socrates speaks whether it is really he or Plato speaking. Masters of Political Thought (London: Harrap & Co., 1942), p. 33.

[10] G. H. Sabine, A History of Political Thought (New York: Holt & Co., 1949), 2nd ed., p. 39.

Virtue Is Knowledge

Implicit in this doctrine are three concepts. First, truth must be objective and unchanging in order for us to attain knowledge of it. Otherwise we could have only opinion, as Plato remarks, and not true knowledge. Second, since virtue is equated with knowledge, the man who knows should be given a decisive role in public affairs. The task of finding good and virtuous rulers is thus simplified by the test of learning.[11] Third, the state should take an active role in educating its people, placing particular emphasis on those who are to be entrusted with the guidance and direction of public life. A more virtuous and well-functioning society will be fostered by training the members of the community to the full extent of their capabilities.

Inequality Among Men

Plato holds no concept of idealistic equality among men in respect to talent and capabilities. He is strongly convinced that nature has made men different in their capacities both for physical and intellectual pursuits and for attaining virtue. His parable of the metals makes this clear:

> Citizens, we shall say to them in our tale, you are brothers, yet God has framed you differently. Some of you have power of command, and in the composition of these he has mingled gold, wherefore also they have the greatest honor; others he has made of silver, to be auxiliaries; others again who are to be husbandmen and craftsmen he has composed of brass and iron.[12]

Some of the practical implications of this view of human inequality are well illustrated in the recent comments of an American educator. Discussing the question whether there should be some point in public education where those unable to go further could be shunted off into trade schools or into doing the humble work that must be done by somebody, he asks, "if a boy is born a truck driver, why don't we start him driving a truck?" Admitting that his remarks sound undemocratic, he observes that "there is nothing more undemocratic than the way the gods have distributed genes among the population of the world."[13]

---

[11] The word "virtue" is generally used in political philosophy in a broad sense to denote both moral and intellectual excellence. Plato divides virtue into four constituent elements: wisdom, courage, temperance, and justice.

[12] Republic, III, 415.

[13] Address by Dr. F. C. Baxter, quoted in Newsweek, June 4, 1956, p. 48.

Platonic theory holds that it would be utterly foolish and senseless to place the inferior individual in a position of public trust for which he is not fully qualified by nature and training. It also holds that such action would unfavorably affect the well-being of the inferior person by depriving him of the guidance of superior minds. "We say that he [the inferior individual] ought to be the servant of the best in whom the Divine rules: not . . . to the injury of the servant, but because every one had better be ruled by divine wisdom dwelling within him; or, if this be impossible, then by an external authority."[14] The title or right to rule should be virtue.

The State as a Natural Institution

What is the state, or phrased in another way, what is the nature of the political association? This is one of the pivotal questions of political philosophy. The whole relationship between the state and the individual depends on the way it is answered. The legitimate role of government will be one thing if the body politic is an entity with an existence and end of its own separate from that of the members who compose it. It will have quite another role if the state is merely a machine or instrumentality that has been fashioned by man to serve his individual convenience. And the function of government will be still different if the civil polity is a natural institution subsidiary to man's development.

Plato holds to an organic concept of the state. He points out that it is not people alone who constitute a body politic, although it is obviously made up of individuals; nor is it people living in geographical proximity, although a defined territory is one of the elements of a state. There must be some bond, he insists, which unites men together in a political association. He finds this bond to be justice, but justice in a different sense than we are accustomed to think of it. He starts his inquiry into the nature of the state by noting that individual man is unable to supply his wants and needs. "A state, I said, arises out of the needs of mankind; no one is self sufficing, but all of us have many wants . . . and [since] many persons are needed to supply them, one takes a helper for one purpose and another for another; and when these partners and helpers are gathered together in one habitation, the body of inhabitants is termed a state."[15]

---

14 *Republic*, IX, 590.
15 *Ibid.*, II, 369.

Men are by nature adapted to different occupations, some to farming, others to the skilled trades, and a lesser number to the various professions and intellectual pursuits. By specializing in that for which each is best suited, optimum progress can be made since all things are produced more plentifully and easily and of a better quality. No individual is a jack-of-all-trades but all — young and old, women and children, craftsmen and laborers, industrialists and farmers, rulers and governed — have their special work marked out for them. It is here that justice lies: in each man fulfilling the role in society for which he is best fitted by the original constitution of his nature.

Plato argues that a system based on his principle of natural skills would create a balanced pattern to fit the intellectual and physical attributes of diverse people. By learning to do well the work that he is born to do, each individual makes his proper contribution to the community and progresses along the path toward his own self-fulfillment. Basic to this approach is a recognition of the community good as a precondition to the good of the individual. The state or social whole is necessary to man. If it is weak and unhealthy, its ability to assist the individual in realizing his maximal perfection is correspondingly impaired. From these premises, the conclusion emerges that the state is a natural institution arising out of the nature of man. It is not, as the sophists taught, a mere product of convention; nor is it, as the fascists were later to hold, a spiritual entity in which man's individuality is completely absorbed.

A second aspect of Plato's theory of the state is also of importance. His definition of justice implies a single whole in which each member acts as a part. This conception permits him to compare the state to the body of man. "The state is the individual writ large." It is an entity composed of different parts that are complementary and mutually dependent and that act together in pursuit of a common end. An injury to any member is an injury to the whole body. If one group in a society is impoverished or abused, the health of the entire community is affected.

The organic view held by Plato does not imply that the state has an existence of its own separate from its component parts. On the contrary, it recognizes that the thoughts and acts of the body politic are simply the thoughts and acts of its members thinking and acting collectively as members. This denial of separate being to the state is sometimes obscured by the unusual stress that Plato places on the unity of the social organism. Political unity, in fact, becomes almost a fetish with him. He repeatedly emphasizes his conviction that the greatest evil to the community is "discord and distraction and plurality," and the greatest good "the bond of unity." This concept dominates the whole organization of his ideal state with its class structure, its division of labor, its communism for the rulers, its educational system, and its completely planned society.

The Purpose of the State

The state comes into being because of the insufficiency of individual man to supply his own needs. It seeks to establish a division of labor that will bring increased material benefits to the individual. Through education and the promotion of the arts and sciences it endeavors to aid him in his intellectual and cultural pursuits, and through its laws it tries to guide him in the path of moral virtue. Its prime task, as envisioned by Plato, is to direct the common life of man in order that all may attain happiness.

The end of the state is not the good of any particular individual or class but the good of all, the common good or general welfare. Plato constantly reiterates that "our aim in founding the State was not the disproportionate happiness of any one class, but the greatest happiness of the whole."[16] Just as the business of the physician is the good of the patient, so the object of the ruler is the welfare of the governed. Throughout Plato's writings, the good of the people and the good of the state are looked upon as coincidental aims. He could conceive of no situation in which the interests of the subjects would conflict with the public interests of the state. He felt that such a conflict could arise only in the case of the rulers, and here he called for rigid safeguards.

The high role which the Republic assigns to the state prompts the reader to ask whether this institution has the capacity to play such a part in the affairs of human life. Plato admits that no existing state does; only the ideal commonwealth modeled after the polis "laid up in the heavens" can enable men to achieve the Good and to perfect their natures.

THE IDEAL STATE

Plato begins his Republic by seeking the definition of justice. He first

---

[16] Ibid., IV, 420.

points out that justice is an important virtue of the state as well as of the individual. Then using this observation to transform the question concerning justice into an investigation of political theory, he somewhat arbitrarily notes that it would be easier to discover this attribute in the larger specimen, the state, than in the smaller, the human individual. For the quantity of justice is likely to be greater and more easily discernible in the large than in the small model. It is imprinted on states in larger characters and is more easily recognizable. "I propose therefore that we enquire into the nature of justice and injustice, first as they appear in the State, and secondly in the individual, proceeding from the greater to the lesser and comparing them."[17] The initial task in this approach is to construct a theoretically perfect state so that perfect justice can be ascertained. Plato proceeds to do this in his prototype of all utopias. As previously indicated, he finds that the just state is one in which each of its component parts performs the function for which it is naturally adapted.

Class Structure

Based on the principle of diversity of talent, the members of the state are divided into three classes: rulers, warriors, and producers.[18] The first is likened to the faculty of reason in man, the second to his spirit or passion, and the third to his sensuous appetite. The rulers determine the entire course of the state through legislation and general direction; the warrior class, which includes both military and administrative officials, guards the state and executes the laws; and the producers, the great mass of common people, provide for the material needs of the social body. This division rests on the assumption that there are basically three types of men: those who are equipped by nature to rule, those who are able to perform administrative and military functions under proper guidance, and those who are capable of working but not ruling.

The class structure which Plato proposes is not a caste system but one which at least theoretically provides for social mobility. Membership in the various categories is to be determined by ability and not by birth or wealth. Each child, no matter how humbly born, is to be accorded

---

[17] Ibid., II, 369. We see here again a typical device of the Greek thinkers, the analogizing between the human body and the body politic.

[18] Plato at times refers to the first two classes collectively as "guardians," and to the second class as "auxiliaries."

the highest training warranted by his natural capacity, and each individual is to be placed in a position corresponding to his ability. It would
thus be possible for the child of a laborer to rise to a high administrative
or military post or for the son of a guardian to be demoted to the working
class. Plato felt, however, that instances of interclass transfers would be
rare. As he remarks in the parable of the metals, a golden parent will
sometimes have a silver son, or a silver parent a golden son, but generally
the species will "be preserved in the children."[19]

The Educational System

Granted that everyone should adopt that form of activity for which
he is specially marked out by nature, how can society put such a plan
into operation? What assurance is there that everyone will submit to
filling his nature-prescribed role, or even that he can determine what
his individual part should be? The main point, Plato answers, is to
establish a comprehensive and thorough system of training. In this way
the talents of the individuals can be ascertained and developed, and the
ethical quality of submission cultivated. The Republic endeavors to outline
such a scheme of education.

Contrary to the practice then prevailing in Athens where education
was considered a private or family affair rather than a state responsibility,
Plato makes it a matter of governmental concern. As his ideal state indicates, he was greatly impressed by many aspects of Spartan life and
government. During his youth he had seen Sparta with its autocratic
rule and highly disciplined citizen body triumph over democratic Athens.
This event had left a deep impression on him. At the same time, he was
a product of the humanistic and cultural traditions of Athenian civilization. These two strains — Spartan and Athenian — met in his political
science. This intermixture is evident in his treatment of education. His
plan for training the youth follows broadly the Spartan example in the
organization of the educational system but departs radically from it in
content. Although highly regimented, the Platonic system, unlike the
Spartan preoccupation with physical training, emphasizes intellectual discipline and the formation of the whole man by imparting to him a
balanced harmony of mind and body.

Apparently all members of the ideal state were to receive the normal

---

[19] Republic, III, 415.

course of education which included reading, writing, arithmetic, music, and gymnastics. There was to be no discrimination practiced against women. Those who possessed the necessary qualifications were to receive the same training as the men and were to be admitted to the same high offices. The preliminary state of education would last until the age of eighteen and would be followed by two years of military training for the able-bodied. The formal process of education would then come to an end for all except a small group of talented students. Those who demonstrated high intellectual potentialities and passed certain qualifying tests during the first two stages would be accepted as probationers for higher offices. For the next ten years this group would undergo a rigorous course of study with emphasis on mathematics. The pruning out process would continue during this time as it had in the earlier stages, thus forming different grades of military and administrative officials. Those who survived this period were to be given an additional five years of training devoted to the study of philosophy. If they failed to demonstrate a philosophic nature under trials and tests, they would be eliminated and assigned to governmental duty in tasks appropriate to their capacities.

The students who successfully completed their philosophical studies would be considered ready to assume high administrative responsibilities in government. They would perform these duties in the service of the state for fifteen years. During this tenure, they would undergo a further series of character tests. If they survived this period with distinction, they would, at the age of fifty, become the guardians or rulers of the state, the philosopher kings, entrusted with the supreme responsibility of statesmanship. In this capacity, they would serve as sovereign legislators, establishing major policies and charting the course of the state. As elder statesmen, they would spend only a portion of their time in the guidance and direction of public affairs; the remainder would be devoted to philosophic contemplation since "the time has now arrived at which they must raise the eye of the soul to the universal light which lightens all things, and behold the absolute good; for that is the pattern according to which they are to order the State and the lives of individuals."[20] Having come out of the cave to witness true reality, the philosopher must then descend into the darkness to impart light and wisdom to the prisoners of the earthly world.

---

[20] Ibid., VII, 540.

The Government

The foremost objective of the Platonic educational system is to produce a class of rulers, pre-eminent in virtue and ability. Governing a
community, Plato observes, is just as specialized a task as treating the
sick. Since people would not relegate the latter task to one without
medical training, neither should they entrust the care of the state to
amateurs. The multitude cannot attain proficiency in political science
any more than it can acquire skill in the science of physics or mathematics. True knowledge is limited to the exceptional few, and it is these
who should rule society.

Plato clearly is no democrat. Only those who are wise and virtuous
are to possess political power in the ideal state, and their views alone
are to prevail in the social order. The average individual must be completely barred from participation in public affairs. He must have no
voice in either the selection of his rulers or the formulation of governmental policy. Once a governing group of the intellectual elite is brought
into being, full and absolute political power should be placed in its
hands. Like artists, the philosopher rulers would fashion the state and
society in the image of its divine prototype. They would begin

> by taking the State and the manners of men, from which, as from a
> tablet, they will rub out the picture and leave a clean surface . . .
> they will first look at absolute justice and beauty and temperance, and
> again at the human copy. . . . And one feature they will erase, and
> another they will put in, until they have made the ways of men, as far
> as possible, agreeable to the ways of God.[21]

Plato nowhere indicates what organs of government will be established,
how policy will be formulated, or how responsibility will be enforced
in the ideal state. These are apparently matters of mere detail that would
rest entirely in the discretion of the experts.

Plato refers to the rule of the philosopher kings as either monarchy
or aristocracy, indicating that both signify rule by the best and that
both forms would be acceptable, dependent on circumstances. In modern
terminology, the type of government proposed by the *Republic* would
be referred to as "benevolent despotism" since the rulers are limited by
no constitution or laws, nor even by the customs of the people. They
simply direct the life of the community as their wisdom dictates. The

---

[21] *Ibid.*, VI, 501.

philosopher king should no more be compelled to follow prescribed rules of law than the expert physician should be bound by the formulas set out in a medical textbook. Plato does not mean by this, however, that the ruler can act arbitrarily and capriciously. Just as the good physician observes the principles of bodily functioning in prescribing for his patients, so the good ruler governs in accordance with the objective principles of justice that are embedded in nature. For it is nature that fixes the limits of human conduct — a concept that, in traditional thought, lies at the heart of true constitutionalism. Plato's rulers would be chosen precisely because they had attained knowledge and therefore virtue (for virtue is knowledge).

Platonic Communism

Plato held that there were two serious defects in the existing governments of his day: the incompetence of public officials (which he felt was largely peculiar to democratic states) and factionalism, or the struggle among opposing groups, classes, and individuals for power. He would eliminate the first weakness through the elaborate educational scheme that was designed to produce a class of experts in statecraft. He would seek to remove the second by a communal system imposed on the ruling classes.

The Greeks were cognizant of the influence that economic motives exert on political action. Plato was not alone in believing that the most serious threat to the unity of the state lies in the dissension that inevitably arises between those who have and those who have not. Each group or faction in the community seeks political power chiefly to further its economic interests. The corrective, as proposed by Plato, is to abolish private wealth for the ruling classes: the guardians and auxiliaries. Devotion to their high public responsibility can tolerate no rival. Since the producers or workers are to have no voice in the government, they can safely be excluded from the communal restrictions. For if the rulers are free from dissension, there is little likelihood that the rest of the city will quarrel either with them or with one another. What Plato fears is the union of political and economic power; what he desires is the union of political power and wisdom.

Plato points out that family ties constitute a second source of dissension in the community since affection and anxiety for one's family is a form of self-seeking that competes with the state for the loyalty of its rulers. The remedy here, as it is in respect to property, is to abolish the family unit for the governing groups. The *Republic* suggests that the guardians and auxiliaries be housed in barracks, be paid nothing other than their board and lodging, and be subjected to regulated breeding.

Plato has a second purpose in mind in abolishing marriage and the family. He argues that no one would tolerate the indiscriminate breeding of fine animals since such breeding would deteriorate the quality of the stock. Why then permit the unselected pairing of human beings when man's efforts should be directed toward the improvement of the race? If progress is to be made in this direction, the children of the rulers must be the issues of temporary unions based on eugenic principles. Immediately after their birth, the offspring must be taken from their mothers and placed in the care of the state. By establishing familial and property communism, private possessive emotions would be minimized and few temptations would remain to deflect the rulers from the path of duty. There would then be no occasion for those in power to "tear the city in pieces by differing about mine and not mine; each man dragging any acquisition which he has made into a separate house of his own, where he has a separate wife and children and private pleasures and pains."[22]

Plato feels that by removing the private interests of the governing classes, all motive for them to use their public power toward any end other than that of the general welfare will be destroyed. His communism, unlike the modern brand, is not economic, but moral and political. It does not seek to destroy private property in order to equalize wealth among the people. It seeks only to communize the property of the ruling classes in order to eliminate the possibility of conflict between their private interests and their public duty. It is interesting to note that in establishing these safeguards, Plato is confessing that few men, even those subjected to the rigorous training and education outlined in the *Republic*, are able to attain true knowledge. A ruler who possesses such knowledge would by that very fact be virtuous and above the temptations that lead to selfish and tyrannical action. He would not have to be checked by such institutional devices as the *Republic* proposes. Even Plato could not overlook the problem that all government faces: the weakness of the flesh.

---

[22] *Ibid.*, V, 464.

The Ideal State: Dream or Possibility

Did Plato fashion a mere utopia, or did he believe that his plan was possible of attainment? When the point was raised, he asked "would a painter be any the worse because after having delineated with consummate art an ideal of a perfectly beautiful man, he was unable to show that any such man could ever have existed?"[23] Whether the ideal state is attainable or beyond human reach is not vitally material to Plato's thinking although it gives it the flavor of unreality. The significant point he seeks to make is that the idea of the perfect polis serves as a standard for existing states. If they do not measure up to the ideal, so much the worse for them. The idea of the perfect state, moreover, serves as a model for the individual to guide his private conduct no matter how bad the community may be in which he actually lives. It will be easier for him to see the pattern of justice and virtue in the larger model than in the smaller cosmos of man.

Plato, however, meant his ideal state to be something more than a mere daydream or imaginary utopia. He conceived it in all seriousness as a practicable and attainable ideal, incorporating in it many social and political features of existing Greek cities. A number of its more radical characteristics had actually been realized in Sparta. He was well aware that a union of knowledge and political power would have to take place before a civil community, such as he visualized, would be possible. The wise man may possess the virtue necessary to exercise power in the best and most enlightened manner, but there is little that he can do to reform society so long as this power resides in unwise hands. Plato admits that the possibility of uniting political power and wisdom is slight and that it could happen only by "some divine chance" since the people do not have sufficient insight to grasp the significance of such a union. Yet the cause is by no means hopeless. There is always the chance that an individual who possesses the true philosopher's temperament might come into political power by inheriting a throne and that he would then set out to reconstruct the state.[24] "Let there be one man who has

---

[23] *Ibid.*, V, 472.
[24] Plato visited Syracuse on several occasions to aid in the education of King Dionysius, a young man in whom he saw the possibilities of a philosopher king. He felt that Dionysius could provide the occasion for radical political reform, but his hopes in this regard failed to materialize.

a city obedient to his will, and he might bring into existence the ideal polity about which the world is so incredulous."[25]

How would such a ruler set about his task of political reform? Plato foresaw that the process of conversion would be slow and gradual. As he describes it, the ruler would have to begin by

> sending out into the country all the inhabitants of the city who are more than ten years old, and take possession of their children, who will be unaffected by the habits of their parents; these they will train in . . . the laws which we have given them: and in this way the State and constitution of which we were speaking will soonest and most easily attain happiness.[26]

The old are too fixed in their habits and beliefs to change; only the young are susceptible to radical molding. Social reconstruction must therefore begin with them.

THE STATESMAN AND THE LAWS

The *Republic* was written by Plato when he was about forty years of age; the *Statesman* and the *Laws* represent the work of his later life. These latter two works deal more with the possible than the ideal. They contain some modification of his political theory in that they restore the general pattern of Athenian democracy as a concession to human frailty. Although the ethical content of his thought remains the same, his attitude toward men has become more tolerant, more understanding of human weaknesses, and more realistic. He does not discard his basic conviction that the best state is one in which everything is placed under the personal and absolute control of the wisest. This is the ideal state "than which there can never be a truer or better." Here is the pattern on which we must ever fix our eyes, which we must cling to and "seek with all our might for one which is like this."[27]

Now, however, Plato expresses doubt that rulers can be found who will be willing to sublimate completely their personal desires and possessions to the interests of the state. Nor is he still certain that the knowledge necessary for a true philosopher king is attainable. "No man's nature is able to know what is best for human society, or knowing, always willing and able to do what is best."[28] Abolishing property and family ties for

---

[25] *Republic*, VI, 501.   [27] *Laws*, 739.
[26] *Ibid.*, VII, 540.   [28] *Ibid.*, 875A.

the rulers remains the most desirable plan, but Plato now cautions that it is to men "we are discoursing and not to gods." His belief in the perfectibility of man through education is supplanted by an awareness that the weakness of human nature makes a new approach to the problem of government necessary.

Having made these concessions to the frailties of man, Plato is compelled to make his ruling group subject to laws which designate the organization and powers of the government. There would be no need of such laws under the rule of the philosopher kings. "We must take things as they are, however, and kings do not arise in cities in the natural course of things in the way the royal bee is born in a beehive — one individual obviously outstanding in body and mind. And therefore it seems men have to gather together and work out written codes."[29] Plato concedes that it would be extremely dangerous to give unlimited power to men buffeted about by passions and temptations. An individual with such power "will be bound to employ it to the hurt and injury and death of anyone he pleases."[30] Somewhat bitter and disillusioned, Plato finds it necessary to accommodate government to the realities of human life.

In the Laws, Plato proposes a mixture of aristocracy and democracy, a balancing of wealth and numbers, in order to stabilize political power. The Council, an administrative body, is to consist of elected representatives from each of four economic classes. Voting is to be compulsory under penalty of fine. A group of thirty-seven judges would constitute the judiciary. The legislative function plays a small role in the proposed state since Plato assumes that the laws would be provided beforehand by a lawgiver such as Solon. The details of the laws would be filled in by the judges and the administrative officials. If major changes became necessary, they would be enacted by the Nocturnal Council, an intellectual aristocracy composed of priests, the ten eldest judges, and some younger members. Changes would be made only in rare instances when great and pressing need existed.

Plato emphasizes that the state which he proposes in the Laws is only the second best, a concession to practical exigencies. Even in this second best state, he still incorporates many of the features of his ideal republic. Although he no longer prescribes an educational program to be pursued under the rigid supervision of the government, he makes it

---

[29] Statesman, trans. by J. B. Skemp (New York: Liberal Arts Press, 1957), p. 80.
[30] Ibid.

perfectly clear that there is no greater sin than ignorance. Those who attain high office must be carefully trained and educated. The rulers would no longer be required to have wives and children in common but they would continue to eat at common tables in which the men and women would be separated. Laws would minutely regulate many aspects of private life. The people would be limited in the amount of wealth that they could possess; poets would be required to submit their works to the censorship of the magistrates; and women as well as men would be taught the use of arms. Throughout the Laws, as in the Republic, runs the indestructible theme that "a man's whole energies throughout life should be devoted to the acquisition of the virtue proper to man."

Plato abandoned hope for the state of the Republic when he became convinced that it was not "within the horizon of practical politics." Yet it is doubtful that his second best polity was any closer to the level of ordinary life, or much more possible of attainment, than his ideal. The tone is still too sublime, too divorced from the political arena, too unaware of the force of popular opinion. The Statesman and the Laws, nonetheless, contain many valuable commentaries on political behavior and institutional arrangements. Aristotle later utilized a number of these observations in the development of his Politics.

SUMMARY

No classical writer is quoted more frequently by modern political commentators than Plato. His thinking continues to have vital relevancy and meaning for the contemporary scene. No one, for example, has better demonstrated the high position of public service in the hierarchy of values. As he emphasized in his allegory of the cave, those who have climbed from the darkness to see the vision of Goodness must not remain on the heights, refusing to return to the mundane affairs of the world. In a remarkable passage, he points out the price that men of ability must pay if they abstain from participation in political life: "Now the worst part of the penalty is that he who refuses to rule is liable to be ruled by one who is inferior to himself."[31]

Plato endeavored to make it clear to all ages that ethics is an integral part of politics. He recognized no double standard of morality, one for political office and one for private life. Politics as such cannot be amoral or morally neutral; it is too deeply involved with human acts. It therefore has moral dimensions and a moral scope; it is concerned with values and norms, with ethical conduct. The student of politics must be interested in more than

---

[31] Republic, I, 347.

what is; he must also be concerned with *what ought to be.* Political philosophy cannot tell him how to fashion or operate political and social institutions but it can direct him toward a good rather than an evil use of them.

Platonic philosophy represented an extreme reaction against the relativism of the sophists. It attempted to establish, through reason and insight, an absolute truth that was good at all times and in all places. It looked upon man as a rational and moral creature with an ultimate destiny that transcends the world of time and space. Man is a spark of the divine, created for the divine. All earthly life has value and meaning only as an education for a higher supersensible existence. Unlike the traditional natural law approach, however, Plato's concept of reality did not permit him to discover truth in the nature of sensible objects since such objects had no real existence for him. His natural law is consequently abstract and mystical rather than concrete and realistic.

Classical thought, as typified by Plato, emphasizes the primary role that education plays in society. It places the responsibility on the state to see that its citizen body is properly trained and educated. Society must not be wasteful of talent. It must reach out and afford ample opportunity to those who for economic reasons are unable to obtain the highest level of education commensurate with their talents. Plato and his colleagues insisted that the minds of the people must be directed toward the good if corruption, crime, and abuse of power are to be minimized and rooted up. They would have fully agreed with the UNESCO slogan that reads: "Since wars begin in the minds of men, it is in the minds of men that we must seek to prevent them."

Plato was the first of the great political theorists; but some of the basic premises that permeated his thinking, particularly his theory of knowledge, made a right understanding of the nature of politics difficult. He assumed, in the light of his theoretical presuppositions, that the life of a community could be fashioned by the rulers in the same manner that an individual shapes his own life. He failed to see that the political life of a state is patterned more by the people themselves than by their political governors. He placed too high a confidence in man's willingness to subordinate his individual desires to the common good. He refused to recognize the merit and ability of the average individual. He assumed that intelligent men could be given political wisdom simply by proper training. Finally, he felt that a body of wise men could be selected through his "winnowing out" process, and that government could then be left in their hands without restraint. History has demonstrated the fallacy of these assumptions.

BIBLIOGRAPHY

Barker, Ernest, *Greek Political Theory: Plato and his Predecessors* (London: Methuen, 1925).
Crossman, R. H. S., *Plato Today* (New York: Oxford, 1939).
Demos, Raphael, *The Philosophy of Plato* (New York: Scribner, 1939).

Doherty, K. F., "God and the Good in Plato," New Scholasticism, October, 1956.

Edelstein, L., "Function of the Myth in Plato's Philosophy," Journal of the History of Ideas, October, 1949.

Field, G. C., "Plato's Political Thought and Its Value Today," Philosophy, July, 1941.

Freeman, Kathleen, The Pre-Socratic Philosophers (Oxford: Blackwell, 1946).

Foster, M. B., The Political Philosophies of Plato and Hegel (Oxford: Clarendon Press, 1935).

Gittler, J. B., "A Note on Greek Sociological Thought Before Plato and Aristotle," Social Science, January, 1948.

Grant, G. P., "Plato and Popper," Canadian Journal of Economics and Political Science, May, 1954.

Grene, David, Man in His Pride: A Study in the Political Philosophy of Thucydides and Plato (Chicago: University of Chicago Press, 1950).

Kelsen, Hans, "Platonic Justice," Ethics, April, 1938.

Levinson, R. B., In Defense of Plato (Cambridge: Harvard University Press, 1953).

Lewis, H. D., "Plato and the Social Contract," Mind, January, 1939.

Lodge, Rupert C., Plato's Theory of Ethics (New York: Harcourt Brace, 1928).

McIlwain, C. H., The Growth of Political Thought in the West (New York: Macmillan, 1932).

McKeown, J. E., "Sociological Misinterpretations of Plato's Republic," American Catholic Sociological Review, October, 1955.

Miller, James W., "The Development of the Philosophy of Socrates," Review of Metaphysics, June, 1953.

Morrow, Glen R., "Plato and the Law of Nature," in Essays in Political Theory, ed. by M. R. Konvitz and A. E. Murphy (Ithaca: Cornell University Press, 1948).

Popper, Karl R., The Open Society and Its Enemies (Princeton: Princeton University Press, 1950).

Poyser, G. H., "Ancient Light on a Modern Problem: the Individual and the State," Hibbert Journal, July, 1953.

Ritter, Constantin, The Essence of Plato's Philosophy (London: G. Allen and Unwin, 1933).

Robin, Leon, Greek Thought and the Origins of the Scientific Spirit (New York: Knopf, 1928).

Ross, David, Plato's Theory of Ideas (Oxford: Clarendon Press, 1951).

Strauss, Leo, "On a New Interpretation of Plato's Political Philosophy," Social Research, September, 1946.

Tarrant, D., "Cave and the Sun," Hibbert Journal, July, 1953.

Taylor, A. E., Plato: The Man and His Work, 6th ed. (New York: Meridian Books, 1956).

Welles, C. B., "Economic Background of Plato's Communism," Journal of Economic History, 1948.

Wild, John, Plato's Theory of Man (Cambridge: Harvard University Press, 1945).

Chapter IV

ARISTOTLE: THE SCIENCE OF POLITICS

"We should consider not only what form of government is best, but also what is possible and what is easily attainable by all" (Aristotle, *Politics*, IV, 1).

FEW men in world history have left a more lasting impression on the thinking of mankind than Aristotle. His writings perennially excite lively interest among philosophers and exert a strong force in contemporary discussions. Much of the history of philosophy could in fact be written around the history of the influence of Aristotle and Plato. Some commentators, such as Coleridge, go so far as to divide all men into Platonists and Aristotelians. Although this division may be somewhat arbitrary and oversimplified, the vigorous philosophical debates which periodically take place between the intransigent followers of the two schools continue to throw much light on present-day intellectual problems.

Aristotle was born in 384 B.C. in Stagira, a small Greek city on the peninsula of Chalcidice. He came from an upper middle class family, his father serving as court physician to Amyntas II, father of Philip the Great. At the age of seventeen, he went to Athens to enroll in the Academy of Plato. He remained in Athens as a member of the school for twenty years, until its founder's death. During the next twelve years, he traveled widely, married, and served for three years at the court of Philip as tutor to the young Macedonian crown prince, Alexander. When the latter was suddenly called to the throne by Philip's murder in 336, Aristotle returned to Athens and set up his own school in the Lyceum, a gymnasium consecrated to Lycian Apollo. The school received the title "peripatetic" because of the shady walks where many of the lectures took place. Most of Aristotle's productive writing dates from the time that he founded the Academy to his death in 322 B.C.

When Alexander the Great died in 323 B.C. during one of his campaigns, anti-Macedonian agitation broke out in Athens. Aristotle, suspect because of his previous association with Alexander, was indicted (as Socrates had been) on the charge of impiety, a capital offense. Since conviction was certain, he fled from Athens to seek sanctuary in Chalcis, a city on the island of Euboea, "so as not to give the Athenians a second chance to sin against philosophy." His exile was of short duration since he died the following year at the age of sixty-two.

The breadth of knowledge displayed by Aristotle, the catholicity of his mind, the vastness of his intellectual achievement, and the influence he exerted on subsequent thought find little parallel in the history of the Western world. The imposing body of his work includes treatises in such widely ranging fields as logic, physics, metaphysics, biology, meteorology, rhetoric, poetry, ethics, and politics. Although he was profoundly influenced by Plato, he broke away from his teacher's influence in certain basic respects. Instead of Plato's distrust of empirical reality, we find Aristotle constantly testing his hypotheses by reference to the sensible and concrete; and instead of Plato's preoccupation with mathematics and its methodology as the correct approach to the social sciences, we find Aristotle seeking his starting point in matter — in historical circumstances, existing facts, and previous experience.

Despite the differences between the two, Aristotle is one with Plato in holding that man is a political animal who can fulfill his nature only in the polis; that the state is a moral institution which exists to aid man in attaining his perfection; and that the true state seeks to further the welfare of the whole and not the good of privileged groups alone. Both thinkers viewed with alarm the instability (stasis) of Greek political life, and both placed great faith in education as a corrective device for the ills of their day.

ARISTOTELIAN THEORY OF KNOWLEDGE

According to Plato, true reality is found only in the archetypal ideas, the universals, such as man in general or the state in general. The particular things that the senses perceive are merely images of the ideas — shadows of reality — which are objects of opinion but not of true knowledge. The universal, in this view, is apart from particulars. It cannot be arrived at by any process of abstracting or disentangling from sensible objects the features common to all of them. It can only be apprehended by the intellect and not by sense experience since it subsists outside the temporal world. Aristotle recognizes that Plato's theory of ideas is insufficient to explain empirical facts. While he agrees that the primary object of the intellect is to know the essences of things, he holds that such essences must not be conceived as different from the objects of experience. As universals, they exist only in the intellect. Hence, unlike Plato's world of ideas, the universals possess no existence or have no independent reality separate from the material objects in which they inhere. Forms are in things; they are not themselves separately existing individual objects.

Aristotle maintains that the essence of an object becomes known to the human intellect through abstraction. In this process, characteristics which are peculiar to some members of a group are disregarded and only those which are common to all are retained. Thus by discarding all the peculiarities which differentiate John, Henry, and James from each other, such as height, weight, and color, the intellect seizes upon those elements which are common to all of them — rationality, sentiency, life, body — and forms them into the idea of man. Knowledge, in this light, begins in the senses but goes beyond sense perception, since the intellect gives knowledge of the essences and properties of things which are more than the mere enumeration or collection of facts and experiences.

The differences in the epistemology of Plato and Aristotle find reflection in their political theory. What the former is asking for is not the best possible state but the ideal polis based upon a model that is far beyond the empirical and historical world. Ernst Cassirer has noted that even though Plato's state provides a pattern for human actions, it has no definite ontological status, no place in reality.[1] As a result, his political philosophy bears at points the same character of unreality as his account of natural things. His exaggerated stress on unity can similarly be traced to his theory of knowledge. Since the idea is more real than the object or species and actually contains it, and since in the logical order the more universal concept is imposed on the less, the lesser societies (individual, family, voluntary association) are properly absorbed in the more universal community, the state.

In contrast to Plato, Aristotle's epistemology enables him to look for the determining principles, the essence and nature, of objects in the objects themselves. His political speculation consequently has the feeling of reality. It seeks the possible and the mean, rather than the impossible

---

[1] *Myth of the State* (New Haven: Yale University Press, 1946), p. 78.

and the extreme. It begins with the particular and the individual, not the universal and the whole. This theory of knowledge conditions the methodology to be employed in an examination of the state in two ways: first, the inquiry must start with an empirical investigation of actually existing political institutions and practices; and second, the study must begin with the parts which make up the whole. Only by proceeding from the simple to the composite can the nature and properties of the whole be properly understood.

THE SPECULATIVE AND PRACTICAL SCIENCES

There is a second difference in the general intellectual approaches to reality that were followed by Plato and Aristotle, a difference which perhaps occasioned a sharper distinction in their political thinking than did their divergent theories of knowledge. Unlike his predecessor, Aristotle differentiates between speculative and practical sciences. The former, which include physics, metaphysics and mathematics, deal with necessary and nonoperable matter — matter which can be known but which cannot be affected by human efforts. There is nothing, for instance, that we can do to change the fact that two plus two are four. The object of these sciences is to see truth simply for the sake of understanding the nature of reality. The end of speculative sciences is to know, and only to know. The knowledge that is so obtained may be used for practical purposes, but such use is only incidental to the object of the science.

The practical sciences, which include ethics and politics, deal with the contingent and operable, with matter that may be affected by the acts of man. As Aristotle notes, "human interference can make them otherwise." The rules which the practical sciences embody are never rigidly universal. They are subject to occasional exceptions because of the contingent character of the facts with which they deal. Their end, moreover, is not only knowledge but action, the use of knowledge to achieve certain goals. Man studies ethics not primarily for the sake of knowing what is good, but for the purpose of acting in a good manner. Similarly, the end of politics "is not knowledge but action"; it is "concerned with nothing so much as with producing a certain character in the citizens, or in other words with making them good."[2] Since the

---

[2] Aristotle, *Politics*, I, 1 and 10. Excerpts from the *Politics* are taken from the Modern Library edition, trans. by B. Jowett (New York: Random House, 1943).

practical sciences deal with the free and voluntary acts of men, they require more than the perfection of reason (knowledge); they require rectitude of the will.

Aristotle points out that unlike the universal truths of the speculative sciences, there is no certainty in the means that man may take to attain his ethical and political goals. One course of action or one set of political institutions may be more effective under given circumstances than another. The statesman must not only know in general what is good for man; he must also be able to judge correctly in a particular situation that a certain act will secure the good. The intellect is capable of giving man the ends and norms, but it cannot give him the practical judgment or prudence to decide in each specific case what means will be more likely to attain the desired end. Nor, and this is equally important, can knowledge alone assure him that he will seek the proper end. Rational insight alone is not sufficient for right action. The strength of the will must be added to it since the will has the power of doing the wrong thing contrary to right insight. Ethical virtue is the continuing state of the will by means of which practical reason rules the desires. How man will act in a given instance therefore depends upon the right ordering of his will and not upon the perfection of his intellect. He may know that absolute integrity in public office is proper behavior, but the passion of avarice may supersede this knowledge.

In repudiating Plato's teaching that scientific knowledge alone qualifies a man to rule (as it would if politics were a speculative science), Aristotle insists that to know is not sufficient and that rectitude of the will and prudence are equally if not more important. The learned man, the expert, is not always the most prudent and virtuous. Virtue is not acquired by study but by moral discipline, practice, and experience. The man who is to be good must be well trained and habituated. Entrusting the conduct of the state to an elite corps of experts would give no assurance of good rule unless the members of this corps were also the most virtuous and prudent.

POLITICAL THEORY

Aristotle's approach to political theory is found chiefly in his *Politics*[3]

---

[3] The *Politics* is not an orderly and integrated book. A large portion of it is probably composed of lecture notes edited by Aristotle's pupils. The order of the

and to a lesser extent in the relevant parts of his *Nicomachean Ethics*, *Rhetoric*, and *Metaphysics*. Underlying his political speculation are four ethical and philosophical premises: man is a rational being with a free will; politics is a practical science; there is a universal moral law which all men are obliged to obey; and the state is a natural institution.

The first two principles have already been commented on; the third requires only a brief reference. Aristotle adhered to the authentic natural law philosophy. In fact, he is responsible for the first disciplined formulation of this concept. Plato had previously taught that man must follow in the main a universal pattern of action if he is to achieve his destiny. His idealism, however, prevented him from basing such a law on the ontological structure of sensible objects. Aristotle's realism, on the other hand, enabled him to bring it "down from the heavens" and give it objective meaning and application.

The fourth Aristotelian premise is closely related to the third. Aristotle looks upon the nature of an object as that which it is capable of becoming. "The nature of a thing is its end. For what each thing is when fully developed, we call its nature whether we are speaking of a man, a horse, or a family."[4] The end of man, as of all being, is the fulfillment of his nature. Standing alone, the individual is incapable of achieving this objective. He needs the assistance of other agencies and institutions for both his material and intellectual needs. Those institutions that are essential for his development, such as the family and the state, are "natural" to him; they constitute part of the universal pattern of human life.

In the *Ethics*, Aristotle observes that man's natural end, that which fulfills his nature, is happiness. He defines happiness as an activity of the soul in accordance with perfect virtue. True happiness can only be attained by leading a life of moral and intellectual goodness. Aristotle emphasizes that a full inquiry into the nature of man is basic to political theory. For if the prime function of the state is to help the individual reach his natural end, it is important that the statesman be aware of this end. And in order to have this knowledge, he must first know the nature of man. "The student of politics must know somehow the facts about the soul, as the man who is to heal the eyes or the body as a

---

books also presents a difficulty. It is generally believed that Book I was written later than the rest and that Books II, III, VII, and VIII were written first.

[4] *Politics*, I, 2.

whole must know about the eyes or the body . . . he must then study the soul."⁵ Once again we are reminded how dependent our political speculation is on the general philosophical premises and the religious beliefs that we hold concerning the nature and destiny of man. Aristotle also makes it clear that the political scientist must draw heavily on other disciplines, such as psychology and economics, if he hopes to acquire an understanding of the state.

The Nature of the State

Aristotle defines the state as "a community of families and aggregations of families in well-being for the sake of a perfect and self-sufficing life."⁶ The term "self-sufficient" implies that the object contains within itself the means to attain its end and that it does not need the help of other agencies in realizing the potentiality of its nature.

Starting from the premise of autarchy or self-sufficiency, Aristotle notes that man individually cannot meet this test. First of all he needs the family to supply his rudimentary needs and to nurture his human growth. The family is an "association established by nature for the supply of men's everyday wants."⁷ But the family alone is not self-sufficing nor can it supply all that man requires for his full development as an individual. Possessing the faculty of speech and of rational communication, man is an essentially social being. "A social instinct is implanted in all men by nature."⁸ As a human being, man can perfect his activity only in communal life. He needs social and political co-operation with all that it implies in the way of better material advantages, educational opportunities, aesthetic, scientific, and moral growth, and expanded knowledge. Harold Laski expressed it well when he said, "Crusoe on his desert island or St. Simon Stylites upon his pillar may defy the normal impulses which make them men; but for the vast majority, to live with others is the condition of a rational existence."⁹ Aristotle stresses this point even more forcefully, declaring that "he who by nature and not by mere accident is without a state, is either a bad man or above humanity."¹⁰

In tracing the development of society, Aristotle observes that some

---

⁵ *Nicomachean Ethics*, I, 12. Selections from the *Ethics* are taken from the *Basic Works of Aristotle*, ed. by R. McKeon (New York: Random House, 1941).
⁶ *Politics*, III, 9.   ⁷ *Ibid.*, I, 2.   ⁸ *Ibid.*
⁹ *Grammar of Politics* (New Haven: Yale University Press, 1925), p. 17.
¹⁰ *Politics*, I, 3.

rudimentary form of social organization has existed wherever human beings were found. Men lived at first in separate families; then groups of
families joined together in village communities for purposes of mutual
help and protection. This form of association, however, was too limited
to care adequately for the most permanent needs of human nature. Self-
sufficiency became possible only when a number of villages pooled their
resources and formed a city state. Thus the same necessity which compels families to unite into villages and villages into "a community large
enough to be nearly or quite self-sufficing" is a natural process founded
on the factual structure of human nature.[11]

Aristotle follows Plato in adhering to an organic concept of the state.
His deep sense of the importance of community is evidenced by his
constant references to the forces and influences which bind men together
in a joint endeavor. The *Politics* describes the polis as "a composite,
like any other whole made up of many parts," each with its proper place
and function and each co-operating with the other for the good of the
entire structure. However, it rejects such unifying devices as property
and familial communism and vigorously criticizes the argument that the
greater the unity of the state the better. Is it not obvious, Aristotle asks,
"that a state may at length attain such a degree of unity as to be no
longer a state — since the nature of a state is to be a plurality, and in
tending to greater unity, from being a state it becomes a family, and
from being a family, an individual?"[12] While the good of the individual
is inextricably bound up with the good of the whole, happiness is not
a conception like that of evenness in number that may be predicated
of the whole number without being predicated of its component parts.

The unity which Aristotle attributes to civil society is a unity of
order, not of simply composition as a living organism. The state is a
moral and not a physical whole. It is composed of individuals, family
groups, and voluntary associations, each of which has operations independent of the whole. Although a soldier functions for the good of
the army, he also has a sphere of activities not connected with his
military duties. The unity of the state lies in a community of mind and
will and purpose on the part of the individual members. The same

---

[11] Aristotle emphasizes the distinction between the gregariousness of animals and
that of men. Only man has speech and only man "has any sense of good and evil,
of just and unjust, and the like; and the association of living beings who have this
sense makes a family and a state" (*Politics*, II, 3).

[12] *Politics*, II, 2.

common good is conceived by different individuals and sought by their co-operative efforts.

Aristotle's doctrine of the common good is not as all-enveloping as that of Plato. It leaves a large sphere of independent action to the individual in his private capacity and to the lesser societies, such as the family and the voluntary associations. It seeks to retain the essential plurality of the state and to make the body politic a functional whole of varied and complementary parts unified by the pursuit of a common aim in which men's natures lead them all to join.[13] The disparate parts of the good state are united and made into a community by education and not by the imposition of a rigid pattern of conformity on the people.

Purpose of the State

The state originates "in the bare needs of life" and continues "in existence for the sake of a good life . . . and not for the sake of life only," for "if life only were the object, slaves and brute animals might form a state."[14] Aristotle constantly returns to the positive function of the state. He strongly insists that the political community does not exist merely to serve as a policeman for preserving order among the citizen body or as a soldier to protect the people against foreign invasion. "A state is not a mere society, having a common place, established for the prevention of mutual crime and for the sake of exchange. These are conditions without which a state cannot exist; but all of them together do not constitute a state."[15]

The opening lines of the *Politics* describe the high role that Aristotle assigns to civil society:

> Every state is a community of some kind, and every community is established with a view of some good; for mankind always act in order to obtain that which they think good. But if all communities aim at some good, the state or political community, which is the highest of all and which embraces all the rest, aims at good in the greater degree than any other, and at the highest good.

The true state must be concerned with the character of its citizens; it must educate and habituate them in the ways of virtue; and it must

---

[13] C. H. McIlwain, *The Growth of Political Thought in the West* (New York: Macmillan, 1932), p. 64.

[14] *Politics*, I, 2.   [15] *Ibid.*, III, 10.

provide them with opportunity to obtain the means — economic, moral, and intellectual — necessary for the good life.[16] These activities are essential if the state is to attain its final purpose: the perfected virtue of its citizens.

The lesser forms of association in the state have functions that are not to be pre-empted by public authorities. The actions of these societies, however, are directed primarily at the mere maintenance of life. They are not self-sufficient, either economically or intellectually. They possess neither the capacity nor the means to enable man to reach his full development. The end of the state, moreover, is the highest to which all other human associations contribute and are subordinate. As one writer recently pointed out, an ethically satisfying state was for Aristotle a requirement for the fullest development of man. "It is not merely a physical requirement but one that human nature will strive for, however imperfectly, in particular and adverse circumstances. It is thus an empirical fact of human behavior, not just a moral postulate."[17]

Kinds of Rule

Aristotle points out that the study of any complex organism or compound should always begin by considering the object in its elements or constituents. Using this approach in his study of the polis, he turns first to an examination of man, the primary element in the state, then to the larger part, the family or household, and finally to the state itself. In the first book of the *Politics*, he examines the various relationships of authority. He is particularly interested in showing that there are different kinds of rule which rest on fundamentally different bases. He criticizes the Platonic assumption that all rule, whether in the family or the state, is the same. He considers it basically erroneous to hold that there is no difference in kind between the authority of master over slave in the household and that of governor over governed in the state. Although there are analogies, political rule is essentially different from other types in that it is the rule of equals over equals. Unlike the household, the subjects in a state are assumed to be responsible and self-governing and not dependent on their rulers in the same sense that

---

[16] Religion was not separated from the state in the Greek polis. The religion was the religion of the city, and the gods were the gods of the city. The role of the polis consequently encompassed both the religious and secular aspects of the citizen body.

[17] Norton Long, "Aristotle and the Study of Local Government," *Social Research*, Autumn, 1957, p. 292.

children are dependent on their parents and slaves on their masters. In his *Ethics*, which was written as a prelude to the *Politics*, Aristotle examines the nature and end of man. He demonstrates that the proper activity of any being is found in that which agrees with its form. Since the form of man (the soul) is rational animality, the end of human life must consist in functions that are proper to man as a rational animal — in activities according to reason. Proceeding with his analysis of this concept, Aristotle emphasizes the necessity of distinguishing between the ruling and subject elements in all things which form a composite whole. Thus in man, the soul is by nature the ruler and the body the subject. Two kinds of rule, despotic and constitutional, are present; "the soul rules the body with a despotic rule, whereas the intellect rules the appetite with a constitutional and royal rule."[18] When the soul commands the bodily limbs to move in a certain direction, they immediately move. They have no voice or discretion in the matter, no initial freedom of movement of their own. The case is quite different in respect to the intellect and passions. Although the rational principle predominates over the sensible passions and appetites in the good man, it does not perfectly control them. The sense appetites are in a certain way more or less on a par with reason; they have a certain initial freedom of movement as well as their proper objects and desires which reason is obliged to recognize.

From the individual, Aristotle turns to the family and the kinds of rule that it embodies. "Seeing that the state is made up of households, before speaking of the state we must speak of the management of the household."[19] Three relationships are here distinguished: master and slave, husband and wife, father and child, each representing a different type of rule. That of master over slave is called despotic. The slave has no choice in the matter and the governance is primarily for the good of the master and not for the good of the slave qua slave. The rule of the husband over wife is called constitutional, that of equal over equal. The woman is in a certain sense free and equal to the man of the household, and her views and wishes must be given due consideration. Yet, because of what Aristotle considers an instability in her prudence, it is better to lodge authority in the husband. The third rule, that of father over child, is called royal. It signifies rule out of love for the child and for his proper good. The child is by nature equal to the

---

[18] *Politics*, I, 5. [19] *Ibid.*, I, 3.

father, but because of his immaturity and his consequent inability to manage his own actions properly, he must be subject to the direction and control of his parents.

The Citizen

Man as a component part of the body politic is referred to as a citizen. "A state is composite like any other whole made up of many parts; these are the citizens who compose it. It is evident, therefore, that we must begin by asking who is the citizen and what is the meaning of the term?"[20] The initial inquiry into the parts of civil society must seek to answer this question. Aristotle first observes that the qualifications for citizenship may be different in the various types of states. "He who is a citizen in a democracy will often not be a citizen in an oligarchy." But whatever the prerequisites, "he who has the power to take part in the deliberative or judicial administration of any state is said by us to be a citizen of that state."[21] This definition is couched in typically Hellenic terms. A citizen must not only be a subject of authority; he must also be capable of exercising it. He must serve in the twin roles of governor and governed. In order to participate in this dual capacity, he must possess the competency to rule as well as the willingness to obey.

Who should be entitled to citizenship? The *Politics* emphasizes that citizenship does not embrace all members of the state. Those who do not possess the qualities of intellect and character necessary to lead a life of virtue should not be entrusted with political rule. Hence those who are "slaves by nature" and even the laborers, merchants, and farmers should not be included in the category of citizens. "The citizens must not lead the life of mechanics or tradesmen, for such a life is ignoble and inimical to virtue. Neither must they be husbandmen, since leisure is necessary both for the development of virtue and the performance of political duties."[22] Men who must toil from morning until night in order to obtain the necessities of life have neither time nor opportunity for acquiring a knowledge of public affairs and cultivating those virtues essential for intelligent participation in political life. "No man can practice virtue who is living the life of a mechanic or laborer . . . or who is a husbandman."[23]

Men employed as artisans and producers are not properly speaking "parts" of the state. They are necessary for its existence in that they

---

[20] *Ibid.*, III, 1.   [21] *Ibid.*   [22] *Ibid.*, VII, 9.   [23] *Ibid.*, III, 5.

provide the material environment within which the citizen body can function. By supplying the material needs of society, they make possible the existence of a leisured and cultivated class that can be entrusted with the administration of public affairs. Professor McIlwain makes a very significant observation in respect to this aspect of Aristotelian thinking. He points out that if the author of the *Politics* is wrong, it is not in his insistence that the citizen must have ample leisure time for acquiring political virtue. His real mistake is in failing to see that the true solution does not lie in denying citizenship to the worker, but in achieving an economic order that will give him the leisure necessary to fit him for the tasks of public life and human living.[24]

Forms of Government

After completing his examination of the parts, Aristotle is ready to consider the whole, the state and its government. Here, as in the lesser components, he differentiates three kinds of rule: despotic, that of a tyrant; constitutional, that of equals over equals; and royal, that of a benevolent monarch. At this point, the *Politics* launches into governmental theory proper with the question, "Whether there is only one form of government or many, and if many, what are they, and how many and what are the differences between them?"[25] The question touches upon one of the central themes of Aristotle's doctrine of constitutions. In answering it, he sets out his celebrated six-forms scheme of government. There are, he asserts, three true forms of constitutions: monarchy, aristocracy, and polity or moderate democracy; and three corrupted forms: tyranny, oligarchy, and extreme democracy or mob rule. In the first group the rule is exercised for the well-being of the governed, and in the latter for the private interests of those in power.

This classification follows the view current at the time that there are three main types of government distinguished by the number of persons who hold supreme political power. Although the *Politics* also equates number with governmental form, it maintains that the more vital distinction is economic. An oligarchy is essentially government by the wealthy; a democracy, rule by the poor. Thus the real difference between the two types is poverty and wealth. "Whenever men rule by reason of their wealth, whether they be few or many, that is an oligarchy,

[24] *The Growth of Political Thought in the West*, op. cit., pp. 71–72.
[25] *Politics*, III, 6.

and where the poor rule, this is a democracy. But as a fact the rich are few and the poor many."[26]

That Aristotle was well aware of the close link between economics and politics is evident from this and similar passages in his writings. Of equal significance, his analysis reveals two distinct claims to political power: one based on the right of property, in which a man's political status is graded according to his "stake in the community"; the other upon the welfare of the many, in which political rights should belong equally to all. As he notes, "few are well-to-do, whereas freedom is enjoyed by all, and wealth and freedom are the grounds on which the oligarchical and democratical parts respectively claim power in the state."[27] Good birth and superior virtue are other claims closely related to political power but they are of much less importance since they are rare and wealth and numbers are more common.

The Best Practicable State

After classifying the various kinds of government, Aristotle next seeks to determine which type is best. In the opening passages of Book VII of the *Politics*, he indicates that the best form of government is one which is most conducive to a happy life for its people. His experience and empirical studies had convinced him that no single model can successfully meet the requirements of different peoples in different historical circumstances. Sketching out an ideal state, as Plato had done, may be good intellectual exercise but it is not enough for the world of everyday affairs. The true statesman "ought to be acquainted not only with what is best in the abstract, but also with what is best relatively to circumstances."[28]

Aristotle insists that constitution makers must take into consideration the character and traditions of the people and the environment in which they live. The political expert cannot wipe the tablet clean and fashion a state according to his own preferences. He must discover the pattern in existing reality, not in metaphysical perambulations; and he cannot overlook the past in planning for the future. Unless he adheres to these principles, the government which he devises is likely to generate more unhappiness than happiness.

If the title to rule is virtue, the best state from an ideal standpoint would be one governed by the most virtuous men. "If there be some

---

[26] *Ibid.*, III, 8.   [27] *Ibid.*   [28] *Ibid.*, IV, 1.

one person, or more than one . . . whose virtue is so pre-eminent that the virtues or the political capacity of all the rest admit of no comparison with his or theirs, he or they can no longer be regarded as part of a state."[29] A person who possesses such a degree of virtue stands above the community "in the relation of a whole to a part." When such an individual or family is found, "then it is just that they should be the royal family and supreme over all, or that one citizen should be king of the whole nation."[30] This line of thinking, Aristotle notes, may be theoretically sound but it is unrealistic. For men are not to be found who excel others "in the same degree in which gods and heroes are supposed to excel mankind." We must therefore turn to the more attainable types of government and inquire

> what is the best constitution for most states and the best life for most men, neither assuming a standard of virtue which is above ordinary persons nor an education which is exceptionally favored by nature and circumstances, nor yet an ideal state which is an aspiration only, but having regard to the life in which the majority are able to share and to the form of government which states in general can attain.[31]

Although Aristotle did not believe that it is possible to outline a governmental pattern that would be universally valid, he felt that political science is capable of discovering the best practicable state — one which on the average and in most historical environments might be expected to work best. Proceeding on this premise, he carefully analyzed the constitutional history and institutions of 158 Greek city-states. Based on this and other studies, he concluded that the best practicable state is one which he calls polity or constitutional rule. It is, in effect, a moderate democracy in which the important offices are filled by election from among qualified persons. He characterizes this form as a fusion of oligarchy and democracy, although he occasionally remarks that it approximates very closely to the aristocratic form. Aristotle's terminology is not always precise when discussing the best practicable state. For example, at several points he speaks of polity as a compromise between oligarchy and extreme democracy — forms which he had previously described as perverted. However, his whole treatment of the subject clearly indicates that his so-called polity is a constitutional democracy with a certain aristocratic element. Contemporary usage regarded oligarchy as the rule of a few and democracy as the rule of many, without placing

[29] *Ibid.*, III, 13.   [30] *Ibid.*, III, 17.   [31] *Ibid.*, IV, 11.

any connotation of good or corrupt on the terms. Aristotle is obviously employing them in this sense when he discusses his best political community.

The major feature of Aristotle's best practicable state is that the middle class holds the balance of power between the rich and the poor, thereby preventing either of the extremes from being dominant. There are three elements in every state: "one class is very rich, another very poor, and a third is a mean." Since it is admitted that moderation and mean are the best, the best political community is formed by citizens of the middle class. Those states, therefore, are likely to be well administered "in which the middle class is large, and stronger if possible, than both the other classes, or at any rate than either singly." Citizens who belong to the middle class are "most secure in a state for they do not, like the poor, covet their neighbor's goods: nor do others covet theirs, as the poor covet the goods of the rich."[32] When either the poor or rich are predominant, or confront each other with no significant middle class between them, the state is irreconcilably divided into hostile camps. Stability in the social order requires that no single claim to political power prevail but that all interests be held together in some kind of balance. Aristotle believes that this equilibrium is best achieved when economic resources are widely distributed among the people.

In the middle class polity, supreme political power is lodged in the whole citizen body. It is the rule of equals over equals, the citizens alike taking their turn of governing and being governed. This arrangement at first glance seems to run contrary to the principle that superiority in virtue is the prime qualification for governing. However, the *Politics* seeks to justify democratic rule on the basis of the collective judgment and wisdom of the people

> For the many, of whom each individual is but an ordinary person, when they meet together may very likely be better than the few good, if regarded not individually but collectively. . . . For each individual among the many has a share of virtue and prudence, and when they meet together, they become in a manner one man, who has many feet, and hands, and senses.[33]

Democratic government for Aristotle was not the ideal but only the most workable form. His personal preference for monarchy is manifest

---

[32] *Ibid.*, IV, 1.
[33] *Ibid.*, III, 11.

throughout the *Politics*. He gave little support to the proposition that democracy is the form of government most suitable to man's nature from a theoretical as well as practical standpoint. His concept of royal rule remained always the ideal, although admittedly an unattainable form. Even his best practicable state is undemocratic by present standards. The equality in public affairs that he speaks of is confined to members of the citizen body, and this group excludes not only the slave and metic but also the mechanic, tradesman, and farmer.

Aristotle is well aware that administrative management calls for professional rather than amateur talent. Although he is not explicit on this point, he indicates that the principal executive offices of the state should be entrusted to a special corps of trained and experienced experts. This group would be chosen for its managerial capacity and technical proficiency, it would be in the nature of a permanent civil service, and it would remain responsible and accountable to the policy-making and judicial organs of the people. In these ways, expertness or excellency in statecraft could be combined with popular rule.

One further question remains in discussing the best practicable state: Should there be any limit to its size? Aristotle is quite definite on this point. There is a limit to the size of states "as there is to other things, plants, animals, implements; for none of these retain their natural power when they are too large or too small, but they either wholly lose their nature, or are spoiled."[34] When the political community is too large, it is too difficult to govern, for "a very great multitude cannot be orderly." The proper size of the state can be ascertained only by experience. It should have enough people to be self-sufficient, but not so many that it is impossible for all the citizens to know one another. If the people are to "judge and to distribute offices according to merit, then they must know each other's character; where they do not possess this knowledge, both the elections to office and the decisions of lawsuits will go wrong."[35] This intimate type of knowledge is obviously impossible in a large state. Apparently the Athenian polis would satisfy Aristotle's requirements of size.

In advancing his theory of the best practicable state, Aristotle was drawing upon his own ethical doctrine of virtue as a mean (courage, for example, stands midway between cowardice and rashness) and on the general Greek tendency toward moderation. His government will be

---

[34] *Ibid.*, VII, 4.   [35] *Ibid.*

democratic since sovereignty rests in the people and the will of the majority prevails, but it will also be aristocratic since the chief public offices will be occupied by men of ability. In like manner, the unity of his body politic will be such as to promote the good of the whole and yet preserve a large sphere of independent activity for the parts. He intended, in short, that his state stand as a happy mean between complete collectivism and excessive individualism.

The Rule of Law

The bill of rights in the constitution of the Commonwealth of Massachusetts concludes with these words, "to the end it may be a government of laws and not of men." The genesis of this historic concept may be traced to ancient Greece. Aristotle was the first notable spokesman for the great tradition of constitutional government — a limited and not absolute government, a government subject to the rule of law. "He who bids the law rule may be deemed to bid God and Reason alone rule, but he who bids man rule adds an element of the beast; for desire is a wild beast, and passion perverts the minds of rulers, even when they are the best of men."[36]

The rule of law is a device to guarantee that political action be based upon right desire. Men are human creatures subject to temptations and passions. Aristotle notes a certain "wickedness of human nature." Because of this weakness, he feels that it would be extremely dangerous to place unlimited power in the hands of the rulers. Just as in man the appetitive faculties occasionally predominate over the rational, so political rule may at times be arbitrary and selfish instead of reasonable and for the welfare of all. Scientific knowledge is not enough to ensure good rule; political science is not independent of the conditions of right appetite. Means must be devised to prevent the perversity of men's desires from gaining mastery of the community. Those who are entrusted with political power must be required to exercise it in accordance with prescribed laws and within designated limitations. The governmental arrangement, moreover, must be such as to militate against the concentration of political power in any one individual or group. It was largely for this latter reason that Aristotle advocates his middle class polity and such limiting devices as frequent rotation in office and selection by lot for the nontechnical offices.

---

[36] Ibid., III, 16.

Aristotle includes in the rule of law not only the enactments of legislative bodies but also customary and natural law. As most Greek thinkers, he looks upon the constitution of a state as a "way of life," an embodiment of the elements that go to make up a political community such as its operative principles and objectives, and its institutions, traditions, and customs. To be legitimate, the rule of the statesman can neither disregard these factors nor flout human rights. Every governing body must continuously give due respect to the constitution or way of life of its people. The true character of the community depends upon the observance of this principle.

The concept of the rule of law or limited government became one of the dominant features of western political life. Today, strengthened by written constitutions, bills of rights, judicial review, impeachment and similar devices, it forms the bedrock of modern democratic government. Aristotle and the middle ages conceived of no legal remedy or sanction for enforcing the rule of law. Resistance, revolution, or the intervention of the Church were the only weapons available against arbitrary government. One of the major contributions of the modern age to the science and practice of politics has been the bridging of this gap by the development of legal and institutional checks on government.

Natural Slavery

Perhaps the most controversial aspect of Aristotle's social thought is his defense of slavery. To understand his position in this respect, it is necessary to note the distinction that he makes between natural and institutional slavery. He describes the natural slave as one "who is by nature not his own but another's man." He is a person so intellectually inferior and so lacking in prudence or practical judgment that he is incapable of governing himself. "He who participates in the rational principle enough to apprehend but not to have such a principle is a slave by nature."[37] Such an individual cannot act rationally on his own initiative; he needs the direction and guidance of others if he is to lead a proper life. He attains the highest mental and moral development of which he is capable, not when left to his own devices, but when he occupies the position of a slave to a virtuous master. It is therefore better for him to "be under the rule of the master."

Just as the farmer and mechanic provide the material means of assur-

[37] *Ibid.,* I, 5.

ing leisure to the citizen class, so the slave frees the master from the performance of menial tasks which interfere with the acquisition of virtue. Aristotle contends that if it is good for the body to be ruled by the soul, there is no reason to deny that the slave has his good in being ruled by the master. Such a person is not wronged by losing a freedom that he is incapable of using properly. This view of natural slavery does not imply inferiority or inequality due to race or social status. It is based on the notion that there are some men who "on their own" are unable to contribute to the common good. It follows Plato's view that there are innate differences in men which fit them for different occupations, and which predetermine some men as slaves and others as freemen.

The second type of slavery described by Aristotle arises by law or convention. It includes the enslavement of prisoners of war, the subjection of a race into servitude, and the institutionalization of slavery such as existed in the southern sections of the United States prior to 1865. Aristotle considers slavery of this kind unjustified since it is based on force and not on nature. Many such slaves are capable of rational judgment; indeed, many of them may well be superior to their masters in intellect and virtue. The enslavement of those taken in war or acquired by purchase is proper only when they are by nature slaves.

The rule of the master "is not a constitutional rule." The slave, qua slave, has no rights; he is under the despotic rule of his master. As a human being, however, he is entitled to the protection of the political community against abuse and maltreatment. There is some analogy here with the practice in modern democracies where those adjudged mentally incompetent are barred from participation in public affairs, and even from the management of their own property, yet are protected by the state against violations of their basic rights. Aristotle insists that the master treat his slave with kindness and benevolence. Any abuse of his authority "is injurious to both; for the interests of part and whole, of body and soul are the same . . . hence where the relation of master and slave between them is natural, they are friends and have a common interest, but where it rests merely on law and force the reverse is true."[38]

While there may be some theoretical justification for Aristotle's position, the difficulty rests in knowing which individuals ought to be slaves and which free, and who is to make the decision. The fact remains that whenever and wherever slavery has existed, it has rested on force, custom,

---

[38] *Ibid.,* I, 6.

or expediency, and not on any distinction of virtue. Despite its benign aspects, Aristotle's view of slavery is cold and harsh. Yet it must be remembered that he knew slavery only in its comparatively humane form. Many of the slaves of his time were household servants or assistants to merchants and artisans. He would even have excluded a number of these from the category of slaves because of their abilities. His intention was to relegate no man to a position inferior to the best of which he is capable.

SUMMARY

Aristotle has been a major influence in molding the western political tradition. His contributions have a timeless and enduring character as the inquiring intellects of all ages bear witness. There are some aspects of his social and political thinking that the modern democrat would reject; there are others, including many of his fundamental premises, that find widespread acceptance. The study of his political thought is more than an academic exercise. It is an excursion into a world of ideas that have considerable relevancy to modern society.

Aristotle followed Plato in emphasizing the moral and ethical nature of the body politic. He was concerned not only with techniques but with the choice of ends. His works remind us that the state, acting through its governmental organs, is more than an agency for enforcing law and order; that it is designed to help men achieve the good life, to create an environment or climate — social, economic, intellectual, and moral — in which man can better fulfill his nature as a rational being. He demonstrates that while the state should not attempt to supplant the private activities of individuals and the lesser social groupings, its energies should be actively and positively aimed at the common good.

The political theory of Aristotle injects a word of caution in the planning of state activities. It warns against attempts to reconstruct society according to some grand blueprint of social reform that shows little respect for the wisdom of experience and little regard for tradition, custom, and the capacities of the people. It points out that such an approach can well lead to the horrors of Aldous Huxley's Brave New World and George Orwell's 1984 in which a "scientific" elite manipulates the mass of mankind in the interests of a complaisant society. "Let us remember," Aristotle cautions, "that we should not disregard the experience of ages." The statesman is not an artist who can shape his clay in the form he thinks best. At the same time, the approach to social and political change should be dynamic and progressive even though not radical. If political institutions are to survive they must be capable of adapting the status quo to the necessities of change.

Aristotle was acutely aware of the role that economics plays in the political process. He recognized that governmental policy making is often no more

84 THE POLITICAL PHILOSOPHY OF THE ANCIENTS

than a ratification of the decisions made by the holders of economic power. His analysis also showed the close relationship between economics and political stability. When great disparity of wealth exists in a state, when widespread poverty is found side by side with great riches, the community is in an unhealthy condition. The bond of justice and the common will that should unify the society are weak or altogether missing in such a state. Dictatorial governments may crush social unrest by force; but the democratic state cannot afford to overlook the economic well-being of any segment of its people. If it does so, it subverts its ethical purpose and opens the door to less desirable philosophies of government.

BIBLIOGRAPHY

Ashley, Winston, The Theory of Natural Slavery According to Aristotle and St. Thomas (South Bend, Indiana: Notre Dame Press, 1941).

Barker, Ernest, The Political Thought of Plato and Aristotle (New York: Putnam, 1906).

Cherniss, Harold, Aristotle's Criticism of Plato and the Academy (Baltimore: John Hopkins Press, 1944).

Hagan, J. J., "Aristotelian Political Philosophy and the Corporate Society," New Scholasticism, April, 1941.

Kelsen, Hans, "The Philosophy of Aristotle and the Hellenic-Macedonian Policy," Ethics, October, 1937.

Lester-Garland, L. V., "Plato, Aristotle and Catholicism," Hibbert Journal, July, 1933.

Long, Norton E., "Aristotle and the Study of Local Government," Social Research, Autumn, 1957.

Marshall, John S., "Aristotle and the Agrarians," Review of Politics, July, 1947.

McCoy, C. N. R., "Logical and Real in Political Theory: Plato, Aristotle and Marx," American Political Science Review, December, 1954.

McIlwain, C. H., Constitutionalism, Ancient and Modern, rev. ed. (Ithaca: Cornell University Press, 1947).

McKeon, Richard, "Aristotle's Conception of Moral and Political Philosophy," Ethics, April, 1941.

———— "Development of the Concept of Property in Political Philosophy: A Study of the Background of the Constitution," Ethics, April, 1938.

Mure, G. R. G., Aristotle (London: E. Benn, 1932).

Olmsted, E. H., "Moral Sense Aspect of Aristotle's Ethical Theory," American Journal of Philology, January, 1948.

Ross, William D., Aristotle, 3rd ed. (London: Methuen, 1937).

Strauss, Leo, "On Classical Political Philosophy," Social Research, February, 1945.

Wheeler, Marcus, "Aristotle's Analysis of the Nature of Political Struggle," American Journal of Philology, April, 1951.

Wormuth, Francis D., "Aristotle on Law," in Essays in Political Theory, ed. by M. R. Konvitz and A. E. Murphy (Ithaca: Cornell University Press, 1948).

Chapter V

THE POLITICAL THOUGHT OF ROME

"To the glory that was Greece, and the grandeur that was
Rome" (Poe, *To Helen*).

ARISTOTLE came at the end of the creative period in Greek thought.
When he died in 322 B.C., the Greek city-state had already lost its political
significance and its traditional role as arbiter of the moral and social
habits of the eastern Mediterranean. The small and self-sufficient polis
had proved incapable of defending itself against the attacks of its more
powerful neighbors. The loose confederations or leagues which the city-
states had entered into in self-defense were no match for the unified
control and the vast resources of the growing empires.

Plato and Aristotle typified the Greek distrust of the large state. They
felt that by going beyond the small and compact polis, the way of life
of one community would be merged with the fortunes of another. They
also felt that the large state destroys the spirit of friendship and the
intimacy that bind a society together. For if people have nothing in
common but mutual defense against an aggressor or the facilitation of
trade "that would not constitute a state." The things which draw men
together in a close union "are created by friendship, for the will to live
together is friendship."[1] This will cannot exist in a large and far-flung
empire.

The conquests of Philip of Macedon and Alexander the Great had
relegated the polis to the position of a small and relatively unimportant
unit in a far larger political system, that of empire. As Professor Dunning
has noted, no longer were the springs of political action to be found in
the assembly or council of a city but at the courts of the Macedonian,
Syrian, and Egyptian monarchs, and in the camps of the Roman consuls.[2]

---

[1] Aristotle, *Politics*, III, 9.
[2] W. A. Dunning, *A History of Political Theories* (New York: Macmillan Co.,
1902), p. 102.

The struggle for power, the domination of military force, and the rapidly changing political picture in a turbulent world caused men, accustomed to the intimacy of the city-state, to feel that they had become outsiders with no part to play in the shaping of political events. Social unrest, arising out of precarious economic conditions, became prevalent during this period. Sparta, for example, underwent three social revolutions in the latter half of the third century B.C. All of these conditions generated a widespread feeling of personal insecurity.

THE PHILOSOPHY OF WITHDRAWAL

Until the Macedonian and Roman conquests, Greek thought had been dominated by civic and religious devotion to the city-state. Greek ethics similarly had centered around men as citizens, as political and social beings. With the changing world scene, a more individual and less social ethic began to predominate. So closely had the speculations of Plato and Aristotle been bound to the city-state that as it declined in importance the philosophy associated with it also fell into disfavor. Political theory was then faced with the task of reinterpreting political and social relations in terms other than those provided by the polis. The spirit of the time, however, was not conducive to such a project.

When political power passed into the hands of the three dynasties that fell heir to the Alexandrian empire,[3] the Greek philosophers turned away completely from political speculation to the problem of individual virtue. They no longer asked the question, "how can a good state be established and operated?" In its place they began to inquire, "how can man be virtuous in a disordered and wicked world?" "How can happiness be attained in an age of perilous and troubled circumstances?"

Instead of attempting to adapt the classical theory of public participation to the new order of things, men began to turn inward and seek within themselves the key to individual happiness. For if the good life could not be attained through politics and social living, it must be sought in other ways. Not until Roman hegemony and order had been

---

[3] Alexander had left no heir, and his sudden death was followed by a prolonged struggle for control among his generals. By 275 three dynasties had managed to carve up the empire: the Antigonids in Macedonia, the Seleucids in the East, and the Ptolemies in Egypt. Toward the end of the century, however, Roman power became predominant and by the middle of the second century B.C. Macedonia itself had become a Roman province and Greece a Roman protectorate.

firmly established over most of the known world of the ancients did men again see in the state the means to the good life.

Epicureanism

Two of the more important schools of philosophy that characterize the interim or transition period between classical Greece and Rome are those of the Epicureans and the Stoics. The first was founded by Epicurus (341–270 B.C.) in an Athenian garden which he had laid out as his school. His philosophy marks a distinct break with that of his Greek predecessors. Discarding the concept of the common good, Epicurus limits himself to a search for means of attaining individual happiness or tranquillity to the exclusion of all other considerations. In line with the prevalent spirit of his day, he seeks to show how man can attain this happiness apart from the state.

The good life, according to Epicurus, consists in the avoidance of care and worry, and in the congenial friendship of a small and select group of companions. Although he holds that pleasure is the chief good and the end of life, he insists that he does not mean the pleasure of the debauchee, but freedom of the body from pain and the soul from anxiety. He and his disciples followed a simple diet — not because they felt that gluttony is wrong but because it leads to physical discomfort. So also with any other sensual or emotional excesses — in the long run they bring disturbance and pain. Man's principal objective should be a life of external and internal peace. This desideratum can be achieved only by living simply and frugally, and by avoiding all forms of public activity.

The philosophy of Epicurus is essentially materialistic. He maintains that the soul is nothing more than a bodily substance composed of intangible particles, like those of breath and heat, scattered throughout the body. Hence there need be no fear of eternity or afterlife, since the soul cannot possibly exist after the death of the body. Denying that there are any intrinsic moral virtues and values or any objective standard of right and wrong, Epicurus teaches that those acts which cause harm are evil only because they expose the individual to discomfort or pain. A philosophy of materialism is essential to his theoretical position, for if happiness consists of freedom from all care and worry, personal moral responsibility and the anxieties of conscience and religion can have no place in man's life.

The implications of such a philosophy for the field of politics are clear. Since participation in public affairs inevitably brings with it burdens and cares, the wise man will not engage in politics. He will rather aim at a life of tranquil obscurity in the company of his friends, holding aloof from participation in the affairs of state and leaving political activity to others. Epicurus and his followers did not deny that political authority is necessary in a community to preserve order, but they were perfectly willing to submit to any form of government, whether it be despotic or constitutional, that would be capable of preserving peace without interfering with their private lives.

Stoicism

The Stoic school, the last of the great academic institutions of Athens, was contemporaneous in origin with Epicureanism. Its history, however, is longer, its doctrine less constant, and its influence much greater. Founded shortly before 300 B.C. by Zeno (340–260 B.C.), stoicism attracted a wide following of educated Greeks and Romans — from the lame and penniless slave, Epictetus, to the strong and wealthy emperor, Marcus Aurelius. Like Epicurus, Zeno was born on the fringe of Greek civilization, in the town of Citium on the island of Cyprus. He was thus free from the persuading influence that life in the Greek city-state exerted on its members. Starting out as a doctrine of withdrawal and of protest against social conventions, stoicism sought in philosophy the entrance into a spiritual realm where the evils and defects of society would little matter. The wise man can attain moral self-sufficiency by suppressing all emotion arising from pain or misfortune and by rigidly controlling himself. Such a person does not need the help of existing institutions; he is able to seek virtue and justice and goodness in himself. By turning inward, the individual can stand in absolute freedom from the mundane world.

As stoicism developed, it gradually assumed more positive aspects than it had shown in its earlier stages. Its idea of a mythical society in which all men enjoy equality under a universal law of nature began to take on meaning in a political context. Instead of the ancient polis, stoic thought substituted the cosmopolis with its world citizenship, its brotherhood of man, and its universal law binding on all people. The ideal state must embrace the whole world so that a man would no longer say, "I am of Athens" or "of Sidon" but "a citizen of the world." The states that exist are temporal necessities, but the wise man holds aloof from them as far as possible, looking to the fraternity of all men in a citizenship of the world. The universal aspects of stoicism appealed to the Romans who seemed destined to bring all races within their political control. To be acceptable to them, stoic philosophy had only to be purged of its remaining element of aloofness toward public life and made more directly applicable to political ideals. The task of revising it in this direction fell to Panaetius of Rhodes (189–109 B.C.)

Panaetius, like his Greek colleague Polybius, was an ardent admirer of the Roman constitution. Both were intimate friends of Scipio Africanus the Younger, and around the three of them gathered a society of distinguished and intelligent Romans. It was this circle that was influential in transmitting Greek philosophy to the new Rome. Panaetius, as the chief interpreter of Greek thought during this period, turned stoic philosophy back in the direction of Plato and Aristotle. By so doing, he succeeded in presenting stoicism to his influential Roman friends in an acceptable form.[4] Instead of the rejection of political activity, Panaetius maintains that the highest vocation of man is the dedication of himself to public life. Stoicism is the school which trains the statesman as well as the philosopher. Coupled with the doctrine of a universal law and world citizenship, this new stoic look appealed so strongly to the temperament and outlook of the Romans that it was transposed into their political and legal system.

Marcus Aurelius, the most prominent of the stoics, represents the new type of stoic virtue. Not only did he spend considerable time in meditation, but he devoted some sixteen hours each day to the governance of the Roman Empire. But what is the good of all this public service if, as stoicism claims, the world does not matter, and if health, riches, and power are in themselves worthless? The answer was clear to Aurelius and the new stoics. Life is like a play or game. What really matters is that the play be properly presented and that the actors properly fulfill their parts. God has given each individual a role: one may be cast as a ruler, another as a lowly slave. The good actor can play either part; his business is to accept the role without joy or complaint and to perform it well. The part in the play, as all things of the world, is entirely worthless. Yet to be good the actor must perform his function, no matter what

---

[4] For a comprehensive and scholarly treatment of the development of stoicism within the Roman Empire see, E. V. Arnold, *Roman Stoicism* (Cambridge: University of Cambridge Press, 1911).

it may be. He must strive for perfection, whether in the role of slave or emperor, since the goodness of nature lies in working toward perfection. By this reasoning, stoicism is able to provide guidance for both the saint and the public servant.[5]

THE GOVERNMENT OF ROME

Rome began its history on the peaks and slopes of the seven hills beside the Tiber River. Legend relates that the city was founded by Romulus, a descendant of Aeneas, in 753 B.C. From a closely knit and compact city-state, Rome expanded into a single empire that encompassed the entire Mediterranean world. From the time of its founding until 509 B.C., the city was governed by kings; from 509 to 27 B.C., it was a republic; and from the latter date to its fall, it was ruled by emperors. Throughout the more than ten centuries of its existence, Rome experienced war and peace, victory and defeat, internal harmony and civil war, glory and shame, good government and despicable political rule, progress and decay. The legacies which grew out of this history are many and varied.

In contrast to Greece, Rome's contribution to the development of formal political theory is slight. Her importance to the field of politics does not arise from any striking originality or any major addition to the world's stock of political ideas. Her significance lies in the great political part that she played in laying the legal foundations of the western world and in her transmission of Greek ideas to western Europe.

The political thought of both the Republic and the Empire was derived chiefly from two sources: Stoic philosophy, as represented by Cicero, Seneca, Epictetus, and Marcus Aurelius; and the Roman jurists of the second and third centuries A.D., such as Ulpian and Gaius, whose political speculations were largely a repetition and elaboration of ideas found in Aristotle. But if the Roman period is not distinguished for its theory, it is noted for its law and, to a lesser extent, its administration. It is in these two areas that Rome left her greatest legacy to the West.

The Republic passed through a long period of development and decline. Democratic in form and theory, it was never at any time, even in its advanced stage, truly democratic in practice. Constitutionally, supreme political authority rested in the assemblies of the people. These, like

---

[5] See Gilbert Murray, The Stoic Philosophy (New York: G. P. Putnam, 1915).

their Athenian counterpart, were mass meetings in which every Roman citizen was eligible to take part. The privilege of participation, however, was virtually meaningless to that portion of the citizen body which lived outside the city of Rome proper, since there was no system of representation. Personal presence was necessary to vote or to make one's opinion heard. The assemblies elected the consuls and magistrates and acted on bills presented to them by the executive officials.

The Roman senate was composed almost wholly of former magistrates and consuls. Theoretically, it possessed no legislative power but served only as an advisory group to the executive officials. Actually, it was the real governing body of the Republic during most of its existence. Dominated by a small group of families through a careful process of manipulation, the senate was aristocratic in composition during its better periods and oligarchic during its declining stages. The popular assemblies were similarly controlled. A system of voting by tribes rather than by individuals enabled an organized minority to direct assembly actions and to elect magistrates with the "right" views and attitudes. Since the executive officials were automatically elevated to the senate at the expiration of their terms, continuity in control and influence over the management of public affairs was assured.

Despite its expansion, Rome remained a city-state in form until the end of the republican era, when citizenship was extended to the provinces. As Roman hegemony spread, an effective system of centralized administrative control was set up. The newly won territory was divided into provinces, each headed by a Roman official with broad powers in civil and political affairs. But despite centralized control, a large degree of autonomy in local matters was permitted to the various units. Roman policy in general was relatively tolerant and noninterventionist. Once the Romans had established their undisputed authority over a people, they then proceeded to raise them gradually to partnership within the empire. Only in a limited sphere of life pertaining to the safety of the state did they demand exacting order and obedience. Although they encouraged the spread of Roman civilization, they made no attempt to enforce uniformity in culture and institutions among the subject people. Much of the success of Roman administration over a widely dispersed empire that embraced more than 50 million people and over 1,300,000 square miles of land can be attributed to the liberal policy displayed toward the provinces.

With the constitutional changes effected by Julius and Augustus Caesar, political power gravitated into the hands of one man. Rome lost its republican character and became an empire, at first in fact, and later also in form. The popular assembly was relegated to an insignificant role, and while the senate retained its important position, it eventually came under the complete domination of the emperor. Even the fiction of the Roman lawyers that "the will of the Emperor has the force of law, because by the passage of the *lex regia* the people transfers to him and vests in him all its own power and authority," was challenged in the third century A.D. by the theory that the emperor's authority was of divine origin. In fact, for a time the emperor was himself worshiped as a god.

CICERO

M. Tullius Cicero (106–43 B.C.) is the outstanding political theorist of the Roman period. Lacking the profundity and originality of talent displayed by his Greek predecessors, he nevertheless exerted a strong influence on the course of western thought. His role was more nearly that of a popularizer of complex ideas than a thinker in his own right. Much of his writing was directly inspired by the political speculations of Plato and Aristotle and by the philosophy of stoicism. Because his works were widely read, he served as the principal medium for transmitting Greek and Roman concepts to medieval Europe. Despite the heavy reliance on his predecessors, Cicero's political writings are of particular significance for two reasons. They show the notions that were generally current in his time, and they demonstrate the application of what is essentially the political philosophy of the city-state to the new context of world empire.

Cicero came from a Roman family of good social position. Educated at home and abroad (he studied philosophy at Athens and Rhodes), he entered politics at the age of twenty-three. In the succeeding years he became the leading lawyer of his time and rose to high public office, serving as governor of a province, consul, and senator. His two major political works are the *De Republica* and *De Legibus*, both modeled after Plato's *Republic* and his *Laws*. He wrote during the declining days of the Roman republic, at a time when the economic transformation brought about by territorial expansion had once again divided the people into two opposing classes, the wealthy nobles and the pauperized commoners. In both his public career and his writings, Cicero sought to restore the Roman constitution to the form that it had during the glorious days of Scipio Africanus and before the revolutionary tribunate of Tiberius Gracchus. His attempt to turn back the clock was a total failure. His importance does not lie in his political accomplishments but in the long-range effects of his writings.

Methodology

Cicero follows the same pattern that Plato employed in his political works. Both the De Republica and the De Legibus are written in dialogue style, with the conversations taking place in the garden of one of the participants during a holiday period. In the De Republica, Cicero puts his views into the mouth of Scipio Africanus the Younger, a statesman of an earlier age, but in the De Legibus he throws off the mask of Scipio (as Plato did that of Socrates in his later writings) and himself assumes the role of the chief character. Unfortunately, both of Cicero's political treatises have come down to us in fragmentary form so that it is difficult at points to piece out the author's thought.[6]

While the form of approach used by Cicero is modeled closely after that of Plato, basic differences in methodology exist between the two writers. Both set forth their conception of an ideal state; but whereas Plato endeavors to arrive at his model polity in much the same way that a sculptor molds his clay, Cicero's approach is historical and empirical. Starting with the assumption that the form of government which existed during the classical period of republican Rome was by far the best, Cicero expresses his intention to "explain the character of this constitution and show why it is the best; and using our own government as my pattern, I will fit to it, if I can, all I have to say about the ideal state."[7] By placing before his readers a description of the Roman state at its birth, during its growth, and at its maturity, Cicero felt that his political science would be more intelligible than if he "would follow the example of Socrates in Plato's work" and himself "invent an ideal state" of his own.[8]

---

[6] The De Republica, with the exception of various quotations found in later works, was lost until 1822, when the prefect of the Vatican Library discovered a substantial portion of the manuscript in a palimpsest containing St. Augustine's commentary on the Psalms.

[7] De Republica, I, xxi. Excerpts from De Republica and De Legibus are taken from the Loeb Classical Library edition, trans. by C. W. Keyes (Cambridge: Harvard University Press, 1928).

[8] Ibid., II, xxx.

Cicero also criticizes Plato's methodology for its reliance on abstract reasoning, a reliance which resulted in a theory of the perfect state that was "quite unsuited to men's actual lives and habits." Following the example of Aristotle, he looks upon the constitution of a state as an organic growth developing with the experience and advance in knowledge that time brings with it. His repudiation of Plato's approach, however, does not imply any rejection of the moral principles which his predecessor had advanced as the foundation of the true state. As Cicero notes, he will endeavor to accomplish his purpose by "employing the same principles which Plato discerned, yet taking no shadowy commonwealth of the imagination but a real and very powerful state"⁹ as the subject of his inquiry. His thinking in this respect is again in the tradition of Aristotle who constantly stressed the close relationship between political institutions and the habits and capacities of the people.

The Nature of the State

Cicero is well aware that an intelligent discussion of political institutions presupposes a knowledge of the nature of the state. "For the qualities of the thing to be considered can never be understood unless one understands first exactly what the thing itself is. Therefore, since the commonwealth is the subject of our investigation, let us first consider exactly what it is that we are investigating."¹⁰ In an oft-quoted and beautifully expressed passage, Cicero defines a state as "the property of a people. But a people is not any collection of human beings brought together in any sort of way, but an assemblage of people in large numbers associated in an agreement with respect to justice and a partnership for the common good."¹¹ Forms of government may vary, but to be legitimate they must always rest on the consent of the people, principles of justice, and the good of the community.

The state comes into being as a natural result of the social instinct of man. "The first cause of such an association is not so much the weakness of the individual as a certain social spirit which nature has implanted in man. For man is not a solitary or unsocial creature."¹² What, therefore, is the purpose or end of the state? Essentially, it is to help man in his task of self-fulfillment and in the promotion of the good life. "Just as the aim of the pilot is a successful voyage, of the physician,

---

⁹ *Ibid.*, II, xxxi.   ¹⁰ *Ibid.*, I, xxiv.   ¹¹ *Ibid.*, I, xxv.   ¹² *Ibid.*

health, and of the general, victory, so the director of the commonwealth has as his aim for his fellow-citizens a happy life, fortified with wealth, rich in material resources, great in glory, and honored by virtue."[13] It is impossible for man to live well "except in a good commonwealth, and nothing can produce greater happiness than a well-constituted State."[14] So also, no nobler form of activity exists than a life dedicated to public service since "there is really no other occupation in which human virtue approaches more closely the august function of the gods."[15]

There is nothing that is new in Cicero's conception of the state. Plato and Aristotle had likewise viewed the body politic as a rational and organic institution founded on law and justice and designed to serve the welfare of the people. They all agree that an individual can realize his natural destiny only in the state, in an association of human beings united in intellect and will in the furtherance of a common objective. Outside of this community, man would be little more than a beast.

The Ideal State

In constructing his ideal state on the model of the Roman Republic, Cicero begins by listing the traditional three types of government — monarchy, aristocracy, and democracy — and then proceeds to criticize each in its pure form. In kingships, the people have too small a share and too insignificant a voice in the administration of public affairs, and the conduct of the state is subject to the nod and caprice of one man. In aristocracies, the liberty of the people is too restricted since they are entirely excluded from sharing in the exercise of political power. In democracies, where all the power is in the people's hands, the very equality which results is dangerous since it recognizes no gradations of merit.[16] Beyond these defects, all three forms are undesirable for another reason. They too easily degenerate into their perverted forms (each containing within itself the germs of its own decay): monarchy into tyranny, aristocracy into plutocracy or oligarchy, and democracy into mob rule.

The ideal form, according to Cicero, is one which is a combination or balanced mixture of the three simple forms. In advancing this concept, he is following Polybius, the Greek historian of Roman institutions, who had attributed the greatness of the Roman state to its constitutional

---

[13] *Ibid.*, V, vi.   [14] *Ibid.*, V, v.   [15] *Ibid.*, I, vii.
[16] *Ibid.*, I, xxvii. Cicero believed that Greece fell because of "immoderate liberty and the license of public assemblies."

arrangement of a mixed type of government. Polybius argues that such a government serves as an effectual check and balance among the different social and economic interests in the state and acts as a safeguard against the decay which inevitably destroys the pure type of government. He believes that by combining the best elements of all three forms, stability can be better assured and the abuse of power rendered less likely. Polybius professes to derive his theory of the balanced form of government from the experiences of the Roman Republic. The consuls represented the monarchic element, the senate the aristocratic, and the popular assemblies the democratic, each acting as a check on the actions of the other.

Adopting Polybius' view, Cicero asserts that although kingship is the best of the three primary forms,[17] a combination of the three simple types was much preferable. "There should be a supreme and royal element in the state, some power also ought to be granted to the leading citizens, and certain matters should be left to the judgment and desires of the masses."[18] In this way there would result "an even balance of rights, duties, and functions, so that the magistrates have enough power, the counsels of the eminent citizens enough influence, and the people enough liberty."[19]

The concept of a mixed form of government had previously appeared in Aristotle's proposal to stabilize government through a balancing of social or economic classes. Cicero and Polybius, while adhering to the same principle of equilibrium, make an important modification in the means of securing it. In doing so they approach more closely to the modern theory of separation of powers. The mixture, as suggested by them, is one not of economic or social but of political power, achieved through balancing the branches of government. True, the senate may generally represent the wealthy and aristocratic classes and the popular assemblies the poorer groups; but the important fact is that the Roman system, unlike the Greek, provided an *institutional* medium for each interest to check and balance the other.

---

[17] Cicero said that the rule of one man, if he be just, is the best ideally speaking, but if he be unjust, it is the worst type. He bases his theoretical preference for kingship on the analogy of nature where the whole universe is ruled by a single mind, and on man where a single element, reason, rules over the other faculties (*De Republica,* I, xxvi–xxviii).

[18] *De Republica,* I, 1.

[19] *Ibid.,* II, xxxiii.

The Natural Law

One of the most important aspects of Cicero's writings is his restatement of the idea of natural law. Here again he expresses little that is new, but speaks under the influence of Plato and Aristotle, and more particularly of the later stoics such as Panaetius. He defines natural law as

> right reason in agreement with nature; it is of universal application, unchanging and everlasting; it summons to duty by its commands, and averts from wrongdoing by its prohibitions. . . . It is a sin to try to alter this law, nor is it allowable to attempt to repeal any part of it, and it is impossible to abolish it entirely. We cannot be freed from its obligations by senate or people, and we need not look outside ourselves for an expounder or interpreter of it. And there will not be different laws at Rome and at Athens, and different laws now and in the future, but one eternal and unchangeable law will be valid for all nations and all times, and there will be one master and ruler, that is God, over us all, for he is the author of this law, its promulgator, and its enforcing judge.[20]

In the De Legibus, Cicero enlarges upon his definition by stating that

> law is the highest reason, implanted in Nature, which commands what ought to be done and forbids the opposite. . . . Law is a natural force; it is the mind and reason of the intelligent man, the standard by which Justice and injustice are measured. But since our whole discussion has to do with the reasoning of the populace, it will sometimes be necessary to speak in the popular manner, and give the name of law to that which in written form decrees whatever it wishes, either by command or prohibition. For such is the crowd's definition of law.[21]

There are two important points to be observed in these excerpts, the first merely repetitious of a principle already noted in classical thought, the second an apparent deviation from the teachings of Aristotle. As to the first, Cicero emphasizes that any law enacted by man, or any custom practiced by the people, which does not conform to the natural law is illegitimate and invalid. "But the most foolish notion of all is the belief that everything is good which is found in the customs or laws of nations."[22] Man may be compelled by the superior physical force of the rulers to obey decrees which contravene nature but he is under no moral obligation to do so.

---

[20] Ibid., III, xxii. [21] De Legibus, I, vi. [22] Ibid., I, xv.

The second factor deals with Cicero's concept of natural law. While his treatment of this subject leaves much to be desired in the way of clarity,[23] he seems to differ radically with Aristotle in stressing the ability of individual human reason to ascertain the natural law. His statement that we need not look outside ourselves for an expounder or interpreter of it illustrates this attitude. Emphasis on the *autarky* or self-sufficiency of human reason is characteristic of all the post-Aristotelian philosophies of conduct, with their basic doctrine that man ought to be completely autonomous and independent.

Professor McCoy has observed that the Stoic conception of the *autarky* of human reason presupposes a self-dependent reason which does not find or discover the laws of nature but is itself the source of such laws.[24] Thus man is subject to no law imposed from without but only to a "natural law" which he in effect gives to himself. Granted the validity of McCoy's interpretation, Cicero actually reduces natural law to that which the majority holds it to be. Cicero, however, disavows such a conclusion in his statement that justice exists in nature and is not founded on the decrees of people. For if it were "then Justice would sanction robbery and adultery and forgery of wills, in case these acts were approved by the votes or decrees of the populace."[25] Yet, in spite of his disavowal, the implications of his insistence on the autonomy of human reason remain.

Unlike Cicero, Aristotle insisted that man is not an intellectually self-sufficient creature; and that while there is an objective moral law, it must be discovered in the ontological structure of things. The form of human life is made determinate through the joint efforts of men as expressed in their acts, habits, laws, and institutions. The individual cannot look solely to his own reason for the correct measure of rightness and wrongness. For him to do so would presuppose that all men are intellectually equal as well as intellectually capable of ascertaining the truth. This mythical equality finds expression in Cicero.

Human Equality

According to classical Greek thought, all men are equal in respect to their

---

[23] In certain passages, his natural law seems to embody a kind of pantheism in which God is identified with human reason.

[24] Charles N. R. McCoy, "The Turning Point in Political Philosophy," *American Political Science Review*, September, 1950, p. 682.

[25] *De Legibus*, I, xv.

specific nature, rationality, but their equality ceases at this point. There are vast differences among them, intellectually, morally, and physically. Plato's class division and Aristotle's doctrine of the natural slave sought to emphasize these differences. When we come to Cicero, we find an entirely new conception of human equality. "No single thing is so like another, so exactly its counterpart, as all of us are to one another. Nay, if bad habits and false belief did not twist the weaker minds and turn them in whatever direction they are inclined, no one would be so like his own self as all men would be like all others."[26]

The Greek political theorists began with the natural inequalities among men. Cicero starts with the assumption that all these differences are in some way contrary to nature. He notes that human reason is common to all of us and "though varying in what it learns, at least in the *capacity to learn it is invariable*. For the same things are invariably perceived by the senses, and those things which stimulate the senses stimulate them in the same way in all men; and those rudimentary beginnings of intelligence to which I have referred, which are imprinted on our minds, are imprinted on all minds alike."[27] Men may, therefore, differ in knowledge, but they are similar in their capacity to acquire knowledge. Furthermore, all men possess not only the faculty of reason but *right* reason. "These creatures who have received the gift of reason from Nature have also received right reason."[28] This is a far cry from the psychology of Cicero's predecessors who based their political philosophy on the inherent differences among men in talent and capacity.

Looking at the world about him, Cicero could hardly deny that inequalities among human beings did exist in fact. To explain away these variations, he contends that it is only the perversions brought about by bad habits and foolish conceptions which cause men to differ from one another. Remove these disabilities, return to a pristine state of nature, and inequalities will vanish. There is a striking anticipation here of the Christian doctrine of original sin, in which evil acts have brought about inequalities and suffering in the natural order. Despite his philosophical presuppositions in this regard, Cicero appears to be under no illusion that such "inequalities can be overcome." As he observes in one passage, since equality of ability is impossible, "the legal rights at least of those who are citizens of the same commonwealth ought to be equal."[29] This

---

26 *Ibid.*, I, x.
27 *Ibid.* (italics added).
28 *Ibid.*, I, xii.
29 *De Republica*, I, xxxii.

view resembles the modern democratic doctrine of equal rights before the law, but legal equality is a quite different matter from that of talents and aptitudes.

Cicero was basically an aristocrat both in temperament and in practice. It will be recalled that he rejected democracy as the best form of government on the grounds that it places everyone on the same level and allows no distinction in rank. Throughout his writings, he continually stresses the need for giving the eminent citizens a place of influence in the political structure. At one point he remarks that he would have no objection to a secret ballot provided the common man showed his vote to "some excellent and serious citizen" before depositing it. Such views are hardly those of one who believes in the innate equality of men. Cicero, loyal to his stoic philosophy, may have thought that such equality existed in the ideal order, but practical statesman as he was, he realized that we must accept men as they are — and men in the concrete order differ radically in talents, capabilities, and virtues. To construct a state on any other premise would be to disregard the basic facts of human psychology.

THE ROMAN LAWYERS

The Roman jurists made no pretense of being political philosophers. Interested primarily in the task of interpreting and applying law to the changing conditions of Roman society, they touched upon such topics as the nature and origin of the state only in so far as they affected or involved consideration of the judicial process. The political speculation which they engaged in was largely a repetition of the theories found in Cicero. What they did say was nevertheless important since the great authority that was attached to Roman law throughout western Europe gave weight and prestige to any general principles associated with it.[30] Consequently, when the jurists employed the concepts of natural law and human equality in their development of the Roman legal system, they assured the spread of these ideas among a wide and receptive audience.

Faced with the task of administering justice to an empire of diversified people during a period of changing economic, social, and political conditions, the Roman lawyers found their solutions primarily in the philo-

---

[30] Sabine, op. cit., p. 169.

sophical concepts prevalent during their time. Stoic in outlook, the jurists had no difficulty in conceiving of an empire in which individuals of different races, with diverse languages and customs, could exist on a basis of equality of rights and privileges before the law. Employing the concept of a universal standard of justice, they sought to determine out of the mass of local customs and practices the general principles that should be applicable to all peoples. In doing so, the Roman jurists were the first to distinguish precisely the different kinds of law.

Gaius, in the second century A.D., speaks of two kinds of law, *jus civile* and *jus gentium*. That which each people has established as law for itself is called *jus civile*; but what natural reason has established among all men, is known as *jus gentium*, as a law used by all nations. Gaius seemingly identifies the *jus gentium* with the natural law. Later jurists, beginning with Ulpian in the third century and continuing on through Justinian in the sixth century, distinguish between the two by recognizing that even that which is generally practiced may be unjust and unreasonable. Behind all particular civil laws and customs are fundamental principles of right embedded in nature itself. These are usually followed by men everywhere, but if some particular local custom or institution should violate the criterion so imposed, the practice must be barred. By incorporating the idea of an objective standard of equity and justice into legal thought and practice, the jurists gave the concept of natural law a character of concreteness that it had previously lacked.

The Roman lawyers contributed to another facet of political thought — that dealing with the source of authority in the state. According to Roman legal theory, all legislative and administrative acts derive their authority ultimately from the people. This view persisted and was accepted as theoretically correct even during the despotic days of the Empire, when power was obtained by every method other than popular consent. Ulpian's famous expression *"Quod principi placuit, legis habet vigorem"* (the will of the Prince is law) was followed by the qualification that the ruler's power is conferred on him by the people. The emperor's will, in other words, is law only because the people desire it to be so. His authority, or what later came to be looked upon as legal sovereignty, is derived from the people by way of delegation. The presence of this concept of "popular sovereignty" in Roman law proved of considerable aid to the later development of democracy.

102 THE POLITICAL PHILOSOPHY OF THE ANCIENTS

SUMMARY

When we come to assess the relevancy that Cicero and the Roman thinkers have for the middle of the twentieth century, several factors seem to stand out. In the first place, the Romans created a political framework which helped to preserve the values of the city-state and to spread the ideas of Hellenism and Christianity throughout the West. This heritage includes an awareness of the high responsibility of public office, a feeling for the dignity and purposiveness of the state, a respect for tradition, a recognition of the organic structure of civil society, and the acceptance of the natural law basis of the state and of political authority.

Cicero and his colleagues contributed substantially to the development of constitutional government. They regarded the state as a *juris societas*, a community of laws. Largely because of their great influence, the state began to assume in western political theory the character of a legal entity exercising its authority within definite limits. Positive law similarly came to be looked upon as representing the practical application of the universal principles of justice and reason, and not merely the arbitrary or capricious will of the lawmakers. As Cicero sums it up, "the function of the magistrates is to govern and to give commands which are just and beneficial and in conformity with the law. For as the laws govern the magistrate, so the magistrate governs the people, and it may be truly said that the magistrate is a speaking law, and the law a silent magistrate."[31] The result is a government of laws as well as of men.

Since the Romans looked upon political authority in legal and constitutional terms, it was possible for them to devise a system of political checks and balances that operated through the governmental organs of the state. Aristotle, as his theory of equilibrium among classes illustrates, had conceived of supremacy within a state largely in terms of social or economic rather than legal or political control. The Romans showed that social and economic forces could be counterbalanced or moderated through governmental arrangements. The modern theory of separation of powers and the American concept of constitutionalism are more understandable in Roman than in Greek terms.

Finally, the notion of individual rights against the state introduced a note into political theory that was not explicit in Greek thought. While the latter recognized the inherent rights of the individual and the wrongfulness of any state action which violated these rights, it could conceive of no legal remedy available to the injured person. Through the development of legal procedures, the Roman system began to display remedial measures which in embryonic form resemble the modern notion of constitutional rights resting on "due process of law."

---

[31] *De Legibus,* III, i.

BIBLIOGRAPHY

Arnold, E. V., Roman Stoicism (Cambridge: University of Cambridge Press, 1911).

Bailey, Cyril (ed.), The Legacy of Rome (Oxford: Clarendon Press, 1923).

Barker, Ernest, Church, State, and Study: Essays (London: Methuen, 1930).

Barnes, H. E., "Theories of the Origin of the State in Classical Political Philosophy," Monist, January, 1924.

Bossier, Gaston, Cicero and His Friends: A Study of Roman Society in the Time of Cicero (New York: G. P. Putnam's Sons, 1925).

Carlyle, A. J., History of Medieval Political Theory in the West, Vol. I (London: Blackwood, 1903).

Chinard, Gilbert, "Polybius and the American Constitution," Journal of the History of Ideas, January, 1940.

Cowell, F. R., Cicero and the Roman Republic (London: Pitman, 1948).

Festugiere, A. J., Epicurus and His Gods, trans. by S. W. Chilton (Cambridge: Harvard University Press, 1957).

Fritz, Kurt von, The Theory of the Mixed Constitution in Antiquity (New York: Columbia University Press, 1954).

Grampp, W. D., "Moral Hero (of the Stoics) and the Economic Man (of modern liberalism)," Ethics, January, 1951.

Hadas, Moses, "From Nationalism to Cosmopolitanism in the Greco-Roman World," Journal of the History of Ideas, January, 1943.

Haskell, H. J., This Was Cicero (New York: Knopf, 1942).

Keyes, Clinton W., "Original Elements in Cicero's Ideal Constitution," American Journal of Philology, October, 1921.

Lear, Floyd S., "The Idea of Majesty in Roman Political Thought," in Essays in History and Political Theory in Honor of Charles Howard McIlwain (Cambridge: Harvard University Press, 1936).

Murray, Gilbert, Stoic, Christian, and Humanist (London: Allan & Unwin, 1940).

Poyser, G. H., "Ancient Light on a Modern Problem: the Stoic Influence on Western Civilization Through Cicero," Hibbert Journal, July, 1953.

Rand, E. K., Cicero in the Courtroom of St. Thomas Aquinas (Milwaukee: Bruce, 1946).

Reesor, M. E., "Stoic Concept of Equality," American Journal of Philology, January, 1954.

Richards, G. C., Cicero: A Study (New York: Houghton Mifflin, 1935).

Rolfe, John C., Cicero and His Influence (Boston: Marshall Jones, 1923).

Smethurst, S. E., "Politics and Morality in Cicero," Phoenix, Autumn, 1955.

Starr, Chester G., "The Perfect Democracy of the Roman Empire," American Historical Review, October, 1952.

Syme, Ronald, The Roman Revolution (Oxford, Clarendon Press, 1939).

Wenley, R. M., Stoicism and Its Influence (Boston: Marshall Jones, 1924).

Wheeler, Marcus, "Cicero's Political Ideal," Greece and Rome, June, 1952.

PART THREE | **THE POLITICAL PHILOSOPHY OF**
THE MEDIEVALISTS

Chapter VI

THE EARLY CHRISTIAN PERIOD

"But seek first the kingdom of God and his justice, and all these things shall be given you besides" (*Matthew* 6:33).

As THE Roman Empire became more despotic and as it slowly traveled the path toward its final collapse, a new force, dynamic and revolutionary, emerged from the East. Known as Christianity, this new element originated among an outcast people in a remote part of the Empire. From its humble beginning it gradually spread in influence until it encompassed the whole of the Roman world. As the followers of Jesus of Nazareth carried the gospels of the new religion to the peoples of the Empire, they brought mankind a new sense of compassion, a new understanding, and a new hope of redemption. The resulting transformation was radical and profound. Never again was the world to be the same. Not only did the teachings of Christianity prove imperishable, but they decisively shaped and determined the future course of western history. The whole complex of modern political and social life in the West is permeated with Christian values and practices.

The early Christians were looked upon with suspicion and hostility. In pagan Rome as in ancient Greece, loyalty to the state involved loyalty to the gods of the state, a view in which the Christians refused to acquiesce. Rejecting the idea that political allegiance implies religious conformity, they protested that they were loyal subjects of the Empire in all but their religion. As time passed, the original small group of Christ's followers grew into an organized movement on a vast scale. Tolerated at first by the Roman government as one oriental sect among others, the Christians were later subjected to persecution because of their persistent refusal to recognize the sole authority of the emperor. However, by the fourth century Christianity had become the religion of the most influential classes in the Empire. Under the edict of toleration issued by Constantine in 313, the new religion was given official recognition. Later when paganism was legally proscribed, Christianity became the official and exclusive religion of the Empire. The two societies, religious and political, now stood face to face on a plane of legal equality. The old antagonisms were for the time being brought to an end, but the problem of defining the nature and character of the resulting relationship, a difficulty unknown to the ancient world, now began to emerge. Before considering this question, it would be helpful to turn momentarily to Seneca, a Roman thinker who epitomizes the pre-Christian dilemma.

SENECA

Seneca (A.D. 4–65) was a wealthy and educated Spaniard who served as tutor to Nero and later as his chief administrative officer. He was perhaps the last of the Roman writers to systematically study stoicism as it found expression among its original interpreters. Although his writings are not considered comparable to those of Cicero, they did enjoy extraordinary popularity at the time of their publication, and for several centuries thereafter. Seneca resigned his high political office when he was in his late fifties in order to devote himself to the exposition of the practical teachings of stoicism. Some time after his retirement, he was accused of conspiring against the emperor and was ordered to commit suicide.[1]

Although Cicero and Seneca adhere to the same basic philosophical beliefs, their outlooks on life are essentially different. Cicero, despite his recognition of sin, remained optimistic and hopeful that Rome could return to her former position of strength and integrity. Seneca, on the other hand, held no such illusions. Thoroughly pessimistic and despondent, he looked upon human nature as corrupt and faulty and as oppressed by vice and misery. He felt that the wise man should withdraw unto himself and devote his time to contemplation. For only in some mystical and theoretical community of the wise can the injustices and inequalities of social life be remedied. Yet Seneca, imbued with the Roman ideal of public service, could not force himself to regard man as altogether exempt from the obligation to serve society. Despite the strong feeling

---

[1] For an account of Seneca and his writings see A. J. Carlyle, *A Story of Medieval Political Theory In The West* (London: Blackwood, 1903), Vol. 1, Chap. 2. Also E. V. Arnold, *Roman Stoicism, op. cit.*

of human wickedness which pervades his thought, he is conscious of a sense of charity, compassion, and tolerance toward his fellow beings. He teaches that the true role of man's life is to be of use to his brethren, either by public service or by participation in humanitarian projects.

There are several remarkable insights in Seneca's thought that are significant to the development of political philosophy. In his *Epistulae Morales*, he pictures a state of nature in which men lived, uncorrupted and innocent, in complete peace and happiness. In this primitive state, they had no need for coercive government; they simply followed nature and voluntarily obeyed the best and wisest men who served as their rulers. However, as time passed, greed came to take hold of the people. Dissatisfied with communal property, they began to desire private possessions and to become self-seeking. The rulers were likewise seized with the lust of authority and property, and from their role as paternal guardians of society they turned to despotism and tyranny. Laws and coercive government then became necessary to curb human vices.

As is evident from this brief résumé, Seneca regarded the institution of society as a by-product of sin. The state and human law are conventional institutions made necessary by man's wickedness rather than by the natural conditions of ideal progress. Coupled with the stoic insistence on the self-sufficiency of the individual, this doctrine was to reappear time and time again in subsequent periods of history.

Although Seneca had virtually no knowledge of the doctrine of Christianity, his idea of man's primitive state parallels the teachings of Revelation in many respects. Because of greed or the lust for power, Adam and Eve destroyed the happiness and well-being of Paradise; and as a result of their sin, the human race fell from its pristine integrity and purity. Haunted with the feeling of human sinfulness (that which I should not, I do) Seneca sought refuge in the hope that compassion and social service will redeem the bestial in man. Yet his belief that no one can escape sin and that virtue consists in an endless struggle for salvation rather than in its achievement is scarcely a palliative for his intrinsic pessimism. It was in this intellectual milieu that Christianity brought new hope to mankind with its theological explanation of man's sinfulness and its doctrine of salvation through grace.

A second aspect of Seneca's thought that foreshadowed the shape of events to come is his concept of the two commonwealths: one the political state with its government and juridical institutions; the other a universal society, a brotherhood of men, whose ties are moral and ethical rather than legal and political, and whose bounds "are to be measured with the circuit of the sun." The universal society must always reject those demands of the political state which interfere with or encroach upon its domain. Implicit in these ideas is the possibility of conflict between the claims of the religious and secular spheres. This possibility soon became a reality in the Christian doctrine of two societies and two loyalties.

EARLY CHRISTIAN POLITICAL AND SOCIAL THOUGHT

Until St. Augustine wrote his great treatise in the first quarter of the fifth century, there was little formal expression of political thought among the Christians, and little organized social action. The attitude of the early followers of Jesus toward the temporal state and society must be sought for primarily in the writings of the New Testament.

The lack of any systematic body of Christian political and social thought during the early years of the new era is hardly surprising. Christianity is a religion, a doctrine of salvation, and not a philosophy or a political theory. As citizens or residents of the Empire, the Christians generally adhered to the prevailing ideas toward the state and government and to the social doctrines of the period.

The Stoics had conceived of man as a citizen of two states, the political entity in which he resides, and the universal state — the brotherhood of man — to which all human creatures belong. For the Christian, this latter realm was not a mere state of mind as the stoics were inclined to look upon it, but a spiritual or supernatural commonwealth that is open to all men if they will but enter it. Unlike the exclusiveness of stoicism, Christianity appealed to the common man as well as the noble, to the simple as well as the wise, to the heart as well as the intellect. No social or intellectual barrier stood in the way of entry to the new fraternity, with its promise of rewards in this world and eternal salvation hereafter.

The universal kingdom of which Christianity spoke is represented on earth by the Church, whose head is the vicar of Christ. The Greek concept of religion as an adjunct of the state lost its applicability in this new context. The Church now stood side by side with the secular government, but its jurisdiction or sovereignty was limited to the spiritual dimensions of man's life. But where does the secular sphere end and the spiritual begin? The answer was not easy to formulate. The full implications of the problem did not, however, become evident during this early period.

THE CHRISTIAN ATTITUDE TOWARD POLITICAL AUTHORITY

Despised and often persecuted, it would not have been strange had the early Christians rejected entirely the things of this world and turned inward to a contemplation of the eternal life. The biblical passages which speak of the renunciation of worldliness, contempt of wealth, and indifference toward slavery are indications of such an attitude. St. James, for example, after condemning the rich who oppressed their workers ("Go to now, ye rich men, weep and howl in your miseries, which shall come upon you. Your riches are corrupted and your garments are motheaten"), then turns to the abused laborers and tells them to be patient, to endure their lot in life, and to await the coming of the Lord.[2] Even St. Paul exhorts the slaves "to be obedient to them that are your lords according to the flesh . . . knowing that whatsoever good any man shall do, the same shall be received from the Lord whether he be bond or free."[3] Endure with fortitude the sufferings of this world since they are but a preparation for the glorious life to follow.

Religious leaders were well aware of the danger that lay in too literal an interpretation of the freedom of the Gospel. It is not difficult to imagine that the Christians, with their enthusiastic spirit and their eyes directed to a future life, might have drifted into an attitude of contempt for secular government, especially when that government was under the control of unspiritual rulers. Although exhortations such as those of St. Paul, "With freedom did Christ set us free: stand fast therefore, and be not entangled again in a yoke of bondage," refer to man's redemption by the sacrifice on the Cross, they could be taken to mean an emancipation from all the ordinary duties and disciplines of this life. Had this latter view gained wide acceptance among the Christians, it might have caused disruptions in the social order; and these would certainly have brought down the wrath of the Empire on the religion of Christ. It was to counteract any such anarchistic tendency that St. Paul found it necessary to stress repeatedly the importance of submitting to lawfully ordained

[2] James 5:1–11.
[3] Eph. 6:5–8.

authority, whether it be that of the state over its citizens or that of the master over his slave.

The attitude of the Christian leaders toward the state and government during this period of religious incubation is of special interest, since it sets the stage for the long church-state controversy that was to follow. St. Paul (A.D. 3–67), who is perhaps the most influential spokesman for the Christian religion in the years immediately following the death of Jesus, took great pains to vindicate the authority of the civil rulers and to disabuse any notion that the new religion was one of withdrawal. In his Epistle to Titus, the bishop of Crete, he urges him to admonish the faithful "to be subject to princes and powers, to obey at a word." And in the famous and oft-quoted passage of Romans XIII, he declares, "Let every soul be in subjection to the higher powers, for there is no power but of God, and those that are ordained of God. Therefore he that resisteth the power, resisteth the ordinance of God." This is strong language since it gives divine sanction to political rule and at the same time indirectly corroborates the Greek conception of the state as a necessary institution.

St. Paul makes it clear that civil law must be obeyed not only because the state has the physical power to compel adherence but, what is more important, because its lawful orders are binding in conscience. "Wherefore be subject of necessity: not only for wrath, but also for conscience sake." Why is obedience to the state so important? St. Paul answers that the purpose of civil government is to suppress evil and to foster and encourage good. It must provide the material conditions in which man can pursue his proper end. As such, the state is worthy of Christian man's loyalty. Pray for kings and all that are in high stations, St. Paul instructs Timothy, "that we may lead a quiet and a peaceful life in all piety and chastity."[4]

Although Christianity from the beginning acknowledged man's obligation toward civil rule, it introduced a new concept to political thought and practice: that of dual authority. Plato and Aristotle had assumed that the religious and social spheres were part and parcel of the same human institutions and subject to the same rule, that of the state. The Christians, however, refused to recognize the all-inclusive nature of secular jurisdiction. Instead, they claimed a separate authority for the Church over the spiritual aspects of human life. Christian man now

---

[4] 1 Tim. 2:2.

became faced with two jurisdictions and two consequent loyalties: one to the state, the other to the church. He was a citizen of the secular society and a potential member of the kingdom of God. How was he to carry out this twofold loyalty?

The underlying basis for resolving the question of secular-spiritual jurisdiction had been given by Jesus when He said "Render to Caesar the things that are Caesar's and to God the things that are God's." St. Paul, in like vein, counseled his listeners to render to all men their dues. "Tribute to whom tribute is due; custom to whom custom; fear to whom fear; honor to whom honor." These eloquent expressions rest on the premise that church and state can stand side by side in peace and harmony, each working for its particular end. The formula so simply stated was destined to go through a long period of interpretation and refinement in the years to follow.

NATURAL LAW AND HUMAN EQUALITY

Two other Christian concepts of social and political significance closely parallel stoic thought: the idea of a natural law and the belief in a universal brotherhood of man. Recognizing that some men would not have direct knowledge of the revealed law of God, St. Paul states that such individuals are nevertheless bound in their conduct by a law higher than that of the state. "For when the Gentiles, who have not the law [that is, the revealed law] do by nature those things that are of the law; these, having not the law, are a law to themselves. Who show the work of the law written in their hearts, their conscience bearing witness to them."[5] Cicero had previously spoken of a law written in man's heart and of right reason in agreement with nature. Such a concept had also been implicit in the thinking of the classical Greeks. Christianity was now to give this law a theological anchorage and make its role more definite in the Divine order of things. Or as one writer has said, Christianity irradiated the stoic ideas of the natural law in the new light of the Fatherhood of God.[6]

The Stoics had conceived of a society existing apart from the political state, a universal brotherhood of mankind in which all men enjoy equality. As evidenced in the writings of Cicero and Seneca, they be-

---

[5] *Rom.* 2:14–15.

[6] J. Bowle, *Western Political Thought* (New York: Oxford University Press, 1948), p. 106.

lieved that sin had destroyed this equality and brought disorder into the world. Christianity in turn introduced the teaching of the universal fatherhood of God and the doctrine of original sin. In his Epistle to the Galatians, St. Paul writes "For you are all the children of God. . . . There is neither Jew nor Greek; there is neither bond nor free; there is neither male nor female. For you are all one in Christ Jesus."[7] At another point, in answer to the queries of certain epicurean and stoic philosophers concerning God, St. Paul replies in poetic terms, "For in him we live and move and are."[8] We are all, regardless of race, color, or social status, members of the mystical body of Christ and as such we share a kinship with the Divine. While there is a certain similarity between these concepts and those of stoicism, Christianity made two things clear. First, it demonstrated that the idea of individual self-sufficiency inherent in stoic thought is inadequate. Since man's nature has been vitiated by sin, he can be redeemed only with the help of grace. He must depend on Divine aid and support if he is to be saved. Second, the new religion taught that man should be concerned not only with his own salvation and well-being, a tendency present in early stoicism, but also with the happiness and welfare of his fellow creatures. As Jesus admonished his listeners "love thy neighbor as thyself."

While stressing that man's true happiness is not of this world, the teaching of Christianity embodied the idea of social justice and of a militant social service in the cause of humanity. As a proscribed sect, the early Christians could not engage in organized social action. It was through Christian personalism or the example of their private lives — charity, modesty, kindness toward the poor and the enslaved, moderate living, fortitude, and courage — that the followers of Jesus sought to influence the social and moral life of their day.[9] Only after the peace of Constantine was the Church free to come out in the open and make her influence felt in the social sphere.

ST. AUGUSTINE

In A.D. 410, the once mighty Roman Empire, which some had thought would stand forever, collapsed with an impact that shocked the civilized

---

[7] Gal. 3:26–28.
[8] Acts 18:28.
[9] See in this connection, P. H. Furfy, "Christian Social Thought in 1st and 2nd Centuries," *American Catholic Sociological Review*, March, 1940, p. 13 ff.

world. Only the eastern or Byzantine portion of the Empire, with its seat at Constantinople, remained. As Alaric and his barbarian Goths sacked and plundered the "Eternal City," men began to realize that the end of a whole civilization and social order was in the making. The city which had taken the whole world captive, was now herself captured. The gradual decline of intellectual and cultural standards, the deterioration of moral discipline, the weakening of civic virtue, and the increasing reliance on slave labor, had all served to sap the strength and vigor of Rome. Only the Church with its growing organization, its corps of trained administrators, and its unbounded vitality was left to fill the void created by the virtual collapse of political rule in the West. The time had now arrived for a more systematic formulation of the position of Christianity in the midst of human society. The task fell to one of the most original and brilliant minds of the Church, Augustine, Bishop of Hippo.

St. Augustine (334–430) was born in Tagaste, a town in North Africa. A pagan during the period of his youth, he was early attracted to the study of philosophy by the writings of Cicero. His mother was a Christian, but he turned first to Manicheanism, which was then flourishing in North Africa, and next to Neo-Platonism. His *Confessions*, written when he was forty-five, relate the story of the dissolute life he led as a youth, his experiences with the Manichaeans and Neo-Platonists in his search for truth, and finally his conversion to Christianity in 387. Eight years after he entered the Church he was consecrated Bishop of Hippo, a town located in what is now Algeria. He died in 430, just as the Vandals were on the point of capturing his city.

The City of God

When Rome fell to the Goths, some of the pagans charged that Christianity was responsible for the debacle. St. Augustine undertook to show the absurdity of this accusation in his great work, *The City of God (Civitas Dei)*. As he tells us

> Rome having been stormed and sacked by the Goths under Alaric their king, the worshipers of false gods or pagans, as we commonly call them, made an attempt to attribute this calamity to the Christian religion, and began to blaspheme the true God with even more than their wonted bitterness and acerbity. It was this which kindled my zeal for the house of God, and prompted me to undertake the defense of

the city of God against the charges and misrepresentations of its assailants.[10]

The *City of God* was begun in 413, and appeared in installments over a period of thirteen years. The first ten books or chapters, out of a total of twenty-two, are directed primarily to a defense of Christianity against the pagan charges. They show that the pagan beliefs, with their weaknesses and inconsistencies, could not possibly have been responsible for the former greatness of Rome; they point out that the Republic was already on the decline, as even Cicero admitted, before the advent of Christianity. "However admirable our adversaries say the republic was or is, it is certain that by the testimony of their own most learned writers it had become, long before the coming of Christ, utterly wicked and dissolute."[11] Had Augustine stopped at this point, his work would scarcely have been of great historical significance. It is in the last twelve books that its real importance lies. In these he sets forth his view of society, and of the political state in the far broader context of the relationship of God to the progress and ultimate destiny of man.

St. Augustine uses the metaphorical vehicle of the two cities to develop his thought. One is the city of good, the other of evil. Neither of them is intended to be descriptive of existing political or religious institutions but of the two forces that contend for man's soul: God and the devil. The title of the work is taken from Psalms. "Glorious things are said of thee, O city of God,"[12] and "Great is the Lord, and exceedingly to be praised in the city of our God, His holy mountain, a beautiful hill, is the joy of the whole earth."[13] St. Augustine explains that "though all these twenty-two books refer to both cities, yet I have named them after the better city, and called them the City of God."[14]

The term "civitas" as used by St. Augustine, is a source of some confusion. The Roman word for state is *republica*, a term always used when Romans such as Cicero speak of a sovereign political unit, whether it be a city-state or a universal empire. Augustine was well acquainted with Cicero's works and had he intended to write of the state as a political community, he would undoubtedly have used the technical term. Instead, he calls his city a *civitas* not a *republica*. That the title

---

[10] *Retractions*, II, 43.

[11] *City of God*, II, 22. Selections from the *City of God* are taken from the Modern Library edition, trans. by M. Dods (New York: Random House, 1950).

[12] 86, 3.   [13] 47, 1.   [14] *Retractions*, II, 43.

"City of God" does not mean a town or area in which people reside seems clear. Professor Barrow has suggested that the term serves as a convenient blank for the reader to fill in as he reads.[15] In one place the idea of a political community will be intended, in another the society of the righteous. The title, therefore, infers that St. Augustine had no intention of developing a theory of the state, much less a theory of the Christian state. Unlike Plato or Cicero, he was not interested in theorizing on the ideal state in the sense of a utopia. His "City of God" can in no way be taken as an ideal commonwealth in the political meaning of the term.

The basic concept underlying the *City of God* is derived from Revelation. All men would have been members of the heavenly city had not the sin of the Garden intervened. Now man can attain membership only with the help of God's grace. "For who will dare to believe or say that it was not in God's power to prevent both angels and men from sinning? But God preferred to leave this in their power, and thus to show what evil could be wrought by their pride, and what good by His grace."[16] Man is free to accept or reject the law of his Creator, but in the end he will be held accountable for his decision. Those who in this world embrace the good belong to the city of God; those who refuse to follow the Divine Will are members of the city of Man. Because some men live according to the flesh and others according to the spirit, two diverse and conflicting cities have arisen.

> Accordingly, two cities have been formed by two loves: the earthly by the love of self, even to the contempt of God; the heavenly by the love of God, even to the contempt of self. The former, in a word, glories in itself, the latter in the Lord. For the one seeks glory from men; but the greatest glory of the other is God, the witness of conscience.[17]

In Augustine's concept of the two cities is the stoic notion of a universal society which transcends all the more limited associations of race, class, and states. The *City of God*, while it includes only the good, is completely indifferent to all boundaries and distinctions among human societies. It "calls citizens out of all nations and gathers together a society of pilgrims of all languages, not scrupling about diversities in the man-

---

[15] R. H. Barrow, *Introduction to St. Augustine, The City of God* (London: Faber, 1950), pp. 20–22.
[16] *City of God*, XIV, 27.
[17] *Ibid.*, XIV, 28.

ners, laws, and institutions whereby earthly peace is secured and maintained."[18] It is a community of Christians that stands above all national and linguistic barriers. It is not a city reserved only for philosophers and sages as the stoic ideal, but a city that beckons all men. Any individual — slave or freeman, nobleman or commoner, Greek or barbarian, educated or uneducated — may belong to the kingdom of heaven by loving and worshiping God. This common love constitutes in a very real sense a social as well as a religious bond between the worshipers. For "he who loves God finds himself in virtue of this very fact in a social relation with all those who love him."[19]

Recognizing that man is subject to the manifold disorders that result from original sin, Augustine continually warns that it is only love or charity, inspired by a common faith in Christ, that unites a people into a true society. "Men will not dwell together in unity unless there lives within them the perfect charity of Christ." He defines charity as a motion of the soul toward the enjoyment of God for His own sake and toward the enjoyment of oneself and one's neighbors because of God. A state that is united only by enlightened self-interest cannot long function. Material goods constitute a divisive force in society. Since they cannot be completely shared, there is a temptation for man to grasp the whole and destroy those who would claim their share. Spiritual goodness, on the other hand, is not diminished when shared. Each individual can possess all without others having less than the whole. In fact, the nature of true goodness is such that, if a man will not share, he cannot possess the whole.[20]

Augustine's preoccupation with love and charity provides the clue to his political thinking. The many individual desires, ambitions, and drives in civil society can be sublimated to the good of the commonalty only by a mutual love of God. "There can be no love of one's neighbor unless there is love of God and love of one's neighbor in God." This love provides the rallying point, the cohesive bond that distinguishes a mob from a true society.

In the city of God, St. Augustine finds an object so complete that all are united in perfect union with Christ. This final and perfect society provides the archetype which should stand as the model for all other

[18] *Ibid.*, XIX, 17.
[19] E. Gilson, *Introduction to Study of St. Thomas* (Paris, 1931), p. 220.
[20] See in this connection, Thomas M. Garrett, "St. Augustine and the Nature of Society," *New Scholasticism*, January, 1956.

groups. Lesser societies and less perfect loves exist in the temporal world. The more these loves are inspired by Christian principles, the more effective they will be in promoting the good and true commonwealth. A people cannot be successfully united, Augustine says, unless they are dedicated to a supreme ideal that transcends individual diversities. Restrictions, discomforts, sacrifices, pain, and even death are tolerated by a people only because they have been sanctified by their relation to a higher good. Augustine finds this transcendental good in the love of God.

The Role of the State

It is sometimes said that Augustine regards the state as necessary only because of man's vitiated nature (the result of original sin). If we start with the premise that the political community has its origin in sin, we can logically say that civil government is a necessary evil, and that the less of it there is, the better off man will be. Or we can echo the words of one theologian who recently said that the state is like a surgical bandage, the abnormal. Those who seek to minimize the role of the state in this way are prone to turn to the writings of St. Augustine for support. The issue raised here is of considerable theoretical interest. For if the state is nothing more than a corrective for sin, theological support is given to the position that the role of government should be limited to keeping order. And if such is the case, the mission of the state as the promoter of the good life becomes suspect.

The *City of God* is quite emphatic in stating that the evils and miseries which men suffer in this world are due to the pollution of human nature by sin. Had there been no sin, there would have been no slavery since, "the condition of slavery is the result of sin"[21] and not of nature. Enlarging on the idea of slavery, St. Augustine indicates that without sin there would have been no occasion for the subjection of one man to the political authority of another. "By nature, as God first created us, no one is the slave either of man or of sin. This servitude is penal, however, and is appointed by that law which enjoins the preservation of the natural order and forbids its disturbance; for if nothing had been done in violation of that law, there would have been nothing to restrain by penal servitude."[22]

---

[21] *City of God*, XIX, 15.
[22] *Ibid.*

Writing in the century following Augustine, Gregory the Great explains that while there would have been no need for coercive government had mankind remained untainted by original sin, the need for political authority to direct the community would still have existed. Some system of authority is necessary to every society. "Even the angels, although free from sin, are yet ordered in a hierarchy of greater and less."[23] St. Augustine is not specific on this point, but his writings indicate that he is in general agreement with the view expressed by Gregory and later reiterated by Thomas Aquinas. In the first place, he agrees with classical thought that man is a social creature and that he needs society to assist him in his development. "The life of the wise man must be social. For how could the city of God . . . either take a beginning or be developed, or attain its proper destiny, if the life of the saints were not a social life."[24] Man, prior to the Fall in the Garden, was no less a social being. "God created only one single man, not, certainly, that he might be a solitary bereft of all society, but that by this means the unity of society and the bond of concord might be more effectually commended him. . . ."[25] The very fact of social living carries with it the necessity for order and direction, for government, in the management of common concerns.

Second, St. Augustine looks upon the state as the chief agency for securing the "tranquillity of order" necessary for man to work out his eternal destiny. This tranquillity signifies more than the absence of strife; it is the harmony which results from the proper ordering of things in their prescribed places. "Order is the distribution which allots things equal and unequal, each to its own place."[26] Such direction would be required even if man were uncorrupted by original sin. The element that would be missing in the state of innocence is coercion, since man in his pristine integrity would willingly and voluntarily obey the regulations laid down for his guidance.

Finally, despite his somewhat detached view of civil society, St. Augustine gives clear indication of recognizing the state as a positive good in the temporal sphere. "It [the state] is itself, in its own kind, better than all other human good. For it desires earthly peace for the sake of enjoying earthly good."[27] Such a peace, while not an end in

---

[23] Quoted in Carlyle, op. cit., I, 127.
[24] City of God, XIX, 5.
[25] Ibid., XII, 21.

[26] Ibid., XIX, 13.
[27] Ibid., XV, 4.

itself or the highest good absolutely speaking, is still the highest secular good since it is an essential means to the attainment of heavenly peace. Moreover, the state is necessary for the achievement of man's temporal end. Its basic purpose "in the well-ordered concord of civic obedience and rule is the combination of men's wills to attain the things which are helpful to this life."[28]

Justice

St. Augustine defines a state as "an assemblage of reasonable beings bound together by a common agreement as to the objects of their lives."[29] It will be a good or bad state according to the ends and objectives it seeks. "It will be a superior people in proportion as it is bound together by higher interests, inferior in proportion as it is bound together by lower." But good or bad, it will continue to be a state "so long as there remains an assemblage of reasonable beings bound together by a common agreement."[30] As the sinner remains a human being although he has violated his nature, so the state remains a political society even though it seeks unworthy objectives and is devoid of justice.

Because Augustine omits the quality of justice from his definition of the state, some commentators infer that he dispenses with the need for it in the secular commonwealth. Such an inference is hardly justifiable. True justice, as Augustine conceives it, consists in more than the willing submission and loyalty of the citizens to the laws of men; it must be a justice that is in conformity with the law of God as well. In the eyes of Augustine, justice of this nature could not possibly exist in a state where the people deny or disregard the claims of the one true God. Such people do not have an adequate idea of objective or absolute justice, and without this knowledge they cannot maintain themselves in sound virtue.[31]

Augustine was seeking a definition of the state which would apply to all alike — to just as well as unjust commonwealths. If Cicero's classical definition of a republic as a group of beings "united by a common regard for law and justice" were true, Rome would not be a state. A pagan commonwealth could not fulfill the requirements of justice as

---

[28] *Ibid.*, XIX, 17.   [29] *Ibid.*, XIX, 24.   [30] *Ibid.*

[31] This point is discussed in M. F. X. Millar, "St. Augustine and Cicero," *Thought*, Sept., 1929, p. 254 ff. Also in C. H. McIlwain, *The Growth of Political Thought in the West, op. cit.*, p. 154 ff.

defined by Augustine. His predominantly religious and theological outlook would not permit him to accept the notion that there can be true
justice in a society which does not recognize Christ as its ultimate
founder and ruler. In discussing the nature of the state, he takes the
opportunity to condemn the purely secular republic and to underscore
the disastrous effects which follow upon an exclusion of God from the
life of the people.

Relationship Between the Two Cities

Augustine's two cities are in fact two societies, the one composed of
all those who are bound together by their common love of God, the
other of those who prefer the love of themselves to the love of God.
At times he speaks of the Church as symbolically representing the heavenly society and of the pagan Roman Empire as the earthly city. Yet
he makes it perfectly clear that he does not intend to equate the heavenly
city with the Church militant and the earthly city with the civil power.
There are many in the Church who do not lead a Christlike life and
who are consequently not members of the heavenly kingdom. Similarly,
there are many presently outside the Church in the earthly city who
will be saved. But whether members of the heavenly city or the earthly
realm, all are commingled during their temporal life in the political
state. Civil society contains the members of both cities, the good and
the evil.

When Augustine speaks of the constant conflict between the two cities,
he is not referring to church and state but to the struggle between the
forces of good and evil. Similarly, when he appears to speak somewhat
disparagingly of the state as typifying the earthly city, he is not condemning the commonwealth as such but only that concept of political
society which views the state as absolute and self-sufficient both in the
spiritual and temporal orders. Rome fell because it was not eternal as
it claimed to be. The state is a provisional and instrumental society; it
is not an end in itself. To view it otherwise is to mistake the relative
and transient for the absolute and permanent. "But such is the stupid
pride of those men who fancy that the supreme good can be found in
this life."[32]

In his quest for salvation, man must make his pilgrimage on this
earth and must enlist the aid of the state for his temporal needs. It is

---

[32] City of God, XIX, 4.

thus incumbent upon the members of the heavenly city who still are sojourning in the secular realm to respect and obey civil rule. They must make "no scruple to obey the laws of the earthly city, whereby the things necessary for the maintenance of this mortal life are administered."[33] Because of the importance of political government, "the apostle also admonished the Church to pray for kings and those in authority, assigning as the reason that we may have a quiet and tranquil life in all godliness and love."[34] Those who are not members of the city of God also enjoy the peace and advantages of the state, but for this class the temporal benefits of political society constitute ends in themselves. To the citizens of the heavenly kingdom, these benefits are but means to the attainment of their eternal destiny.

Although a member of the kingdom of God is obliged to obey the civil laws and be loyal to the state during his terrestrial sojourn, this obedience and loyalty is limited to the secular sphere. Whenever the state interferes in matters of religion and hinders in any way "the worship of the one supreme and true God," the obligation of obedience ceases. Political society is not the ultimate authority in matters of faith and morals. It is the Church as the agent of Christ on earth that occupies this role.

Augustine has little to say about the organization of political society. He feels that the form of government is immaterial; in this mortal pilgrimage "what does it matter under whose government a dying man lives, if they who govern do not force him to impiety and iniquity."[35] His personal preference for monarchy is indicated in other passages in which he points out that peace and order require the unifying control and direction of a single head. Just as peace cannot be adequately maintained in a household "unless all the members of the same domestic circle be subject to one head, so too in civil society the tranquillity of order is best served by having a city or nation under the direction of a king."[36]

THE NATURE OF ST. AUGUSTINE'S POLITICAL PHILOSOPHY

St. Augustine stood at the crossroads of history. Through him were channeled all of the main currents of the classical world: Hebraic, Greek, and Roman. To him fell the task of interpreting and modifying these

---

[33] *Ibid.*, XIX, 17.
[34] *Ibid.*, XIX, 26.

[35] *Ibid.*, V, 17.
[36] *Ibid.*, XIX, 12.

great intellectual and cultural forces in the light of Christian Revelation. St. Augustine is primarily a theologian, not a political philosopher. His thinking tends to absorb the natural in the supernatural. Thus the City of God embodies a theological and not a political conception of society. Yet it is in this very fact that its contribution to political philosophy is found.

The social thought of antiquity had identified man's total social relations with the political unit of which he was a part. Stoicism and the other philosophies of withdrawal had later stressed the self-sufficiency of the individual to the almost total exclusion of the state. Christianity struck a balance between these two extremes. On the one hand, it made clear that man's life does not exhaust itself in strictly political patterns but that there is a private sphere — that of conscience and of man's relation to his God — which lie outside the domain of the state. On the other hand, it supported the ancient idea that man is a social creature who needs the state and society for his temporal development. It was Augustine who first sketched out in broad terms the nature and relationship of these two spheres. Unfortunately, his failure to speak more precisely on this question permitted the proponents both of papal claims and temporal sovereignty to draw on his writings for support during the years to follow.

St. Augustine made no pretense of devising a complete political theory. Nevertheless by picturing the world and human society in the light of Revelation, he gave a Christian idiom to the state and to political rule that remained unchallenged until the modern era. His attitude toward the state is not cynical or cavalier although at times it seems to border on these qualities. His objective is to place civil society in its proper perspective in a hierarchy of values. The temporal order is of importance to him as a Christian only in relation to the supernatural sphere. The state may be a means for attaining perfection in the temporal order, but man must never forget that this order is only fleeting and temporary, a preparation or testing ground for the life to come. Augustine's de-emphasis of the temporal sphere was prompted by his reaction to the declining moral tone of his day, a decline that had contributed to the fall of the Empire. By this de-emphasis he brought into sharp focus the claims of the spiritual realm and the precedence of the spirit over the flesh. No political leader or theorist could thereafter act or write in disregard of these factors.

The most important facet of Augustine's political philosophy is the theological anchorage that it gives to the realm of human rights. The classical writers could speak of the prerogatives which man must enjoy in order to attain his temporal self-perfection. They could also demonstrate that these rights stemmed from and were embedded in the ontological structure of nature. But beyond this point they could only grope for the transfinite sphere which they somehow conceived to exist. Even Aristotle expressed dissatisfaction with the limitations of human reason. Augustine now fills this void with the aid of Christian Revelation. Coming as a complementation and enlargement of classical thought, Revelation brought with it the doctrine of a personal God from whom all rights flow, an explanation of man's fall and the hope of his redemption through grace, and the teaching of an ultimate destiny not of this world.

Man's possession of an immortal and perfectible soul gave more meaning to the doctrine of human rights. Not until Revelation established that men have an inherent moral duty to pursue an end that transcends the state did it become clear that they possess inalienable rights which the state is bound to respect. The *City of God* was the first work to give systematic and formal articulation to these elements that were implicit in the Christian tradition. In doing so, it placed the social and political realm in a new and dynamic perspective.

SUMMARY

The pre-Christian social and political thinkers had gone as far as natural reason was capable of taking them. The majority of them believed that man was a perfectible creature but they could not understand his apparent inability to attain this perfection. In some of them, such as Aristotle, this failure to reach full understanding evoked an awareness of the limitations of human reason; in others, such as Seneca, it brought on an intense feeling of frustration and a negative submission to the pattern of human events. All of these men, in one fashion or another, were trying to reach a theological truth by natural reasoning. With the advent of Christianity, Revelation came to supplement the reason of man in his quest for truth and justice, and to explain in theological terms that which before had seemed vague and uncertain.

Christianity introduced no new political philosophy, no new conception of the state. It did raise the question of a twofold loyalty and the need for demarcating the two spheres: temporal and spiritual. It also brought with it a message of hope and charity and a new sense of the brotherhood of man. The communities which it fostered fulfilled many of the social and moral needs which had remained unsatisfied during the period of transition from the old to the new order. And most important, Christianity took ultimate values out of politics and placed them in their proper perspective.

We cannot find in this early period any complete and formalized Christian theory dealing with the nature and purpose of the state, with democracy, or with constitutional government. For the most part, Christianity accepted without modification the basic political principles as enunciated by the classical writers of Greece and Rome. Yet, in doing so it imbued them with a new spirit and a new significance, in the light of their place and role in the Divine plan. So strong was the influence of the new religion in this regard that the political thought of western Europe has remained to this day predominantly in terms of the Christian outlook.

BIBLIOGRAPHY

Bevan, Edwyn, Hellenism and Christianity (London: Allan & Unwin, 1921).

Bourke, Vernon, "Political Philosophy of St. Augustine," Proceedings of American Catholic Philosophical Association, 1931.

Burleigh, John, The City of God: A Study of St. Augustine's Philosophy (London: Nisbet, 1949).

Chroust, A. H., "Philosophy of Law of St. Augustine," Philosophical Review, March, 1944.

Cochrane, C. N., Christianity and Classical Culture (Oxford: Clarendon Press, 1940).

Coulton, George G., Studies in Medieval Thought (London: Nelson, 1921).

Cranz, F. E., "St. Augustine and Nicholas of Cusa in the Tradition of Western Christian Thought," Speculum, April, 1953.

Deferrari, R. J., and Keeler, M. J., "St. Augustine's City of God: Its Plan and Development," American Journal of Philology, April, 1929.

Figgis, John N., The Political Aspects of St. Augustine's City of God (London: Longmans, Green, 1921).

Friberg, Hans D., Love and Justice in Political Theory: A Study of St. Augustine's Defense of the Commonwealth (Chicago: University of Chicago Press, 1944).

Garrett, Thomas M., "St. Augustine and the Nature of Society," New Scholasticism, January, 1956.

Lloyd, Roger, "The Christian Contribution to Social Order," Quarterly Review, October, 1945.

Loetscher, Frederick W., "St. Augustine's Conception of the State," Church History, March, 1935.

Mommsen, Theodor, "St. Augustine and the Christian Idea of Progress," Journal of the History of Ideas, July, 1951.

Niebuhr, Reinhold, Christian Realism and Political Problems (New York: Scribner's Sons, 1953).

O'Connell, James, "The Social Philosophy of St. Augustine," Irish Ecclesiastical Review, November, 1954.

Pegis, A. C., "Some Permanent Contributions of Medieval Philosophy to the Notion of Man," Royal Society of Canada, Proceedings and Transactions, 1952.

Chapter VII

THE TWO SWORDS

"Behold, here are two swords" (Luke 22:38).

THE long span between the collapse of the Roman empire and the advent of the modern national state is referred to as the middle ages or the medieval era. It is a period characterized by feudal government, by the idea of unity or cosmopolitanism (despite the decentralized political control which in reality existed), by a strong sense of religion and otherworldliness, by the Christian permeation of many aspects of society, and by a simple economic order. What is of more significance, it is an age of formation and fermentation, an age that has spawned many of the social and political institutions, and even modes of thought of the modern era. A knowledge of the historical background of the middle ages is indispensable to a full understanding and appreciation of its political philosophy.

The middle ages produced little in the way of formal and systematic political theory. One would search in vain for treatises such as Aristotle's *Politics* or Cicero's *De Republica*. The inquirer would find the *Policraticus* of John of Salisbury and the *De Monarchia* of Dante; but these and other similar works were generally oriented toward topics that had aroused little interest in classical thought. This observation does not imply that the medieval period was devoid of political speculation or that it is of little importance in the development of political philosophy. Medieval political thought was particularly concerned with the limits on governmental authority and the relationships between the state and other institutions. These issues had not been of pressing concern in the closely interwoven societies of Greece and Rome.

The crucial issue during the middle ages revolved about the relative positions of church and state. In seeking to define the respective roles of these institutions, both papal and imperial claimants were led into

127

discussions of fundamental political questions pertaining to the origin and nature of the state and the source and scope of civil authority. The relationship between the political and ecclesiastical orders depends basically on the way these questions are answered. It is one thing, for example, to say that the state receives its authority through the church; it is quite another matter to hold that political rule comes into being and exists independent of the religious order. The logical consequences of these two views are patently and radically different.

In examining medieval political theory, attention will be focused on three major aspects: the relationship between church and state; the nature of governmental authority; and the idea of a universal commonwealth of Christian men living in peace and harmony in an ordered society under God and sustained by an all-embracing objective.[1] Such a sketch of the political theory of the middle ages is admittedly organized from a limited point of view. It glosses over the development of political institutions and movements such as the feudal system and the forces destructive of that system. Yet political theory is distinctively medieval only so long as it is engaged in treating the relationship of civic society to Christendom as a whole. Just as the boundary between ancient and medieval theory was crossed when the concept of the city-state gave way to the idea of empire, so the line between medieval and modern theory was traversed when the conception of universal Christendom as embodied in the Holy Roman Empire was superseded by the idea of the national state.[2]

THE GELASIAN DOCTRINE

As noted previously, neither St. Augustine nor any of the other Church Fathers attempted to give explicit theoretical formulation to the relative positions of church and state. St. Optatus, in the latter part of the fourth century, had admonished the schismatic Donatists of North Africa that the empire was not in the church but the church in the empire. (The Donatists had indignantly protested against imperial interference on behalf of the papal power, contending that the emperor had no concern with church affairs.) During the same period St. Ambrose had emphasized that the civil magistrate had no authority over ecclesiastics

---

[1] The first aspect will be treated here, and the latter two in succeeding chapters.
[2] See the article on political theory in *Cambridge Medieval History* (London: Cambridge University Press, 1929), Vol. VI, Chap. 18.

in religious matters. Neither Optatus nor Ambrose, however, had made any attempt to construct a comprehensive statement covering the proper relationship between the two spheres, but had merely set forth policies for meeting particular situations as they arose.

There were at least three possible theories of the relationship between the two powers that might have been pursued: (1) the identification of church and state, in which event a religious or civil theocracy would have resulted; (2) hostile opposition or a perpetual struggle for advantage, in which case both authorities would have suffered; (3) distinction between the two spheres, with a division of jurisdiction. It was this last alternative which prevailed. To the medieval mind the relationship between church and state appeared to be a question of mutually adjusting two sets of offices within a single society, the *respublica Christiana*. For the medievalist, therefore, the problem was not one involving two completely separate societies confronting each other, but one of divided jurisdiction between *regnum* and *sacerdotium* — kingship and priesthood — over the same society.

The first effort at a formal definition of church-state relations, and the one that has proved most enduring, was made by Pope Gelasius I in 494. His formulation became known as the doctrine of the "two swords." Gelasius points out that before the coming of Christ there were some who were legitimately both kings and priests, such as Melchizedek. "But Christ, knowing the weakness of human nature and being concerned for the welfare of his people separated the two offices, giving to each its peculiar functions and duties. Thus the Christian emperor needs the ecclesiastic for the attainment of eternal life, and the ecclesiastic similarly depends upon the government of the emperor in temporal matters."[3] Writing to the Roman Emperor Anastasius, the Pope further notes that, while there are two powers by which the world is governed,

the burden laid upon the priests is the heavier, in that they will have to render an account at the divine judgment even for the kings of men. . . . So far as concerns the rule of public order, the leaders of religion themselves obey your laws, recognizing that the imperial authority has been conferred upon you from on high. . . . With how much greater zeal then ought you to obey those who are set in charge of the sacred mysteries?[4]

---

[3] Quoted in Carlyle, *op. cit.*, Vol. 1, p. 190.
[4] *Ibid.*, p. 191.

The views expressed by Gelasius are of considerable importance to the course of medieval political philosophy since they came to be regarded as the embodiment of the traditional and classical position on church-state relations. Three points in his exposition should be particularly noted. First, he firmly repudiates the idea of a theocratic state, that is one in which the priests exercise political as well as spiritual authority. Second, he distinguishes between the *regnum* and *sacerdotium* and their respective jurisdictions, making clear that the relationship between the two is that of independent though closely related orders, each drawing its authority from God and each supreme in its own sphere. Third, he is conscious that the line of demarcation between the two powers cannot always be drawn with completeness and finality, and that in certain relations each must have authority over the other. Gelasius does not state where the final power rests to decide whether a specific issue belongs to the religious or political jurisdiction, or when intervention by one in the affairs of the other is justified. His emphasis on the heavier burden of the clergy was later taken to mean that the primacy of decision in these matters belonged to the *sacerdotium*. Few medievalists would have denied the pre-eminence of the spiritual over the temporal; the difficulty came in ascertaining just what this pre-eminence involved.

THE INVESTITURE CONTROVERSY

The political struggle between empire and papacy was long and complex. Two historical instances, the investiture controversy between Gregory VII and Henry IV and the conflict between Boniface VIII and Philip the Fair, stand out as important highlights in the development of the "two swords" doctrine. They also illustrate the two divergent views which vied for recognition: the first holding that the solution to the problem of church-state relations can be found in the harmonious co-ordination of the two powers without the institutional subordination of one to the other; the second contending that the answer lay only in an institutional organization flowing from a single apex of authority.

From the time of Gelasius to the middle of the eleventh century, the Popes took a restrained, and at times deferential, attitude toward the temporal power. Gregory the Great (540–604) fixed the policy that was generally followed during the early years of this period by declaring that he would obey the commands of the emperor if they did not violate the laws of the Church; and that even if such orders were contrary to canon law, he would accede to them if he could do so without sin. The fact that Gregory himself had been forced to assume the duties of a political ruler in Italy because of the feebleness of the secular power may have been responsible for his highly respectful attitude toward civic authority. Whatever the reason, the precedent which he set exerted persuasive influence during the first several centuries of the medieval era.

As time passed, the difficulty of drawing a clear line between matters which were to be regarded as spiritual and those which belonged to the temporal sphere became increasingly evident. In practice, the secular power exercised a certain measure of authority over strictly spiritual affairs by intervening on occasions when the Church was being badly administered. This interference was tolerated and even encouraged by a disposition on the part of some of the popes to seek the aid and support of the civil power in the internal government of the Church. At the same time, it was universally recognized that the Church had jurisdiction over all temporal authorities in spiritual matters and that any person, including the emperor, who refused to obey the divine law would subject himself to the discipline of the ecclesiastical arm. This power was exercised with great restraint during the early years of the middle ages, although a tendency to use it in matters other than those strictly spiritual was not entirely absent.

The era of relative harmony between the two powers was followed by a period of crisis from the eleventh to the fifteenth century. During this stage, the Gelasian doctrine was repudiated in fact, if not in theory, and excessive claims were made by adherents of both church and state. The controversy over investitures marked the beginning of the struggle. The historical circumstances surrounding this phase of the conflict are of special interest because they epitomize the virtually insoluble difficulties which political and religious practices cast in the way of an harmonious relationship between *sacerdotium* and *regnum*.

In medieval society the high spiritual and secular offices (other than papacy and kingship) were frequently merged in the same person. Under the feudal system many of the churchmen became holders of land, and consequently vassals of the king. Since the ecclesiastics were the best educated and best trained administrators of their day, the king constantly drew upon them to fill important posts in his government. As a result of such practices, the higher clergy — the bishops and abbots

— not only became lords of great fiefs, but integral parts of the developing structure and machinery of secular government. It is quite understandable that under such circumstances the king would insist upon a share in the selection and appointment of the bishops. Theoretically, these officials were elected by the clergy and the people as provided by canon law; actually, from the sixth century on, the right of the ruler to approve and even pick candidates was generally recognized. Canon law also provided that a newly elected prelate be invested by an archbishop with the ring and staff, the symbols of his spiritual office. In practice, the ring and staff were usually carried to court immediately upon the death of a bishop, and the king then conferred them on the successor to the office.

When Gregory VII assumed papal authority in 1073 he well realized that the Church would have to exercise complete control over her own officers if she was to fulfill properly her spiritual mission. He saw clearly the ambiguity of a situation in which high ecclesiastics were not only chosen by a secular ruler but were invested by him with the title to their spiritual office. A man of deep religious conviction, Gregory was greatly disturbed by the abuses, such as simony, or the buying of ecclesiastical offices, then existing in the Church. His first step in stamping out these practices was to forbid the lay investiture of bishops, thereby emphasizing the primary jurisdiction of the Church over her officers. When the Emperor, Henry IV, refused to abide by this decree and in fact tried to secure the removal of Gregory from office, the Pope countered by excommunicating him, declaring him deposed as emperor, and absolving his vassals from their feudal oaths of allegiance to him. For the first time the issue of regnum and sacerdotium was clearly drawn, and pamphleteers on both sides jumped eagerly into the fray.

Gregory's action in deposing the emperor raised the essential question whether the Church, in pursuit of her proper ends, had the right to intervene directly in the secular sphere. Gregory took the position that he was acting within the scope and spirit of the traditional Gelasian doctrine. He contended that his act of deposition was to protect the independence of the Church within the twofold system contemplated by Gelasius. Henry, on the other hand, charged that the Pope was attempting to wield both powers. Calling attention to the accepted doctrine that the emperor's power as well as that of the pope was derived from God, Henry asserted that he was responsible for its exercise solely to God and that he could not be deposed except for heresy.

> You have laid hands upon me also who, though unworthy among Christians, am anointed to kingship, and who, as the tradition of the Holy Father teaches, am to be judged by God alone and not to be deposed for any crime, unless I should wander from the faith, which God forbid.[5]

There can be little question that Gregory did in fact exercise a political power when he declared the emperor deposed. From the standpoint of theory, the pope and those who supported him still adhered to the doctrine that the two spheres could operate without the institutional subordination of one to the other. However, they went further than any of their predecessors in interpreting the primacy of the spiritual to include direct intervention in the political order whenever necessary for the furtherance of a spiritual cause.

DIRECT PAPAL POWER

As late as the thirteenth century, no responsible churchman had asserted in principle a supremacy of papal authority over secular rulers in temporal matters. The actions of Gregory VII and the strong popes who succeeded him (notably Innocent III, Gregory IX, and Innocent IV) in exercising sweeping jurisdiction over the temporal order de facto set the stage for a papal claim of jurisdiction de jure as well. The bitter controversy between Boniface VIII and Philip the Fair of France at the close of the thirteenth century provided the occasion for such an assertion. The immediate cause of the dispute arose out of the Church's claim to financial and judicial immunity. The first issue was joined when Philip attempted to raise money for his war with England by imposing taxes on the French clergy. The Church had long maintained that she could not be taxed without her consent. Boniface, in the bull Clericis Laicos (1296), reiterated this position by forbidding the clergy to pay the tax.

The second issue was whether a member of the clergy could be tried in the secular courts for an alleged offense against the state. The events surrounding this dispute led to the issuance of the famous bull Unam

---

[5] Quoted in Carlyle, op. cit., Vol. IV, p. 186, n. 1.

Sanctam, which some commentators feel took the most advanced ground on papal imperialism ever written into an official document. While the bull is subject to contradictory interpretations, it contains language strongly indicative of a theocratic view:

> Truly he who denies that the temporal sword is in the power of Peter, misunderstands the words of the Lord, "Put up thy sword into the sheath." Both are therefore in the power of the Church, the spiritual and the material. . . . The one sword then, should be under the other, and temporal authority subject to the spiritual power. . . . If, therefore, the earthly power err, it shall be judged by the spiritual power. . . . But if the supreme power err, it can only be judged by God, not by man.[6]

These words seem to imply that the temporal power comes from God through the pope, mediante papa, and that the king is therefore minister sacerdotii, or agent of the church for the exercise of secular functions. They also seem to imply that papal power is full (plenitudo potestatis) in the sense that it is above all other authority and contains all power, temporal and spiritual. No other power is legitimate unless subjected to the supreme rulership of the pope, and no other authority can in turn react upon papal jurisdiction.

While there are other statements of Boniface which seem to contradict such an extreme position, the canonists of the period who defended him and who undoubtedly influenced him in his stand were quite unequivocal. Discarding the Gelasian doctrine, they maintained that the secular power is institutionally subordinated to the papacy and that the authority of the king is derived from the church. Two works published in 1301 are worthy of notice in this respect since they constitute the best exposition of extreme papal claims: De ecclesiastica potestate, written by Egidius Colonna (also referred to as Egidius Romanus) and De regimine Christiano by James of Viterbo.

Egidius Colonna

Egidius, archbishop of Bourges, portrays the universe as an organic unity with a common hierarchical structure in which all created things are related to each other in a divinely established and controlled order. Human law is subordinate to divine law, nature to grace, and political

---

[6] Quoted in E. F. Henderson, Select Historical Documents of the Middle Ages (London: Bell and Sons, 1896), p. 436.

to theological authority. Egidius refers to this preordained relationship of superior to inferior as *dominium*. Standing at the apex of the hierarchical order, God possesses this *dominium* over his whole creation. Any lesser being or institution can be said to exercise legitimate authority only in so far as it is received from God through His grace. Since the church is the representative of God on earth and the dispenser of His grace, any *dominium* which man exercises must be derived from her.

Egidius borrowed his concept of an ordered universe from St. Augustine's "tranquillity of order" which "allots things equal and unequal, each to its own place." But whereas Augustine had spoken of this order as a reflection of the divine law governing the relationships of the universe in general and had made no claim for institutional jurisdiction of one agency over another, Egidius holds that this organic order necessarily demands that all human institutions be subject to the theological power. And whereas Augustine had defined justice as subjection to God, Egidius takes this to mean subjection to the pope as the vicar of Christ in all matters, political as well as religious. Thus, while lesser institutions such as the state have their proper jurisdiction and function, they are in the last analysis subject to the superior directive power, to the *dominium*, of the overlord. In this way all human relations are reduced to a single unified system of control under papal headship, and rulers are made mere subordinates of the pope, even in the secular administration of their political units.

James of Viterbo

The approach employed by James of Viterbo in his defense of papal claims differed somewhat from that of Egidius, but the conclusions which he arrived at were fully as extreme. Starting with the conception of the world as a single *regnum* or realm, James identifies this kingdom with the visible church. In every *regnum* there are two powers, sacerdotal and regal. The former, that of administering the sacraments, is shared by all priests; the latter, that of jurisdictional power, was bestowed upon Peter and his successors in the grant of the keys. "And I will give to thee the keys of the kingdom of heaven. And whatsoever thou shalt bind upon earth, it shall be bound also in heaven: and whatsoever thou shalt loose upon earth, it shall be loosed also in heaven." This power is truly regal since the highest act of authority is to judge, and all other powers flow from judgment. (Gregory VII had expressed a somewhat similar view when he cited the words of St. Paul. "Know you not that we shall judge angels? How much more things of this world?") The successor of Peter is "king of kings both secular and spiritual. . . . Like Christ whose vicar he is, he is called chief of the kings of the earth, which means those who are upon the earth."[7]

James, as the other supporters of papal supremacy, makes no pretense of claiming that both swords are actually in the hands of the Church. He recognizes that the king in practice wields the secular sword but he emphasizes that he does so as *minister sacerdotii* or agent of the spiritual arm. The temporal sword, in short, belongs *de jure* to the pope who in turn delegates it to the temporal ruler for the performance of those functions in the *respublica Christiana* which cannot fittingly be exercised by ecclesiastical hands. Its use, therefore, is always under the general direction and at the sufferance of the spiritual power. This radical subordination of the secular to the religious jurisdiction as instrument to cause or agent to principal was utterly foreign to the medieval tradition.

THE EXTREME REGAL POSITION

On the side of the king, equally extreme arguments in defense of the temporal jurisdiction were advanced during the late middle ages, especially by the civilian lawyers. Most of the temporal claims relied heavily on history and on the *Digest* of Justinian for support. It became common for the defenders of the king to argue that the *regnum* was older than the church and hence could not have received its authority from her; that, on the contrary, whatever temporal power the church possesses rests on the grant or permission of the secular ruler. The texts of Justinian that considered the *jus sacrum* (canon law) as part of the *jus publicum* (public law) were cited as authority for this position. The lawyers did not deny, as indeed no medieval thinker would, that the church is the instrumentality through which salvation is secured. They simply attempted to interpret the Gelasian doctrine in such a way as to effect a complete compartmentalization between the temporal and spiritual spheres. In this rigid division, the jurisdiction of the clergy was limited to a purely sacramental function, while the king's control extended without qualification to the temporal possessions and affairs of the clergy.

---

[7] *De regimine Christiano*, II, 3.

The tendency to confine the church to the sacristy and to limit the spiritual authority to ethical and religious instruction culminated some twenty years after the Boniface-Philip quarrel in the *Defensor Pacis* written by Marsilius of Padua. Going so far as to maintain that excommunication belongs wholly to the secular power, Marsilius posits a thoroughgoing control of the temporal over the spiritual. In fact, he takes the position that religion is subject to state control in the same manner as any other social institution. Denying that Peter enjoyed any pre-eminence in jurisdiction over the other Apostles, Marsilius concludes that neither Peter nor his successors have any jurisdictional power, even in spiritual matters, over the people or clergy. All that they possess is a sacramental power, the power to exercise their *priestly* functions, which all clergymen enjoy equally. Hence, whatever authority of a directive or controlling nature is exercised by the ecclesiastical hierarchy must be conferred on it by human law (just as the state grants certain powers to private corporations by charter or law).

Although Marsilius seeks to separate absolutely the temporal and spiritual spheres and to limit the latter to a purely sacramental function, he actually makes a complete identification of church and state falling under a single omnicompetent authority. His papal opponents had done virtually the same thing; only in this case the tables were turned. The supreme jurisdictional power is vested in the state rather than in the pope, while the latter's authority over the internal structure and affairs of the church is totally undermined. Marsilius' views are sometimes cited as a defense of religious liberty, but any such notion disregards the fact that his position logically subjects religion to a thoroughgoing regimentation by the civil power.

JOHN OF PARIS: THE VIA MEDIA

In addition to the extreme and at times radical stand taken by the lawyers, there were also more moderate and well-reasoned views expressed by some ecclesiastics in answer to the pro-papal arguments of Egidius and James. The most representative and influential work in this respect was the treatise *De potestate regia et papali* written in 1302 by a French Dominican, John of Paris.[8] Basically, his work follows a middle course

---

[8] There is no translation of this work available in English. Pertinent quotations from it are found in Carlyle, *op. cit.*, Vol. V, Chap. 10.

in its approach to the church-state problem. It seeks to show that the true relationship of the two powers lies between an excessively spiritual concept of papal authority that denies the church any jurisdiction whatsoever in temporalities, and the opposite concept that attributes to the pope complete temporal dominium under the *mediante papa* theory. John assumes, as does the Gelasian doctrine, that the spiritual power must enjoy some measure of jurisdiction in the temporal order, since it is by nature superior to the secular. The task is to define the character of this primacy and the manner of its exercise.[9]

To show that secular government is independent in its own right, John adopts the Aristotelian view that the state originates in the social nature of man and that it is necessary for the achievement of the "whole life" of the human individual. Moreover, since human beings live in civil society and community because of a natural instinct, that instinct must have been implanted in men by God. And since political power (*regnum*) is essential to the proper existence of such a community, it must itself be natural and therefore from God. Thus the king has a distinct power, proper to himself, which he receives from God and not from the pope.

In seeking to determine the proper sphere of civil society, it is necessary to show both the origin of the state and the end or purpose for which it is ordained. Here again John of Paris follows Aristotle in holding that the objective of the state is that good which can be achieved by nature, namely a life according to virtue. From these premises the conclusion emerges, as John Courtney Murray has so aptly observed, that

> the civil community is temporal, not ultimate in its finality; the content of its common good is the "human things" that make up "the whole life" of man in this world. Moreover, this order of human life . . . is an order in its own right with a certain relative autonomy of its own. The "virtue" which is its object is "acquired moral virtue." . . . The civic life of virtue in this sense "has in itself the nature of a good (*rationem boni*) and is desirable for its own sake" even though it is not the ultimate good in the highest order.[10]

---

[9] The analysis of John of Paris is based largely on John Courtney Murray's writings on church and state, particularly his article "Contemporary Orientations of Catholic Thought on Church and State in the Light of History," *Theological Studies*, June, 1949; reprinted in *Cross Currents*, Fall, 1951.

[10] "Contemporary Orientations of Catholic Thought on Church and State in the Light of History," *Cross Currents*, Fall, 1951, p. 28.

The civil rulers are actually serving as ministers of God in their efforts to promote peace, justice, and the common good in the temporal sphere. As such their duties are not merely legal and administrative, but moral as well. These functions, however, are restrictive ones clearly fixed by the ends of the state, which ends are of themselves necessarily contained within the limits of the natural, the terrestrial, the temporal.

Turning next to the spiritual power, the *sacerdotium*, John starts from the universally accepted premise that the temporal life is not man's ultimate end; that he is further destined to a higher and supernatural goal, that of eternal life. Just as the responsibility of the state is to assist man in reaching his natural perfection, so the church has the function of leading man to his supernatural goal through the dispensation of the sacraments. The ends, while quite distinct, are not wholly independent. Virtuous living in this life (which the state should foster and encourage) necessarily bears a direct relation to the higher goal. Similarly, the practice of religion aids man in the attainment of his temporal fulfillment by inculcating moral virtues. Such interdependency, however, does not deny that in the hierarchy of values the spiritual end is superior to the temporal. It was at this point, as John recognized, that the medieval attempts to arrive at a clear theoretical formulation of church-state relations usually broke down. For if the sacerdotal power is higher than that of the temporal, it must by virtue of its superior position enjoy some kind of precedence over the latter. The source of much dispute lay in the definition of this primacy.

In seeking a solution to this problem, John warns against indiscriminate argument from one kind of order to another, as from the superiority of spiritual over temporal ends to the political jurisdiction of the spiritual over the secular power. Pointing out that an order of dignity does not necessarily involve an order of jurisdiction, he goes on to emphasize that the spiritual enjoys a primacy of dignity only and not of causality over the temporal. By this he means that the secular power, while of inferior status in the order of ends or values, is not contained in and set up by the spiritual power, as extreme papal claims implied. The royal power is not from the pope either in itself or in its executive use; it is from God and from the people who elect the king. Both powers are derived independently of each other from a source higher than either, the Divine Ruler of the universe.

What does the primacy of dignity imply, and what jurisdiction if any does it give the spiritual over the temporal in the practical order of things? According to John of Paris, the primacy enjoyed by the spiritual is exercised "indirectly." The church does not intervene directly in the affairs of the state, but as the teacher of faith and morals she influences the temporal order by guiding men in the ways of virtue. Although the jurisdiction of the church is purely spiritual, she is able to reach into the temporal order indirectly by the repercussions which her teachings have on the actions of men, whether they be rulers or subjects. The pope does not establish the monarch, but each in his own way is established by God; nor does he direct the king *per se*, as king, he directs him *per accidens*, inasmuch as the ruler ought to be a believer in Christ. In this capacity the king is instructed by the pope about matters of faith, not about governmental affairs. While the transcendent position of the spiritual order does not remove it from all contact with the temporal, it does determine the manner in which its primacy is to be effective.

The interpretation given by John to the classical Gelasian doctrine posits no direct authority for the spiritual over the temporal sword but only moral jurisdiction over conscience. Such a view does not assume, as that of the civil lawyers tended to do, that the church should be confined to the sacristy and have no concern with the state. On the contrary, it holds that the church would set spiritual norms for temporal affairs through her power to administer the sacraments, to teach the word of God, and to interpret the Divine law. Under certain circumstances the pope could impose a spiritual sanction or penalty which might affect the political order. He could, for example, excommunicate a king as he could any other church member for a grave ecclesiastical offense. This, however, would be the extreme penalty that he could inflict; he would have no power whatsoever to depose a secular ruler.

The state, John repeatedly emphasizes, is a purely natural institution which in no way requires the sanctification of the church to be legitimate. The primacy of the spiritual does not imply that the state is merely an instrument or arm of the church for the attainment of the latter's end. It is not the function of the civil power to heal fallen man by subjecting him to the influence of ecclesiastical authorities. Its objective is that set forth by nature itself, the temporal common good, an end that is specifically lay and not religious. The state does have a moral function, as Aristotle pointed out, to assist man in reaching his temporal perfection, a perfection which consists in a life of moral and intellectual virtue — but this moral obligation is wholly in the natural order. The church, on the other hand, does not have the task of teaching the prince his politics. Her responsibility is to teach him the fundamental principles of what is right and wrong, principles which should underlie and govern political behavior.

John of Paris views church and state, juridically speaking, as separate and distinct societies which find their unity only in their common origin from God. The goals of both the temporal and eternal are necessarily related since they are both ends of the same man. But the jurisdiction of the *sacerdotium* over the higher order of man's spiritual life does not mean institutional dominium over the inferior order of his temporal life. The situation is analogous to that of the household where the tutor in morals is superior in the dignity of his calling to the household physician, yet each derives his position independently from the common master.

The doctrine of church-state relations as advanced in *De potestate regia et papali* is summed up by a contemporary philosopher in the following passage

> By his essential conception of the ecclesiastical power, John of Paris joins himself to the purest tradition of the Middle Ages, since he authorizes its intervention in the political sphere. But at the same time he shows himself entirely modern by the manner in which he understands this function of the spiritual power, and by his reduction of it to the exercise of a spiritual power.[11]

SUMMARY

To some, the long theoretical dispute over the proper relationship of church and state may appear to be of no more than historical or academic interest in the development of political thought. Such an assumption would hardly be correct since the problem involved in the controversy is significantly relevant to the contemporary scene. No one would deny that the modern setting is radically different from that which existed during the middle ages. When John of Paris penned his treatise there was only one church universally accepted throughout the western world, while the nation state was just beginning to emerge as the political unit of the future. Today, man lives in a world of many religions and many nation states. Yet despite the changed historical environment, the basic problem of the relationship between the temporal and spiritual spheres continues. The setting of the play may be new, but the plot remains

---

[11] J. Riviere, *Le problème de l'Eglise et de l'Etat au temps de Philippe le Bel* (Louvain, 1926), p. 281.

essentially unchanged. One need only examine the vast literature on church and state which has appeared during the past decade to realize how great current interest is in this question.

In interpreting what he conceived to be the true relation between the two swords, John of Paris maintained that both powers with their different missions must be maintained on distinct planes. His position does not imply a complete cleavage or compartmentalization between the two spheres (a compartmentalization some individuals achieve in their own minds by looking upon their religion as divorced from the ordinary business of living), but a close and harmonious relationship in which each would work respectively for the natural and supernatural ends of man. In terms of this theory, the civil power has no direct concern with man's conversion or his salvation; its political task ceases on the threshold of the spiritual domain. The state contributes to man's supernatural goal only indirectly by creating conditions of material life, of culture and education, of social justice, of civic virtue and public morality — conditions that will enable the supernatural work of the religious sword to be freely developed. Conversely, the jurisdiction of the religious order stops at the gate of the secular power. The church is free to form the conscience of her members; and they as citizens are free to work for a social order of justice and charity that conforms to the dictates of their consciences.

The medieval controversy over the problem of church and state involved in essence two basically different concepts. On the one side was the view that the state is the universal community and the church is a lesser society or limited association of individuals for restricted ends. On the other side was the view that the church is the universal community and the state a lesser association for limited ends. John of Paris sought to put each of these theories in its proper perspective. While he recognized that both church and state have autonomous spheres of activity, he also realized the close inter-dependence between the two realms and the impossibility of any absolute separation of one from the other. Christopher Dawson's observation is pertinent here.

> The philosopher and the theologian may say that both (Church and State) are perfect societies with their own rights and their proper autonomous spheres of action. But this is only true juridically speaking, not psychologically or morally. The Church is socially incomplete unless there is a Christian society as well as an ecclesiastical congregation, and the State is morally incomplete without some spiritual bond other than the law and the power of the sword.[12]

BIBLIOGRAPHY

Bonacina, Conrad, "The Catholic Church and Modern Democracy," *Cross Currents*, Fall, 1951.
Calhoun, R. L., and Bainton, R. H., *Christian Conscience and the State* (New York: Social Action, 1940).

---

[12] "Education and the State," *Commonweal*, Jan. 25, 1957, p. 425.

Carlyle, R. W., and A. J., A History of Medieval Political Theory in the West, Vol. 5 (London: Blackwood, 1928).

Cour, R. F., "Recent Teaching of the Supreme Court on the Subject of Church and State," American Catholic Historical Society Records, December, 1957.

Domenach, Jean M., "Religion and Politics," Cross Currents, Summer, 1956.

Ellis, J. T., "Church and State in the United States: A Critical Appraisal," Catholic Historical Review, October, 1952.

Figgis, John N., The Divine Right of Kings (Cambridge: Cambridge University Press, 1934).

Gurian, W. A., and Fitzsimons, M. A. (eds.), The Catholic Church in World Affairs (South Bend: Notre Dame Press, 1954).

Hardy, E. R., "Servant of the Servant of God: Gregory the Great," Church History, March, 1943.

LaCroix, Jean, "Religious Conscience and Political Conscience," Cross Currents, Fall, 1952.

Ladner, G. B., "Aspects of Medieval Thought on Church and State," Review of Politics, October, 1947.

Lecler, Joseph, The Two Sovereignties (New York: Philosophical Library, 1952).

Lewis, Ewart, "Organic Tendencies in Medieval Political Thought," American Political Science Review, October, 1938.

Murray, John C., "The Problem of Pluralism in America," Thought, Summer, 1954.

Rommen, Heinrich, "Church and State," Review of Politics, July, 1950.

Ruff, G. E., The Dilemma of Church and State (Philadelphia: Muhlenberg Press, 1954).

Tellenbach, Gerd, Church, State and Christian Society at the Time of the Investiture Contest, trans. by R. F. Bennett (Oxford: Blackwell, 1940).

Ullman, Walter, Medieval Papalism: The Political Theories of the Medieval Canonists (London: Methuen, 1949).

Weigel, Gustave, "The Church and the Democratic State," Thought, Spring, 1952.

Whitney, J. P., "Pope Gregory VII and the Hildebrandine Ideal," Church Quarterly Review.

Yanitelli, V. R., "Church — State Anthology: The Works of Father Courtney Murray," Thought, 1952.

Chapter VIII

ST. THOMAS AQUINAS:
THEOLOGIAN AS POLITICAL PHILOSOPHER

"Yet it is natural for man, more than any other animal, to be a social and political animal, to live in a group" (St. Thomas, *On Kingship*).

AFTER the fall of Rome and up to the capture of Constantinople in 1204, there was little intellectual exchange between the civilizations of the western and eastern halves of the old empire. During this period, the West knew little of Aristotle beyond his treatise on logic. In the East, however, the tradition of Aristotelian learning was kept alive, first at Constantinople and later at the Arabic and Jewish centers of learning. When the Moors overran Spain in the eighth century, they brought with them Arabic translations of many Greek works. After the Spanish Christians recaptured Toledo in 1085, the Archbishop established a college to translate the Arabic texts into Latin. Through this medium the complete works of Aristotle began to enter western Europe during the latter half of the twelfth century. Sometime later his Greek texts were brought from the East by the returning Crusaders, and in 1260 the *Politics* was translated into Latin from the Greek by William of Moerbeka.

The rediscovery of Aristotle's works effected a radical change in the tenor of medieval political thought. The Christian doctrine of the social and political relations of man as a creature and child of God became merged with the Greek concept of man and the state as seen through pagan eyes. In the process, a balance was struck between the spiritual and secular aspects of political society.

THE STATESMAN'S BOOK

John of Salisbury (1120–1180), an English scholastic philosopher, served as secretary to Thomas Becket during the latter's ill-fated tenure as Archbishop of Canterbury. He was educated in the universities of Paris and Chartres, where he came in contact with some of the works of Cicero and Plato. His *Policraticus* or *Statesman's Book*, completed in 1150, is of importance to the history of political philosophy chiefly for two major reasons. First of all, it is the only systematic summation of medieval political speculation up to the time of St. Thomas, and as such it is representative of the thought of the early medieval period. Second, since it was written shortly before the *Politics* of Aristotle became known to the West, it provides a convenient means of comparing the political speculations of the early and late middle ages and of assessing Aristotelian influence on the political thought of medieval Christendom.[1]

Although the *Policraticus* is oriented primarily toward a defense of papal supremacy, it embodies a more formal and comprehensive discussion of the civil community than any other work of its day. Its general approach and treatment as well as the tendencies it evidences are, nevertheless, typical of the pre-Thomistic period. Representing an advanced ecclesiastic position, John argues that the prince is merely "a minister of the priestly power, and one who exercises that side of the sacred offices which seems unworthy of the hands of the priesthood. For every office existing under, and concerned with the execution of, the sacred laws is really a religious office, but that is inferior which consists in punishing crimes, and which therefore seems to be typified in the person of the hangman."[2] The primary duty of the king is to protect the church; next to that he must preserve peace and administer justice.

John's position has added significance apart from its insistence on a jurisdictional primacy of the spiritual over the temporal. It graphically illustrates how the classical view of the state as a natural institution for the perfection of man had become submerged during the middle ages into the conception of a church society in which the civil authority was relegated to the position of an ecclesiastical agency. Since the office of the king was looked upon as essentially a "religious office," a large portion of the *Policraticus* is devoted to a treatment of the religious and moral duties of the monarch. John's writings also indicate an inclination to consider the state as a divinely instituted remedy or corrective for sin (its role is that of the hangman), a view that gained considerable acceptance

---

[1] The important portions of the *Policraticus* have been translated by John Dickinson, *The Statesman's Book of John of Salisbury* (New York: Knopf, 1928). Selections are taken from this edition.

[2] *Policraticus*, Book IV, Chap. 3.

during the early middle ages. With the reception of Aristotle in the thirteenth century, these tendencies ran headlong into the formidable philosophical barrier that the Greek master had so ably constructed.

The general attitude of John of Salisbury toward political authority may also be seen by contrasting his treatment of tyrannicide with that later given by St. Thomas. According to John, a ruler who oppresses the people and governs by force is a tyrant and may lawfully be killed by a private individual. "He who takes the sword shall perish by the sword." No violation of law or morality is committed by resisting and slaying the ruler who usurps power and oppresses justice. "To kill a tyrant is not merely lawful, but right and just. . . . Tyranny, therefore, is not merely a public crime but, if there could be such a thing, a crime more than public. And if in the crime of *lese majeste* all men are admitted to be prosecutors, how much more should this be true in the case of the crime of subverting the laws which should rule even over emperors?"[3]

Taking a contrary view to that of John, St. Thomas asserts that public action, not individual violence, is the proper remedy against tyranny. "To proceed against the cruelty of tyrants is an action to be undertaken not through the private presumptions of a few but rather by public authority."[4] Stressing the preservation of the state and of political rule, he warns that "should private persons attempt on their own private presumption to kill the rulers, even though tyrants, this would be dangerous for the multitude as well as for the rulers. This is because the wicked usually expose themselves to dangers of this kind more than the good, for the rule of a king no less than that of a tyrant, is burdensome to them."[5]

St. Thomas feels that it would be detrimental to civil order if private individuals could assume the right to murder their rulers whenever they believe them to be tyrants. He recognizes, however, the right to revolution when: (1) the oppression by the ruler is of a serious character; (2) there is a reasonable chance of the revolt succeeding; and (3) there is some assurance that the revolution will not provoke greater social evils than those it attempts to eradicate. Revolution under these conditions is more in the nature of a public than a private act. It does not tolerate the assassination of the tyrant. If he is overthrown, the new public au-

---

[3] *Ibid.*, Book III, Chap. 15.

[4] *On Kingship*, Book I, Chap. 6. Translated by G. B. Phelan (Toronto: The Pontifical Institute of Medieval Studies, 1949).

[5] *Ibid.*

thority would have the right to punish him. In his discussion of tyrannicide, Thomas attempts to distinguish between private individual action and public collective action, a distinction that John of Salisbury fails to make.

One interesting feature of the *Policraticus* is its emphasis on the organic nature of the state. Although this aspect is a by-product of John's efforts to show the subordination of secular to ecclesiastical authority, it once again directed attention to the close unity of human society. John likens the monarch to the head of the body, the clergy to the soul (to which the head is therefore subordinate), the senate to the heart, the eyes, ears, and tongue to the judges, the hands to the administrative officials, and the farmers, artisans, and workers to the feet. All of these parts must work in harmony if the health of the body is to be maintained.

> Then and then only will the health of the commonwealth be sound and flourishing when the higher members shield the lower, and the lower respond faithfully and fully in like measure to the just demands of their superiors, so that each and all are as it were members one of another by a sort of reciprocity, and each regards his own interest as best served by that which he knows to be most advantageous for the others.[6]

John made no attempt to identify the state as a biological organism; his description is one of analogy only. Yet by pushing this analogy as far as he did, he exposed the traditional organic concept of society to the danger of misinterpretation.

ST. THOMAS AQUINAS

It is not uncommon to hear St. Thomas referred to in such terms as the dominant thinker of the middle ages, one of the world's great philosophers, the apostle of the mind, or the pre-eminent guardian and glory of the Catholic Church. The works of the angelic doctor stand as impressive testimonials to the validity of these encomiums. Born near Naples in 1225 of a noble Italian family, Thomas received his early education at the Benedictine monastery of Monte Cassino and his later training at the University of Naples. In 1244 he joined the Dominican Order and was sent to Paris to study theology under Albert

---

[6] *Policraticus*, Book VI, Chap. 21.

the Great, an early leader in the Aristotelian revival. By the time he was twenty-five, he himself was teaching at the university as a full professor. He served as adviser to the papacy and during the later years of his life he was asked to reorganize the University of Naples. He died in 1274 at the age of forty-nine.

Continuing the task which Albert had inaugurated, Thomas sought to assimilate the science and philosophy of Aristotle with the revealed truths of Christianity. Some writers have described the process as a Christianizing of Aristotle, or as an effort to graft onto the teachings of the Church the newly rediscovered wisdom of pagan Greece. Maritain has observed that St. Thomas could enthusiastically accept Aristotle since the latter's metaphysical principles are based on objective reality, and hence are capable of being universally adopted.

The writings of St. Thomas constituted the principal medium through which Aristotelian political ideas were reincorporated in western thought. Like Augustine, however, Thomas is primarily a theologian rather than a political philosopher. His major efforts are aimed at demonstrating that the whole of human knowledge forms one vast pattern of thought with the particularized sciences at the base, philosophy above them, and theology at the apex. All these sources of knowledge are blended into a harmonious unit in which reason and faith, science and religion, co-operate in furthering the discovery of truth. In this universal synthesis, divine revelation in no way contradicts that which the philosopher discovers by the use of natural reason; it merely completes the pattern of knowledge of which science and philosophy form the beginning. Theology and philosophy are equally valid, each in its own sphere. Spiritual wisdom from above illumines rational wisdom from below; revelation is an auxiliary of the reason.

While the political aspect of man's life could not be overlooked in the monumental task which St. Thomas undertook, the objective of his work did not require or call for a full-blown treatise on political theory. The closest that he came to a systematic formulation of his ideas on the state occurred in his uncompleted work On Kingship. However, many clues to his political thinking can be gleaned from his Commentaries on the Ethics and Politics of Aristotle. These works together with certain passages in the Summa Theologica, the Contra Gentiles, and the Nicomachean Ethics provide the principal sources for an examination of his political philosophy.

The Nature of the State

For St. Thomas, as for Aristotle, the bedrock of political philosophy is nature. Starting with man, he demonstrates that his end is fixed and determined by his nature. His will is necessarily inclined toward the perfection of his form as man. But unlike other created being, man is able by virtue of his reason to apprehend his end and thus to direct himself toward it.

> . . . all things participate to some degree in the eternal law insofar as they derive from it certain inclinations to those actions and aims which are proper to them. But, of all others, rational creatures are subject to divine providence in a very special way; being themselves made participators in providence itself, in that they control their own actions and the actions of others.[7]

This end of man is the foundation of the natural moral law, and by it all human actions are judged. Whatever leads toward the perfection of man's nature is good, whatever diverts from it is evil.[8]

Having established this moral basis, St. Thomas makes the transfer into the realm of political philosophy by noting that man is naturally a social and political animal. He is a social being because he is not self-sufficing; he cannot procure through his own efforts the means to attain his proper end as a rational creature. He needs the help and guidance of others to accomplish this objective. His natural insufficiency is partially overcome by the family and small social groupings such as the village in which his elemental needs can be met; but it is only in an organized society that his natural longing for knowledge, culture, and virtue can be satisfied and the acme of his well-being attained.

Man is also a political animal because the very existence of social living, of society, necessitates some form of civil authority. The multiplicity of individuals must be brought into an organized co-operative arrangement so that their efforts can be united in pursuit of a common goal. The organic character of the state is implicit in this thinking. Following Aristotle, Thomas finds the unity of political society in the moving principle or internal compulsion that forms and organizes the

---

[7] *Summa Theologica,* I–II, q. 91. a. 2. Excerpts from the *Summa* are taken from *Basic Writings of St. Thomas Aquinas* (New York: Random House, 1944).

[8] For a more extended discussion of this point see W. Farrell, "Natural Foundations of the Political Philosophy of St. Thomas," *Proceedings of the American Catholic Philosophical Association,* 1931, pp. 75–85.

member parts into a social whole. It is the community of purposes, interests, and mutual objectives which amalgamates the people into a body politic.

The "ordering" toward an end which Thomas speaks of implies a directing authority.

> If, then, it is natural for man to live in the society of many, it is necessary that there exist among men some means by which the group may be governed. For where there are many men together and each one is looking after his own interest, the multitude would be broken up and scattered unless there were also an agency to take care of what appertains to the commonweal.[9]

The naturalness of subordination to authority is further demonstrated by the fact that some men are born with the capacity to rule, others have the aptitude to carry out various functions under the direction of a supervising official, and still others have only the ability to follow. "Among men an order is found to exist inasmuch as those who are superior by intellect are by nature rulers."[10] The wisdom and order of nature is here seen, for if all men were born leaders (or contrariwise, followers) the formation of an integrated social whole would be virtually impossible.

It is evident from what has been said that St. Thomas views the state as an agency for supplying the temporal needs of man and assisting him in his task of self-fulfillment. Like Aristotle, he advocates in principle a wide role for civil government in the life of the community. The state comes into being to furnish those human needs which the individual and lesser social groupings are unable to supply for themselves. Its task, however, is to supplement the efforts of individuals and groups, not to supplant or abolish them.

The immediate end of the state is to preserve an orderly society by maintaining internal and external peace and by insuring the satisfaction of man's corporal necessities. Its ultimate end — that which gives true meaning to the common good — is the temporal perfection of its members. To pursue this latter goal, it must foster virtuous living by promoting the intellectual, moral, and cultural growth of man. Life according to virtue is life according to reason. Thus the functions of the state are positive and dynamic. As the pilot who steers his ship toward a

---

[9] *On Kingship*, Book I, Chap. 1.
[10] *Contra Gentiles*, III, 81.

distant goal, so should the state direct and co-ordinate the efforts of the community in its pursuit of the virtuous life.

Can it be legitimately said, as many of the medievalists did, that political rule is merely a divine remedy for sin and that there would have been no need for civil authority if the original state of innocence had endured? St. Thomas is emphatic in repudiating any such notion. Discussing this matter under the question "Whether in the State of Innocence Man would have been Master over Man," he points out that the term "mastership" has a twofold meaning. In one sense it refers to the power exercised over slaves; in the other it refers to the ruler's direction of free men. The first kind of authority, in which the slave is ordered to the master's use, would not have existed in the state of innocence; the second type of rule, that for the benefit of a free subject by directing him toward his proper welfare, would have existed even in the Garden of Eden

> First, because man is truly a social being, and so in the state of innocence he would have led a social life. Now a social life cannot exist among a number of people unless under the governance of one to look after the common good; for many, as such, seek many things, whereas one attends only to one. . . .
> Secondly, if one man surpassed another in knowledge and justice, this would not have been fitting unless these gifts conduced to the benefit of others.[11]

St. Thomas believes that inequalities in talent and capacity would have existed among men even in the state of innocence. Nature made all men equal in liberty, and not in their natural endowments. Such being the case, some guidance and direction of the social community by those of superior ability is required in order to achieve the common end of the members. If each man were left free to pursue his end in such ways as he saw fit, the diversity of methods employed would create disorder and confusion.

Although St. Thomas is in general agreement with Aristotle as to the nature and purpose of the body politic, he accepts the Aristotelian notion of the state as the "perfect society" only in a qualified sense. To a Christian, there are needs of man that cannot find their fulfillment in the political order. As a moral being, the individual is ordained ultimately to a supernatural goal that transcends the temporal sphere.

---

[11] *Summa Theologica,* I, q. 96, a. 4.

Since the care of this final and ultimate end is beyond the capacities of natural institutions, the task of directing man toward it is the responsibility not of human but of divine government. The Christian Church as a divine institution charged with the care of man's soul must be substituted for the ancient concept of a civic religion. Ewart Lewis has succinctly summed up the new element which St. Thomas introduced:

> In Aquinas's thought, two tendencies were held in quiet harmony: on the one hand, an appreciation of secular and natural values as good in themselves; on the other, an acknowledgement of the pre-eminence of spiritual goods, to which all lesser goods were finally ordained. As revelation completed the work of reason, as grace fulfilled nature, so the Church must supplement and guide the state.[12]

St. Thomas is nowhere clear as to how this guidance is to be institutionally accomplished. He has sometimes been classified as a champion of papal supremacy, but actually his comments on the institutional relationship between spiritual and secular authority are fragmentary and inconclusive. What he is primarily interested in demonstrating is the end to be sought and not the specific means for attaining it.

The Source of Political Authority

No medieval thinker would have denied that all authority, temporal as well as spiritual, has its ultimate source in God. Nor would few have questioned the belief that the spiritual power of the pope is conferred on him directly by a divine act. However, when it came to the question as to how political power in the concrete reaches the secular ruler, there was much less consensus. To stop with the assertion that political authority comes from God is to leave unanswered the crucial question as to how this power is morally and legitimately obtained by those who actually exercise it.

Although St. Thomas does not explicitly discuss this question, it is clear that he considers political authority to exist originally in the whole people organized as a civic community. "To order anything to the common good (which is the true function of the political authority) belongs either to the whole people, or to someone who is the vice-regent of the whole people."[13] The people do not receive this power by a special act of divine intervention, as does the pope, but through the

---

[12] Medieval Political Ideas, op. cit., Vol. 1, p. 151.
[13] Summa Theologica, I–II, q. 90, a. 5.

natural law. Such authority exists in the political community as a property or attribute of its nature. Once there is a uniting of minds and wills for the establishment of a state, authority simultaneously comes into being as a necessary and natural product of this union.

Reason, according to Thomas, demonstrates that supreme political power rests in the people organized as a community; it does not show that it is determinately placed in any particular person or group. The people in turn are free to create the type of government they desire and to confer on the holders of public office the authority to rule the community. The government, whether it be a king, parliament, or direct democracy, exists solely as the representative or vice-regent of the people. It has "no power to frame laws except as representing the people."[14]

The ruler's only legitimate title to power is that which he receives as a result of a transfer by the free rational act and consent of the community. In this sense, both the state and political authority may be said to be of immediate human origin. Dominion or political control is derived from human law. The people are morally obliged to give their consent to the establishment of political authority with respect to common needs and ends as rationally conceived. They are not, in other words, free to withhold consent to the creation of civil government since its existence is essential to their development as human beings.

The implications of such a theory are evident. The prince is to be considered part of the community, not somebody outside or above it. The people as a political unit is supreme or sovereign and the king is its representative or servant. The power which he exerts is derived from the people by way of delegation or grant.

This transfer is in the nature of a contract or pact between the ruler and the people, although the agreement is more implied than expressed. The idea of such a political contract was not unknown before Thomas. It found expression in such characteristic statements as that made by Archbishop Hincmar of Rheims in a letter to Louis III: "You have not chosen me to be a prelate of the Church, but I and my colleagues, with the loyal subjects of God and your ancestors, have chosen you to rule the kingdom on the condition that you shall keep the law."[15] This and other similar passages in the literature of the period indicate that in medieval political thought the king had a definite obligation to conform to both human law and the law of God.

---

[14] *Ibid.*, I–II, q. 97, a. 3, 3.　　　　[15] Quoted by Carlyle, *op. cit.*, Vol. I, p. 244.

But is the ruler's obligation a legal as well as a moral one, and if so, how can it be enforced by the community? The difficulty here lay in the generally accepted Roman law principle of *legibus solutus* which holds that the king is above human law and free from coercion. Bracton, an English jurist of the thirteenth century, expressed the prevailing idea in his famous and oft-quoted statement that "no writ runs against the king." There was, in short, no legal or institutional means of enforcing the community's interest in the government of its king. The only sanctions available against the ruler who flagrantly violated his pact with the people was insurrection or, as John of Salisbury proposed, private tyrannicide. This freedom from external compulsion to obey the laws did not, of course, discharge the ruler morally from any of his duties and obligations to the people. In this latter sense, he remained under the law.

In discussing the question of royal obligation, St. Thomas distinguishes between the coercive and directive force of the law. As to the first, he notes that it would be proper to say that the ruler is exempt from the law since there is no institutional means available to compel obedience by punitive sanctions. "Thus is the sovereign said to be exempt from the law because none is competent to pass sentence upon him, if he acts against the law."[16] As to directive force, Thomas states that the ruler is subject to law in that he is obliged in conscience to follow the law of the realm. "But as to the directive force of law, the sovereign is subject to the law by his own will, according to the statement that whatever law a man makes for another, he should keep for himself. . . . Hence in the judgment of God, the sovereign is not exempt from the law, as to its directive force; but he should fulfill it voluntarily and not of constraint."[17] Thus while the supreme power of the ruler is beyond the legal control of the people, his moral responsibility to observe the law remains in full effect. This duality is reflected in the many medieval treatises that were designed to inspire the king with ideals appropriate to his position or as one writer has put it, to persuade the king to accept voluntarily the bridle that could not by legal means be forced on him.[18] "It is a thing greater than empire that a prince submit his government to the laws."

---

[16] *Summa Theologica*, I–II, q. 96, a. 5, 3.
[17] *Ibid.*
[18] Lewis, *op. cit.*, I, 248.

The Best Form of Government

By supporting the theory that political power belongs originally to the community, St. Thomas has no intention of expressing any preference for democracy. In his view, all forms of government, whether they be monarchy, aristocracy, or democracy, depend for their legitimacy on the voluntary consent of the people from whom they derive their authority. It is not essential to popular sovereignty, as he defines it, for the people themselves to carry on their government or participate in its management. They may transfer these functions *in toto* to a monarch or to a group of wise men, but whatever action they take, the element of popular sovereignty remains intact. The government may exercise supreme political power but it does so only as the agent and representative of the community.

Medieval thought in general oriented toward kingship as the ideal form of government, and St. Thomas follows this pattern. Holding that monarchy is the most desirable type ideally speaking, he bases his choice on three grounds: the necessity for unity, the analogy with nature, and experience. The welfare of the community lies in the preservation of its unity and order. This integrity can best be achieved and maintained by a single ruler rather than by several, since the possibility of disagreement always exists where authority is divided. Similarly, since art imitates nature, political society should follow the example of nature where all things are governed by one, such as the heart is the principal mover of the body, and a single God is the ruler of the universe. Finally, Thomas observes (without attempting to cite empirical proof) that provinces or cities which are not ruled by one person are usually torn with dissension.[19] This defense of monarchy offered nothing that was new; it merely restated arguments that had long been advanced.

St. Thomas, like Aristotle, was realistic and practical in his thinking. He was quite aware that while monarchy *per se* may be the ideal form of government, it too has its drawbacks and its deficiencies. For one thing, placing the care of the community in the hands of a paternal monarch discourages any popular motivation or initiative in public affairs and consequently lessens the social sensibilities of the people. "For it frequently happens that men living under a king strive more sluggishly for the common good inasmuch as they consider that what they devote

[19] *On Kingship*, Book I, Chap. 2.

to the common good, they do not confer upon themselves but upon another under whose power they see the common goods to be."[20] A second defect of monarchy rests in the danger so forcefully phrased by Lord Acton that power tends to corrupt, absolute power tends to corrupt absolutely. In words reminiscent of the *Politics*, St. Thomas notes that "since the power granted to a king is so great, it easily degenerates into tyranny, unless he to whom this power is given be a very virtuous man; for it is only the virtuous man that conducts himself well in the midst of prosperity."[21] But since "perfect virtue is to be found in few,"[22] the best practicable form of government must be sought elsewhere.

In his work *On Kingship*, St. Thomas suggests that some scheme should be worked out to prevent political rule from degenerating into tyranny.[23] Unfortunately, he does not develop the idea, since the fragmentary treatise jumps abruptly at this point to another question. In a passage in the *Summa Theologica*, however, he presents the idea of a mixed government similar to that previously proposed by Cicero.

> Accordingly, the best form of government is in a state or kingdom wherein one is given the power to preside over all, while under him are others having governing powers. And yet a government of this kind is shared by all, both because all men are eligible to govern, and because the rulers are chosen by all. For this is the best of polity, being partly kingdom, since there is one at the head of all; partly aristocracy, insofar as the number of persons are set in authority; partly democracy, that is, government by the people, insofar, as the rulers can be chosen from the people, and the people have the right to choose their rulers.[24]

St. Thomas probably intended to elaborate on this idea of a mixed constitution in his unfinished treatise *On Kingship*. Influenced as he was in his political thinking by Aristotle, it is reasonable to assume that he believed in royal rule as the best form of government absolutely or ideally speaking, but felt that in the practical order monarchy must give way to some mixed type which would embody a balancing of interests or forces. The government which he sketchily describes in the *Summa Theologica* would presumably meet this need. It would minimize the danger of tyrannical abuse by providing a check or limitation on the

---

[20] *Ibid.*, Book I, Chap. 4.
[21] *Summa Theologica*, I–II, q. 105, a. 1, 2.
[22] *Ibid.*
[23] Book I, Chap. 6.
[24] *Summa Theologica*, I–II, q. 105, a. 1.

monarch; it would make the people feel that they had a stake in the community and its common good by permitting a degree of popular participation; and it would encourage good government by placing able citizens in positions of public authority where they could not only carry out administrative functions but also could keep the monarch "temperate" or "moderate" (*temperetur potestas*).

That it was the intention of St. Thomas to propose a mixed government as the best practical type is further strengthened by other considerations. He apparently accepts the Aristotelian view that both the monarchical and aristocratical forms overlook the fact that one man or a selected elite, no matter how virtuous, can never be as good as the whole community which comprises them as one of its parts.[25] He also realizes that as a matter of political reality forms of government must be suitable to the talents, the culture, and the social maturity of the people concerned. In this connection, he quotes with approval St. Augustine's statement

> If a people have a sense of moderation and responsibility, and are most careful guardians of the common welfare, it is right to enact a law allowing such a people to choose their own magistrates for the government of the community. But if, as time goes on, the same people become so corrupt as to sell their votes and entrust their government to scoundrels and criminals, then the right of appointing these public officials is rightly forfeit to such a people, and the choice devolves to a few good men.[26]

The Pattern of the Law

The great and distinctive contribution that St. Thomas made to the development of political philosophy is found in his comprehensive analysis of law rather than in his treatment of the nature of the civil community. His theory of the state and political authority was formulated within the conceptual pattern of his general system of law. The modern world is accustomed to think of law as the product of the will of those charged with the care of the public weal. Law in this view must be conceived of within the framework of the state, and not the reverse as Thomas did. He and all other medievalists looked upon the political community in terms of a law whose existence and content are independent

---

[25] This point is made by D. Bigongiari, *The Political Ideas of St. Thomas Aquinas* (New York: Hafner, 1953), p. xxix.

[26] *Summa Theologica*, I–II, q. 97, a. 1.

of human decision. The Germanic concept of the folk and its law best expresses this notion.

When the Germanic tribes overran the Roman empire, they brought with them their own notions of law and government. Among these ideas was the concept that law is not made by any individual or group but already exists in nature. As such, it finds expression in the immemorial traditions and customs of the people. The function of the ruler is not to legislate or enact law in the modern sense but rather to discover it. Customs and usages frequently demand clarification in order to resolve apparent conflicts or to meet new situations. On such occasions, the king with the aid of his counselors inquires into the practices of the community, decides what the custom really is, and then promulgates his decision in the form of an assize or law.

The Germanic idea that the law belongs to the people does not mean that law is a product of their will and subject to change at their volition. It simply means that the community is fashioned by its law in much the same way that a human body is governed by its principles of organization.[27] The difference between current and medieval thinking on law is that "whereas the modern democrat is prepared to respect a law insofar as he can regard himself as its author, medieval obedience was founded on the opposite sentiment, that laws were respectable insofar as they were not made by man."[28]

St. Thomas' conception of the universe as an orderly and integrated hierarchy called in turn for a system of law that would govern and bind together each level of the grand structure. He found this master pattern in his fourfold classification of law: eternal, divine, natural, and human.

Eternal Law — St. Thomas looks upon eternal law as the Divine reason which governs and orders the whole of creation. It is the eternal plan of God's wisdom, "the plan of government in the Chief Governor," from which "all the plans of government in the inferior governors must be derived." These plans of the lesser governors "are all the other laws which are in addition to the eternal law. Therefore all laws, in so far as they partake of right reason, are derived from the eternal law."[29] This

---

[27] For an excellent discussion of this matter see Sabine, *op. cit.*, Chap. XI.

[28] H. M. Reade, "Political Theory to c. 1300," *Cambridge Medieval History, op. cit.*, Vol. VI, p. 616.

[29] *Summa Theologica*, I, II, q. 96, a. 3.

law is called eternal since "the divine reason's conception of things is not subject to time."

Natural Law — Thomas firmly repudiates the identification of natural and divine law made by some of the medieval canonists. He defines natural law as that part of the eternal law which is presented to the reason of man. Since all creation is ruled by divine providence, all things partake in some way in the eternal law from which they derive their respective inclinations to their proper acts and ends. In the case of man, this means the desire to lead a life in which his rational nature may be realized. As examples of this inherent propensity, St. Thomas mentions the inclination in man to live in society, to seek good and avoid evil, to educate his children, to search for truth, and to strive for intellectual development.

The natural law has a different significance for man than for the rest of created being. Irrational creation is governed by the physical laws of nature in a necessary and immutable order in which each natural object conforms without understanding. Rational beings are subject to the eternal law in a different way in that, unlike any other nature, they move themselves precisely because they have knowledge of the end.[30] Hence, "all things to which man has a natural inclination are naturally apprehended by reason as being good, and consequently as objects of pursuit, and their contraries as evil, and objects of avoidance."[31]

St. Thomas does not look upon the natural law as a complete code of rules and regulations which can be determined with exactness and finality. He is careful to point out that the natural law sets forth only the broad principles for the guidance of human acts and that these principles require specific application to individual events as they occur in the order of reality. While these first principles are universal and permanent, their bearing on social and political institutions may vary as changing circumstances affect their intrinsic justice or their utility. As in the application of any principle, the more one descends from the general to the particular, the more difficult becomes the task of determining the proper application of the principle. "Man has a natural participation of the eternal law, according to certain common principles, but not as regards the particular determinations of individual

---

[30] The rational creature has "a share of the eternal reason whereby it has a natural inclination to its proper act and end; and this participation of the eternal law in the rational creature is called the natural law" (*Summa Theologica*, I–II, q. 91, a. 2).

[31] *Ibid.*, q. 94, a. 2.

cases."[32] He, accordingly, has need for a more detailed system of rules and regulations to govern the conduct of society. It is the function of human law to meet this need.

Human Law — Human or positive law (that issued by the ruler or other lawmaking agency) is the detailed application of natural law precepts to particular situations. "From the precepts of the natural law, as from the common and indemonstrable principles, the human reason needs to proceed to the more particular determination of certain matters. These particular determinations, devised by human reason, are called human laws."[33] The relationship between natural and human law determines the moral validity of the latter. Human law is justified only in so far as its provisions do not conflict with the general precepts of the natural law. "Every human law has just so much of the nature of law as it is derived from the law of nature. But if at any point it departs from the law of nature, it is no longer a law but a perversion of law."[34]

The question arises in later political thought whether human law can be rigidly deduced from the principles of the natural law in geometrical fashion. Documenting his refutation of this notion, Thomas states that human law is derived from natural law in two ways: as a conclusion from principles, and as a determination from principles.[35] The first is similar to the method of the speculative sciences whereby demonstrated conclusions are drawn from certain principles, and here the analogy with mathematics is close. For example, the conclusion that it is wrong to murder another can be deduced from the primary natural law precept "do good and avoid evil." The conclusion that the culprit should be punished can be arrived at by the same process. Wrongdoing cannot be left unpunished in the interest of a peaceable and orderly society. However, the best way of punishing the violator cannot be similarly determined. This decision can be reached only by the second method, a determination from the first principles. Here, experience and factual evidence as to the efficacy of the various types of punishments and their general effect on the community, the extenuating circumstances in the particular case, and other data of like nature are required before an intelligent judgment can be made. The precept that the wrong doer should be punished is immutable, but its application varies in concrete instances.

---

[32] Ibid., q. 91, a. 3, 1.   [33] Ibid., q. 91, a. 3.   [34] Ibid., q. 95, a. 2.
[35] This distinction is discussed by St. Thomas in Summa Theologica, I–II, q. 95, a. 2.

The conception of human law presented by St. Thomas is entirely compatible with the medieval idea that the law is found and not made. He defines law as "an ordinance of reason for the common good, promulgated by him who has the care of the community."[36] Law according to reason implies that it is found in the nature of things; that it is "just, possible to nature, according to the customs of the country, adapted to place and time."[37] In other passages, St. Thomas shows that he considers positive law as nothing more than the promulgation or codification of custom. By the actions of the people "especially if they be repeated, so as to make a custom, law can be changed and set forth. . . . For when a thing is done again and again, it seems to proceed from a deliberate judgment of reason. Accordingly, custom has the force of a law, abolishes law, and is the interpreter of law."[38] Custom, moreover, should not be abrogated by the rulers except in extreme cases where the practice clearly is unjust or its observance extremely harmful to the common good, or where some very great benefit would be conferred by the new enactment. A law which is made, in the sense that it embodies the arbitrary will of the governors and disregards the established customs and traditions of the people, is unreasonable and improper. The primary task of the lawgiver is to clarify and promulgate custom (which medieval thought regarded as a branch of natural law) and in this sense the law is found rather than made.

Divine law — St. Thomas refers to that portion of the eternal law which God has revealed to man through the Old and New Testament and in church dogma as divine law. The Ten Commandments are an example of this branch of law. Divine law is a gift of grace rather than a discovery of natural reason. The need for it is explained by St. Thomas in the following passage:

Besides the natural and human law it was necessary for the directing of human conduct to have a divine law . . . it is by law that man is directed how to perform his proper acts in view of his last end. Now if man were ordained to no other end than that which is proportionate to his natural ability, there would be no need for man to have any further direction, on the part of his reason, in addition to the natural law and humanly devised law which is derived from it. But since man is ordained to an end of eternal happiness which exceeds man's natural ability . . . therefore it was

---

[36] Ibid., q. 90, a. 4.
[37] Ibid., q. 95, a. 3.
[38] Ibid., q. 97, a. 3.

necessary that, in addition to the natural and human law, man should be directed to his end by a law given by God.[39]

Even in respect to man's natural end, the divine law supplements reason in its quest for truth and justice since human reason is fallible and therefore subject to error:

By reason of the uncertainty of human judgment, especially on contingent and particular matters, different people form different judgments on human acts; whence also different and contrary laws result. In order, therefore, that man may know without any doubt what he ought to do and what he ought to avoid, it was necessary for man to be directed in his proper acts by a law given by God, for it is certain that such a law cannot err.[40]

As grace perfects nature, so does the divine law perfect the natural law. It illuminates the path that man must tread if he is to attain his temporal and spiritual self-fulfillment. Revelation adds to reason but it does not supplant it. Both faith and reason are part of the grand structure which Thomas describes.

SUMMARY

Divorced from their historical milieu and stripped of those accidental attributes peculiar to the period, the social teachings of St. Thomas, are of timeless significance. No other single thinker of the medieval era has left so deep an impression on political speculation. The modern scholar may reject his teachings, but he cannot disregard them. To the Christian, the political philosophy of St. Thomas is of special importance since it helps substantially to clarify, both in the light of revealed and natural truth, the role and position of the state, and man's duty and relation to it. Aristotle had relied on natural reason for his explanation of civil society; St. Augustine had viewed the state primarily in theological terms; St. Thomas combines both forms of knowledge in presenting to Christian man a meaningful picture of political rule placed in its true perspective in the ordered hierarchy of the universe.

Perhaps the most significant contribution that St. Thomas made to political thought is his restoration of the classical conception of the state as a natural and not a divine or religious institution. As a Christian theologian he regards man as a rational and moral creature with an ultimate and eternal end to be found in union with God. At the same time, he is careful to point out that man also has a natural end, a goal to be sought for and attained in this world. In seeking the fulfillment of his nature as a rational being, man is also traveling the path toward his eternal goal. "Through virtuous living man is

[39] *Ibid.*, q. 91, a. 4.
[40] *Ibid.*

further ordained to a higher end which consists in the enjoyment of God."
And in pursuing his supernatural destiny, he is simultaneously achieving his
natural perfection.

St. Thomas demonstrates that it is neither necessary nor possible to connect
the origin of the state with any supernatural act. In his thinking, God remains
as the first and ultimate, but not the proximate cause of the state.[41] This
cause is to be found in the social instinct of man, an instinct that is not only
natural, as the gregariousness of animals, but also a rational product depending
upon a free and conscious activity. By virtue of his nature as a moral being,
man has the fundamental obligation to build up an order of right and justice
by his own efforts. Despite the Fall, he has not lost the faculty of pursuing
his natural perfection. The existence and dignity of a purely natural sphere of
ethical values as embodied in the natural law has not been vitiated by sin.
It is within this natural sphere that the state finds its *raison d'être* and its
justification. The fact that man needs the help of divine grace even for the
achievement of his natural end does not impair the dignity of the temporal
order, for grace does not destroy nature, it perfects it (*gratia naturam non
tollit, sed perficit*). So conceived, the state is not the result of the Fall and
it does not bear the stigmata of sin.

The whole tenor of Thomas' political speculation is based on the premise
that state power is of a limited nature and subject to law. The same idea is
implicit in the thought of the ancient Greeks, but the middle ages, with its
conception of God as the ultimate source of all authority, gives new meaning
and a stronger foundation to this principle. The unyielding insistence which
St. Thomas and the medievalists placed on the conformity of human law
to the natural and divine law better prepared the state for the later institutionalization of limited government, through such devices as written constitutions and judicial review.

BIBLIOGRAPHY

Bigongiori, Dino (ed.), *Political Ideas of St. Thomas Aquinas: Representative
Selections* (New York: Hafner, 1953).
Chesterton, G. K., *St. Thomas Aquinas* (New York: Sheed and Ward, 1933).
Chroust, A. H., "The Corporate Idea and the Body Politic in the Middle
Ages," *Review of Politics*, October, 1947.
Conover, Milton, "St. Thomas Aquinas as a Social Realist," *Social Science*,
June, 1954.
———— "St. Thomas Aquinas in Some Recent Non-Scholastic Writers on
Political Philosophy," *New Scholasticism*, January, 1956.
D'Entreves, Alexander P., *The Medieval Contribution to Political Thought*
(Oxford: Oxford University Press, 1939).
Dougherty, George V., *The Moral Basis of Social Order According to St.
Thomas* (Washington: Catholic University Press, 1941).

---

[41] See Ernest Cassirer, *The Myth of the State, op. cit.*, p. 114.

Farrell, Walter, "Natural Foundations of the Political Philosophy of St. Thomas," Proceedings of the American Catholic Philosophical Association, 1931.

Gilby, Thomas A., The Political Thought of Thomas Aquinas (Chicago: University of Chicago Press, 1958).

Gilson, Etienne, Reason and Revelation in the Middle Ages (New York: Scribners, 1938).

Hearnshaw, F. J. C. (ed.), The Social and Political Ideas of Some Great Medieval Thinkers (London: Harrap, 1923).

Jaffa, Harry V., Thomism and Aristotelianism: A Study of the Commentary by Thomas Aquinas on the Nicomachean Ethics (Chicago: University of Chicago Press, 1952).

Jaszi, Oscar, and Lewis, J. D., Against the Tyrant: The Tradition and Theory of Tyrannicide (Glencoe: The Free Press, 1957).

Maritain, Jacques, Scholasticism and Politics (New York: Macmillan, 1940).

Martinez, Marie L., "Distributive Justice According to St. Thomas," Modern Schoolman, May, 1947.

Murphy, Edward F., St. Thomas' Political Doctrine and Democracy (Washington: Catholic University Press, 1921).

Parsons, W. R., "Medieval Theory of the Tyrant," Review of Politics, April, 1942.

Stephenson, Carl, "The Problem of the Common Man in Early Medieval Europe," American Historical Review, April, 1946.

Ward, L. R., "St. Thomas' Defense of Man," Proceedings of the American Catholic Philosophical Association, 1945.

PART FOUR | POLITICAL PHILOSOPHY DURING THE ERA OF TRANSITION

Chapter IX

THE POLITICAL THOUGHT OF THE RENAISSANCE AND REFORMATION

"An historic event has taken place; the world has been changed. Even the most stable European state finds itself in the midst of an entirely new movement" (Jules Michelet, *History of France*).

THE chronological characterization of any period can at best be only a rough approximation. Just as the ancient world cannot be separated from the middle ages by any sharp line of demarcation, neither can the latter be marked off from the modern era by a given historical moment. The religious, social, and political climate that distinguishes the medieval from the modern period was not molded in a year, a decade, or even a century. It was only by a slow and gradual process, a long period of fermentation, running over the course of many years that the change was eventually wrought. The two great movements which mark the transition from the old to the new are known as the Renaissance and the Reformation. Both affected radically the attitude and outlook of man, the one in the secular, the other in the religious sphere. In a sense, these two forces were partners in a revolutionary effort that destroyed the foundations of medieval unity and led to the establishment of the modern national state.

THE RENAISSANCE

Many dates, depending on the purposes of the particular author, have been used to designate the period of the Renaissance. In general, its boundaries are fluidly fixed around the fourteenth to the sixteenth century. Economically, the period was characterized by a shift from a purely agricultural society to the beginnings of a capitalistic and commercial system. Coined money instead of barter came into common use and trade began to expand rapidly. Socially, the middle class — the bourgeoisie, the merchant — began to come into its own as the center of social and economic life shifted from the manor to the growing towns. Scientifically, the Renaissance was an age of great advancement marked by the invention or importation from the East of iron-casting, the compass, movable printing type, and gunpowder, and by the discovery of the solar system and the theory of blood circulation. A similar revolution in geographic knowledge was brought about by the explorations of Vasco da Gama, Columbus, and Magellan.

Intellectually and culturally, the Renaissance witnessed a quickening of interest in the arts and letters, and a corresponding inattention to ethics, metaphysics, and theology. The orientation was toward the secular and "secularism" rather than toward the religious and spiritual. Otherworldliness gave way to a preoccupation with the things and problems of this life. As Professor Hallowell has noted, the skill which had previously been directed to the building of magnificent cathedrals proclaiming the glory of God was now directed to singing the praises of men.[1] From the standpoint of politics, the era of transition witnessed the breakdown of the feudal system and the development of the national state, with its absolutist tendencies. It also evidenced a growing awareness that the dream of universal empire in the West (so eloquently expressed by Dante in his De Monarchia) was impossible of realization.

In a narrow sense, the Renaissance signified a revival or rebirth of antiquity as demonstrated by the renewed interest in classical art and literature. In a broader and more proper meaning, it described an age when man's energy and spirit surged forward in a new momentum. The cultural stimulus which classical antiquity provided was more a consequence than a cause of man's changed outlook. The new age of "humanism" was one of self-confidence and individualism, reflecting not only an increased consciousness of the human personality but of its environment as well, a consciousness that is expressed in the pictorial art and poetry of the period. It was also an era in which man sought to break free from traditional authority in order to assert more fully his autonomy as an individual.

Man's dignity in the eyes of the medievalist had consisted in the fact

---

[1] J. H. Hallowell, Main Currents in Modern Political Thought (New York: Holt & Co., 1950), p. 32.

that he alone of all created beings was capable of knowing and giving praise to God. To the Renaissance mind, man rather than God became the focal point of attention. Although religion continued to occupy an important place in the lives of the Christian humanists, such as Erasmus, it was no longer the all-embracing, all-dominant factor that it has been during the middle ages. And to the increasing number of pagan humanists, God was completely displaced by man as the source of all power. For man to submit to any authority that he himself had not created would be unbefitting his dignity as a rational being. "I will not imitate things glorious, no more than base; I'll be my own example."

The new spirit affected profoundly the political thinking of the period. No better illustration of this can be found than the works of Niccolo Machiavelli, the famous son of the Renaissance. A less well-known example is the political writings of Marsilius of Padua, who lived in the late middle ages or early Renaissance period. Although the latter remained within the idiom of the medieval tradition, he presented a political philosophy that was anticipatory of the great Florentine, and was distinctly "modern" in its approach. Since Machiavelli repudiated the medieval tradition of politics in its entirety, the works of Marsilius are of interest in providing a transitional step from the old to the new. As a modern commentator has observed, the *Defensor Pacis* of Marsilius presents both the vestiges of medieval political ideas and the germs of modern thought in such fashion that their interrelations are brought out with great clarity.[2]

MARSILIUS OF PADUA

Marsilius' ideas on the relationship between church and state have already been considered;[3] only that aspect of his writing which pertains to his general political philosophy is of concern here. Marsilius follows Aristotle's ideas on the state and society in much the same way that St. Thomas does, but his conclusions differ radically from those of the latter. The divergence results primarily from the fundamentally different concept of the relationship between faith and reason held by the two thinkers. Thomas maintains that faith complements reason and that therefore certain truths in the supernatural order, such as the existence

---

[2] Alan Gewirth, *Marsilius of Padua* (New York: Columbia U. Press, 1951), Vol. 1, p. 10.
[3] See *ante*, Chapter VII.

of God and the divine origin of political authority, are subject to rational demonstration. Marsilius, on the other hand, regards faith and reason as two completely separate spheres of truth, so distinct in fact that contradiction between the two is possible.

From the standpoint of political philosophy, Marsilius' position means that the state must be studied from a purely secular standpoint without any reference to the supernatural aspects of man's life. By thus widening the gap between faith and reason, the divine creation and end of man are "no longer in any sense susceptible of rational proof, and consequently the entire divine order exercises no control whatsoever upon a political doctrine established by rational demonstration."[4] St. Augustine and many of the medievalists had emphasized the theological aspects of the state, sometimes to the exclusion or at the expense of the natural. St. Thomas had sought to reconcile the natural and the theological in his political speculation. Marsilius rejects both these approaches by stressing the secular aspects of the state to the total exclusion and without reference to the spiritual.

The Nature and Purpose of the State

Marsilius holds to the organic theory of the state as commonly understood. "Even as an animal that is well disposed in accordance with nature is composed of certain proportionate parts ordained to one another, which communicate their actions mutually to one another and to the whole, so a state that is well disposed and instituted in accordance with reason is constituted in a similar way."[5] His conception of the unity of this organism is, however, more in accord with the nominalistic tendencies of later medieval thought than it is with traditional theory. Aristotle had attributed to the state a unity of order, a formal unity that is a proper object of rational thought, although it creates no new substance and leaves its parts still capable of individual and self-motivated action.[6] Marsilius denies any such metaphysical reality to the state, asserting that its unity consists simply in the acceptance by the people of a common government.

The Paduan also differs with his predecessors over the purpose of

---

[4] A. Gewirth, op. cit., p. 70.

[5] Defensor Pacis, I, Chap. 2, sec. 3. Selections from the Defensor Pacis are taken from Alan Gewirth's translation, op. cit.

[6] See ante, p. 70.

the state. He interprets the good or sufficient life as one of economic and social security and of the fulfillment of man's natural desires without particular reference to ethical and moral values. He views the state primarily as an agency for satisfying the material needs of man. His accent is on the useful things of life, with no mention of the state as the promoter of moral and intellectual virtues. The emphasis has been shifted from ends to means. Politics loses its normative character and turns its attention away completely from the ultimate goals of civil society to those means necessary for the operation and preservation of the state.

The new twist which Marsilius gives to the political community results from his basic psychology. Interpreting the social instinct to be merely a biological urge, he states that the "natural" instinct for the sufficient life consists essentially in the satisfaction of man's physical and biological desires — desires which he shares with "every genus of animals."[7] Since the "natural" is purely biological, man's desires will be neither rational nor free; they will be as necessary and determined as those of an animal. Given these premises, it is possible to construct a science of politics with a degree of certitude similar to that enjoyed by the physical sciences.

Popular Sovereignty

St. Thomas had located political authority in the community as a whole and had looked upon the ruler as the delegate or vice-regent of the people for the actual exercise of this power.[8] Marsilius takes a similar view, but his concept of law gives his theory of popular sovereignty a coloration quite different from that of his predecessor. The crux of his theory rests in the concept that lawmaking power has its ultimate source in the civic community.

> The legislator, or prime and proper effective cause of law, is the people or body of citizens, or its more weighty part, through its choice or will orally expressed in the general assembly of citizens, commanding or determining, in regard to the civil actions of men that something be done or not done, under penalty of temporal punishment.[9]

---

[7] See Professor Gewirth's analysis of this point, op. cit., pp. 54–66.

[8] See ante, p. 153.

[9] Defensor Pacis, I, Chap. 12, sec. 3. When Marsilius uses the expression "more weighty part" he means more than a numerical majority. Although he nowhere describes in detail how the voting is to be weighted, he makes it clear that both quantity and quality must be taken into consideration in making the determination.

This passage suggests that Marsilius considers the essence of the law to be the coercive command and not right reason. He makes no mention of law as a product of reason; instead he emphasizes its origination in human will. He does not deny that the best law is that which is made for the common benefit of the citizens; but the test for making this determination is simply the "utility" of the law, that is whether it would be beneficial in terms of satisfying the "natural" or biological desires of the people.

Form of Government

Marsilius adopts the Aristotelian definition of citizenship as "any man who participates in the civil community, in the principate or the council or the jury, according to rank. By this definition boys, slaves, sojourners, and women are excluded from the category of citizens."[10] This citizen body makes up the "legislator" or the supreme lawmaking authority in the state. It may itself exercise this power as in a direct democracy, or it may transfer it to a smaller group of experienced men. "The whole corps of citizens, or its weightier part, either makes law itself directly, or entrusts this task to some person or persons, who are not and cannot be the legislator in the absolute sense, but only for specific matters, and temporarily, and by virtue of the authority of the prime legislator."[11] It is usually expedient for the people to make this delegation since lawmaking can "more thoroughly be carried out by the observations of those who have opportunity for leisure, the elders and those more experienced in practical affairs who are called 'the prudent' rather than by the opinions of artisans, who have to direct their activity toward acquiring the necessities of life."[12]

Marsilius justifies the vesting of primary lawmaking authority in the people on the Aristotelian principle that the collective judgment of the many is better than that of a single individual or of a few. "For a greater number can give more attention to a defect in a proposed law than can any part of that number, since the whole of any body is at least greater in mass and in virtues than is any of its parts separately."[13] Since in most cases it would be impractical for the whole citizen body to assemble for lawmaking purposes, it is necessary that a smaller group of prudent and expert men be elected to perform this function. The laws drafted by

---

[10] *Ibid.*, I, Chap. 12, sec. 4.
[11] *Ibid.*, I, Chap. 12, sec. 3.
[12] *Ibid.*, I, Chap. 12, sec. 2.
[13] *Ibid.*, I, Chap. 12, sec. 5.

this agency should then be referred to the people for their approval or rejection. This process resembles the modern referendum, or the practice of referring certain laws to popular vote.

Once the laws have been enacted, their execution must be entrusted to the political rulers. Marsilius is largely indifferent whether the administration of public affairs be placed in the hands of a king or an aristocracy, although at one point he expresses a preference for monarchy. Whatever the type, the choice of the ruler belongs to the citizen body, since the law is to ruler as form to matter, and since the citizens generate the form, it belongs to them to determine the matter of that form.

Significance of Marsilius

Although Marsilius still spoke in classical and medieval terms, the orientation which he gave to political philosophy is startlingly "modern." Reading his Defensor Pacis, the present-day scholar cannot help but be amazed at the many points in which he anticipates later theorists such as Machiavelli, Hobbes, Austin, Bentham, and Rousseau. This modernity expresses itself in at least four different aspects of his thinking:

1. Marsilius conceives of political power not in ethical and intellectual but in utilitarian and biological terms. The raison d'être of the state is not to be found in ultimate ends and values but in the means for satisfying the common biological desires of the people. The basic question of politics is no longer whether governmental institutions and functions are legitimate in terms of ethical and rational norms but whether these institutions are capable of accomplishing the immediate material ends of society. Marsilius assumes that the political ends which the community seeks are just and for the benefit of the general good since these objectives are initially defined by the "natural" appetites common to all men.

Professor Gewirth points out that Marsilius' view of state functions as those which are conducive to the maintenance of order, the promotion of trade and commerce, and the freedom of the citizen in exercising his proper activities makes him the first thorough spokesman of the bourgeois state. While the traditionalists looked upon security only as a necessary condition for the attainment of moral and intellectual perfection, the emerging age tended to discard this higher goal for the state. In the new view, "the typical citizen is no longer the theologically or aristocratically virtuous man but rather the bourgeois merchant or artisan desiring above all else to be secure in what he has, and requiring for this security that he be free in the sense of controlling the laws and government under which he lives."[14] The Epicurean had asked only peace and security of the state; he had no desire to take part in its operations. The bourgeois realized that if he was to have the security he desired, he must himself control the organs of government.

2. Marsilius' psychology had the effect of discarding natural law as a norm and condition for political legitimacy. He did not, as Machiavelli was later to do, hold that it is immaterial whether the ends which government pursues are moral or immoral so long as they contribute to the preservation of the state. Yet by discarding the traditional view that political authority is limited by rationally apprehended ends, and by equating man's biological desires with the good, he was forced to accept the proposition that whatever the will (based on the "natural" appetites) of the weighted majority decrees must per se be legitimate and just.

3. The theory of law held by the Paduan is a forerunner both of the Austinian concept of law as the command of the sovereign and the doctrine of popular sovereignty as it found expression in Rousseau. Human law, as Marsilius views it, is solely a product of the will and not of reason. Its essential element is its coercive nature; its source rests in the will of the people. Conformity of the law to reason is no longer a necessary attribute. A government acting in accordance with a duly enacted law would be acting legitimately even though the law was morally unjust. In medieval thought, such an enactment would lack the character of true law, and hence its enforcement would rest on power alone and not on right.

4. The procedure which Marsilius employs in his study of the state stresses an aspect of political theory that had received little attention during the middle ages. Preceding thinkers such as John of Salisbury, John of Paris, and Thomas Aquinas had outlined the source and objectives of political rule but had dealt only in vague terms with the institutional means of conducting, limiting, and controlling civil power. Marsilius approaches his subject in reverse fashion. At the points where his forerunners are vague, he is precise; but where St. Thomas and the others carefully indicate the moral limits beyond which the state cannot go, Marsilius merely observes that political power belongs to the people without setting any limits on its exercise.

---

[14] A. Gewirth, op. cit., p. 308.

THE REFORMATION

On October 31, 1517, an Augustinian friar, Martin Luther, nailed his historic ninety-five theses to the door of the castle church at Wittenberg. In the religious upheaval which followed, the unity of the Christian faith in western Europe was shattered and the Catholic Church was reduced to the status of one among many confessions. The causes of the Reformation were deep-seated and complex. Moral, doctrinal, economical, and political factors contributed to the chain of events which occurred in the wake of Luther's action at Wittenberg. Although the movement was primarily a religious one, it had far reaching consequences in the political order.

The reasons for Luther's revolt against the Roman Church, and the doctrinal differences which he introduced, are only of indirect importance to the development of political thought. What is perhaps most significant from this standpoint is that Luther found it necessary to enlist the aid of the German princes in the furtherance of his religious cause. The immediate result of this action was inevitable: religion became more dependent upon the secular authorities than it had been at any period during the middle ages. Since this reliance came at a time when the individual rulers were seeking to capitalize on the growing nationalistic tendencies of the era, the support of the reformers strengthened and enhanced the position of the secular authorities, and thereby unwittingly contributed to the establishment of the absolute state.

For more than one thousand years there had been only one Church in the western world standing as the teacher and guardian of revealed truth. When the split came, men were not conditioned to accept a state of religious toleration. On the side of the churchmen there was a strong belief that the purity of religious doctrine must be preserved by public authority, even to the extent of using force if necessary in the suppression of heresy. Similarly, on the side of the statesmen it was believed that religious unity was an indispensable condition of public order. The idea that men of varying faiths could live side by side in harmony or that political unity could be maintained amidst religious diversity was as yet an untenable concept.

The strange principle of *cujus regio, ejus religio* (whoever rules the territory determines the religion), which was established in the Religious Peace of Augsburg in 1555, provides a graphic expression of this feeling.

Under the terms of the treaty, the ruler's choice determined the established religion of his territory. His subjects had to submit to the choice or emigrate to another state. In the middle ages the universal church had taught the true faith for the state to establish. The Peace abandoned this time-honored parallelism by subjecting religion to state control, thus creating the idea of a state-established religion.

The Reformation has much to offer in the way of political ideas, even though these ideas are not always cast in a political idiom. The competing positions of the religious reformers with respect to clerical authority and church institutions inevitably involved considerations of the political and social order. Three stages may be noted in the development of the political thought of the Protestant writers of the Reformation: (1) the acceptance of the doctrine of nonresistance to secular rule, (2) the theoretical justification of theocracy, and (3) the shift from the doctrine of nonresistance to that of active opposition against tyrannical government. The first found its best expression in Luther, the second in Calvin, and the third in the writings of the Monarchomachs.

MARTIN LUTHER

In his powerful *Address to the Christian Nobility*, published in 1520, Luther indicates his acceptance of the traditional principle that political power resides in the whole community and that those who exercise it do so with the consent of the people. Because all Christians are "of equal standing, no one must push himself forward and without the consent and choice of the rest, presume to do that for which we have equal authority. Only by the consent and command of the community should any individual person claim for himself what belongs equally to all."[15] At the same time, Luther also holds to the proposition that political power is divinely ordained. Like his medieval predecessors, he could see no inconsistency in the theory that political power is at the same time from God and from the people. However, as he became more dependent on the princes for support, he tended to emphasize the divine origin of political authority and to disregard the role of popular consent.

Proceeding next to the relationship between church and state, Luther seeks to show that both clergy and laity are subject as individuals to the

---

[15] *Address to the Christian Nobility of the German Nation*, translated by B. L. Woolf, *Reformation Writings of Martin Luther* (New York: Philosophical Library, 1953), Vol. 1, p. 115.

complete jurisdiction of the state in all matters not strictly of a religious or spiritual nature. "Since the secular authorities are ordained by God to punish evildoers and to protect the law-abiding, so we ought to let them free to do their work without let or hindrance everywhere in Christian countries and without partiality, whether for pope, bishops, pastors, monks, nuns, or anyone else."[16] This authority in the secular ruler extends even to the correction of abuses existing in the ecclesiastical organization. If reform is needed in the church and the pope fails to act "let anyone who is a true member of the Christian community as a whole take steps as early as possible to bring about a genuinely free council. No one is able to do this better than the secular authorities, especially since they are also fellow Christians, fellow priests, similarly religious, and of similar authority in all respects."[17]

Largely because of the rapid growth of Lutheranism in Germany, its founder was forced into the position of assigning to the state primacy of jurisdiction over the ecclesiastical sphere. Although Luther's theoretical statements are not entirely explicit on this point, his actions are clear. When it became imperative that a specially trained ministry and some form of organization were needed to preserve doctrinal integrity and to promote the orderly growth of the new religion, he turned to secular government for assistance. Barred from establishing an ecclesiastical hierarchy by his bias against institutions,[18] and unwilling to accept a purely democratic church organization because of his distrust of popular rule, he was compelled to adopt the secular alternative.

Under Luther's system as it was finally worked out, overseers or superintendents were appointed by the princes to visit and inspect the parishes and to advise the local pastors in matters of dogma and administration.

> While we cannot issue any strict commands as if we were publishing a new form of papal decrees. . . . We hope that they [pastors] will not ungratefully and proudly despise our love and good intention, but will willingly, without any compulsion, subject themselves in a spirit of love to such visitation. . . ."[19]

---

[16] *Ibid.*, p. 116.

[17] *Ibid.*, p. 122.

[18] Luther's teaching of the priesthood of all believers and his doctrine of justification by faith alone implied that the religious community should not be subjected to ecclesiastical governance.

[19] *Instructions for the Visitors of Parish Pastors*, in *Luther's Works*, American edition (Philadelphia: Muhlenberg Press, 1958), Vol. 40, p. 272.

Closely related to this same area of inquiry is the question of whether the secular arm should be used to suppress heresy. Luther first took a negative position on the grounds that the ruler has no right to interfere in the spiritual life of the individual. This is the work of the bishops for heresy cannot be checked with temporal force. However, he later reversed himself on this point when some of the more fanatical sects, such as the Anabaptists, took the new religious formula "freedom of the Christian individual" literally and threatened religious stability in those states where Lutheranism had become the established creed. He then began to hold that government cannot tolerate subversive religious beliefs since these in turn may lead to civil strife. Public authorities must fix a limit of toleration for heretical beliefs and must use force when this limit is passed.

Luther's reliance upon secular authority to police the church and to enforce a degree of religious uniformity had important consequences. A religion which had denied itself the power of an ecclesiastical organization was now forced to rely on political rulers who were unhampered by the traditional restraints of religious institutions.[20] As a result of this new orientation of the church-state question, the Lutheran churches became in effect state churches managed by the princes, much like secular branches of the government — a result far different from that envisaged by their founder. The German princes were not slow to take advantage of the new theory in order to further their own interests and nationalistic aspirations.

Perhaps the most important aspect of Luther's political theory, as distinguished from his political actions, is his doctrine of nonresistance to political rule. The citizens, he asserts, owe the duty of full obedience to their government. Even if the ruler is tyrannical and abuses his office, the people have no right to rebel against him. It is improper for a Christian to set himself up against his government for any reason. If the ruler demands obedience in things outside the temporal sphere, the subject is under no moral compulsion to obey. Yet even in this case he has no right to resist actively, but must suffer the penalty inflicted on him for his disobedience.

The fact that the German princes owed political allegiance to the emperor presented a theoretical difficulty for the doctrine of passive

---

[20] See S. Wolin, "Politics and Religion: Luther's Simplistic Imperative," *American Political Science Review*, March, 1956, p. 33.

obedience. As late as 1529 Luther had plainly indicated that he did not approve of resistance by a prince to the emperor, for the latter is "the lord and government placed above the princes." To rise against him with armed forces is a form of sedition and disobedience. The question became a practical one in 1530 when the Catholic emperor Charles V threatened to proceed against the heretical Protestant princes. The latter now objected strenuously to the restriction which Luther had placed on resistance. They argued that the emperor was chosen by the German electors and ruled with their co-operation, and that consequently he had no right to impose his will on them over their objections. Submitting to this reasoning, Luther stated that the issue between the princes and emperor was primarily a legal or constitutional one which could better be decided by jurists than by theologians. The distinction was at best a dubious one, but by employing it Luther sought to preserve the integrity of the doctrine of obedience, while at the same time acceding to the political exigencies which confronted him.

Luther has often been charged with inconsistencies in his political thinking. We must remember, however, that he was first of all a theologian — the founder of a great religious movement — and what political theory he did express was wholly related to his religious aims. His dramatic break with Rome was not paralleled by any new social or political philosophy. To him the relation of man's soul to God was of far more importance than man's position in the temporal world. He felt that if man stood in the proper relation to his Creator, his relation to society would right itself.[21] Yet he knew that in the historical intermixture of politics and religion in the sixteenth century, religious reforms could not be accomplished in total disregard of political considerations.

Luther's religious radicalism stands in strange contrast to his extreme conservatism in political affairs. He rigorously questioned and even attacked ecclesiastical authority but constantly stressed the duty of the subject to obey faithfully the commands of the state. On the religious side he advocated far-reaching reforms while on the political side he urged quietism and passivity. Yet this apparently contradictory position is not illogical in the light of Luther's teaching. His theological doctrine may have militated against an ecclesiastical authority but his concept of human nature called for a strong civil rule. Men may be spiritually

---

[21] See H. J. Grimm, "Luther, Luther's Critics, and the Peasant Revolt," *The Lutheran Church Quarterly*, XIX, 1946, 115–132.

sovereign over their souls but they are essentially depraved. It is necessary to keep the sword constantly hanging over their heads and to place them under compulsion to render full obedience. For it would be dangerous to order and stability if individuals were entrusted with the discretionary right to decide when and under what conditions they will submit to secular rule. Order must be imposed at all costs on the fallen world of man.

JOHN CALVIN

Unlike Lutheranism, which was politically conservative and deferential to state authority, Calvinism sought to penetrate all aspects of public as well as private life with the influence of religion. Its founder, John Calvin (1509–1564) came from a bourgeois family in northeastern France. He studied at the University of Paris and received a law degree at Orleans. In 1534 he broke with Catholicism and fled to Basel where two years later he published his *Institutes of the Christian Religion*, undoubtedly the greatest Protestant work on systematic theology produced during the Reformation period. The last chapter of the book deals with his political philosophy. The principles he sets forth can best be understood in the light of the interpretation which they received in actual practice. A rather unique opportunity is afforded in this connection, since Calvin was able to put his political doctrines into operation in the city-state of Geneva where he sought to establish a model Christian government.

Calvin agrees with Luther as to the divine ordination of secular rule and the duty of passive submission to such authority. It is impossible to resist the magistrate without, at the same time, resisting God Himself. Even the tyrannical ruler is to be tolerated and obeyed since obedience is due to the office and not to the person. An impious king is "a judgment of God's wrath upon the world." There are several passages in Calvin's writings which suggest that in certain cases inferior magistrates can properly resist a tyrannical ruler. Private persons are never permitted to resist; this right can be exercised only by officials, such as the Roman tribunes, whose constitutional function is the protection of the people against the wrongdoing of kings. "For if there be, in the present day, any magistrates appointed for the protection of the people and the moderation of the powers of the king. . . . I am so far from prohibiting them, in the discharge of their duty, to oppose the violence or cruelty of kings. . . ."[22] These passages were later utilized by his followers to justify active resistance in countries such as Scotland, Holland, and France, where Calvinism was in the minority.

Luther believed that civil government is primarily an instrument of repression or a remedy for sin, and not a promoter of virtue. The political order in his view is superfluous to the true Christian. Calvin, on the other hand, seeks to bridge the alleged dialectical opposition between the religious and secular societies and to re-establish the moral status of the political order without making it appear as a substitute for religious society.[23] Condemning the sectarian view that political government is "a polluted thing which has nothing to do with Christian men," Calvin underscores the large role which he assigns to the state.

> . . . civil government is designed, as long as we live in this world, to cherish and support the external worship of God, to preserve the pure doctrine of religion, to defend the constitution of the Church, to regulate our lives in a manner requisite for the society of men, to form our manners to civil justice, to promote our concord with each other, and to establish general peace and tranquility.[24]

Returning to the classical concept of the role of the statesman, he declares that "no doubt ought now to be entertained by any person that civil magistracy is a calling not only holy and legitimate, but for the most sacred and honorable in human life."[25]

By restoring the high status of political society in the order of crea- tion — a position that Luther denied to it — Calvin was able to reinvest the political order with dignity and respect even for the true Christian. His purpose in doing so was purely religious. If the power of the state could be linked with the objectives of the religious society, an important means of furthering these goals would thereby be established. Govern- ment would then have as its function not only the preservation of life and order but the enactment of laws "to regulate a man's life among his neighbors by the rules of holiness, integrity and sobriety." It would see to it "that idolatry, sacrileges against the name of God, blasphemies against his trust, and other offenses against religion may not openly appear and be disseminated among the people."[26]

---

[22] *Institutes of the Christian Religion*, IV, xx, 31. Excerpts taken from *John Calvin, On God and Political Duty* (New York: Liberal Arts Press, 1956).

[23] See in this connection S. Wolin "Calvin and the Reformation: The Political Education of Protestantism," *American Political Science Review*, June, 1957, p. 428 ff.

[24] *Institutes*, IV, xx, 2.   [25] *Ibid.*, IV, xx, 4.   [26] *Ibid.*, IV, xx, 3.

Calvin makes it quite clear, however, that decisions as to religious matters lay outside the purview of the political rulers. "For I do not allow men to make laws respecting religion and the worship of God . . . though I approve of civil government which provides that the true religion contained in the law of God be not violated and polluted by public blasphemies with impunity."[27] All questions pertaining to religion, including the interpretation of Scripture, must be confined strictly to the appropriate officials of the church. So long as the civil government comes under the direct or indirect control of the religious society, the church will be safe in the world and the world safe for the church.

Calvin objects in principle to any union of church and state, although he admits that the two powers are bound to assist each other in the execution of their respective tasks. How far the state is to aid the spiritual sword is made clear by the practices that he inaugurated at Geneva. The religious authorities were free to set their own standards of doctrine and morals in accordance with their interpretation of Scripture. Once this was done, it became the duty and responsibility of the civil authorities to enforce these standards. In Geneva and Puritan Massachusetts this meant rigid regulation of private conduct in social as well as religious matters. The state under clerical guidance had the function of purging its citizenry of erroneous dogmas and of enforcing standards of piety and conduct in such matters as dress and recreation. Attendance at church services was compulsory, the wearing of jewelry and gay colored clothes was prohibited, and all forms of entertainment were rigidly restricted and supervised.

In Calvin's practice, if not in his theory, the church is to dominate the state with the latter serving primarily as an instrument for the establishment of God's glory. He envisioned a world ruled by the Old Testament — one in which the church would mold and direct the state and government of men. To those who contend that the state should confine itself to the administration of natural justice and natural law, Calvin retorts "as though God appointed rulers in his own name to decide secular controversies and disregarded that which is of far greater importance — the pure worship of himself according to his law."[28]

Luther deviated from the traditional doctrine of the two swords by entrusting primary responsibility for the care of the religious society to the civil authorities rather than to an ecclesiastical hierarchy. In so doing,

---

[27] *Ibid.*   [28] *Ibid.*, Book IV, xx, 9.

he had unwittingly permitted the spiritual sword to come under the control and domination of the temporal. Calvin also deviated from the spirit of the Gelasian doctrine but in a way that differed radically from Luther's defection. By making the state a virtual agent of the religious authorities, he combined both swords in the same hands, only in this case the hands were those of the religious and not the temporal authorities. The result was a theocratic government that ran counter to the concept of the natural and autonomous sphere of state authority.

THE MONARCHOMACHS

The term "monarchomachs" refers to the theorists of the sixteenth and seventeenth centuries who maintained the right of active resistance against tyrants. While those who fell within this category held no single or unified system of political philosophy, all of them were antiabsolutist in their thinking. They generally held that all authority comes ultimately from God but more immediately from the people who, in some way, are the monarch-makers (monarchomachi). They considered the ruler to be limited by divine, natural, and civil law, and held that when he violates the law he becomes a tyrant. They also maintained that government is created by a contract between the ruler and ruled. The monarchomachs included in their numbers both Protestant and Catholic writers. The unknown author of the Vindiciae and John Ponet are representative of the former, and Juan de Mariana of the latter.

When the Catholic monarchs of the post-Reformation period undertook to stamp out heresy in France, the Protestant Huguenots, a sect that drew its inspiration from Calvin, were placed on the defensive. As the opposition between the monarchy and its Huguenot constituents came to a crisis, Protestant writers began to discard the doctrine of passive submission and to argue for the right of active resistance against a tyrannical ruler. The most influential work of this nature was the famous Vindiciae contra tyrannos, or the Grounds of Right against Tyrants, published anonymously in 1579.

The Vindiciae proceeds upon the theory that the secular ruler, although his position is a divinely ordained one, derives his power immediately from the people and is therefore accountable to them. The relationship between king and people is governed by a twofold covenant: the first in which God is one party and the king and people jointly the other; the second between the king on one side and the people on the other. In the first contract both ruler and subject pledge their faithfulness to God as His people. In the second pact, which is of a political nature, the people agree to obey the king so long as he rules justly and well.

The covenant with God imposes a duty on the state to support the true worship. If the king disregards this religious responsibility, the people have a clear right to resist or even depose him. Conversely, if the people are heretical, the king may proceed against them. Each must be kept within the divine law of God. (The difficulty lies in establishing who is heretical and who is not. In the French controversy, for example, both the king and the antiroyalist pamphleteers maintained that they were upholding the true word of God.) More significant than the views of the Vindiciae on resistance is the fact that its author makes no attempt to justify the principle of religious toleration. The same can be said of those who followed him in advocating resistance against the growing absolutism of the monarchy in sixteenth-century France.

In England, John Ponet's A Shorte Treatise of Political Power (1588) represented the Protestant shift from the doctrine of unlimited obedience to that of active resistance. Ponet wrote to justify the deposition of Mary who was "intent upon enforcing the demands of a false religion." He argues that political authority is merely a delegation of power from the people and that if the ruler is a tyrant, he cannot be ordained of God since it is evident that the people erred in choosing him. Ponet, as other writers of the period, was able to offer no workable method short of rebellion for expressing and enforcing the popular will in the face of royal tyranny.

The literature prompted by the religious wars also included many tracts against monarchical absolutism by Catholic writers such as Boucher and Rossaeus in France and Mariana in Spain. Unlike most of the other monarchomachs, the Spanish Jesuit Mariana wrote in a country in which there was no difference of creed between rulers and subjects. In his De rege et regis institutione (1599), he observes that government is the natural result of the impulsion to fulfill human needs. Hence the community must always be able to control the political rulers who have been created to serve its needs.

Together with the other antiabsolutist writers, Mariana feels that individuals should not take action against tyrants on their own initiative. It is the responsibility of the representative body in the community — the estates general or parliament — to determine whether the prince has become a tyrant. Once this official body has made such a finding, the people are free to rise up against the ruler; in fact, any private citizen may then assassinate the tyrant. But what if the ruler prevents the assembly from meeting or acting? In that case, Mariana says, the private citizen is justified in taking matters into his own hands and killing the tyrant at his discretion. Mariana concedes that there are latent dangers in his doctrine which could well strike at the root of political authority. He argues, however, that men will put up with a great deal before they will rise up against a ruler. And it is a salutary restraint upon princes to let them know that they are subject to assassination if they become oppressive.

SUMMARY

With the new spirit of individualism and the changed outlook introduced by the Renaissance and Reformation, the traditional principles of political philosophy had either to be replaced or adjusted to serve the changing character of the western world. Political speculation could no longer be cast in terms of one religion and one state; it had to accommodate itself to many religions and many states. The Reformation, and indirectly the Renaissance, not only destroyed the unity of religion but in doing so wrote the final chapter in the ill-fated hope for political unity. The historical circumstances which compelled the Protestant churches to ally themselves with the growing territorial states and their nationalistic aspirations strengthened the movement toward political particularism. Moreover, by the emphasis which they placed on the exalted position of the secular ruler, the early reformers helped to enhance the office of the political sovereign, and inadvertently to encourage the tendency toward state absolutism.

The transformation of political philosophy from the old order to the new was not accomplished with ease or rapidity. The relative unity which political thought had enjoyed for almost a millennium had been shattered, and the pieces had once again to be reassembled as they had in the days following the collapse of the city-state. While there had been differences in theory during the medieval period, there had been essential unanimity with respect to the fundamental concepts underlying civic life. The moral nature of man, the ethical mission of the state, the existence of an objective moral law, the idea of limited government, and the separate spheres of church and state were premises denied by few.

With the new ideas introduced by the Reformation and more especially the Renaissance, traditional principles came under vigorous attack in one form or another. As they did so, the stream of speculative thought split into separate channels, leading to the formulation of the divergent political philosophies to which the western world has fallen heir. Traditional thought continued on its course of development, adapting itself to the new historical environment; but its features became more difficult of ascertainment as they became gradually immersed in the new wellspring of modern ideas.

BIBLIOGRAPHY

Acton, John, *The History of Freedom and Other Essays* (London: Macmillan, 1907).

Allen, J. W., *A History of Political Thought in the Sixteenth Century* (New York: MacVeagh, 1928).

Armstrong, E., "The Political Theory of the Huguenots," *English Historical Review*, January, 1889.

Carlson, E. M., "Luther's Conception of Government," *Church History*, December, 1946.

Dodge, G. H., *The Political Theory of the Huguenots of the Dispersion* (New York: Columbia University Press, 1947).

Gewirth, Alan, *Marsilius of Padua and Medieval Political Philosophy*, 2 vols. (New York: Columbia University Press, 1951).

Gilmore, M. P., *The World of Humanism* (New York: Harper, 1952).

Hearnshaw, F. J. C. (ed.), *The Social and Political Ideas of Some Great Thinkers of the Renaissance and Reformation* (London: Harrap, 1925).

Hudson, Winthrop S., *John Ponet: Advocate of Limited Monarchy* (Chicago: University of Chicago Press, 1942).

Mackinnon, James, *Calvin and the Reformation* (London: Longmans, 1926).

Mueller, William, *Church and State in Luther and Calvin* (Nashville: Broadman Press, 1954).

Murray, R. H., *The Political Consequences of the Reformation* (London: Benn, 1926).

Richter, Werner, "Calvinistic Conception of the State," *Theology Today*, July, 1948.

Rommen, Heinrich A., "The Natural Law in the Renaissance Period," *Notre Dame Lawyer*, Summer, 1949.

Schwiebert, E. G., "Medieval Pattern in Luther's Views on the State," *Church History*, June, 1943.

Southgate, W. M., "Erasmus: Christian Humanism and Political Theory," *History*, October, 1955.

Tawney, R. H., *Religion and the Rise of Capitalism* (New York: Harcourt Brace, 1926).

Taylor, Henry O., *Thought and Expression in the 16th Century* (New York: Macmillan, 1920).

Troeltsch, Ernst, *The Social Teaching of the Christian Churches*, Vol. 2, trans. by O. Wyon (New York: Macmillan, 1931).

Waring, L. H., *The Political Theories of Martin Luther* (New York: Putnam, 1910).

Weber, Max, *The Protestant Ethic and the Spirit of Capitalism*, trans. by T. Parsons (London: G. Allen, 1930).

Chapter X

MACHIAVELLI: THE NEW SCIENCE OF POLITICS

"And in the actions of men, and especially of princes from which there is no appeal, the end justifies the means" (Machiavelli, *The Prince*, Chap. 18).

No FIGURE in political philosophy has been the subject of more varied and contradictory appraisal than Niccolo Machiavelli, the Florentine statesman turned writer. At one extreme, he has been denounced as the teacher *par excellence* of political chicanery and treachery, as the incarnation of cunning and naked force in political affairs, and as the forefather of modern totalitarianism. Shakespeare's Iago was purportedly modeled after him, and Niccolo, transformed into "Old Nick" has become an epithet equally applicable to both Machiavelli and the Devil himself. To many, his name is a synonym for unscrupulousness in politics.

At the other end of the spectrum, the author of *The Prince* has been lauded as a fervid Italian patriot dedicated to the common good of his countrymen, as a great democrat, and as a thinker who has contributed immensely to the cause of human freedom and the dignity of man by freeing political philosophy from the shackles of the past. Modern scholarship has treated him with more kindness than his contemporaries did, sometimes to the point, it would seem, of distorting his true significance.[1]

However we may view Machiavelli and whatever interpretation we may

[1] An example of this is found in G. Ferrero, "Machiavelli and Machiavellianism," *Foreign Affairs* (April, 1939), pp. 569–577, where the author passes over Machiavelli's statements on political conduct as nothing more than "bad-tempered explosions." In a similar vein, James Burnham in *The Machiavellians* (New York: John Day, 1943) observes that the harsh opinion of Machiavelli which has been more widespread in England and the United States than on the Continent "is no doubt natural because the distinguishing quality of Anglo-Saxon politics has always been hypocrisy, and hypocrisy must always be at pains to shy away from the truth" (p. 77).

187

place upon his thought, two things are clear: one, he is a typical son of the Italian Renaissance with its secular and this-worldly spirit, its classical perspective, and its scientific amoralism; two, he has proved to be one of the most influential political writers of all times. Read with fascination by statesmen and political leaders from the days of the Medici to the era of modern totalitarianism, he has served as a source of theoretical justification for power politics and for political actions of an infamous and immoral character.

Napoleon Bonaparte declared that Machiavelli's writings were the only political works worth reading. Mussolini considered the Florentine his spiritual and intellectual godfather, and studied his writings carefully. Hitler is reported to have kept a copy of The Prince by his bedside, and to have asserted that he ranked its author with the composer Richard Wagner as among the important influences shaping his thought. Machiavelli would probably have shuddered at some of the deeds later perpetrated by those who claimed to be guided by his principles. He was a sincere and honest man whose personal life was morally impeccable. Yet, by divorcing ethics from politics and by excluding the question of morality from public affairs, he helped to clear the way theoretically for the absolutist and later the totalitarian state with its incredible disregard of human rights.

BACKGROUND OF MACHIAVELLI'S WRITINGS

Machiavelli was born at Florence in 1469 of a well-known and noble family. His father was a lawyer who occasionally held public positions in the city-state of Florence. Little is known of Niccolo's education, but it is reasonable to assume from his station in life and the knowledge displayed in his writings that he received the liberal education normally given members of his class. In 1498 he was appointed to one of the principal secretaryships of the Florentine Republic, a post which he held for fourteen years. The range of his duties gave him an insight into both the internal management of the state and the conduct of foreign affairs. In addition to his domestic duties, he was frequently sent on missions to foreign powers where he came into contact with such political figures as Louis XII of France, and Emperor Maximilian of Germany. A keen observer with a penetrating and inquiring mind, he utilized his experiences to learn how the politics of his day actually operated. Few, if any, of his contemporaries could lay claim to so extensive and intimate a knowledge of public affairs.

The political situation in Italy during Machiavelli's lifetime was a troubled one. The peninsula was divided into five separate states: Milan, Venice, Naples, the Papal States, and Florence. Not only was the country torn by internal dissensions among these various city-states, each plotting for control, but it was also a pawn in the larger battle of power politics. France, Germany, and Spain were the principal protagonists seeking hegemony over the peninsula. In the interest of self-preservation, the Italian city-states usually allied themselves with one of the great powers; consequently, their individual positions came to depend largely upon the fortunes of their protector. The Florentine Republic was allied with France under this arrangement. Hence, when the French were driven from Italy in 1512 by the other powers, the Medici (who had been expelled in 1494) were able to regain control of the city and put an end to republican government. Machiavelli was arrested in the purge which followed, and after a short imprisonment he was banished to his country home near San Casciano. It was here that he wrote his great works including The Prince, the Discourses, a History of Florence, and a first rate comedy entitled Mandragola. He never gave up his hope of returning to public life; but while he was assigned to perform some minor tasks during the reign of the Medici, he received no further public appointment even after the republic was restored in 1527.

Machiavelli lived and was part of a turbulent era in Italian politics. Factional strife within the cities as well as difficulties and jealousies among them led to constant warfare, to the rise of despots, to violence and treachery in public office, and to conspiracies and assassinations. Political morality reached a low ebb as individuals and states contended for power. While these internal events were taking place, the problem of dealing with the foreign states was always present. Obviously helpless before the forces of the great powers, the small Italian city-states became adept in the use of craft and diplomacy, playing off one country against another. Machiavelli had the opportunity to observe all of this at first-hand. His teachers of politics include men like the ruthless but able Cesare Borgia, who thought nothing of having his own brother and brother-in-law assassinated when it served his interest to do so. It was against such a background of intrigue and violence that Machiavelli fashioned his political philosophy.

THE NEW METHODOLOGY

The main concern of political thinkers up to the time of the Renaissance centered around ends and norms, around "what ought to be" rather than "what is." They were usually interested in the construction of an ideal state or in writing handbooks for the moral guidance of the princes. In so far as political thought is concerned, they were prone to follow the speculative method of Plato rather than the empirical approach of Aristotle. When they did discuss means and institutional devices, they generally dealt with them in broad and abstract terms and with little attempt to validate them in experience. Since the days of the classical Greeks, the moral content of politics had remained strong but the formulation of causal theory had made no noticeable advance. Marsilius was perhaps the first medievalist to emphasize the importance of studying the means in politics; but his contribution in this direction was not great, since he supported his observations by citing Aristotle's findings instead of making empirical investigations of his own.

With Machiavelli, a radically new methodology is introduced to the study of politics. The change rests not so much in his orientation toward the analysis of concrete political behavior since Aristotle centuries before had carefully collected factual data as a prerequisite to theoretical formulation; it lies rather in his attempt to remove political reality totally from its ethical context. Before him, political speculation had one central question: the end of the state. Machiavelli ignores the matter of ethical ends. He studies the political process solely for the purpose of determining the efficacy of institutional practices and devices in terms of stabilizing political power. He is not concerned with the morality or immorality of political actions as they lead to or deviate from the moral goals of man. He insists that the question of means can and should be treated in a scientific manner without regard to the goodness or badness of the ends.

Machiavelli has little sympathy for the Greek-medievalist orientation, with its emphasis on the way things ought to be in the political order. His approach is somewhat paradoxical since he attempts to divorce ethics from politics and yet at the same time he actually makes ethical judgments in the political sphere. He is not content merely to observe contemporary politics and to describe men's social behavior. Although his judgments and preachments are couched in pragmatic terms, they contain within themselves a certain moral urgency, and even an ethical imperative. He constantly criticizes the world of his day and repeatedly tells statesmen how they ought to act. As he is fond of pointing out, the methods which have proved most successful in attaining and preserving political power should be carefully studied and analyzed. These means ought then to be used by the rulers. It is in fact their moral obligation to employ them in order that society may be stabilized and the general welfare of the people promoted.

Machiavelli employs the comparative method in his approach to the study of politics, relying largely on history for his empirical data. In his introduction to the Discourses, he expresses his intention to relate "what I have arrived at by comparing ancient with modern events, and think necessary for the better understanding of them, so that those who read what I have to say may the more easily draw those practical lessons which one should seek to obtain from the study of history."[2] His primary emphasis is not on pure research but on the discovery of universal rules of action that could become the basis of success. His aim is to create a science of politics, meaning by this a body of rules that governments can follow and rely on absolutely. In the process, he gives his readers a collection of concrete maxims or principles that rulers must observe in various circumstances if they wish to succeed. Thus to him, political science means the science of practical statecraft.

In line with his general objective, Machiavelli formulates certain hypotheses or general propositions which he presumes to discover from a reading of Livy's works. He then proceeds to test these assumptions in the light of examples taken from ancient and contemporary history. By using this approach, he seeks to arrive at laws of cause and effect which possess universal validity. Given such laws, man would be able to forecast in present circumstances the effects of causes analogous to those found operative in past situations. Similarly, given like circumstances and an effect that man wishes to bring about, he could introduce the appropriate cause to produce the desired result.

Machiavelli was concerned primarily with a methodology that could be applied to the discovery of causal sequences within the domain of politics and social behavior. At several points in his writings he indi-

---

[2] Discourses on the First Ten Books of Titus Livius, translated from the Italian by L. J. Walker in The Discourses of Niccolo Machiavelli (London: Routledge & Kegan Paul, 1950).

cates that the laws applicable to the political order are similar to those which operate in the physical universe. It is assumed, he states, that "all our actions resemble those of nature"; hence it is just as impossible in politics for a "slender trunk to support a heavy branch" as it is in nature. So also medicine is "nothing but a record of experiments performed by doctors of old upon which the doctors of our day base their prescriptions," while the civil law is "nothing but a collection of decisions made by jurists of old, tabulated for our instruction." There is something in common, he observes, between the behavior of man and the process of nature; hence the laws which are applicable to one should also be applicable to the other.

As indicated above, one of the important assumptions underlying the Florentine's approach to the establishment of a political science is the constancy of human nature. Men at all periods have been moved by the same passions and their reactions have always been similar. "For there is nothing in this world at present, or at any other time, but has and will have its counterpart in antiquity; which happens because these things are operated by human beings who, having the same passions in all ages, must necessarily behave uniformly in similar situations."[3] Historical change is not an evolutionary development, but a perpetual repetition of past situations and events. This view of historical recurrence permits Machiavelli to turn to history for the discovery of general rules and political precepts. It also enables him to regard these findings as possessing universal validity since they have reference to events that are most certain to recur.

> If the present be compared with the remote past, it is easily seen that in all cities and in all peoples there are the same desires and the same passions as there always were. So that, if one examines with diligence the past, it is easy to foresee the future of any commonwealth, and to apply those remedies which were used of old; or, if one does not find that remedies were used, to devise new ones owing to the similarity between events.[4]

MACHIAVELLI'S PSYCHOLOGY

The seemingly divergent views in the political writings of Machiavelli can be reconciled only in the light of his theory of man. It is not surprising that his intimate experience in the corrupt politics of his day

---

[3] *Discourses, op. cit.*, III, 43.   [4] *Ibid.*, I, 39.

gave him a rather dim and contemptuous picture of human nature. One must take for granted "that all men are wicked and that they will always give vent to the malignity that is in their minds when opportunity offers." It is common knowledge that they never do good unless necessity drives them to it.

> Those who have discussed the problem of civic life demonstrate . . . that whoever organizes a state and arranges laws for the government of it must presuppose that all men are wicked and that they will not fail to show their natural depravity whenever they have a clear oppor- tunity, though possibly it may lie concealed for a while.[5]

Men are "ungrateful, voluble dissemblers, anxious to avoid danger and covetous of gain."[6] They are animals motivated primarily by self-interest, personal aggrandizement, fear, vanity, and the lust for power. Only by shrewdness and a calculating ruthlessness can the individual hope to cope with his environment and satisfy his appetites and instincts.

Machiavelli could point to some of the medieval thinkers who looked upon man with a substantial measure of distrust. He could not, how- ever, have cited any precedent for the view of human nature which he expresses in the famous passage of the lion and the fox. Discussing the ways in which a prince must keep good faith with his subjects and those with whom he deals, he points out that there are two ways of fighting, "the one by law, the other by force; the first method is that of men, the second of beasts." Since the first is often insufficient, the ruler must occasionally resort to the second. "It is therefore necessary for a prince to know well how to use both the beast and the man . . . to use both natures." In the employment of his animal nature, man should learn to imitate both the fox and the lion since "the lion cannot protect him- self from traps and the fox cannot defend himself from wolves." A good ruler must

> be a fox to recognize traps and a lion to frighten wolves. Those who wish to be only lions do not understand this. Therefore, a prudent ruler ought not to keep faith when by so doing it would be against his interest, and when the reasons which made him bind himself no longer exist.[7]

In a penetrating analysis of Machiavelli, Charles N. R. McCoy sug-

---

[5] *Ibid.*, I, 3.
[6] *The Prince, Modern Library Edition* (New York: Random House, 1940), p. 61.
[7] *Ibid.*, p. 64.

gests that the Florentine considers the animal and rational nature of man as two unrelated principles of action. By his animal nature man acts like a beast, and by his rational nature he acts like a man. For a man to act like a beast, moreover, requires intelligence and demands the exercise of the rational principle in behalf of the animal nature. The lion can never act as a fox, but man, precisely because he is a rational being, is able to assume the character and qualities of several different beasts as the occasion demands. By failing to perceive that man is substantially a rational animal, Machiavelli fails also to see that the animal passions and appetites in man are ordered under the rational principle, and that there is a right desire, a right fear, and a right use of force which are properly attributable to man as man.[8] It is, in other words, proper for man to use force in certain circumstances when reason demands such action. When man so acts under the rational principle, he is acting in a mode suitable not to beasts but to man. Only when the passions are not so ordered, can man be said to act as a beast. Machiavelli, on the contrary, assumes that to be forceful and fearful is always to act as a beast; and a beast is not subject to reason.

The logical implications of Machiavelli's position are clear. By separating the two natures and placing them on a virtual par, man's so-called animal nature is released from subordination to the rational and prudential principle and is left free to be its own directive force. Such a position virtually drafts the rational side of man into the service of the animal principle in such a way that reason becomes a mere instrumentality for satisfying the desires of the sensual appetites. An animal with reason at its command and disposal can be a far more dangerous creature than the most ferocious of wild beasts.

THE END JUSTIFIES THE MEANS

Modern scholarship generally holds that Machiavelli's first interest and his primary objective is the good of the Italian people. There is no reason nor any necessity for denying this appraisal. The classical indictment of the Florentine is not directed against his motives but against the theoretical framework which he fashioned and its logical untenability. Machiavelli follows the ancient tradition in distinguishing between king-

---

[8] "The Place of Machiavelli in the History of Political Thought," *American Political Science Review*, Aug., 1943, p. 633.

ship and tyranny — the one embodying a rule for the common benefit of the governed; the other consisting of a rule for the personal gratification of the governor. The good ruler is one "whose intention is to govern not in his own interests but for the common good, and not in the interest of his successors but for the sake of that fatherland which is common to all."[9]

Leaving aside for the moment the vital question as to how Machiavelli defines the common good, it will be enlightening to examine the means which he advocates for the attainment of social and political objectives. His position in this regard is frank and clear. In the *Discourses*, he sets forth as a sound maxim that "reprehensible actions may be justified by their effects, and that when the effect is good, as it was in the case of Romulus, it always justifies the action." Romulus is to be commended for murdering his brother Remus since "what he did was done for the common good and not to satisfy his personal ambition."[10] This same idea, which dominates the whole of Machiavelli's theory, is repeated in *The Prince*, where he flatly states that in human actions "the end justifies the means."[11]

Given a good end, which the statements in the *Discourses* presuppose, all necessary means may be used to attain it. The ruler is under no compulsion to debate whether his actions are morally proper or whether there are ethical limits beyond which he may not go. There are no crimes in politics, only stupid mistakes. Freed from the need for moral considerations, the prince can devote his full energy to empirical decisions. All the methods of the tyrant are legitimately thrown open to him. The only restriction is that he employ them for a proper end (the common good as defined by Machiavelli) and that he have reasonable grounds to assume that the selected means will be conducive to the attainment of the desired objective.

In classical and Christian thought, the means must always be commensurate or proportionate to the end. To speak of evil means and a good objective is incomprehensible. Actions which deviate from the natural or divine law are considered morally wrong and no end, no matter how elevated, can possibly justify them. The traditional belief that certain acts are intrinsically wrong regardless of the end for which they are performed is well expressed by Aristotle in the following passage:

---

[9] *Discourses, op. cit.,* I, 9.   [10] *Ibid.*   [11] *The Prince, op. cit.,* p. 66.

But not every action nor every passion admits of a means; for some have names that already imply badness, e.g., spite, shamelessness, envy, and in the case of actions, adultery, theft, murder; for all of these and such like things imply by their names that they are themselves bad, and not the excesses or deficiencies of them. It is not possible, then, ever to be right with regard to them; one must always be wrong. Nor does goodness or badness with regard to such things depend on committing adultery with the right woman, at the right time, and in the right way, but simply to do any of them is to do wrong.[12]

Machiavelli's treatment of ends and means marks an abrupt break with this past. He himself acknowledges the radical innovation of his approach:

I break away completely from the principles laid down by my predecessors. But my intention being to write something of use to those who understand, it appears to me more proper to go to the real truth of the matter than to its imagination . . . for how we live is so far removed from how we ought to live, that he who abandons what is done for what ought to be done, will rather learn to bring about his own ruin than his preservation.[13]

Machiavelli seeks to avoid the logical difficulty implicit in the question of ends and means by isolating the political sphere for separate analysis and by emancipating its laws from the regulation of morality. No recognition of natural law, only a challenge to it, is found in this line of thinking. The whole cast of the new social philosophy prohibits the regulation of political and social conduct by reference to any transcendent moral norm. It would be patently inconsistent to link a doctrine of unmitigated expediency to the existence of a natural law. One or the other must be relegated to the scrap heap. Machiavelli's choice is clear and unequivocal.

PUBLIC AND PRIVATE MORALITY

If it is true, as Machiavelli seems to hold, that moral considerations can be restricted to the individual's private life, it would then be possible to place the governance of the state upon a wholly amoral and pragmatic basis. And if such is the case, the ruler would act under a double standard of conduct. As a private individual, his behavior should conform to his religious and moral convictions. When he acts in the capacity of a public official, his actions must be regulated solely by practical consequences without regard for moral considerations. This dichotomy be-

---

[12] *Nicomachean Ethics*, II, 6.   [13] *The Prince, op. cit.*, p. 56.

comes especially noticeable at a time of national crisis, "for when on the decision to be taken wholly depends the safety of one's country, no attention should be paid either to justice or injustice, to kindness or cruelty, or to its being praiseworthy or ignominious. On the contrary, every other consideration being set aside, that alternative should be wholeheartedly adopted which will save the life and preserve the freedom of one's country."[14]

The question of public and private morality is one of the most important issues raised by Machiavelli. Are the rules of morality different for the statesman than they are for the private individual? Is there a double standard of ethics or a special political morality that gives the public official more latitude than the private individual? For the traditionalist, the answer is an emphatic no. He recognizes no bifurcated standard of conduct but regards evil as always evil whether committed in a public or private capacity. In terms of Christian ethics, the morals of the statesman qua statesman and those of the individual qua individual are governed by precisely the same laws. Since the application of these laws may differ in given historical situations, prudence may dictate that the government official follow a course of conduct in a matter of public concern different from that which he would pursue were the matter one of private relations. In either case, the standard would remain the same.[15]

By isolating the political sphere for separate analysis and by divorcing political from private morality, Machiavelli is able to view the state and society in a purely amoral and detached manner. Man's ethical concerns and religious beliefs matter little in the formulation of a public philosophy since they belong to an entirely different arena. Machiavelli would have enthusiastically applauded Hitler's insincere pre-war treaties and Stalin's cleverly devised purges of the 1930's as strokes of master statesmanship. No moral scruples would have caused him to condemn these acts. They would have been perfectly justified in his eyes since their objective was the retention and stabilization of political power.

NOTION OF THE COMMON GOOD AND VIRTUE

Machiavelli's use of traditional terminology, such as the common good

---

[14] *Discourses, op. cit.*, III, 41.
[15] For an interesting discussion of this point in nontechnical terms see Joyce Cary, "Political and Personal Morality," *The Saturday Review*, Dec. 31, 1955.

and virtue, has contributed greatly to the difficulty in interpreting his thought. To resolve the differences which appear to be irreconcilable in his writings, it is necessary to compare his use of the terms common to the history of political thought with the traditional meaning attached to them. Once his understanding of these common expressions is clearly understood, the consistency of his political theory becomes more evident.

In the Graeco-medieval concept of the common good, two basic elements are present: the good must be for the commonalty, not for the benefit of the ruler or for any particular individual; and what is good for the community is that which is rooted in and measured by the natural law, not that which is based on the arbitrary will of man. Machiavelli accepts the first attribute but rejects the second. He insists that the political ruler must not act for his own advantage but for that of the people. At the same time he determines the validity of the prince's action not by any moral standard, but by the pragmatic test of success measured in terms of stabilizing and preserving political power. If everything that is successful is good morally speaking, Machiavelli's differences with the main stream of western thought would not be great; but the inconsistency of trying to equate success with goodness is too patent. Traditionally, goodness or badness is a matter to be determined in the light of the natural and divine law. By rejecting this standard, Machiavelli severs the notion of the common good from its ancient and moral source. He maintains that if a ruler acts out of love for his country and is successful, his efforts are in the interests of the common good. The traditionalist insists that simply because a ruler acts in behalf of the people, it does not necessarily follow that his acts are good; all that can be said is that they fulfill the element of commonalty.

Machiavelli's use of the term "virtue" has caused similar difficulties. No word occurs with greater frequency in *The Prince* and the *Discourses* than *virtù*. The notorious Cesare Borgia is described as a man who rose to power because of his great virtue. So also, the Roman general Severus is depicted as a person of eminent virtue despite his extreme cruelty and rapaciousness. It is quite apparent that Machiavelli employs the term in a purely political sense without any ethical significance. He describes *virtù* almost wholly in reference to the means one might employ in order to attain a chosen end. The virtuous man is marked by his skill in choosing effective means, in utilizing them with strength and vigor, and in resolutely seeking to achieve his goal, whatever it might be. The virtuous prince is the successful, efficient, and able ruler. Whether he attains his objectives by corrupt, wicked, or even treacherous means is of no matter so long as his actions are designed to benefit the people. Thus Agathocles, a Sicilian ruler, is criticized by Machiavelli for killing his fellow citizens and betraying his friends because these acts were performed for his personal aggrandizement and not for the good of his country.

Machiavelli also occasions some confusion by insisting that the prince should ordinarily be truthful and honest. Yet here again, these statements are nothing more than expressions of the pragmatic attitude that "honesty is the best policy." The reason for being truthful or honest in public life is not that such conduct is ethically proper but that it is the most expedient way of acting under the particular circumstances. "Thus it is well to seem merciful, faithful, humane, sincere, religious, and also to be so; but you must have the mind so disposed that when it is needful to be otherwise you may be able to change to the opposite qualities."[16] It is useful or good policy, in other words, for one to possess such attributes because generally they are of assistance in attaining desired ends. Dishonesty and corruption often lead to the downfall of those who resort to their use.

THE PRINCE AND THE DISCOURSES

Another major problem in trying to understand Machiavelli arises from the apparently flagrant contradictions that exist between The Prince and the Discourses. From a reading of the latter, we discover that the Florentine's chief concern is the good of the Italian people; in the former we are furnished with what is sometimes characterized as a "handbook for tyrants." Modern scholarship endeavors to reconcile the two by pointing out that The Prince must be read in the light of the Discourses. An example of this is found in Max Lerner's introduction to The Prince in which he insists that when we talk of Machiavelli we must keep the Discourses in mind as well; and that if we are to judge a man, it is fairer to judge him by the book which contains his whole system of politics rather than by the pamphlet which he dashed off to influence or win the graces of a particular personage.[17]

The argument for considering the two works together is certainly

---

16 The Prince, op. cit., p. 65.
17 Modern Library edition, op. cit., p. xxxvi.

valid, but in following this procedure cognizance must be taken of the manner in which Machiavelli uses traditional terms. If, for example, the investigator finds that the Discourses point to the common good as the primary end of political action, and if he accepts that term in its traditional sense, he cannot by any feat of legerdemain reconcile the two works. For when he comes to The Prince, he immediately discovers (if he has not already done so in the Discourses) that the ruler is permitted to use immoral means to achieve the general welfare. Thus only if the common good is understood in an amoral sense, as Machiavelli means it to be throughout his political writings, does The Prince become intelligible in the light of the Discourses. If tyrannical rule is necessary to attain the common good, then tyranny shall it be. If the people have to be forced to be "free," then let force be used.

There is a second discrepancy between the two works that relates to the type and form of governmental rule. In the Discourses, Machiavelli declares himself in favor of a republican form of government presumably with a large area of personal freedom and political participation for the individual. Conversely, The Prince deals exclusively with states ruled by a single person with supreme and absolute power. In seeking to reconcile these two approaches, some commentators contend that although Machiavelli considered a republic as the ideal form of government, he recognized that such a type can exist only when the historical circumstances and the political characteristics of a people are favorable. Since the Italy of his day was disunited and torn with strife, and since the people as well as their public officials had sunk into a state of extreme political corruption, the time was inopportune for republican government. Hence, the argument goes, Machiavelli was reluctantly compelled to insist that the only type of rule which would be successful in Italy would be that of a virtual tyrant who could crush all opposition and unify the country.

An interpretation of this kind may seem reasonable, but it overlooks the fact that Machiavelli's psychology and the basic principles which underlie both of his major political works scarcely permit any form of government other than that which he describes in The Prince. If man is by nature perverse and thoroughly corrupt and if morality has no place in public life, then a ruthless and absolute tyrant is needed to suppress the viciousness of the people and to maintain order. It would be ridiculous to entrust any degree of political power to a mass of people possessed of the nature which the Florentine attributes to them.

By looking upon political rule as an independent force governed by its own functional laws and dissociated with whatever moral principles might apply to men's private actions, Machiavelli's political philosophy opens the door to unlimited state action — to fascist totalitarianism as well as Hobbesian absolutism. His theoretical framework commits him, in short, to the necessity of absolute power, preferably perhaps in the hands of a benevolent prince, but absolute regardless of who might hold it. Therefore, even when *The Prince* is interpreted within the framework of the *Discourses*, the antidemocratic character of Machiavelli's thinking still remains unmistakably evident.

FORTUNE

Machiavelli's plan to formulate universal laws of political conduct and social behavior starts from the premise of the physical scientist that all natural events obey the same invariable laws. It seeks to show that the political scientist works with history to discover the laws governing the social order in much the same manner that the chemist studies with cold detachment the action and reaction of physical substances. Machiavelli feels that by following this process, definite guides can be found to the concrete problems which face the contemporary statesman. Yet in spite of the confidence with which he approaches his subject, he is too much of a realist to disregard the element of unpredictability in human affairs. He is well aware that while man may anticipate the future to a certain degree, he cannot foretell it with any high measure of certitude. This factor of unreliability poses the problem of how the principle of universal determinism can be made applicable to the field of politics, as *The Prince* and the *Discourses* seek to make it.

Ernst Cassirer has pointed out that the clear dichotomy between Machiavelli's "scientism" and the actual conduct of human affairs was one of the great puzzles that his political theory was forced to face. The Florentine on occasions had found his political experience in flagrant contradiction to his general scientific principles, and he had seen that even the best political advice is sometimes ineffective. A ruler may be observing the lessons of the past with due diligence only to be thwarted in his designs by a sudden and unexpected change in the course of affairs. Did these vicissitudes mean that there is no necessity in political events and that, contrasted with the physical realm, the social and political order is governed by mere chance? Cassirer believes that Machiavelli saw this apparent contradiction clearly but that his logical and rational method was unable to solve it and, in fact, deserted him at this point. Forced to admit that human actions are not entirely describable in terms of reason or scientific principles, Machiavelli turns for explanation not to the Christian concept of Divine Providence but to the essentially pagan idea of Fortune, "an impetuous river that when turbulent inundates the plains, casts down trees and buildings, removes earth from this side and places it on the other."[18]

Presumably, Machiavelli feels that if man could understand the role that Fortune plays in history, he could master and utilize it for his own advantage, "for if one could change one's nature with time and circumstances, fortune would never change."[19] The ruler who is able to adapt his actions to the needs and spirit of the times, who can act cautiously when caution is demanded and impetuously when impetuousness is called for, can control and harness Fortune to his own use. Those who are not afraid to resist the demands of Fortune and who refuse to be subdued by her are destined for success. "Fortune is a woman, and it is necessary, if you wish to master her, to conquer her by force; and it can be seen that she lets herself be overcome by the bold rather than by those who proceed coldly. And therefore, like a woman, she is always a friend to the young, because they are less cautious, fiercer, and master her with greater audacity."[20] Little of the scientific method remains evident in this mythical description; yet is Machiavelli to be blamed for failing to explain the inscrutable truths of the universe in empirical terms?

THE NATURE OF THE STATE

Machiavelli has little to say about the nature and organization of the state. Although he treats it as existing in its own right without reference to any higher order, he never asks the question, "what is the state?" The conception of the community as an organic growth which the political rulers can affect only to a limited degree is entirely absent in his thinking. He shows no awareness of the corporate character of the

---

[18] *The Prince, op. cit.*, p. 91.   [19] *Ibid.*, p. 93.   [20] *Ibid.*, p. 94.

body politic. His distrust of human nature leads him to place the political ruler outside the group and even to free him from the morality enforced within the society. Despite his expressed preference for the Roman Republic, his state approaches closer to the leviathan of Hobbes than the organic commonwealth of the classicists.

There are no specifically formulated ideas as to the range of state functions in Machiavelli's writings. His theory certainly includes no conception of the principle of subsidiarity as an operative standard to be applied in the interest of individual self-fulfillment. Apparently, he would permit an area of freedom to the people so long as it did not interfere with the safety and stability of the political order. Yet if legislation and social organization must proceed from the fact that man is basically evil, the range of political liberty that can safely be allowed is indeed narrow. At any rate, whatever freedom the people possess to exercise initiative in the political community would be granted in the interest of expediency and not of ethical right.

SUMMARY

In a prefatory note to an article which appeared several years ago in the *Saturday Review*, the editors remarked that "the politician lives in a world of half truths, complexities, and impurities not because he is a liar or a crook but because that's the way he finds the world."[21] Machiavelli would have fully concurred with this observation since it expresses so well the point that he was seeking to emphasize. If a man desires to improve the social order, he must not blind himself to the realities of human conduct. As a political scientist, he must study and try to understand things as they are, he must face the unpleasant as well as the agreeable, he must realize that political theory cannot be formulated in an ivory tower. Only if man thoroughly understands the functioning of the social and political processes in a time and space context can he hope to contend with the evil that exists and to lead society toward a better life. Machiavelli's insistence on empirical research to determine the "what is" in the political order came as a wholesome leaven to an age that was far too inclined to overlook the necessity of experiential investigation. Unfortunately, however, the Florentine's real significance in the history of western civilization does not lie in his contributions to social methodology but in his philosophical justification for political amorality.

Prior to Machiavelli, there had been rulers who had acted in a corrupt, ruthless, and tyrannical style; but no political thinker had sought to justify such actions on philosophical grounds. Before Machiavelli rulers had felt guilty

---

[21] See Joyce Cary, "Political and Personal Morality," *op. cit.*

or at least shameful in using such methods. After him, they could feel that in employing injustice for establishing order they were accomplishing their duty as political heads of state. Few expressions in political history have had greater significance than the passage in The Prince which sums up the doctrine known as Machiavellianism. "A man who wishes to make a profession of goodness in everything must necessarily come to grief among so many who are not good. Therefore it is necessary for a prince, who wishes to maintain himself, to learn how not to be good, and to use this knowledge and not use it, according to the necessity of the case."[22] For Machiavelli, the doctrine "live as the world lives" is the same as the ordinary vulgar belief that morality does not pay. Such a doctrine is clearly an invitation to immorality. Its only purport is to reduce the conduct of good men to the standards of the worst.[23]

The good prince must be one who is not attached to the principles of morality since the observance of such laws might hamstring him in his efforts to achieve the common good. But who is to be the judge of this common good? Obviously, no one but the prince himself. And "if the common good could justify all those things that are recommended in Machiavelli's book, if it could be used as an excuse for fraud and deception, felony, and cruelty, it would hardly be distinguishable from the common evil."[24]

Machiavelli is often referred to as the father of "power politics," a term that has assumed such great importance in the modern era. Power is for those who have the skill to seize it and the ability to hold it. The traumatic experience with the politics of his day undoubtedly blinded Machiavelli to the fact that the mystery of power is not the whole of politics, for the pertinent reason that the lust for power is not all there is to human values. Thus, while the author of The Prince was not oblivious to other factors in politics, his picture of political reality was certainly out of focus.[25]

Power politics existed long before Machiavelli's time. What he did was not only to recognize its existence and raise its problems to the level of scientific study but, more importantly, to free it from all moral limitations. This detachment followed from his basic premise that politics has a value system of its own which is different from that of personal ethics. He looked upon power as the nexus of this system since without power the realization of social goals is impossible. Hence anything which is conducive to the acquisition, retention, and expansion of political power is justified even though it may be distinctly evil from the viewpoint of private morality and religion.

Traditional thought finds no quarrel with the observation that power is a necessary element in government, but it insists that power is only a means for the attainment of given ends — ends that are determined by the nature

---

[22] The Prince, p. 56.
[23] H. Butterfield, The Statecraft of Machiavelli (New York: Macmillan, 1956), pp. 112–113.
[24] Ernst Cassirer, The Myth of the State, op. cit., p. 145.
[25] See Eric Voegelin, "Machiavelli's Prince: Background and Formation," Review of Politics, Apr., 1951.

of man. The use of power to achieve these goals must be commensurate and proportionate to the objectives. The force of the state must be rightful force, and its goodness or badness must be determined by its conformity to moral norms, and not solely by its success or lack of success in achieving political victories. The peculiar connotation which is today attached to the term "power politics" — that naked force or measures of pure expediency can and in fact should be used if necessary to attain the purposes of the state — is distinctly the offspring of Machiavellian political philosophy.

BIBLIOGRAPHY

Abraham, H. J., "Was Machiavelli a Machiavellian?" Social Science, January, 1953.
Burnham, James, The Machiavellians (New York: John Day, 1943).
Burns, E. M., "Liberalism of Machiavelli," Antioch Review, September, 1948.
Butterfield, Herbert, The Statecraft of Machiavelli (New York: Macmillan, 1956).
Cassirer, Ernst, The Myth of the State (New Haven: Yale University Press, 1946).
Ferrero, Guglielmo, "Machiavelli and Machiavellianism," Foreign Affairs, April, 1939.
Gilbert, Allan H., Machiavelli's Prince and Its Forerunners (Durham: Duke University Press, 1938).
Gilbert, Felix, "The Humanist Concept of the Prince," Journal of Modern History, December, 1939.
———— "The Composition and Structure of Machiavelli's Discorsi," Journal of the History of Ideas, January, 1953.
Hancock, W. K., "Machiavelli in Modern Dress: An Inquiry into Historical Method," History, September, 1935.
Kraft, J., "Truth and Poetry in Machiavelli," Journal of Modern History, June, 1951.
Maritain, Jacques, "The End of Machiavellianism," Review of Politics, January, 1942.
McCoy, Charles N. R., "The Place of Machiavelli in the History of Political Thought," American Political Science Review, August, 1943.
Strauss, Leo, "Machiavelli's Intentions," American Political Science Review, March, 1957.
Voegelin, Eric, "Machiavelli's Prince: Background and Formation," Review of Politics, April, 1951.
Whitfield, John H., Machiavelli (Oxford: Blackwell, 1957).

Chapter XI

THE SOVEREIGN STATE

"Behind the Western bars
The shrouded day retreats,
And unperceived the stars
Steal to their sovran seats"
(Robert Bridges, *The Clouds Have Left the Sky*).

THE outstanding political fact of the sixteenth and seventeenth centuries is the substitution of the national state for the dynastic feudalism of the middle ages. As western Christendom developed into separate and competing states, the tradition of European unity was gradually discarded. In the transformation, political speculation became cast within the framework and in terms of the new political unit. Just as the center of political thought in antiquity was the city-state and in the middle ages universal empire, so the national state became the central concept of modern political theory.

During the medieval period there had been no clear conception of the state as a sovereign body exercising supreme power within its own borders and enjoying complete independence from other political entities that existed outside its territorial limits. The presence of two spheres of authority — church and state — each with its own organization and legal system, the decentralizing effects of feudalism on political control, and the fiction of universal empire made the idea of national sovereignty difficult of comprehension. Professor Merriam cites four obstacles that stood in the way of a strong doctrine on the nature of sovereignty during the middle ages: (1) the idea of the dominance of divine and natural law over positive law; (2) the church-state conflict; (3) the prevalent idea in favor of a mixed form of government; and (4) the feudal condition of the state.[1]

---

[1] Charles E. Merriam, *History of the Theory of Sovereignty Since Rousseau* (New York: Columbia University Press, 1900), p. 13.

The classical writers and the medievalists realized the necessity of a supreme power in the body politic. They knew that there must be some person or agency at the top with power to make final political decisions which are not appealable to any higher governmental authority. They did not, however, view this supreme power as absolute; they regarded it as subject to divine, natural, and customary law. With the appearance of the national state and its centralized monarchy, the traditional idea of a supreme political power began to undergo basic modifications that radically changed its character. The first evidences of change appeared in the political thought of the late sixteenth century.

The new development proceeded along two lines, the one theological, the other essentially juridical, both lending theoretical justification to the growing trend toward absolutism. The first, known as the divine right theory, holds that the ruler receives his authority directly from God; the second, the theory of "genuine" sovereignty, maintains that a determinate authority standing above the law and the community must exist somewhere in the state. Except for a brief flourish in France and England, the first theory met with little acceptance in western thought. In an age when religion was being placed on the defensive, no political doctrine grounded on a purely theological foundation could hope to endure. On the other hand, the lay concept of sovereignty as the *sine qua non* of the state grew in importance and significance.

The present chapter will first examine the theory of divine right and then turn to two writers, Jean Bodin and Hugo Grotius, as representatives of the new concept of the state: the one dealing with the internal aspects of sovereignty, the other with its external character.

THEORY OF THE DIVINE RIGHT OF KINGS

Medieval thought had stressed the sacredness of secular rule and the necessity of submission to it so long as it remained just. While the Protestant thinkers of the Reformation had placed even greater emphasis on the divine character of political authority, the concept had generally persisted that the king's power came both from God and from the people. None of the reformers had attempted to formulate in specific and theoretical terms the idea that the ruler received his authority by a direct act of divine intervention and therefore stood outside and above the community. So long as the doctrine of passive obedience predominated in the growing national states, the supporters of royal absolutism were content to leave existing theory undisturbed. However, when religious spokesmen, both Protestant and Catholic, began to advance the doctrine of active popular resistance to tyrannical rule, some royalist supporters countered by seeking to invest the king with a special sanctity.

A typical proponent of the theological argument was William Barclay, a Scotch Catholic who had taken refuge in France. In his treatise, *De regno et regali potestate*, published in 1600, Barclay undertook a theoretical exposition of the source and nature of royal authority. Admitting that the form of government, and even the manner of selecting the prince, is a matter to be determined by human law, he maintains that once this has been settled, God bestows political authority directly on the ruler. This authority is superior to that of the whole people and cannot be violated or controlled by them. The actions of kings are reserved for Divine judgment; others must answer to the king for their acts, but he is accountable only to God. Those who claim authority to judge or resist the monarch are guilty of a great offense against God.[2]

James I of England writes in a similar vein: "Kings are breathing images of God upon earth . . . the state of monarchy is the supremest thing upon earth; for kings are not only God's lieutenants upon earth, and sit upon God's throne, but even by God himself they are called God."[3] Answering the claim that Parliament is the lawmaking organ of the realm, James replies that this body is but the creation of the royal will and its part in legislation is entirely subordinate. It can make no law without the approval of the king; and since the king is in effect the author of the law, he is necessarily above the law. To resist the monarch is contrary both to the divine law as revealed in Scripture and to human reason for not only is the king appointed by God but he is the binding force that holds the state together.

The divine right theory means in essence that the ruler receives the temporal sword through the divine law in the same manner that the pope, according to Catholic dogma, is invested with the spiritual sword. Such a doctrine removes the question of political power from the arena of nature and reason and places it in the realm of the supernatural and theological. James admits this when he says that the royal office is a "mystery" into which neither lawyers nor philosophers may inquire.

---

[2] For an account of Barclay's thought see Carlyle, *op. cit.*, Vol. 6, p. 455 ff.

[3] See Charles H. McIlwain, *The Political Works of James I* (Cambridge: Harvard University Press, 1918).

JEAN BODIN: THE THEORY OF THE SOVEREIGN STATE

The divine right pamphleteers had advanced a theory of sovereignty founded on a theological basis, but the doctrine was foredoomed to failure in an era when secular tendencies were on the ascendant. The new age was receptive only to a theory of state authority that was divorced from any divine roots. Thus even though the divine right doctrine and the concept of legal sovereignty had similar objectives — the theoretical justification of strong if not absolute rule — the influence of the former on political speculation was relatively meager and short-lived while the impact of the latter on the future course of state development was profound.

The name generally associated with the origin of the modern concept of sovereignty is Jean Bodin (1530–1596). Born in Anjou, France, of a well-to-do middle class family, Bodin studied philosophy and languages in Paris and law at Toulouse, where he spent ten years as student and teacher. In 1561 he left the teaching profession to engage in the practice of law in Paris. Ten years later he entered the household of the King's brother, the Duke of Alençon, to serve as counselor. Here he came into contact with the world of high politics, and like Machiavelli, he made good use of the opportunities of his position to extend his knowledge of state affairs. Bodin's political thinking was developed under pressure of personal experience. He lived at a time when the prolonged religious struggles, culminating in the St. Bartholomew Massacre of 1572, had brought France to the brink of disaster. Early in his career he became associated with a small group of distinguished lawyers and administrators including the French chancellor, Michel de L'Hopital. His own superior, the Duke of Alençon was the official leader of this party which was known as the *Politiques*.

The *Politiques* realized that the state would be torn asunder if the religious wars continued. They were also aware that the division of Christianity had become too deep to be cemented together by force and persecution. They held that the state is primarily concerned with the maintenance of order and not the preservation or establishment of the true religion. Some contemporary philosophers were maintaining that genuine Christianity does not require the extermination or physical coercion of opponents of the faith; it asks only that they be convinced by reason, converted by instruction, or quietly tolerated. The Politiques were motivated by no such feelings. They did not commend religious toleration as morally or theologically correct; they advocated it merely as a policy of expediency rendered necessary by the historical exigencies of the day.

Standing between two extremes — Catholics and Huguenots — the Politiques sought to provide a middle ground that would prevent the division of France into two irreconcilable camps and that would permit political unity despite religious diversity. They were convinced that the only hope of accomplishing this objective lay in the creation of a strong central authority standing above all religious sects and political factions. They knew that such an authority must possess the means of enforcing peace and order and the unqualified right to demand obedience. Since the monarchy appeared to be the only agency capable of assuming such a role, they directed their efforts toward strengthening the royal power and elevating it as the center of national unity. Bodin was the chief theoretician in this movement.

Bodin's best known work is his *Six Books of the Commonwealth*. Ten editions of this work in the French version and three in Latin appeared during his lifetime. The book was also translated into Italian, Spanish, German, and English. It is of major significance as the first treatise dealing with the modern theory of sovereignty. The work displays the vast erudition of its author but it is of excessive length, rambling in style, and at points confusing in thought if not contradictory. Yet in spite of these drawbacks, the *Commonwealth* offers the most mature statement of political philosophy in the sixteenth century. With irreconcilable views being expressed on all sides as to the nature of political power and civic obligation, Bodin undertook to set forth the fundamental principles on which a permanent social order must be based. He believed that the first task was to obtain a clearer understanding of political authority. He felt that before such insight would be possible, some principle of order had to be discovered that would reconcile human liberty and state authority as well as satisfy conscience and reason. He purported to find this basic element in his doctrine of sovereignty.

Nature of the State

Unlike Machiavelli, Bodin does not rush into a discussion of the means of attaining and preserving political power. He considers it essential to establish first of all the nature and ends of the state before turning

ctives. "The man who does not
define his subject, has no hope
more than the man who shoots
hit the mark."[4] Bodin, however,
-ded approach, particularly that
of ends. He starts out by in-
the good and virtuous life of its
t of the subject altogether. His
eans of preserving the state re-
ans of promoting the good life
he gives to the state vanishes with
ized power as a true state. His
tions, is essentially Machiavellian.
y ordered government of several
ests by a sovereign power."[5] He
nents to be observed here: right
and that which is of common
in accordance with the laws of
nity that distinguishes it from a
or happy life which the ancients
t a necessary term of the definition
e sought. For "a commonwealth
with poverty, abandoned by its
ought low by every sort of mis-

that the family rather than the
te. It is "not only the true source
it also its principal constituent."[7]
It is, morever, a natural community from which all the more complex
societies arise. Authority over the members of the family is vested in
the head of the household. Bodin is convinced that human beings, as a
result of the Fall, are wicked and rebellious. He believes that man's
chief need is discipline to curb his factious and evil spirit. This attitude
leads him to stress authority and power whether it be in the father
of a family or the ruler of a state. He urges that paternal authority be
strengthened even to the extent of life and death over the children.

---

[4] Six Books of the Commonwealth, I, 1, trans. by M. J. Tooley (Oxford: Blackwell).
[5] Ibid.   [6] Ibid.   [7] Ibid., I, 2.

Only in this way can the habit of obedience be instilled in them, so that later they will become obedient citizens of the ruler. "Children who stand in little awe of their parents, and have even less fear of the wrath of God, readily set at defiance the authority of magistrates."[8] The training of the good citizen must start in the nursery.

The well-ordered family "is a true image of the commonwealth." The model for political governance is found in the rule of the father over his household. Just as in the family, subordination to the will of the father is essential to the well-being of the home, so is obedience to the ruler necessary to the stability of the state. And as the father has absolute authority over his family, so the ruler of the commonwealth must have complete jurisdiction over his subjects. "For a family is like a state: there can be only one ruler, one master, one lord. If several persons were in positions of authority, they might issue contrary orders and continual turmoil would result."[9]

While Bodin follows Aristotle in stressing the family as the primary unit of society, he refuses to accept his predecessor's distinction between the rule of the father over his household (one of superior over inferior) and political rule (one of equals over equals). In Aristotelian thought, the rule of the father is not based on the consent of his children, but the rule of civil government to be legitimate must rest on the consent of the governed. By disregarding this distinction, Bodin is able to employ the analogy of the household to suit the purposes of his political theory.

According to Bodin, the state has its origin in force and violence. Before there were any forms of political association, each head of a family "was sovereign in his household, having power of life and death over his wife and children." But something like a Hobbesian state of nature prevailed. "Force, violence, ambition, avarice and the passion for vengeance armed men against one another."[10] These unsatisfactory conditions led groups of families to unite for their common defense and other mutual advantages and to recognize a sovereign political power, a *puissance souveraine*. The recognition of such an authority was more often accomplished by force than by voluntary acceptance. Aristotle and others are wrong, Bodin asserts, in thinking that the first rulers were chosen for their justice and virtue. On the contrary, they were men who possessed the physical force necessary to subject others to their will.

---

8 *Ibid.*, I, 3–4.   9 *Ibid.*   10 *Ibid.*, I, 6.

Sovereignty

Bodin holds that the element which distinguishes the state from all other forms of human association is sovereignty. There can be no true commonwealth without sovereign power to unite all its several members. An absolute and supreme authority which is subject to no other human power must be located somewhere in the body politic. This is the first and most fundamental principle of Bodin's political theory. He calls attention early in his work to the necessity of defining the concept of sovereignty "because although it is the distinguishing mark of a commonwealth and an understanding of its nature fundamental to any treatment of politics, no jurist or political philosopher has in fact attempted to define it."[11] His effort to remedy what he considers the failure of his predecessors is unfortunately not free from difficulties.

Sovereignty, as Bodin defines it "is the absolute and perpetual power vested in a commonwealth"; it is "supreme power over citizens and subjects unrestrained by the laws."[12] The essential qualities of sovereignty are absoluteness, permanence, and indivisibility. The person or agency possessing sovereignty cannot be limited by any other power or by any human laws. A sovereign prince has no mortal peer; "he acknowledges no one greater than himself save only God." Sovereignty is permanent since there are no time limits placed on its exercise. Once it is vested in the ruler, he enjoys it for his lifetime. "So that sovereignty is not limited either in power, charge, or time certain." Finally, sovereignty is indivisible since divided sovereignty would be a contradiction in terms. "Just as Almighty God cannot create another God equal with Himself, since he is infinite and two infinities cannot co-exist, so the sovereign prince, who is the image of God, cannot make a subject equal with himself without self-destruction."[13]

The peculiar and essential mark of sovereignty is the power to make laws. "The first attribute of the sovereign prince is the power to make law binding on all his subjects in general and on each in particular" and he exercises this power "without the consent of any superior, equal, or inferior being necessary."[14] The medievalists looked upon law as found rather than made. They regarded it not so much as a command of a governmental authority but as a custom expressive of the life of the

---

11 *Ibid.*, I, 8.   13 *Ibid.*, I, 10.
12 *Ibid.*   14 *Ibid.*

community.[15] Bodin breaks with the past in this respect by relegating custom to a subordinate position. He is emphatic in his assertion that it has force "only on suffrance and during the good pleasure of the sovereign prince and so far as he is willing to authorize it . . . the force of both statutes and customary law derives from the authorization of the prince."[16]

The sovereign is bound neither by the laws which he or his predecessor made nor by the practices of his people. Such laws and customs, even though they may be based on sound reasons, depend solely on his free will. The element of reason so strongly stressed by St. Thomas in his definition of law is given an inferior and gratuitous role, while the will of the legislator becomes the primary factor. Bodin was not the first to think of law in terms of a command made by the political ruler but his theory represents a much sharper enunciation of the concept.

Up to this point, Bodin's doctrine of sovereignty appears to be an expression of absolute and unlimited power in the state. He has, however, no intention of going this far as he plainly indicates. If absolute power is used in the sense of exemption from all law, "there is no prince in the world who can be regarded as sovereign, since all the princes of the earth are subject to the laws of God and of nature and even to certain human law common to all nations."[17] The ruler is therefore bound by those civil laws that "embody the principles of natural justice" since laws of this kind, "though published by the prince's authority, are properly natural laws."[18] He is also subject to certain constitutional or fundamental laws of the realm (*leges imperii*). These laws forbid the sovereign to alter the Salic law pertaining to royal succession, to alienate any part of the public domain, or to take private property without the consent of the owner.

It is not difficult to reconcile Bodin's divine and natural limitations on political power with the absolute character of sovereignty, since these restrictions would still leave the ruler standing above human law and accountable only to God. The confusion lies in the other qualifications which he makes since these include matters solely of human law. If sovereignty is essentially the power to make laws, and if such power cannot be divided or legally conditioned, it is illogical to subject the ruler to laws which he has not made and which he cannot change.

---

[15] See *ante*, pp. 157–158.
[16] *Six Books of the Commonwealth, op. cit.*, I, 10.
[17] *Ibid.*, I, 8.
[18] *Ibid.*

Bodin's theory has consistency only if these human restrictions are viewed as embodiments of natural law. Jacques Maritain has so interpreted the Bodinian concept of sovereignty, maintaining that its author places the ruler under obligation to respect the *leges imperii*, because human laws of this nature actually enforce natural law itself.[19] He believes that Bodin erroneously considers such laws to be part of the natural law even though they contain limitations which do not have their source in man's nature, such as the inability of the sovereign to change the line of succession to the throne or to dispose of any part of the realm.

Bodin is careful to point out that while the rightly ordered state faithfully observes the natural and divine law, a commonwealth does not cease to be a true state if it violates these precepts. He objects to Aristotle's classification of governments into good and bad forms, maintaining that there are only three types of government and that these are distinguished by the location of sovereignty: in one man, in several, or in the multitude. Whether the political rule in a state is good or bad is only an accidental attribute. "If one adopts the principle of distinguishing between commonwealths according to the particular virtues and vices that are characteristic of each, one is soon faced with an infinity of variations." Bodin also rejects the idea of a mixed state on the ground that such a type with its division of powers cannot exist. Since sovereignty is by its very nature indivisible "how can a prince, a ruling class, and the people all have a part in it at the same time."[20] Under a mixed constitution there would be constant dispute as to whether sovereignty is vested in the prince or in a part or in the whole people. An examination of the so-called mixed state, Bodin claims, will reveal that sovereignty actually rests with the people and that the governing officials are merely serving as their agents. Such a commonwealth should properly be classified as a democracy.

The Significance of Bodin

In appraising Bodin's political philosophy, two questions might appropriately be asked: (1) is there anything new in his idea of sovereignty that distinguishes it from prior theory?; and (2) granting that he introduced a new element in the concept of political authority, what influence

---

[19] "The Concept of Sovereignty," *American Political Science Review*, June, 1950, p. 344.
[20] *Six Books of the Commonwealth*, op. cit., II, 1.

did it have on the future development of political thought? Bodin remained to a certain extent tributary to the medieval tradition, as evidenced by his insistence on the ruler's subjection to the natural and divine laws and to other specified limitations. The prince in this sense remains under the law. "It is a true mark of royal power that the ruler himself is just as obedient to the laws of nature as he desires his subject to be to him. . . . If the subjects obey the law laid down by their king, and he in turn obeys the laws of nature, then it is really the laws that rule."[21] Because Bodin imposes these restrictions on the ruler, some commentators feel that he stands at the crossroads between the medieval notion of the ruler as subject to the directive although not the coercive power of human law and the modern notion of the sovereign as completely free from any law on earth.[22] Maritain, on the other hand, contends that Bodin may rightly be considered as the father of the modern theory of sovereignty. Construing Bodin's doctrine to mean freedom of the sovereign from human law, he asserts that this is the essence of absolute rule; and absolutism is alien to medieval thought. "Yet the fact remains that Bodin's sovereign was subject only to Natural Law, and to no human law whatsoever, as distinct from Natural Law, and that is the core of political absolutism."[23]

If the classical and medieval concept of the state as a community of individuals having laws and a constitution of its own is correct, Bodin's attempt to identify sovereignty with the ruler is a logical impossibility. Sovereignty according to the traditional or organic view of the state rests in the political community and not in any individual who might be exercising public power at any particular time. To circumvent this difficulty, Bodin maintains that the people as a body politic absolutely and unconditionally divests itself of its total power in order to transfer it to a ruler. It is not a delegation but a total surrender of power. "The people have renounced and alienated its sovereign power in order to invest him with it and put him in possession, and it thereby transfers to him all its powers, authority and sovereign rights, just as does the man who gives to another possessory and proprietary rights over what he formerly owned."[24]

---

[21] Ibid., II, 3.
[22] See M. A. Shepard, "Sovereignty at the Crossroads. A Study of Bodin," Political Science Quarterly, 1930, pp. 580–603.
[23] "The Concept of Sovereignty," op. cit., p. 344.
[24] Six Books of the Commonwealth, op. cit., I, 8.

By this act of complete divestment, the sovereign assumes a position above and transcendent to the political whole in much the same way that God transcends the cosmos. Regardless of Bodin's intention, the implications of his thinking helped to lay the groundwork for the doctrine of pure absolutism. To arrive at such a doctrine, his theory had only to be stripped of the remaining restrictions that he had sought to retain. This surgical operation was skillfully performed later by Thomas Hobbes.[25]

A CRITIQUE OF "SOVEREIGNTY"

Since the question of absolute and unlimited political power in the state has been raised in a new form by Bodin, Maritain's perceptive criticism of sovereignty is briefly referred to at this point.[26] Maritain holds that sovereignty has two meanings: a right to supreme independence and power which is a natural right; and a right to an independence and power which is supreme absolutely and transcendentally. The first is compatible with traditional thought, the second deviates radically from it. The right of the body politic to full autonomy means that it governs itself with comparatively supreme independence. No one of its parts can, by usurping government, substitute itself for the whole and infringe upon its freedom of action. Externally, this right means that the state enjoys comparatively supreme independence with respect to the international community. The body politic derives its right to full autonomy from its nature as a perfect and self-sufficient society. The right is natural in the sense that it cannot be taken away without its consent.

The second meaning attached to sovereignty is peculiar to absolutism. According to it the power of the sovereign is not only supreme in relation to any other part of the political whole but is supreme absolutely speaking as being above and outside the whole in question. So conceived, sovereignty is a property which is absolute and indivisible, which cannot be participated in or admit of degrees, and which belongs to the Sovereign independently of the political whole, as a right of his own. Nothing remains here of the traditional view that the power of the state is only relatively supreme as proper to a given whole with respect to its parts.

---

[25] Bodin's work was translated into English and used as a textbook at Cambridge within a few years after its appearance in France. There is little doubt that it influenced Hobbes' thinking, particularly in the matter of sovereignty.

[26] "The Concept of Sovereignty," op. cit., pp. 343–357.

Maritain defines government as a party and an instrumental agency of the body politic. He points out that government has no right of its own to supreme independence and power. It has a right only to such comparatively supreme independence and power as it receives from the body politic. The acquisition of these prerogatives does not involve a transfer of title or ownership but a delegation of trust from the people. It is not necessary that this right be uprooted from the citizenry in order to be transferred to a ruler. A right may be possessed by one as belonging to his nature and by another as participated in by him. The prince is possessed of the right to rule only by participation in the people's right of self-governance.

The prince and others who exercise political authority are vicars or deputies of the people, performing in behalf of them a right which still exists in the commonalty. They are but a part of the political community at the service of the common good; they receive their right to rule within certain fixed limits from the people who exercise their fundamental right to govern themselves. This inherent right is in turn limited by the very nature of the civil community. Thus sovereignty in the first but not in the second meaning of the term can properly be attributed to the body politic or state; but in neither sense does it apply to the prince or government.

HUGO GROTIUS

Bodin was interested in the concept of sovereignty primarily as it applied to political power within a given territorial state. He said little as to the external aspect of sovereignty or the autonomy of the body politic in relation to other states. His definition of sovereignty, however, implied that each state has above itself no earthly power which it should be compelled to obey. Hugo Grotius (1583–1640), the great Dutch lawyer, takes this assumption for granted in his efforts to establish an international law.[27] He starts from the premise that formal or juridical equality exists among states and that they enjoy complete independence both of one another and of any supranational authority. Legally, all states, regardless of size or strength, stand on a basis of equality in the family of nations. To be eligible for membership in this group, a political unit must conform to certain standards of civilization. It must have a govern-

---

[27] Grotius was preceded and influenced in his efforts to formulate international law by the sixteenth-century Spaniards, Francisco de Vitoria and Francisco Suárez.

ment that is capable of entering into and observing treaties, and it must show evidence of stability and permanency. These are the principal characteristics of international status that are still recognized today.

The problem which Grotius faced was one of establishing a principle of order among a group of autonomous political units that operate in the same world but are legally subject to no superior power. He describes his task as one of demonstrating that there is a common law among nations, which is operative in both peace and war. To accomplish this objective, he had first to show how this law is determined and how it can be made binding on sovereign entities. If one accepts the theory that law is the product of the will of a lawgiver, a law of international scope is not possible without a supranational agency having legislative jurisdiction over the states. In the Prolegomena to his well-known work *De Jure Belli ac Pacis*, Grotius refutes any such notion of law by appealing to the long tradition of Greco-Christian political thought with its recognition of a transcendent moral law or an essential justice that is discovered in the nature of reality. He maintains that this natural law governs not only the internal operations and functions of the body politic but also determines the fundamental relations among states and their conduct toward each other.

The "Modernization" of Natural Law

While Grotius' analysis of the law of nations is beyond the scope of a treatise on political theory, his discussion of natural law as the basis of international order requires some examination. He defines natural law as "a dictate of right reason, which points out that an act, according as it is or is not in conformity with rational nature, has in it a quality of moral baseness or moral necessity; and that in consequence, such an act is either forbidden or enjoyed by the author of nature, God." Grotius goes on, however, to emphasize that his reference to God adds nothing to the definition and could well be omitted. "The law of nature . . . is unchangeable even in the sense that it cannot be changed by God. Measureless as is the power of God, nevertheless it can be said that there are certain things over which that power does not extend."[28] Man's infallible moral guide is in his reason which would correctly guide him even if there were no God, or "if He had no interest in mortal affairs."

---

[28] *De Jure Belli ac Pacis*, Book I, Chap. 1, sec. 10. Published in English under title *The Law of War and Peace* (Oxford: Clarendon Press, 1925).

For the principles of the natural law "are in themselves manifest and clear, almost as evident as are those which we perceive by the external senses."[29] Grotius apparently does not mean to imply (as his successors were soon to do) that morals and geometry are equally certain or that natural law can be rendered mathematically demonstrable, yet he does attempt to give a degree of precision to reason that it had not previously known. He speaks, for example, in terms of certain axiomatic propositions from which a wholly rational system of rules governing human conduct could be constructed.

Grotius clearly had no intention of denying the existence of God. Living in an age of religious controversy, he was probably trying to free natural law from any theological dimensions in order to prevent it from becoming involved in doctrinal differences. It is doubtful that he seriously intended to divorce natural law from the Divine Reason, since he indicated over and over again that God constitutes its ultimate source. Some writers, however, have interpreted him in this way. One of the more prominent of them is Samuel Pufendorf (1632–1694), a German jurist who wrote on international law several decades later. Pufendorf applauds Grotius for divorcing natural law from theology and religion by grounding it solely in the social nature and reason of men.

A theory which endeavored to sever the moral law from its theological foundations was amenable to the growing secular and scientific spirit of the day. By making the natural law independent of the authorship of God, secular man is able to accept it in the same way that he accepts a physical law of the universe without being compelled to submit to the authority of any supramundane reason. Similarly, Grotius' references to the possibility of a more precise method for discovering the contents of the natural law appealed to the current scientific temper. It remained for others, such as Pufendorf and Hobbes, to develop the implications contained in these ideas.

Significance of Grotius

Grotius' importance lies in the field of international law rather than political philosophy. Yet in an age when the question of national sovereignty was being raised in its most advanced form, the principles underlying correct behavior among autonomous states assumed increasing signif-

---

[29] *Ibid.*, sec. 39.

icance in the political arena. In accepting the independent character of the state, Grotius did not believe that it was necessary to establish a supergovernment standing above national units in order to preserve peace. At the same time, he realized that the international community can no more exist in peace and harmony without law than can the domestic society within a state. As one still within the pale of medieval influence, he looked to natural law as the primary source of the law by which sovereign states are guided and rightly ordered in their communication and association with each other.

Grotius also recognized the role played by custom and treaty; but what is important in his thinking from the standpoint of political philosophy is his insistence that states, despite their absolute character and the absence of any universal legislator, are subject to law and to a natural order. International law has not only the force of an agreement among states, such as might be evidenced in treaties, but also the force of a law which political rulers are under moral obligation to obey. Since Grotius provided for no institutional organ to promulgate and enforce this law, his critics have argued that his international law was not "real" law but only moral preachments. Modern scholarship treats him more kindly by acknowledging that the law of nations owes to natural law not only its beginning but also the concept, without which international law could not have been realized, that even sovereign states are subject to law.[30]

The content which Grotius attributes to the natural law conforms substantially to that which had been understood during the classical and medieval periods. The significance of his treatment of this subject lies both in his claim (at least as interpreted by some of his contemporaries) that the natural law exists independently of God and in his indication of a new method of arriving at its contents. Later theorists of the seventeenth and eighteenth centuries were to enlarge upon the premises implicit in his methodology by formulating a "scientific" or "rational" method of determining the principles and rules governing social and political conduct. From all indications, Grotius did not intend to deviate from the traditional concept of natural law, but only to enlarge upon those aspects that he considered helpful in establishing a theoretical foundation for an international order. His efforts succeeded

[30] See, for example, C. Eagleton, International Government (New York: The Ronald Press, 1957).

in giving to political speculation (which still persisted in the idiom of natural law) a character that was appealing to the more liberal and rationalistic elements of the modern world and also to the devotees of the new secular learning. Concomitantly, his efforts helped to pave the way for a radical departure from the very tradition of natural law that he was seeking to preserve.

Professor Hallowell has made the interesting suggestion that Grotius' findings as to the contents of natural law met with little dissent from his contemporaries since there was substantial agreement on what was morally self-evident; but what they regarded as self-evident was acceptable to them because it appealed not only to their reason but to their Christian consciences. That these same principles appear less reasonable to many persons in the twentieth century is due, not to the fact that the man of the present is more rational than his seventeenth-century ancestor, but that his conscience is less firmly rooted in Christian convictions.[31]

SUMMARY

The historical conditions which prevailed during the period of the Renaissance and Reformation necessitated a readaption of the theoretical schema of political science. The disintegration of the feudal system and the virtual collapse of western European unity paved the way for the emergence of the national territorial state. With it, although not so much a result as a cause, came the social and economic changes which molded the western world into a lay, industrial, and capitalistic culture. Bodin grasped the need for adjusting the theoretical framework of politics to meet the demands of a changed society. His solution to the new order with its particularistic tendencies was a strong central power capable of unifying the divergent forces and energies within the state and directing them toward a common goal. He sought to provide the necessary philosophical basis and justification for such a power in his theory of sovereignty. As he remarked, this is a new concept not mentioned in any of the Greek or medieval thinkers. For better or for worse, Bodin had fastened onto political theory a doctrine that was destined to play a major role in the modern world.

When Grotius wrote his treatise on international law several decades after Bodin's death, he sought to establish a law that would govern the relations among sovereign states — states that recognized no higher human power. There was no mention of empire or of any supranational government in his writings. The existence of separate, independent, autonomous, and sovereign states was taken for granted. He was aware that the formulation of any law

---

[31] *Main Currents in Modern Political Thought, op. cit.,* pp. 96–97.

applicable to the external relations of these political units had to proceed upon such an assumption. But legal autonomy and autonomy in fact are two quite different matters. With the passage of time, the actual interdependence of sovereign states became increasingly more evident. The political order could not remain unaffected as the social and economic pattern grew in complexity and as it began to transcend the territorial limits of national states. As these developments took place, man began to suspect the adequacy of a political form based on a theoretical foundation of national sovereignty.

Bodin and Grotius still wrote within the shadow of the medieval tradition. The ruler or sovereign, in their thought, is under a moral obligation both to God and the community. He is free only to employ moral means in the interest of the common good. Bodin sharply distinguished between the true sovereign who rules in the interest of justice and in accordance with the natural law, and the sovereign who disregards such principles. Machiavelli, who had preceded Bodin and Grotius by almost a century, had torn away from the ancient tradition, but his ideas had been too "advanced" for his age and had received almost universal condemnation. Only as the medieval influence receded could a theory that disregarded the ethical content of politics hope to win more than nominal acceptance. The time for this change was near at hand.

BIBLIOGRAPHY

Aufricht, Hans, "On Relative Sovereignty," Cornell Law Quarterly, March, 1945.

Campbell, D. W., "Sovereignty and Social Dynamics," American Political Science Review, October, 1934.

Cohen, H. E., Recent Theories of Sovereignty (Chicago: University of Chicago Press, 1937).

Cole, Kenneth C., "The Theory of the State as a Sovereign Juristic Person," American Political Science Review, February, 1948.

Connor, J. T., "Notion of Sovereignty in a Democratic State," American Catholic Philosophical Association Proceedings, 1939.

Dickenson, John, "A Working Theory of Sovereignty," Political Science Quarterly, December, 1927.

Farrell, W., "Philosophy of Sovereignty," American Catholic Philosophical Association Proceedings, 1939.

Greenleaf, W. H., "James I and the Divine Right of Kings," Political Studies, February, 1957.

Holsti, R., "Sociological Theory of Sovereignty," Institute of International Relations Proceedings, 1930.

Jouvenal, Bertrand de, Sovereignty: An Inquiry into the Political Good, trans. by J. F. Huntington (Chicago: University of Chicago Press, 1957).

Kirchheimer, Otto, "In Quest of Sovereignty," Journal of Politics, May, 1944.

Korff, S. H., "The Problem of Sovereignty," American Political Science Review, August, 1928.

McIlwain, Charles H., "A Fragment on Sovereignty," Political Science Quarterly, March, 1933.

Niemeyer, G., "National Sovereignty and Individual Behavior," *Journal of Politics*, August, 1947.

Parsons, Wilfrid, "St. Thomas Aquinas and Popular Sovereignty," *Thought*, September, 1941.

Pennock, J. R., "Law and Sovereignty," *American Political Science Review*, August, 1937.

Reynolds, Beatrice, *Proponents of Limited Monarchy in the 16th Century* (New York: Columbia University Press, 1931).

Riesenberg, Peter, *Inalienability of Sovereignty in Medieval Political Thought* (New York: Columbia University Press, 1956).

Spahr, Margaret, "Sovereignty Under Law," *American Political Science Review*, April, 1945.

Ullman, Walter, "The Development of the Medieval Idea of Sovereignty," *English Historical Review*, October, 1951.

PART FIVE | **THE POLITICAL PHILOSOPHY OF**
THE SOCIAL CONTRACT ERA

Chapter XII

HOBBES: THE SOVEREIGN LEVIATHAN

"Let them curse it who curse the day, who are ready to raise up a Leviathan" (*Job* 3:8).

THE philosophical seeds which had been sown during the period of the Renaissance began to flower in the seventeenth century, "the century of genius." The emancipation of the individual mind from the medieval "shackles" of authority was accompanied by a growing confidence in the ability of man to master the problems of the universe. The great progress made in the physical sciences strengthened the conviction that a natural order exists not only in the physical but in the social world as well, and that there are laws of human behavior as certain and precise as the laws of physics. Only a proper methodology for ascertaining the content of this immutable social order was yet lacking. Once a systematic approach could be developed, the veil of mystery surrounding human affairs would be torn asunder. And when this stage is reached, Francis Bacon's declaration that "knowledge is power" (*nam et ipsa scientia potestas est*) would assume a meaning and significance that it had not previously known.

The early seventeenth century purported to find the proper method of studying the political and social order in rationalism, a movement that reached its climax during the Age of Enlightenment of the eighteenth century. Exalting the autonomy and self-sufficiency of reason, the new theorists held that the human mind is capable of deducing social truths from certain axiomatic principles in much the same way that the mathematician can construct a completely rational system of theorems by analytical inference. The beginnings of such a tendency had already been noticed in prior thinkers such as Grotius, but the first clear and explicit expression of the new approach was given by Rene Descartes (1596–1650), the Jesuit educated Frenchman, who has been rightly called the "father of modern rationalism."

227

THE NEW METHODOLOGY

Descartes wrote no treatise on political philosophy, but his method of arriving at knowledge affected in one fashion or another the course of political thought for many decades thereafter. A brief examination of his relevancy to political philosophy should logically precede a discussion of such seventeenth century theorists as Hobbes, Locke, and Kant. In his famous *Discourse on Method* published in 1637, Descartes states his determination to sweep from his mind all the opinions which he had previously embraced and to discard all traditional principles and doctrines. Once he accomplishes this, he will begin afresh his search for truth, rejecting as absolutely false everything to which he could imagine the least ground of doubt. Proceeding on the assumption that knowledge has its source in universal and necessary principles which may be intuitively discovered by reason, he asserts that only what the mind apprehends with perfect clearness and distinctness can be considered true. These principles, moreover, must be such that all other truths can be derived from them by necessary inference. The first truth that so occurs to the mind is the proposition "I think, therefore I am" (*cogito, ergo sum*). Descartes believed it possible to construct a whole body of knowledge by way of deduction from this fundamental axiom.

The traditional thinkers of the classical and medieval eras had assigned a high role to reason, but they had recognized its limitations and the necessity for its reliance on observation and the accumulation of empirical facts. Descartes refuses to accept this approach. Influenced by the mathematical type of reasoning which was assuming great popularity in his day, and by the Renaissance skepticism of the senses, he rejects judgments based on sense perception of the material world and instead starts with immaterial entities. He seeks to justify his position on the basis that pure intelligence does not depend upon the senses for its proper data but operates apart from them in the formulation of ideas. It is possible, therefore (and in fact necessary in his view) to establish facts about the existing world quite independent of experience.

Descartes introduces into philosophy a dualism of body and mind that is alien to traditional thought. In his conception there are two different and complete substances in man, the thinking mind and the extended body.[1] The self is the mind alone; it is not only distinct in reality from

[1] See in this connection, James Collins, A *History of Modern European Philosophy* (Milwaukee: Bruce, 1954), p. 183 ff.

the body but can exist without it. This dualism justifies both a mechanistic philosophy of nature and a spiritualistic philosophy of mind. On the one hand, the human body divorced from the mind is itself nothing more than a machine, the movements of which can be explained just as mechanically as the operations of a clock. On the other hand, the mind is an immaterial substance that provides the source of its own ideas independent of the senses. External objects only arouse or stimulate it to produce ideas by itself and out of its own capacities. Thus the body and mind interact on each other solely in a physiological way.[2] This dualism or separation of mind and matter led in subsequent thinking to the emphasis upon one to the exclusion of the other. The result was either materialism or idealism.

During the Christian era the necessity for supplementing reason and human activity by faith, in much the same way that grace fulfills nature, had been universally accepted. Important as reason was to man, it was not considered either autonomous or infallible. However, with the advent of the new philosophy of human competency, reason came to assume the supreme role in the universe, either by a *priori* processes as the rationalists claimed, or as an adjunct to scientific investigation as the empiricists were soon to demand. It is a far cry from the middle ages to the proud, self-reliant, and autonomous personality of the new thinker. The seventeenth-century philosopher ceases to turn from the world as did St. Augustine; sure of his own personality, he returns to his ego, believing himself to be the rational creator of the world.[3] As even Descartes avows (although in the last analysis his good sense led him to acknowledge a wisdom greater than that of man), he is seeking to discover the knowledge by means of which "we might render ourselves the lords and possessors of nature."

THOMAS HOBBES

The first notable evidence of the effects of Cartesian dualism on political thought occurs in the works of Thomas Hobbes. Born in 1588, the son of a ne'er-do-well and quarrelsome parson who was forced to flee

---

[2] Descartes's dualism raises the problem of how two separate and distinct substances can form a unified composite such as man. His answer is that while unity of composition between the two substances is a fact manifested to us by our experiences, the nature of the union remains incomprehensible. The only explanation he can offer is that this is the way God has so constructed man.

[3] J. P. Mayer, *Political Thought* (New York: Viking Press, 1939), p. 159.

from his parish and his family, Hobbes lived to the ripe age of ninety-one. He was a precocious youngster who learned Greek and Latin when he was six and entered Oxford at the age of fifteen. He later said that he profited little from his years at the university; indeed he was appalled at the "frequency of insignificant speech" which he heard there. Sometime after graduation, he became tutor to the oldest son of Lord Cavendish, a member of one of the most aristocratic families in England. Most of his life was spent in the service of this family in one capacity or another. His duties permitted him to travel widely and to associate with the leading scientists and men of letters of his day. Just before the outbreak of the English civil war, he deemed it prudent to move to Paris because of his pamphlets defending the absolute rights of the king. Early in 1652, after residing eleven years in France, he made his peace with the Commonwealth and returned to England, where he spent the remainder of his life.

Like Bodin, Hobbes lived during a turbulent era, and like his French predecessor he was deeply impressed with the need for a strong political power to bring order out of the disturbances that were threatening civil society. The shattering of medieval unity had affected Britain in much the same way that it had continental Europe. The Tudor monarchy had profited by the breaking of all external political and spiritual chains, but the same forces that had permitted the establishment of the modern state had also awakened a new spirit of independence and self-assertion among the people. Although the marriage between bourgeoisie and monarchy had enabled the latter to attain its position of political supremacy, the marriage contained within itself the seeds of conflict. As the king's power increased, the merchant and landowner began to see the dangers inherent in an unlimited and uncontrolled political power. Similarly, the question of a religious monopoly in the state began to create difficulty in an age when the Bible had become the fountainhead of truth, and the right of individual interpretation was widely claimed.

By the time of the Stuarts, these forces were becoming manifest in England. The forthcoming epoch was a violent one in which the excesses of the rulers were matched by the turbulences of their subjects. England enjoyed no real internal peace from the time that James I ascended the throne in 1603, the year that Hobbes entered Oxford, until the closing decades of the century. It was in an environment such as this that Hobbes wrote his major political treatise, the Leviathan.

Hobbes' masterpiece contains the first great general and comprehensive political philosophy produced by an English thinker. Previous British writers such as John of Salisbury, Thomas More, and Richard Hooker had written important political works; but in each instance their treatment of government had been more limited and specialized and their political speculation largely incidental to other objectives. The *Leviathan* was politically conceived and politically oriented. It is sometimes described as an attempt to justify Stuart absolutism, but actually it sought to lay the theoretical foundations for absolute government in general, whether by a monarch, a Cromwellian dictatorship, or even by a parliament.

The drawing on the frontispiece to the *Leviathan* is extremely fascinating as well as descriptive of the general theme of the book. Towering in the background of a neatly arranged town is the upper portion of the figure of a huge giant wearing a crown and holding in his extended hands a sword and a crozier: the one the symbol of secular and the other of ecclesiastical office. The waist and arms of the figure are made up of a mass of small people with their eyes raised toward the face of the king. At the top of the page is a quotation from *Job*, "There is no power upon earth that can be compared with him who was made to fear no one." On the lower half of the page is the inscription "Leviathan, or the Matter, Form and Power of a Commonwealth Ecclesiastical and Civil, by Thomas Hobbes of Malmesbury." On each side of this title are emblems and scenes representative of temporal and spiritual power such as the crown and the miter, and the castle and church. The symbolic significance of the drawing becomes more apparent as the reader pursues his examination of Hobbes' political thought.

Methodology

The first of the four books or parts of the *Leviathan*, entitled "Of Man," is devoted to an analysis of human psychology.[4] Hobbes is well aware that a theory of the state must be grounded on a theory of the nature of man. In his introduction he observes that there are two ways of approaching the study of human nature; the first by observing the actions of other men, the second by introspection. The empirical approach of experimental psychology is indicated in the first method, but Hobbes was too immersed in an age of rationalism to pursue it diligently. While

---

[4] The second part is titled "Of Commonwealth," the third "Of a Christian Commonwealth," and the fourth "Of the Kingdom of Darkness."

he is interested in discovering how men react to their circumstances and in formulating a theory of human behavior, he employs a method quite unlike that of modern psychology. Instead of examining many individual cases, he looks for universal truths by a careful study of a single example: himself. He states that this procedure is preferable since "whosoever looks into himself, and considers what he does, when he does think, opine, reason, hope, fear, etc., and upon what grounds; he shall thereby read and know, what are the thoughts and passions of all other men, upon the like occasions."[5] Unlike Descartes, he believes that knowledge is acquired through the senses and is not innate; it has its real source in sensation. Yet, by holding a mechanistic conception of nature, he is able to assume that the reactions of human beings to given stimuli are similar. Thus by examining his own passions and actions, he is actually studying man in general. He is reading in himself not this or that particular man, but mankind.

When he speaks of methodology, Hobbes means the most expeditious way of discovering effects from known causes, or causes from observable effects. Deeply impressed by the scientific discoveries of his day, he believed it possible to create a theory of man and the state equal in clarity and definiteness to the physical laws of the universe. He saw no reason why the social scientist could not treat of human actions and passions just as the physicist treats of weights and solids. He realized that such an approach presupposes a mechanistic psychology which on the one side denies freedom of will, and on the other asserts that man's actions are determined by his sense-impressions and by his automatic responses to these impressions. He also saw that an exact science of human behavior, and hence an exact political science, is possible only if such behavior can be reduced to material particles moving in accordance with certain physical laws. To establish this point, he endeavors to demonstrate that the principles of mechanical causation are applicable to all phenomena, including the human intellect and will.

Psychology of Man

In constructing his general psychology, Hobbes starts by describing man's passions and ethics in terms of motion. Maintaining that only the body and its movements are real, he asserts that sensation must consist

---

[5] *Leviathan*, edited by M. Oakeshott (Oxford: Blackwell), p. 6. Excerpts from the *Leviathan* are from this edition.

in the movement of particles. External objects exert pressure upon the sense organs and thereby generate a motion that continues inward until it reaches the organic center in the brain. Here a reaction to the motion takes place resulting in an outward endeavor or act upon the part of the sentient subject toward the perceived object. "The cause of sense is the external body or object, which presses the organ proper to each sense, either immediately as in the taste and touch; or mediately as in seeing, hearing, and smelling; which pressure, by the mediation of nerves, and other strings and membranes of the body, continues inward to the brain and heart, and causes there a resistance, or counterpressure, or endeavor of the heart, to deliver itself."[6] External stimuli or motion, in other words, act upon the human brain in such a way as to cause automatic and largely predetermined responses.

Hobbes was faced with the task of reconciling his mechanistic description of organic reaction with the universally accepted fact that man is distinguished from the rest of the physical world by the faculty of reason. He attempts to do this by claiming that man's appetites and passions fix the ends to be pursued while reason plays a purely instrumental function to his desires. Thus the appetite sets a particular goal and this in turn leads to a searching of the individual's thought for an appropriate sequence of means to accomplish the projected end. Hobbes does not clearly explain whether the presence of the rational faculty introduces an indeterminate element in what otherwise would be a system completely determined by nature and environment. But regardless of his position on this point, his philosophy must be viewed as a form of naturalism inasmuch as it denies any basic difference between man and the rest of nature.

Hobbes' second psychological assumption is that man is naturally moved toward certain objects and away from others. The first are objects of desire, the second of aversion. Those toward which his appetites move him are good and pleasurable; those which repel him are evil and painful. In this connection, it is necessary to distinguish between voluntary motions and vital motions. The latter, "such as are the course of the blood, the pulse, the breathing . . . to which motions there needs no help of imagination," are purely automatic responses that require no mental intervention. The former consist of such actions as walking and speaking, and these depend upon "a precedent thought of whither,

---

[6] *Ibid.*, I, 1.

which way, and what."[7] The process of voluntary motions differs little in animals or men. Man, in fact, is an animal like all other animals and as such is constantly exposed to manifold impressions which automatically call forth desires and aversions. He has no more power than the beast to determine freely his own wishes or acts of choice. However, because of his reason he is much less at the mercy of momentary sense-impressions. He can envisage the future much better than can animals and can assess the consequences of alternative courses of action precisely because his appetite has reason at its service. In view of Hobbes' psychology, this distinction between vital and voluntary acts does not appear very meaningful since both classes of activity remain essentially physical and reducible to the principles of mechanics.

The third proposition underlying Hobbesian psychology is the relatively equal capacity of men for attaining their objectives. Unlike most advocates of despotic government, Hobbes regards men as naturally equal. Deficiency in the intellectual ability of an individual is generally compensated for by greater physical strength or cunning or by some other quality. "Nature hath made men so equal, in the faculties of body and mind, as that though there can be found one man sometimes manifestly stronger in body, or of quicker mind than another; yet when all is reckoned together, the difference between man and man is not so considerable, as that one man can thereupon claim to himself any benefit, to which another may not pretend, as well as he."[8] Coupled with man's vanity, this very equality is a disturbing element in human relations since each individual believes himself capable of satisfying his own desires.

Finally, Hobbes regards man as naturally and fundamentally selfish, quarrelsome, power-hungry, cruel, and perverse. These characteristics are largely the result of man's efforts to gratify his appetites, since only by satisfying his desires can the individual achieve happiness. This process is a continual and perpetual one, a "progress of the desire from one object to another, the attaining of the former being still but the way to the latter." Men want assurance, a feeling of security, that they will be able to gratify not only their immediate but their future desires as well. "The object of man's desire is not to enjoy once only, and for one instance of time, but to assure forever the way of his future desire." In order to achieve this end, man needs power. All mankind, therefore, has "a perpetual and restless desire of power after power that ceases only in

---

[7] *Ibid.*, I, 13.   [8] *Ibid.*

death." This incessant struggle for power is not always caused by the fact that "a man hopes for a more intensive delight than he had already attained to; or that he cannot be content with moderate power: but because he cannot assure the power and means to live well, which he hath present, without the acquisition of more."[9] A vicious circle is thus created from which flows strife, enmity, hatred, and bitterness.

The State of Nature

Starting from these psychological premises, Hobbes concludes that the normal condition of human life is one of unceasing conflict, of a fiercely competitive struggle for power and prestige, and of war "of every man against every man." In this prepolitical state of nature, the individual is completely free to do anything which he deems necessary for his own preservation and security. "There is nothing that he can make use of that may not be a help to him in preserving his life against his enemies; it follows that in such a condition every man has a right to everything; even to one another's body."[10] The self-centered individual finds himself in a world with other similarly motivated men who are striving after their own satisfactions. With limited material goods available, several men will inevitably desire the same thing. And since men are roughly equal in their ability to preserve themselves and to satisfy their appetites, no individual can be secure. "From this equality of ability, arises equality of hope in the attaining of our end. Therefore if any two men desire the same thing, which nevertheless they cannot both enjoy, they become enemies; and in the way to their end . . . endeavor to destroy or subdue one another."[11] A few men are willing to recognize this equality and to accept the fact that other individuals are just as capable of resisting encroachments as they are of imposing their wills on them. The vast majority, however, are led by vain conceit to overestimate their own ability and strength, and hence they attempt to outdo their fellow creatures at all costs. The result is perpetual conflict since the very equality of men prevents any one from gaining permanent ascendancy over the others.

In this state of nature, which Hobbes intends as a description of the relations among men in the absence of a sovereign political power, there are no legal or moral laws to govern human behavior. Neither principles of right or wrong nor of justice or injustice have any place, since there

[9] Ibid., I, 11.   [10] Ibid., I, 14.   [11] Ibid., I, 13.

is no objective standard of conduct. Whatever man desires is perforce good and just; what repels him is evil and unjust. Nor is there any security for the individual other than what his own strength and ingenuity furnishes him. Under such conditions "there is no place for industry because the fruit thereof is uncertain: and consequently no culture of the earth . . . no arts, no letters, no society; and which is worst of all, continual fear and danger of violent death."[12] If anyone doubts that nature has so constituted man, let him reflect on his own experiences, Hobbes advises. When he goes to bed at night, he bars his doors and windows, he puts his valuables in strong vaults, and he pays large taxes to provide for a police force and a standing army. Given man's nature as pictured in the Leviathan, it is not difficult to visualize the intolerable condition of a society without the political commonwealth and its suppressive powers. The life of man in such a state of nature "would be solitary, poor, nasty, brutish, and short."[13]

The Laws of Nature

Having described the precarious condition of man in his natural state, Hobbes employs his mechanistic philosophy to generate a countermotion that will drive men into political society. The passions and the reason supply the necessary impetus and the means of emerging from the primitive state of anarchy. The strongest passion in man is fear of death and this is followed next by the desire for commodious living. These two passions incline men to seek peace, since war is a constant threat to the life and material possessions of the individual. As the passions dispose men toward peace, reason points out the way to obtain this desideratum by formulating certain rules for making life secure. "And reason suggesteth convenient articles of peace, upon which men may be drawn to agreement. These articles are they, which otherwise are called the laws of nature." A law of nature, as Hobbes defines it, is "a precept, or a general rule, found out by reason, by which a man is forbidden to do that which is destructive of his life, or taketh away the means of preserving the same."[14]

Man has a natural right (in the sense of liberty) to seek out whatever will satisfy any of his desires. Hobbes contends that each individual acts in order to secure what he considers the greatest good or least evil available at the time of acting. But so long "as this natural right of everyman

---

[12] Ibid.   [13] Ibid.   [14] Ibid., I, 14.

to everything endures there can be no security to any man . . . of living out the time which nature ordinarily allows men to live." Reason therefore dictates that man should "seek peace and follow it."[15] This is the first and fundamental law of nature. From it is derived the second law which ordains "that a man be willing, when others are so too, insofar as for peace and defense of himself he shall think it necessary, to lay down this right to all things; and be contented with so much liberty against other men as he would allow other men against himself."[16] The third law, a corollary of the second, is that men keep their covenants. Otherwise, "the right of all men to all things remaining, we are still in the condition of war."[17] Hobbes enumerates seventeen more laws of nature which are essentially precepts of conduct designed to contribute to the preservation of peace.

The natural law for Hobbes is something quite different from what it had been for his predecessors. What he refers to as natural law is merely a set of materialistic principles for developing a workable society out of the actions and interactions of human individuals. Expressed somewhat differently, it is a body of rules or counsels of prudence whereby man is enabled to overcome his fear of death and to enjoy comfortable living. The new concept rejects any transcendent test of good or evil. Whatever is the object of man's desires is good, whatever the object of his hate evil. The measure of goodness or badness is purely subjective, "for these words of good, evil, and contemptible are ever used with relation to the person that uses them; there being . . . [no] common rule of good and evil, to be taken from the nature of the objects themselves."[18]

No obligation exists on the part of the individual to obey Hobbes' rational precepts. To disregard them is simply foolish and inconsistent with man's natural desire to preserve his life. In his natural condition of freedom, an individual may be deterred from performing an act because he does not have the necessary power or physical means; he is never prevented from acting by any consideration that the contemplated deed is morally wrong.

There are additional differences between the Hobbesian and the older concept of natural law. Hobbes distinguishes between man's natural right, or the freedom to do as he pleases, and natural law, or the course of action he must follow to avoid self-destruction. He considers the latter as a set of voluntary restrictions which man places on his natural right of liberty for the sake of expediency. In traditional thought, natural rights are those basic privileges which flow from the natural law. There is no dichotomy between the two as Hobbes proposes. Natural law establishes the order within which man's natural rights are determined and made legitimate. Hobbes, moreover, does not regard natural law as law in the true sense of the term. "For the laws of nature . . . are not properly laws, but qualities that dispose men to peace and obedience."[19] Anticipating later developments, he looks upon law as the command of a sovereign agency that has the authority to make rules and the power to enforce them. Natural law becomes law strictly speaking only after a state is established and the ruler commands men to obey these precepts of reason.

The Social Contract

Since the individual is inclined to seek peace for his own preservation and since reason dictates that orderly living is not possible so long as the state of nature persists, men must obviously seek some arrangement that will remove them from their primitive condition. According to the second precept of Hobbes' natural law, men can assure their self-preservation only if they are willing to covenant with each other to give up their absolute natural right to all things. However, in view of man's selfish and depraved tendencies, such an agreement runs counter to all the emotions that lead to perpetual warfare. Thinking themselves cleverer than their fellow men, individuals would break the rules whenever it appears to their advantage to do so. Hobbes points out that man cannot be relied on to keep his covenants without some external sanction — that of force. Agreements "without the sword are but words and of no strength to secure a man at all."[20] The only solution is to create a common or public authority with sufficient coercive power to compel adherence to the social covenant. Such an authority can be established if each individual, in consideration of others doing likewise, transfers his natural right of liberty to a beneficiary who is not a party to the contract. This divestiture is made as though each person should say to the other, "*I authorize and give up my right of governing myself to this man, or to this assembly of men, on this condition, that thou give up thy right to him, and authorize*

---

[19] *Ibid.,* II, 26.
[20] *Ibid.,* II, 17.

all his actions in like manner. This done, the Multitude so united in one person is called a Commonwealth, in Latin Civitas."[21]

The nature of the political state created by the covenant can be gathered from the definition of the commonwealth as "One person of whose acts a great multitude, by mutual covenants one with another, have made themselves every one the author, to the end he may use the strength and means of them all, as he shall think expedient, for their peace and common defense."[22] Apparently everyone who voluntarily joins the assembly of men for the purpose of creating a state implicitly agrees to follow the majority decision in the selection of the sovereign. "For if he voluntarily entered into the congregation of them that were assembled, he sufficiently declared thereby his will, and therefore tacitly covenanted to stand to what the major part should ordain."[23] Once a majority agreement as to the ruler is obtained, "everyone, both he that *voted for it* and he that *voted against it,* shall *authorize* all the actions and judgments of that man or assembly of men in the same manner as if they were his own."[24] The activist role of the people in the political process ends with the selection of the first sovereign. The matter of succession is thereafter determined solely by the holder of the office.

Several features of Hobbes' definition of the social contract are of peculiar significance. First, the covenant is not one between ruler and ruled, but an agreement among individuals to relinquish the state of nature and to create a civil society. Previous thinkers had spoken in terms of a political covenant between the people or community and the king or government. Viewing man as a social creature, they had looked upon life in an organized society as the natural mode of living. The contract which they sometimes referred to was one between the community as a unit and the ruler. It was not one to create a political society, since they regarded such a society as a natural institution that comes into being without the necessity of contract.

Second, Hobbes' social contract is made by individuals who are naturally solitary and antisocial. This view is reminiscent of the Sophist claim that man is naturally nonsocial and that justice arises from the mutual agreement to refrain from mutual injury. Hobbes' theory of the social compact seems to suggest that men have no natural interests in common; yet his argument shows that they all have a mutual and vital interest in the

---

[21] *Ibid.*
[22] *Ibid.*

[23] *Ibid.,* II, 18.
[24] *Ibid.*

preservation of civil society. For without this society, man's life would be in constant peril. Since men rationally unite in pursuance of a common end — self-preservation — why may they not be considered similarly united in respect to other ends also? And if this is true, is not civil society with its co-operative devices natural to man?

Third, the unity of the people which is created by the social covenant is a consequence rather than a cause of sovereignty. The efficient cause of the state is, in the first instance, the individual wills contracting singly with each other. These wills are made one only as a result of their contract and the erection of a common power, which alone is the "people." Hence the importance of the words "one person" in Hobbes' definition of the commonwealth.[25] The multitude is reduced to one not through the organic unity of the people but through the creation of the political sovereign in whom the entire strength of the individual subjects is conferred. This unity is real and not merely moral. Not consent but submission of the wills of all to the will of one creates civil society.

The permeation of Hobbes' political philosophy by the stark determinism of seventeenth-century physics can here be seen. Before individuals enter into the social contract, they are nothing more than a disordered mass. After the compact, the political community that is created by a chance collection of human individuals is held together artificially by the unlimited power of the sovereign, just as material atoms are controlled by physical force. So conceived, the state becomes "the great *Leviathan*, or rather (to speak more reverently) the *Mortal God* to which we owe under the *Immortal God* our peace and defence."[26]

Fourth, there is no place for unanimous consent in Hobbes' version of the social contract. Many men, a multitude, are required to create a sovereign sufficiently powerful to enforce internal order and defend against external aggression. The minority has no choice but to submit to the new master or be destroyed by its preponderance of power. Hobbes was forced to resort to the fiction of a social contract because a theory of society in terms of individual interests was a foregone conclusion in the mental climate of his day. The difficulty inherent in his version of state origin is to explain how an individual can be deprived of his alleged natural right to full freedom if he refuses to enter into the covenant. Hobbes attempts to explain this away by noting that those who do not consent to the pact remain in a state of nature and are

---

[25] See James Collins, *op. cit.*, p. 197.   [26] *Leviathan*, II, 17.

therefore subject to whatever action the sovereign may take for the protection of the civic body. Whether an individual "be of the congregation or not, and whether his consent be asked or not, he must either submit to their decrees or be left in the condition of war he was in before; wherein he might without injustice be destroyed by any man whatsoever."[27]

Sovereignty

The party to whom the individuals transfer their authority is known as the sovereign. His position carries with it certain basic rights and powers. The subjects cannot withdraw their grant of authority without his permission because they have irrevocably covenanted to be bound "every man to every man, to own and be reputed author of all that he that already is their Sovereign shall do and judge fit to be done." Since the sovereign is not a party to the contract, there can be no breach of covenant on his part, "and consequently none of his subjects by any pretense of forfeiture can be freed from his subjection."[28] Whatever the sovereign does is *per se* right and just and cannot be questioned by the people. In order to justify this attribute of sovereignty and yet maintain the pretense of individual liberty, Hobbes employs the novel device (later used by Rousseau) of making every man the author of the acts of the sovereign.[29] Whenever the latter acts, it is in effect the individual acting. "By this institution of a Commonwealth, every particular man is author of all the Sovereign does; and consequently he that complains of injury from his Sovereign, complains of that whereof he himself is author."[30]

The sovereign is above criticism and his policies immune from public debate. Full power of censorship over all expressions of opinion and doctrine is vested in him. "It is annexed to the sovereignty to be judge of what opinions and doctrines are averse and what conducive to peace; and consequently on what occasions, how far, and what men are to be trusted withal in speaking to multitudes of people; and who shall examine the doctrines of all books before they be published."[31] The position of the sovereign is also above the civil laws of the commonwealth. "For having power to make and repeal laws, he may when he pleases free himself from that subjection by repealing those laws that trouble him and making new."[32]

---

[27] *Ibid.*, II, 18.   [29] See *post*, pp. 296 ff.   [31] *Ibid.*
[28] *Ibid.*   [30] *Leviathan*, II, 18.   [32] *Ibid.*, II, 26.

Hobbes sums up the unlimited authority which he attributes to the sovereign in the following passage:

His power cannot, without his consent, be transferred to another. He cannot forfeit it. He cannot be accused by any of his subjects of injury. He cannot be punished by them. He is the judge of what is necessary for peace and judge of doctrine. He is sole legislator and supreme judge of controversies, and of the times and occasions of war and peace.[33]

By the authority conferred on him, the sovereign has the right to use as much power and strength as he deems necessary to maintain peace at home and protection against enemies abroad. There is no moral law, no tradition or customs, no fundamental restriction that can be raised against the power of the leviathan. All the reservations which Bodin retained in his theory of sovereignty are here flatly discarded. Once the citizen has entered into the social pact and chosen the ruler, not only does his political power come to an end, but he loses all his civil rights.

Hobbes' conception of sovereignty recognizes a sphere of private activity which should remain relatively free from state interference. This area of individual freedom includes the right "to buy and sell, and otherwise contract with one another, to choose their own abode, their own diet, their own trade of life, and institute their children as they themselves think fit."[34] There are also certain acts which the subject may legitimately refuse to perform. He has the right, for example, to disobey if the sovereign commands him "to kill, wound or maime himself; or not to resist those that assault him; or to abstain from the use of food, air, medicine, or any other thing without which he cannot live."[35] Since men enter into a social contract for the protection of their lives, it would be inconsistent for them to invest the sovereign with the right to annihilate them. In both the state of nature and civil society, man cannot be obliged to destroy himself or to refrain from resisting those who attempt to kill or injure him. For similar reasons, no man is obliged to incriminate himself. "If a man be interrogated by the sovereign or his authority concerning a crime done by himself, he is not bound (without assurance of pardon) to confess it; because no man . . . can be obliged by covenant to accuse himself."[36]

What value do these individual rights have if the sovereign is not accountable to his subjects? Actually, they have none, since they are

---

[33] *Ibid.*, II, 20.
[34] *Ibid.*, II, 21.

[35] *Ibid.*
[36] *Ibid.*

both ethically and legally meaningless. Although Hobbes concedes a sphere of private activity to the individual, the unlimited power which he vests in the state places no legal or philosophical barriers in the way of a ruler who might arbitrarily decide to assume control over every aspect of human life. Unless the subject has the physical power and means to resist encroachment on his private rights, in which event it could be said that a true sovereign no longer exists, he has no choice but to acquiesce or pay the penalty for disobedience.

Rebellion of the subjects is never lawful, although an individual may resist any attempt on his life by the ruler. However, if an uprising does occur and the sovereign proves incapable of suppressing it, the covenant apparently terminates and the subjects are restored to the state of nature. "The obligation of subjects to the sovereign is understood to last as long, and no longer, than the power lasts by which he is able to protect them. For the right men have by nature to protect themselves, when none else can protect them, can by no covenant be relinquished."[37] If the sovereign loses effective control of his society, the people are thrown back upon their own resources and are free to turn to a new leviathan who can protect them.

SUMMARY

Bodin's doctrine of sovereignty had acknowledged certain limitations on the power of the ruler. Hobbes discarded all such limitations by giving the first statement of "genuine" sovereignty known to political thought. His writings saddled upon the field of politics a concept that has led to the most extreme forms of state domination, and that has made effective international government impossible of attainment. He no doubt felt that a desperately ill society, one plunged in disorder and turbulence, called for desperate remedies. If his analysis of human nature is correct, if the basic drives in man are fear and lust for power, and if man's natural condition is antisocial, quarrelsome, and completely selfish, perhaps the *Leviathan* is justified and the apologia later offered for fascism and totalitarianism sound. As one writer has remarked, the natural depravity of man presented by Hobbes asks and deserves the totalitarian answer that the *Leviathan* offers.[38]

Hobbes' theory demonstrates the logical consequences of the antitraditional view that there is no disposition in man to place his passions and appetites under the rational principle. Reason, in his thinking, is no longer a judge of the proper ends to be sought; it is only an instrumental agency for pointing out the way to achieve the objects of one's desires more swiftly and fully.

---

[37] *Ibid.*   [38] J. Bowle, *op. cit.*, p. 331.

The psychical life of man is reduced to the mechanics of attraction and repulsion, such as love-hate and courage-fear, which serve as the foundations of human behavior. In the process, the Cartesian distinction between the knowing subject and the known object is carried to extremes, with the mind becoming merely a passive reflector of external phenomena.

Limited government and the rule of law lie at the heart of Greek-medieval thought. Hobbes rejects both of these concepts in his effort to construct a theory of the state that will ensure order and security. His notion of sovereignty can tolerate no restriction on the power of the political leviathan. Unlike the traditional appeal to law and to the good sense of the average man to obey social regulation, the new doctrine appealed to absolutism in fear of anarchy. Given Hobbes' concept of human nature every man is in reality a tyrant. The question then is, do you want many tyrants, in which case no citizen is secure, or one tyrant that is capable of enforcing peace and order among all the populace.

Despite his absolutist tendencies, Hobbes is a forerunner of modern individualism. His basic premise that the common good is not a natural end for men but merely a pure figment of the imagination haunted political philosophy for more than two centuries. His individualism found political expression in the doctrine of the social contract, a doctrine based on an intellectual recognition by isolated individuals that they would personally gain through some form of association. Hence, man creates civil society for much the same reason that he fashions a saw or hammer to be used as an instrument for his own purposes. The state in this light is little more than an artificial contrivance, lacking the moral and organic unity that brings men together in a continuing endeavor for their mutual growth and development.

Despite his reference to natural law, there is no room in Hobbes' theory for any independent moral standard by which human behavior may be approved or condemned. The precepts of conduct which he offers are not moral norms for judging political acts, but general rules of behavior which can be relied on only when enforced by civil government. By abolishing the moral test, Hobbes cleared the way for the purely utilitarian and pragmatic standards which later were to assume great popularity. The social philosophy which he formulated ends by deriving moral duties from political necessity.

BIBLIOGRAPHY

Arendt, Hannah, "Expansion and the Philosophy of Power," Sewanee Review, October, 1946.

Balz, A. G. A., "Indefensibility of Dictatorship — and the Doctrine of Hobbes," Journal of Philosophy, March, 1939.

Chroust, A. H., "The Origin and Meaning of the Social Contract Doctrine as Expressed by Greek Philosophers," Ethics, October, 1946.

Fichter, J. H., "Thomas Hobbes on Absolutism," Modern Schoolman, March, 1939.

Gerhard, W. A., "The Epistemology of Thomas Hobbes," *The Thomist*, October, 1946.
Gotesky, R., "Social Sources and the Significance of Hobbes' Conception of the Law of Nature," *Ethics*, July, 1940.
Gough, J. W., *The Social Contract*, 2nd ed. (New York: Oxford University Press, 1957).
Grene, M., "On Some Distinctions Between Men and Brutes," *Ethics*, January, 1947.
Herz, John H., *Political Realism and Political Idealism* (Chicago: University of Chicago Press, 1951).
Jessup, B. E., "Relation of Hobbes' Metaphysics to his Theory of Values," *Ethics*, April, 1948.
Kaplan, M. A., "How Sovereign is Hobbes' Sovereign?" *Western Political Quarterly*, June, 1956.
Laird, John, *Hobbes* (London: Benn, 1934).
Lamprecht, Sterling P., "Hobbes and Hobbism," *American Political Science Review*, February, 1940.
Levy, A., "Economic Views of Thomas Hobbes," *Journal of the History of Ideas*, October, 1954.
Nagel, T., "Hobbes' Concept of Obligation," *Philosophical Review*, January, 1959.
Oakeshott, Michael, *Leviathan* (Oxford: Blackwell, 1946).
Stewart, H. L., "Personality of Thomas Hobbes," *Hibbert Journal*, January, 1949.
Stewart, J. B., "Hobbes Among the Critics," *Political Science Quarterly*, December, 1958.
Strauss, Leo, *The Political Philosophy of Hobbes* (Chicago: University of Chicago Press, 1952).
Trevor-Roper, H. R., "Fear as the Basis of Hobbes' Political Philosophy," *New Statesman and Nation*, July, 1945.
Warrender, Howard, *The Political Philosophy of Hobbes* (New York: Oxford University Press, 1957).
Watkins, J. W. N., "Philosophy and Politics in Hobbes," *Philosophical Quarterly*, April, 1955.
——— "The Posthumous Career of Thomas Hobbes," *Review of Politics*, July, 1957.
Windolph, F. L., *Leviathan and Natural Law* (Princeton: Princeton University Press, 1951).

Chapter XIII

JOHN LOCKE: THE STATE LIMITED

"To understand political power right, and derive it from its original, we must consider what state all men are naturally in" (Locke, Second Treatise of Civil Government, II, 4).

HOBBES's Leviathan had received a cold reception on all sides. His view that man was under no moral obligation in the state of nature and his cavalier attitude toward religion were particularly shocking to his English contemporaries.[1] Supporters and opponents of the monarchy alike repudiated his views, often with bitter invective. Those who sought to uphold the Crown were not averse to his absolutism but to the grounds on which he based it. His materialism and his theory of the social contract were hardly compatible with the doctrine of divine rights. On the other side, his support of unlimited sovereign power evoked strong protest from the Parliamentarians. No one but Hobbes seemed particularly satisfied with the new twist that he had given to political philosophy.

During the latter part of Charles II's reign, the doctrine of divine rights and passive obedience again came into prominence. Theoretical support was given to its revival by the posthumous publication of Sir Robert Filmer's Patriarcha in 1680, during the controversies that led to the Whig revolution. Although Filmer sought to sustain his defense of divine rights on more rationalistic grounds than his predecessors had, his rejection of the natural freedom and equality of all men placed him outside the main current of seventeenth-century philosophy. Hobbes had endeavored to stay within this stream by harnessing the dogma of natural equality and the device of consent in support of authoritarianism. The efforts of both Filmer and Hobbes were doomed to failure as the tradi-

[1] See John Bowle, Hobbes and His Critics (New York: Oxford University Press, 1952) for an account of the political criticisms directed against the Leviathan by Hobbes' contemporaries.

tional concept of constitutionalism and limited rule began to reassert itself in English political life.

In the early part of the century, James I had been able precariously to maintain his position of supremacy despite increasing opposition. His successor, Charles I, was not so fortunate. Forced to summon parliament in 1640 for financial reasons, Charles became involved in a series of disputes with that body that led to civil war and to his eventual execution. In the ensuing period Oliver Cromwell, the leader of the parliamentary army, emerged as the strong man. The republican form of government that had been established after the execution of the king was soon converted into a virtual dictatorship. As Lord Protector, a position created under the Instrument of Government (England's first and only written constitution), Cromwell enjoyed a position as absolute as that of any Tudor or Stuart. On his death in 1658, the system which he had established fell to pieces. Two years later, the Stuart dynasty in the person of Charles II was returned to the throne, and the contest between king and parliament began anew.

The opponents of Charles's government sought to secure the passage of an "exclusion bill" that would have removed the Catholic Duke of York, the future James II, from succession to the throne. It was at this time that the Tory supporters of the House of Stuart resurrected Filmer's *Patriarcha* in their efforts to provide a theoretical basis for monarchical legitimism. The Whig justification for the exclusion act rested on the premise that it was parliament's duty to alter the succession because the people allegedly did not want James as their king. This position implied that government rests on popular consent, whereas the *Patriarcha* denied that such consent is the basis of political authority. The Tory efforts to sustain this latter view on theoretical grounds marked the swan song of the divine right doctrine.

Charles II had succeeded in retaining a substantial measure of power largely because of the disunity among his opposition. When James II inherited the throne and attempted to restore political and other privileges to the members of his faith, he provided the one ground on which the opposing factions could unite. Since there were no constitutional means of deposing the monarch, revolution was the only course open. Men of varying shades of opinion accordingly joined in an invitation to the Dutch Stadtholder, William of Orange, to "bring over an army and secure the infringed liberties" of Englishmen. In the "Glorious Revolution" which followed, James fled to France while William and his wife Mary (the daughter of the deposed king), were proclaimed joint sovereigns of England. The constitutional settlement, effected by parliament and set out in the Bill of Rights of 1689, placed certain conditions and limitations on royal tenure. The monarchy was preserved but it was now a monarchy dependent on legislative sanction. By its actions in the post-revolutionary period, parliament demonstrated that it had become theoretically as well as actually sovereign. Under title of right, it had made and unmade kings and prescribed the conditions under which they were to hold office. These are the marks of a supreme political power, not of a subordinate agency.

THE LEVELERS

The parliamentary victory meant that Whig constitutionalism, not Tory authoritarianism, was to determine the development of eighteenth-century England. It would be wrong, however, to assume that democracy had been established in the process. The victory meant simply that political control had been shifted from the king to a narrow oligarchy of propertied interests, with parliamentary suffrage no more liberal than it had been during the late middle ages. The political disqualification of all but a small segment of the population had already evoked cries of protest. As early as the period of the civil wars, the less prosperous elements of the middle class had started to press for a more democratic government. Originating in the ranks of the Cromwellian army, the Leveler movement, as it became known, was the first organized manifestation of a growing political consciousness among the lower economic classes. Dissatisfied with the conservative plan of reform advocated by the army officers, the Levelers under the leadership of John Lilburne and Richard Overton demanded widespread political changes. The reforms which they proposed included universal suffrage, representation in parliament on the basis of population instead of wealth, and constitutional limitations on the power of government over individual rights. Their ideas were embodied in a written document, "The Agreement of the People," drafted in 1647.

The Levelers, many of whom were small property owners and shopkeepers, had no intention of seeking the abolition of property rights but only the curtailment of political monopoly by the privileged classes.[2] The proposals which they made met with instant opposition from the army officers, such as Cromwell and Ireton, who represented in the main the landholding and corporate interests of England. This group was committed by conviction as well as economic status to a modification, but not an abolition, of England's traditional structure. Its members looked upon parliament as the protector of property and vested rights; and hence they considered dangerous and subversive any scheme that would divest them of political control. The Manifestoes issued by the Levelers in support of their demands for political reform anticipated in large measure the constitutional patterns that later were to stir England and America.[3] But in seventeenth-century Britain, their ideas were considered destructive of the country's economic and social interests. Faced with such a threat, the landed Anglican and the Presbyterian businessman cast aside their differences to join forces in defense of the status quo. The time had not yet arrived for the democratization of England.

JAMES HARRINGTON

James Harrington (1611–1677), a contemporary of Hobbes, represents a more conservative and scientific approach to British political reform than that employed by the Levelers. In his *Oceana*, he outlines a scheme for the formation of a new republican government to be established in the Commonwealth of Oceana, a fictitious country that obviously refers to England. He employs the medium of a political utopia in his efforts to construct a comprehensive science of politics that would account for all political phenomena. The underlying basis of his theory is that the form of government appropriate to a state depends upon the distribution of property, and that in the long run government must inevitably reflect the manner of this distribution in a community. Whatever class owns a preponderance of the land must by sheer economic necessity command the power to control government. When one man owns more land than all others in the community combined, an absolute monarchy is usually

---

[2] In addition to the Levelers, there was a more radical and extremist group known as the Diggers. Led by Gerrard Winstanley, the Diggers contended that private property is one of the primary causes of social evil and corruption and should therefore be abolished. They advocated the common ownership of all land and the distribution of its produce on an equitable basis.

[3] See D. M. Wolfe, ed., *Leveller Manifestoes of the Puritan Revolution* (New York: Nelson & Sons, 1944).

found; when ownership is in the hands of a small nobility, a mixed or limited monarchy is common; and when landholding is widely dispersed, a commonwealth or popular form of government normally exists.

Historically, Harrington's thesis that property is the key which determines the character of government finds a large measure of verification. Aristotle had realized the importance of this factor, but he had warned that to permit government to be determined by property is to make politics subservient to economics. Despite his theory of economic causation, Harrington is likewise unwilling to see government placed wholly at the mercy of economics. Although he feels that in the interest of stability, supreme political authority must rest with those who own most of the land in the community, he advocates the distribution of property within limits so as to favor a particular form of government. Thus in his *Oceana*, he proposes a system to ensure wider ownership among the upper middle class — a group that he regards as best equipped to govern. He believes that this plan would make it possible to secure the proper economic basis for a commonwealth. The aristocratic class would play a predominant role but it would be subject to constitutional restrictions. Moreover, it would not hold a disproportionate amount of property in the community. For if a state is to be stable, great variations in wealth must not exist among classes; such differences tend to destroy the equilibrium that holds a society together.

While Harrington believes that order in a state depends upon the existence of a sovereign power, he also insists that ways be devised to prevent the arbitrary or selfish use of this power. Institutional means must be available to check the rulers if the objectives of civil government are to be achieved. This political balance is supplementary to the economic balance. It can be attained through such devices as indirect elections, the secret ballot, rotation in office, and written constitutions that are superior in status to other laws. He is convinced that there must be a "government of laws and not of men," and that the saying "give us good men and they will make us good laws" is the maxim of a demagogue. His *Oceana* is designed to ensure proper use of the enormous power that must necessarily be vested in the state.

JOHN LOCKE

Despite their basic differences, both the Levelers and Harrington helped to cast the ancient conception of natural right and consent into a new mold. Influenced by the egoistic tendencies of the period, both were inclined to emphasize individual rights at the expense of the traditional notion of the primacy of the common good. The Levelers viewed civil society as a mass of free individuals co-operating, not out of a sense of fellowship and common destiny but primarily from motives of self-interest. Harrington similarly felt that government should be designed to protect an enlightened egoism. These threads were woven together into a more formal and articulate theory of political individualism in Locke's theoretical justification of the 1688 constitutional settlement.

After six years of exile, John Locke (1632–1704) returned to his native land on the same boat that brought the Princess Mary to join her husband William of Orange on the English throne. He was born in Wrington in the county of Somerset, of Puritan parents. His father was a small landowner and lawyer who had fought in the civil war on the side of the Parliamentary party. Locke was educated at Oxford, where he received the bachelor's and master's degrees. He subsequently studied medicine, and in 1667 became personal secretary and physician to the first Earl of Shaftesbury, who organized the Whig party. During his patron's tenure as Lord Chancellor, Locke received several important public appointments that gave him practical experience and insight into the realities of politics and administration. Ill health caused him to retire to France for four years, and this enforced leisure gave him the opportunity to develop his own philosophical views. Shortly after Locke returned to England, Shaftesbury became involved in a plot against the king and was forced to flee the country. Although Locke played no part in the conspiracy, he fell under suspicion and was obliged to seek safety in Holland. Early in 1689 he returned to England and the following year published his major political opus, *Two Treatises of Government,* a work which is sometimes referred to as the bible of modern liberalism. It was written in defense of the revolutionary settlement, or as its author expresses it to "establish the throne of our great restorer, the present King William, to make good his title in the consent of the people." The first book is a refutation of the divine right theory of Filmer; the second sets forth Locke's own constructive ideas on the nature of the state and its authority.

State of Nature

Like his predecessor Hobbes, Locke rests political obligation on a social contract. He begins his treatise on political philosophy by positing an original state of nature which he refers to as the great natural community of mankind. This condition, as he describes it, is one of living together under the guidance of reason but with no designated political authority. "Men living together according to reason without a common superior on earth with authority to judge between them are properly in the state of nature."⁴ In this prepolitical society men are free, equal, and independent. Each individual possesses the natural liberty "to be free from any superior power on earth, and not to be under the will or legislative authority of man."⁵ Each man is the equal of every other human being, not necessarily in respect to virtue or capacity but in the fact that he is absolute lord over himself and subject to no other human authority.

While the state of nature is one of liberty, it is not one of license. Nor is it a community of savages, but of civilized and rational anarchists. Though man in this state has "an uncontrollable liberty to dispose of his person or possessions, yet he has not liberty to destroy himself, or so much as any creature in his possession, but where some nobler use than its bare preservation calls for it."⁶ Unlike the Hobbesian conception, Locke's state of nature is not one of war. Peace prevails, although it is a precarious peace. This state, moreover, is not devoid of law. Man's freedom and conduct are regulated by the natural law, which to Locke means "real" law and not mere qualities disposing man to seek peace as a matter of self-preservation. "The state of nature has a law of nature to govern it, which obliges every one; and reason, which is that law, teaches all mankind who will but consult it, that being all equal and independent, no one ought to harm another in his life, health, liberty, or possessions."⁷

How is a law of this kind to be enforced in the state of nature without some form of governing agency? Locke recognizes the need for sanctions other than those of a moral character since "the law of nature would, as all other laws that concern men in this world be in vain if there were nobody that in the state of nature had a power to execute that law, and thereby preserve the innocent and restrain offenders."⁸ He observes that nature has not failed in this respect since she provides a

---

⁴ *Second Treatise of Civil Government*, III, 19. Excerpts from Locke are taken from the World's Classics Edition (Oxford: Oxford University Press, 1947).

⁵ *Ibid.*, IV, 22. ⁷ *Ibid.*, II, 6.

⁶ *Ibid.*, II, 5. ⁸ *Ibid.*, II, 7.

remedy for anarchy by making every man an executioner of the law with authority to punish wrongdoers.

Man being born as has been proved, with a title to perfect freedom and an uncontrolled enjoyment of all the rights and privileges of the law of nature, equally with any other man, or member of men in the world, has by nature a power not only to preserve his property, that is, his life, liberty, and estate, against the injuries and attempts of other men, but to judge of and punish the breaches of that law in others.[9]

There are certain serious defects, Locke admits, in a societal system that must depend on self-execution of the natural law. First, "there wants an established, settled, known law received and allowed by common consent to be the standard of right and wrong, and the common measure to decide all controversies between them." Although the natural law exists and can be known to all rational creatures if they but take the trouble to discover it, men do not reflect sufficiently under unsettled social conditions and are biased by their own interests in determining what the law is. Hence, in the prepolitical state the natural law is deprived of its proper promulgation. Second, "there wants a known and indifferent judge with authority to determine all differences according to the established law." It is unreasonable for men to be judges in their own cases since self-interest will tend to make them partial to themselves and their friends. Finally, "there often wants power to back and support the sentence when right, and give it due execution."[10] Since an individual must depend on his own capacity to enforce his natural rights, a just claim may be left unsatisfied when the claimant does not possess sufficient physical force to execute the law. Under such circumstances man's enjoyment of his personal and property rights is uncertain and insecure.

The Social Contract

Despite the freedom and independence which man enjoyed in the state of nature, the shortcomings of that condition impelled him to unite in political society. Although Locke touches upon man's social nature and his inclination to seek the company of others, he insists that the individual is driven into political society by inconveniences of his natural condition rather than by nature itself. "To avoid those inconveniences which disorder men's properties in the state of nature, men unite into societies that they may have the united strength of the whole society

---

[9] *Ibid.*, VII, 87.   [10] *Ibid.*, IX, 124–126.

to secure and defend their properties, and may have standing rules to bound it by which everyone may know what is his."[11]

Since men are "free, equal and independent" it follows that no man without his consent can rightfully be subjected to the political authority of another. To supply this element of assent, Locke follows the prevailing pattern of his day by employing the device of the social contract. Men agree with one another to enter into society and to establish a body politic under one supreme government. By this compact, the people transfer to the newly created community the power to execute the natural law, a power which they individually enjoyed in the state of nature. "Because no political society can be, nor subsist, without having in itself the power to preserve the property, and in order thereunto punish the offences of all those of that society; there, and there only, is political society, where every one of the members has given up this natural power, re-signed it up into the hands of the community."[12] And by consenting to the agreement to form a body politic, each person obligates himself to submit to the majority will. "For, when any number of men have, by the consent of every individual, made a community, they have thereby made that community one body, with a power to act as one body, which is only by the will and determination of the majority."[13]

Several features of Locke's social contract should be noted. First, the motivating principle behind the agreement is not fear of destruction but a desire to avoid the annoyances of the state of nature. Men are not refugees from an earthly hell seeking protection in the strength of an all powerful sovereign; they are merely seeking an institutional device that will make more secure the rights they already possess. Second, the individual does not surrender to the community his substantive natural rights, but only his right of executing the law of nature. Third, the right which the individual resigns is not given to any particular person or group but to the community as a whole. The contract is one to form a political society. Once this society is established, it must then proceed to set up a government. It goes about this task by drafting a trust in-strument that creates a government with "fiduciary power to act for certain ends." The political community is at the same time both creator and beneficiary of this trust. As creator it sets the limits of the trustee's power; as beneficiary it is the recipient of the advantages accruing from the exercise of this power. Although unanimous consent is required for

---

[11] *Ibid.*, XI, 136.   [12] *Ibid.*, VII, 87.   [13] *Ibid.*, VIII, 96.

the original social contract, the will of the majority prevails in the formation of the government and in subsequent lawmaking.

Limited Government

Locke's description of the social compact indicates that he had no intention of vesting arbitrary and absolute power in the hands of the government as did Hobbes. His aim is to justify limited rule under a government that derives its authority from the people and holds its power in trust for their benefit and welfare. In such a political system, public officials as well as private citizens must come under the law and be subject to its sanctions. This means that the powers of government must be limited by law and exercised in accordance with it.

Recognizing that in any organized community there can be only one supreme political agency, Locke assigns this role to the legislative branch of government. He avoids the pitfalls in the problem of sovereignty by describing the legislature as a trustee of the law for the people. In this capacity it may rightfully claim political supremacy while the community itself enjoys a reversionary sovereignty as the beneficiary of this trust. Since political authority is of a fiduciary nature, "there remains still in the people a supreme power to remove or alter the legislative" when it acts contrary to the terms of the trust. "For all power given with trust for the attainment of an end being limited by that end, whenever that end is manifestly neglected or opposed, the trust must necessarily be forfeited, and the power devolve into the hands of those that gave it, who may place it anew where they shall think best for their safety and security."[14]

Locke lists four specific limitations on the powers of the legislature: (1) It is obliged to obey the natural law which "stands as an eternal rule to all men, legislators as well as others."[15] (2) It must rule according to law and not by arbitrary decrees. "For all the power the government has, being only for the good of the society, as it ought not to be arbitrary and at pleasure, so it ought to be exercised by established and promulgated laws, that both the people may know their duty, and be safe and secure within the limits of the law, and the rulers, too, kept within their due bounds."[16] (3) It cannot levy taxes on the property of the people without their consent. "'Tis true, governments cannot be

---

[14] *Ibid.*, XIII, 149.   [15] *Ibid.*, XI, 135.   [16] *Ibid.*, XI, 137.

supported without great charge, and 'tis fit everyone who enjoys his share of the protection should pay out of his estate his proportion for the maintenance of it. But still it must be with his own consent, i.e., the consent of the majority, giving it either by themselves or their representatives chosen by them."[17] (4) It cannot delegate its lawmaking authority to other hands. "The power of the legislative, being derived from the people by a positive voluntary grant and institution, can be no other than what that positive grant conveyed, which being only to make laws, and not to make legislators, the legislative can have no power to transfer their authority of making laws, and place it in other hands."[18]

The various limitations which Locke places on political rule indicate how rich a storehouse of ideas he provided for American political thought. All of the following can be attributed, at least in part, to his influence: the Declaration of Independence with its emphasis on the inalienable rights of man, including the right of the people to alter or abolish their government when it becomes destructive of human ends and values; the colonial argument of no taxation without representation; and the distinctly modern principle of unlawful delegation of legislative power which is frequently invoked in American constitutional law.

The Purpose of Government

Closely allied to the question of limited rule is that of the purpose or end of government. The answer to this question seemed clear to Locke. He believed with many of his English contemporaries that the protection of property is the principal, if not the whole, business of the state. To support this position he seeks to show that there is a natural right of property which exists antecedent to the establishment of civil society. Property in the state of nature is common in the sense that each individual has the right to obtain his subsistence from whatever nature offers. Once, however, he appropriates property by adding his labor to it, such as by cultivating a field, he acquires a private interest in it. By expending his energy on the fruits of nature he makes them a part of himself. He acquires a right to that "which he hath mixed his labor with." It is a right which he brings with him when he enters society. The primary function of government is to protect this property right.

---

[17] *Ibid.*, XI, 140.
[18] *Ibid.*, XI, 141.

Locke explains that when he uses the term property, he employs it in an all inclusive sense to mean "life, liberty and estate."[19] Nevertheless, he gives the right of property in the sense of land and goods special prominence among these prerogatives.[20] His thinking evidences no effort to distinguish between the relative positions of property rights and human values. Both categories are placed on the same plane and spoken of in the same voice. Little regard is paid to the traditional conception of a hierarchy of values with different levels of rights. Under this latter view, the right of the individual to develop his moral capacities and to maintain his dignity as a human person stands at the hierarchical apex. Lower in the scale are other values, such as property, that are indispensable to the realization of the primary objective. If government is barred from recognizing such gradation of values and is obliged to consider all rights on the same plane, it cannot rightfully restrict one to the advantage of the other.

What then is the purpose and function of the state? Locke holds that civil government would be unnecessary if it were not for the inconveniences of the state of nature — inconveniences which hinder man in the enjoyment of his life and property. Since man enters into political society to correct these deficiencies, the functions of government are necessarily limited to this end. Hence, the proper role of government can be determined simply by ascertaining the shortcomings which force man into political society. Locke points out that these deficiencies revolve around the insecurity of man's life and property in the state of nature. Prepolitical society is "full of fears and continual dangers" and peace and quiet are uncertain. All that is needed is some organized power to ensure order and settle disputes.

Like most of the Whigs of his day, Locke is not an advocate of *laissez faire* but a mercantilist. He does not believe that economic relationships automatically balance and adjust themselves. He feels that some governmental regulation of trade is necessary to protect and foster commercial interests. The functions of government, however, are essentially of a negative rather than positive character. Government is to protect property, keep order, and provide a peaceful environment in which individuals can freely pursue their own ends. Social betterment and the

---

[19] *Ibid.*, XV, 173.
[20] See, in this connection, J. W. Gough, *John Locke's Political Philosophy* (Oxford: Oxford University Press, 1950), p. 85.

removal of economic inequities are outside its jurisdiction. Locke speaks of the common good, but his treatment of it is ambiguous and unsatisfactory. His emphasis is almost wholly on private initiative and individual right, to the neglect of public interests and the general well-being. In the last analysis, the egoism inherent in his political philosophy tends to reduce the common good to the aggregate sum of individual goods.

Majority Rule

Long before the eighteenth century, the principle that government must rest upon the consent of the governed had become incorporated into western thought. Locke makes this theory the basic point in his solution to the problem of civic obligation. No man, he observes, can be subjected to the will of another without his own consent. Unanimity is required to form the social compact and to make the individual a member of a commonwealth. There is no obligation, moral or otherwise, on the individual to enter society; the impelling motive is merely that of expediency. Anyone who refuses to join the pact may go his own way and provide for himself elsewhere. Presumably the community could rightfully enforce his departure, although this aspect is not clear. At any rate, once an individual has agreed to the original contract, he is thereafter bound to accept the decisions of the majority. "And thus every man, by consenting with others to make one body politic under one government, puts himself under an obligation to everyone of that society to submit to the determination of the majority and to be concluded by it."[21]

Locke's recourse to majority rule calls for explanation. If government rests on consent, why should the decision of the majority be received as the act of all? Why, in other words, should an individual be compelled to act contrary to his wishes or his good judgment simply because a numerical majority has so decreed? Locke's answer is a practical one: the community cannot otherwise continue to exist if each person is free to reject those laws in which he has not concurred. "For that which acts any community, being only the consent of the individuals of it, and it being one body, must move one way, it is necessary the body should move that way whither the greater force carries it, which is the consent of the majority, or else it is impossible it should act or continue one body."[22]

---

[21] *Second Treatise of Civil Government*, VIII, 97.   [22] *Ibid.*, VIII, 96.

After the social pact is freely concluded, the element of individual consent disappears and is replaced by the will of the majority. Again, the justification for the changed character of man's freedom is sheer necessity. But why in the original contract should unanimous consent be required and in subsequent acts of government only majority approval demanded? If majority consent is justified as a necessary expedient to prevent anarchy, is it not also justified on similar grounds to end the chaotic conditions in the state of nature? Some of Locke's commentators say that he avoids this difficulty by including in the social pact an agreement to submit to the will of the majority. If he had this in mind, he certainly took little pains to emphasize it, apparently recognizing the artificiality of attempting to preserve the formal principle of consent in this manner.

There is a second difficulty implicit in the doctrine of majority rule, a difficulty that Locke is well aware of and for which he attempts to provide a corrective. The problem is an obvious one: what guarantee is there that the majority will not on occasions exploit its superior power and violate the rights of individuals? That majorities can be just as tyrannical as absolute princes was later to be tragically demonstrated during the French Revolution. Locke argues that the individual's rights are less seriously threatened by majority rule than by monarchical absolutism, an argument supported by historical experience. Yet from a philosophical standpoint, it makes little difference whether man is subject to the unqualified power of a leviathan or the unrestricted will of the majority. The logical consequences in each case would be the same.

Locke's philosophy takes account of this theoretical difficulty by recognizing that behind the civil law (law expressing the will of the majority) stands the natural law. This law endows the individual with certain basic rights which he does not lose on entering political society. Majorities as well as absolute monarchs are morally obligated to respect these rights. If they fail to do so, their acts lose all title to legitimacy, and brute force then replaces right in the governance of man.

Natural Law

If, as Locke states, civil rule is limited by the natural law, the logical and ultimate outcome of his political philosophy must be dependent on his understanding of the character of this law. It will be recalled that Hobbes looked upon the laws of nature as mere conclusions or theorems which conduce to self-preservation.[23] These precepts are not binding until they are enacted into civil law by a sovereign power. Locke, on the contrary, holds that there are certain moral rules established by God which are valid, whether observed by governments or not. Such limitations are inherent in the fiduciary relationship which characterizes political rule. If government violates them and endeavors "to take away and destroy the property of the people, or to reduce them to slavery under arbitrary power," it puts itself into "a state of war with the people, who are thereupon absolved from any further obedience, and are left to the common refuge which God hath provided for all men against force and violence."[24] This remedy is revolution.

On the basis of these statements it appears that Locke unconditionally rejects the Hobbesian view of natural law in favor of the traditional concept. However, there are certain tendencies in his work which militate against this conclusion and which raise the presumption that his natural law provides no more of a philosophical barrier against the abuse of human rights than did that of his predecessor.[25] Despite his more optimistic view of man, his state of nature is basically no different than that described in the Leviathan. Nature is full of fears and dangers, and man has a natural right to "do whatever he thought fit for his preservation" within the bounds of the moral law. Since reason teaches that life and property cannot properly be preserved in such a condition, man enters civil society to overcome these difficulties. Man may be less warlike and there may be fewer dangers in the Lockean than in the Hobbesian state of nature, but these are largely matters of degree. The compulsion to enter civil society in order to avoid the dangers and inconveniences of the prepolitical state exists equally in each case.

The crucial and only important difference between Hobbes and Locke in their approach to the state appears to be the latter's insistence on the binding character of the natural law regardless of civil sanction. Yet a closer examination raises doubt as to whether there is a substantial difference even in this respect.[26] Characteristic of those who adhere to

---

[23] See ante, p. 237.

[24] Second Treatise of Civil Government, XIX, 222.

[25] For a comparison of the thought of Locke and Hobbes in this regard, see H. Johnston, "Locke's Leviathan," Modern Schoolman, Mar., 1949, pp. 201–210.

[26] For a carefully reasoned discussion holding that there is no substantial difference between Locke and Hobbes in respect to their theories of natural law, see Leo Strauss, "Locke's Doctrine of Natural Right," The Philosophical Review LXI (1952), pp. 475–502.

the empiricism of eighteenth-century epistemology, Locke rejects the possibility of innate ideas. "All our ideas come from experience." Complex ideas are constructed from simple ideas by various operations of the mind in much the same way that one sorts individual playing cards into new combinations or puts together bricks to make a house. Man, according to Locke, is able to know the moral law by observation and by the "light of nature." This natural light is vaguely defined as a combination of sense and reason working together to discover the law of God.

Locke's approach to human knowledge, and more specifically to man's ability to know the moral law, is highly restricted. All the facts which we know are derived through our senses. Yet we do not know these facts immediately but only through the ideas which the mind has of them. Our knowledge is therefore real only so far as there is conformity between our ideas and the reality they represent. But how do we know that our ideas agree with outside reality? Locke's epistemology prevents such knowledge since by his own definition all knowledge is only of the relations of ideas in our mind.

Locke's strict empiricism causes him to reject any habitus of moral principles in man and to deny that the natural law can be known from man's natural inclinations toward truth and virtue. He looks upon conscience as nothing more than an individual's own opinion or judgment of the moral rectitude of his own acts; as such, it supplies no sanction to the natural law. Nowhere does he purport to show what the metaphysical relationship is between God and the human mind. Hence his conception of reason as a guide to individual and social morality tends to result in a relative standard defined by the majority view at any given time and place. Considered in its entirety, his thinking appears to replace the traditional idea of natural law with a moral teaching that is based on the desire or instinct for self-preservation.[27]

The Organization of Government

Whatever may be said of Locke's metaphysics, his political philosophy seeks to demonstrate that the natural rights of individuals may better be protected under limited than absolute government. His causal and practical theory, while incomplete and sketchy, is designed to achieve constitutional government through the establishment of institutional safe-

---

[27] See Leo Strauss, "Locke's Doctrine of Natural Law," *American Political Science Review*, June, 1958.

guards against arbitrary rule. Underlying his thought is the belief that the government of political society must be constructed in such a way that it will be least incapable of oppressing its citizens. Locke purports to see the ideal framework for governmental organization in the constitutional settlement of 1688. This arrangement made Parliament legally supreme, but retained the king as chief executive with certain prerogatives and powers.

In discussing the imperfections of the state of nature, Locke notes that prepolitical society lacked a public agency to promulgate, adjudicate, and execute the natural law. When later he describes the organization to be established for the commonwealth, he does not follow the same division in listing the three categories of governmental powers. Instead, he speaks of the legislative, executive, and federative or treaty-making powers. These latter two functions are to be vested in the same department of government. No mention is made of the judiciary as a separate and independent branch.

This division of powers is necessary partly for reasons of convenience. Since the legislature may do its work in a relatively short period, there is no need for it to remain in session at all times. The administration of the laws, on the other hand, is a daily and continuing job that requires the executive department to function all the year around. But more important than convenience, the functional separation of legislative and executive powers is essential as a check on arbitrary rule "because it may be too great a temptation to human frailty, apt to grasp at power, for the same persons who have the power of making laws, to have also in their hands the power to execute them."[28] Locke belongs to a long line of theorists who believe that one of the weaknesses of mankind is a tendency for those in authority to seek ever greater power.

The legislature in Locke's scheme of government is to be elected from time to time by popular vote. It is legally omnipotent; there is no appeal from its decisions to any higher tribunal. Its power, however, is limited to the public good of society. If it abuses its position, the people have the right to resist. Parliament, in other words, is to remain at all times responsible to the people who are the true holders of political sovereignty. Their sovereignty is normally in abeyance; it becomes active only when the government has been overthrown by revolution. In such case, the government (but not civil society, which once created, is permanent) is

---

[28] *Second Treatise of Civil Government*, XII, 143.

dissolved and political power or legal sovereignty reverts to the people. They in turn would provide for a new government just as they had established civil rule following the original social compact.

Although the legislative branch is to be elected by the people, it is not necessary that there be a wide suffrage. Locke is no more a democrat than the average Whig of his day. He was perfectly satisfied with the constitutional settlement of 1688, which gave a virtual monopoly of political power to the propertied class. He felt that this group was far better qualified than the masses to direct the course of British government. Sovereignty of the people does not mean democracy or universal suffrage to him, but merely a conditional right of revolution in the people should government breach its trust.

In answer to the question as to who shall judge whether the prince or legislator is acting contrary to his trust, Locke categorically replies, "the people." Just as the master has the right to determine whether his servant is acting properly, so the people have the authority to judge whether their political deputies are acting according to the trust reposed in them. If the prince or governors decline to submit to this way of determination, "the appeal then lies nowhere but to Heaven" — meaning revolution. Presumably heaven will give victory to the better cause. The people must decide for themselves whether it is advisable to resort to this drastic remedy. Locke contends that the right of revolution in the people will not lead to governmental instability as some of his contemporaries claimed. He believes that people will not rebel for slight reasons; in fact they "are more disposed to suffer than right themselves by resistance."

SUMMARY

The political thought of the seventeenth century is distinguished by two major doctrines pertaining to the origin of government: divine right and social contract. The first maintains that God has bestowed political power on certain persons and that an act of rebellion against them is not only treasonous but immoral. The second holds that civil government is the result of contract among individuals. Locke is one of the leading exponents of the latter theory. He saw in it a means of defending on philosophical grounds the cause of constitutional government against the claims of absolutism.

Locke's approach to the state and government is not unlike that of Hobbes, although the conclusions he arrives at are quite different. Both look upon civil society in essentially mechanistic terms. They view it as an institution that would be wholly unnecessary were it not for the inconveniences or evils which exist in the state of nature. The concept of community is entirely missing in their writings. In its place is the notion of a group of isolated individuals living together for reasons of security and convenience.

Locke, no more so than Hobbes, mentions the intellectual and moral requirements or the perfection of human personality that make the state a necessary and therefore distinctly natural institution for man. He does recognize the natural law but tends to overlook the fact that it calls for duties as well as rights and that it enjoins the common good as well as the protection of private interests. This tendency to equate private with public good was later to play a significant role in western thought. As Professor Sabine has noted, Hobbes and Locke by a strange and undesigned co-operation helped to fasten on social thought the presumption that individual self-interest is clear and compelling while public or social interest, the common good, is thin and unsubstantial.[29]

Locke's impact on subsequent political theory and practice has been great. He became the philosophic godfather of the American Revolution and a source of inspiration to the Founding Fathers; he gave theoretical formulation in terms of contemporary thought to the principles of limited and constitutional government; and he helped set the stage for institutional control of the rulers. On the other side of the coin, the weaknesses inherent in his political philosophy helped to pave the way for the exaggerated individualism which became one of the basic tenets of eighteenth- and nineteenth-century liberalism. These defects also contributed to the deterioration of the sense of community and encouraged the emphasis on property over human values. Locke's civil society, despite the moral premises on which he seeks to base it, remains an artificial contrivance, not the natural state of man — an uneasy cohesion of individual atoms held together not by any intrinsic principle of moral unity but by an external force. For Hobbes this unifying element had been supplied by the power of the leviathan; for Locke it was furnished by the will and strength of the majority.

BIBLIOGRAPHY

Cherno, M., "Locke on Property: A Reappraisal," Ethics, October, 1957.
Crossman, R. H. S., Government and the Governed (London: Christophers, 1939).
Czajkowski, C. J., The Theory of Property in John Locke's Political Philosophy (South Bend: University of Notre Dame Press, 1941).
Gibb, M. A., John Lilburne, the Leveller (London: Drummond, 1948).
Gough, J. W., John Locke's Political Philosophy (Oxford: Clarendon Press, 1950).
Frank, Joseph, The Levellers (Cambridge: Harvard University Press, 1955).

---

[29] A History of Political Theory, op. cit., p. 529.

Hamilton, W. H., "Property — According to Locke," Yale Law Journal, April, 1931.

Johnston, H., "Locke's Leviathan," Modern Schoolman, March, 1946.

Kelsen, Hans, "Foundations of Democracy: Property and Freedom in the Natural Law Doctrine of John Locke," Ethics, October, 1955.

Kendall, Willmoore, John Locke and the Doctrine of Majority Rule (Urbana: University of Illinois Press, 1941).

Lamprecht, Sterling P., The Moral and Political Philosophy of John Locke (New York: Columbia University Press, 1918).

Lewis, H. D., "Original Contract," Ethics, January, 1940.

Monson, C. H., Jr., "Locke and His Interpreters," Political Studies, June, 1958.

Murphy, W. F., "The Political Thought of Gerrard Winstanley," Review of Politics, April, 1957.

Neilson, F., "Locke's Essays on Property and Natural Law," American Journal of Economics and Sociology, April, 1951.

Reinhardt, I. J. F., "Political Philosophy from John Locke to Thomas Jefferson," University of Kansas City Law Review, December, 1944, and February, 1945.

Rotenstreich, Nathan, "Rule by Majority or by Principles," Social Review, Winter, 1954.

Rowen, H. H., "Second Thought on Locke's First Treatise (Confusion of Property and Political Power)," Journal of the History of Ideas, January, 1956.

Simon, W. M., "John Locke: Philosophy and Political Theory," American Political Science Review, June, 1951.

Strauss, Leo, "Locke's Doctrine of Natural Law," American Political Science Review, June, 1958.

Waldman, T., "Note on John Locke's Concept of Consent," Ethics, October, 1957.

Yolton, J. W., "Locke on the Law of Nature," Philosophical Review, October, 1958.

Chapter XIV

THE AGE OF ENLIGHTENMENT

"Nature and Nature's laws lay hid in night, God said: 'Let Newton be,' and all was light" (Pope, *Epitaph Intended for Sir Isaac Newton*).

THE eighteenth century has often been labeled the "philosophical century." It was a period of intense intellectual activity in which the quest for the hidden truths of the universe was accelerated with crusading zeal. Reason became the high priest of a new intellectual cult; but it was no longer the reason of the past. It was a new reason, supremely self-confident, convinced of its autonomy, and certain that it had discovered the key to unravel the innermost mysteries of the universe. Human omniscience now became regarded as an attainable goal. As Cassirer has so well noted, "the whole eighteenth century is permeated by this conviction, namely, that in the history of humanity the time had now arrived to deprive nature of its carefully guarded secret, to leave it no longer in the dark to be marveled at as an incomprehensible mystery but to bring it under the bright light of reason and analyze it with all its fundamental forces."[1] The influence of the Enlightenment on social and political thought was so substantial that its effects were felt well into the nineteenth century, despite the challenging protestations of more sober minds.

Reason traditionally had recognized its limitations and its ultimate dependence on the Divine Mind. With Descartes this reliance had been virtually disavowed as human reason began to assert its complete autonomy. In Cartesian philosophy, thought starts from an intuitively grasped certainty and proceeds by strict systematic deduction to piece out the whole pattern of knowledge.[2] The eighteenth century completed the process of emancipation started by Descartes. Impressed by the great

---

[1] *The Philosophy of the Enlightenment* (Princeton: Princeton University Press, 1951), p. 47.

[2] See *ante*, p. 228.

scientific discoveries of the age, the philosophers of the Enlightenment turned to the model of contemporary natural science. In so doing they sought to make the same methods which lead to exact insights into the nature of the physical world applicable without reservation to the social aspects of mankind. Impressive efforts were made to convert philosophy into a natural science. In the process, philosophical questions were placed on the same level with other problems and regarded as answerable by similar means. Only the measurable facets of reality were considered as real.

Newtonian physics, which had apparently succeeded in discovering the mechanical laws of nature, gave encouragement to the belief that social, political, and economic events could be treated in scientific fashion. What science had achieved in the material world, it could also accomplish in the social sphere. Once the laws governing human behavior are discovered, they can be incorporated in a social science analogous to physics or biology. How men should live and act, or what makes them happy and satisfied, are simply factual questions that can be investigated as any physical phenomenon. Through a social science the good society can be created with the same assurance that nuclear energy can be utilized for various purposes. For men, just as atoms, are objects of nature, and subject to similar laws.

The leaders in the new movement were a group of French thinkers and writers known as the philosophes. Although they had various political and social ideas, they were united by their faith in science, their acceptance of Locke and Newton, and their antagonism toward the Catholic Church.[3] The philosophes, such as Voltaire, Diderot, Helvetius, and Holbach, many of them the darlings of the salons, stress in brilliant style the concept of a world governed by inevitable and impersonal law — a world, moreover, that is progressing steadily toward a more glorious era. They regard this universe as intelligible and capable of being subdued to the uses of mankind. Similarly, they envision the new scientism as the means of enabling the human creature to become the master and possessor of nature. As knowledge increases and as man discovers the laws of the universe, he places himself in a position where, if he cannot fully control reality, he can at least manage it in the interest of human happiness and well-being.

---

[3] Kingsley Martin, *The Rise of French Liberal Thought* (New York: New York University Press, 1954), p. 93.

Carl Becker, in his penetrating analysis of the philosophes, lists the four major characteristics of their "religion": (1) man is not naturally depraved, he is naturally good and disposed to follow reason; (2) the end of human existence is the good life on earth, not the beatific life after death; (3) man through his own efforts, guided solely by reason and experience, is capable of achieving this objective on earth; (4) the first and essential condition of human living is the freeing of men's minds from ignorance, superstition, and intolerance.[4] This last goal can be accomplished only by scientifically studying the phenomena of nature — by sweeping away the cobwebs of medieval superstition and letting in the light of reason.

For the eighteenth century, the power of reason and the notion of inevitable progress came to usurp the places formerly held by Christian redemption and Divine Providence. The new movement took on the character of a messianic enterprise or religious crusade. This metamorphosis was clearly evidenced by the transference from a religious to a secular state of mind — a transference that reached its climax during the French Revolution when the crucifix in the Paris cathedral was torn down and an altar erected for the worship of "Reason," the god of triumphant man. The ancient belief that man and his world are derived from and dependent upon a transcendent power was dissipated in the new order of thought. In its place came a practical terrestrianism, "characterized sometimes by a resigned acceptance of a truncated spirituality, sometimes by a simple agnostic matter-of-factness, unconcerned with that of which it is largely unaware, and sometimes marked by a heroic search for significance in the 'absurdity' of it all."[5] Since western culture had developed primarily from Christian roots, this process of secularization took the concrete form of a de-Christianization.

Although the Enlightenment was by no means confined to France, the most culturally advanced nation of the period, it found its most characteristic and articulate expression there. To illustrate the significant aspects of the movement, four French writers have been chosen for brief examination: Voltaire for his critical and highly skeptical attitude toward religion; Quesnay as the founder of the "physiocratic" theory of economics; Condorcet for his idea of progress; and Montesquieu for his

---

[4] *The Heavenly City of the Eighteenth Century Philosophers* (New Haven: Yale University Press, 1932), p. 102.

[5] T. F. O'Dea, "The Secularization of Culture," *Commonweal*, Apr. 20, 1956.

political theory. In addition, one English thinker of the Enlightenment, David Hume, is considered because of his logical positivism and his attempt to apply Newtonian methods to the study of human nature.

VOLTAIRE

Francois Marie Arouet (1694–1778), known by his assumed name of Voltaire, was educated by the Jesuits in the Collège Louis-le-Grand. A leading figure of the eighteenth-century Enlightenment, he was one of the most productive as well as popular writers of his day. His writings reached far beyond the borders of his native France. Everyone who read at all, read him. The "new" philosophy was consequently assured of a wide audience. Prior to the publication of Voltaire's *Lettres philosophiques* in 1773, the ideas of the philosophes were known only to a small group of French thinkers. With the appearance of the *Lettres*, many thousands of readers came into contact with the dogma of scientific rationalism for the first time. Newtonian physics and Lockean psychology were brought down from the citadels of learning to the salons and the market place. The results on the thought and action of the period were profound.

In his later years, Voltaire wrote that he would die with three theological virtues: his faith in human reason which is beginning to develop in the world; the hope that ministers in their boldness and their wisdom will at length destroy customs which are as ridiculous as they are dangerous; the charity which makes him grieve for his neighbor, complain of his bonds, and long for his deliverance. This outlook, he states, is more akin to the gospel of the New Testament than is the teaching of its orthodox interpreters. Organized religion, as he put it, is narrow, intolerant, and cruel. Every sensible person ought to hold it in horror. Man must be snatched from the tyranny of the clerical impostors and inspired with the spirit of tolerance and freethinking.

The early philosophes did not deny the existence of God. Following the English deists, they held that creation implies a creator, and that the operation of nature according to certain fixed principles necessarily assumes the existence of some intelligent Being or first cause. Once this impersonal force had fashioned the world, immutable laws came into existence to govern it. "I shall always be convinced," Voltaire remarks, "that a watch proves a watchmaker and the universe proves a God." This idea of a first cause, of a Being who created and started the world in motion and then withdrew to the side lines was contrary to the Christian concept of a personal deity continually active and creative.

As Professor Hallowell has noted, Deism could not long retain its impossible position perched precariously as it was between orthodox Christianity and atheism.[6] Some of the later philosophes such as Baron d'Holbach (1723–1789) took the next logical step by discarding altogether the idea of a creator and adopting the view that the universe was the result of an accidental combination of atoms. Yet even this thoroughgoing materialism could not dispense with the impelling necessity felt by man for some transcendent object of worship. Holbach sought to fill this need by extolling nature as the object of veneration while others turned to a religion of humanity — to a worship of man. In place of the love of God, "they substituted the love of humanity; for the vicarious atonement, the perfectibility of man through his own efforts; and for the hope of immortality in another world, the hope of living in the memory of future generations."[7] As Voltaire observes, even if there were no God it would be necessary to invent one.

The new outlook which Voltaire typifies did not include any radical ideas in the field of politics and government. Although the men of the Enlightenment spoke out against oppression of all kinds and taught that all men have equal rights to liberty and property, they had no faith in the capacity of the average man for self-government. Voltaire's reference to the masses as "les canailles" (scum) may not have been typical, yet it was expressive of the suspicion that he and his colleagues held for the "common" man. Impressed by the British constitution which had become a symbol of freedom on the Continent, Voltaire saw the solution to the problem of government in an enlightened monarch (that is, one enlightened by the philosophes) who would carry out the necessary reforms. Despotism would be guarded against by extending the franchise to the upper middle class and by setting up certain constitutional checks. By these means, the political ideals of the philosophes could be attained: "an enlightened and tolerant State, which guaranteed civil liberty to every individual: a State whose policy was entirely secular, and which was always on its guard against the encroachments of any Church: a State in which the only laws were reasonable applications of a single, universal and evident law of nature."[8]

---

[6] Main Currents in Modern Political Thought, op. cit., p. 124.
[7] Carl Becker, op. cit., p. 130.   [8] Kingsley Martin, op. cit., p. 147

QUESNAY

The emphasis on freedom and the belief in a "natural order" carried over into the field of economics. Reacting against the mercantilistic policies which had characterized government since the rise of the absolutist state, a group known as the Physiocrats turned for support to the scientific rationalism of the day. The founder of the physiocratic school, Francois Quesnay (1694–1774), belongs more to the classical tradition than he does to the Enlightenment. He believes in the existence of an objective order and in man's ability to comprehend that order, but he nowhere subscribes to the simple deductive approach to social questions.[9] Insisting that France's ills were primarily economic, he set out to show how these could be corrected. His disciples, however, soon turned physiocratic thinking toward the easy rationalistic treatment of economic and social problems. In the process, the original premises of the school's founder were quickly overlooked or rejected.

Starting with the notion that the organization of society is governed by fixed and ascertainable laws, the physiocrats argue that the state should not attempt to interfere with or regulate the production and distribution of goods. They maintain that natural law applies to the circulation of money just as much as it does to the circulation of blood. No physician would attempt to interfere with the natural course of the circulatory system in man. He might study and examine it in order to enlarge his knowledge of the human body and its operations but he would never attempt to tamper with its natural functionings. Similarly, no government should be so foolish as to interfere with the natural operation of economic or even social laws. To do so would be to flaunt the forces of nature and to act contrary to her laws.

The Physiocrats were more concerned with economic liberty than they were with political rights. They had no interest in democratic government or popular participation in the political arena. Their idea was a benevolent despotism — a state administered by an hereditary monarch whose function would not be the creation of new laws but the maintenance of a framework within which the laws of nature might freely operate. Holding to the doctrine earlier expressed by Hobbes that pleasure and pain are the motivating factors in human action and that each man

---

[9] See in this connection, Thomas P. Neill, "Quesnay and Physiocracy," *Journal of the History of Ideas*, Apr., 1948, pp. 153–173.

is the best judge of his own interests,[10] the Physiocrats conclude that a healthy and happy society can result only if governmental restrictions are reduced to a bare minimum. In Lockean fashion, they assert that the function of the state is to safeguard the natural rights of the individual to life, property, and the pursuit of happiness. Government's role is simply to permit the free operation of social and economic laws by preventing the invasions of individual liberty which sometimes occur in society. The welfare and happiness of the community will be greatly enhanced if the natural harmony that is inherent in the social order is given free play and not interfered with by human regulation. Governmental attempts to curb economic processes violate natural law and lead to misery and chaos.

Mercier, a disciple of Quesnay, sums up the essence of the new economic philosophy in revealing fashion:

> Each of us, by favour of this full and entire liberty, and pricked by desire of enjoyment, is occupied, according to his state, in varying, multiplying, perfecting the objects of enjoyment which must be shared amongst us, and thus increases the sum of the common happiness by increasing his private happiness. And so each in the sum total of the common happiness would take a particular sum which ought to belong to him. We must admire the way in which every man becomes an instrument to the happiness of others, and the manner in which this happiness seems to communicate itself to the whole. Speaking literally, of course, I do not know if in this State we shall see a few unhappy people, but if there are any, they will be so few in number and the number of the happy will be so great that we need not be much concerned about helping them.[11]

Soon to become known as "liberalism," this line of thinking emerged as one of the dominant forces in nineteenth century political thought. Physiocratic thinking provided the doctrinal basis for the position of the merchant and manufacturing classes. These groups had become so self-sufficient by the middle of the eighteenth century that they were anxious to free themselves from the mercantilist policy of state control. The idea of a natural law of economics served their purposes admirably.

CONDORCET: THE THEORY OF PROGRESS

The belief that man is essentially good, that he is capable by virtue

---

[10] See ante, p. 232 ff.   [11] Quoted in K. Martin, op. cit., p. 234.

of his reason of fully understanding reality, and that he can manipulate his environment through science gave encouragement to the idea of "progress." Is there any reason why man cannot attain the knowledge and means to control his future, to establish the perfect society on earth, and to achieve complete happiness? None whatsoever, is the answer of the eighteenth century. The attainment of these objectives will be made possible as soon as more is learned about the laws which govern the social order and as the science of society becomes better formulated and understood. This optimistic view is well expressed by the Marquis de Condorcet (1743–1794), a French philosopher and mathematician. In his *Outlines of an Historical View of the Progress of the Human Mind*, he sketches the development of man from a barbarian past to a perfect future ushered in by the French Revolution.[12] It is his thesis that man will attain perfection by the use of reason and facts. Nature has set no limits to the perfection of the human faculties; the perfectibility of mankind is indefinite.

According to Condorcet, the story of progress is identical with that of knowledge — knowledge that results from the accumulation of experience. Each generation knows more than the last, and passes on this widened area of truth to its successors. As science and truth prevail in the process, the errors and superstitions fostered by the priests and despots for selfish and vested interests are gradually overcome. If the passage from a rude society to a state of civilization has at times been a painful struggle, it has been a necessary course in the gradual advance of the human species toward absolute perfection. The outlook for the future, moreover, need occasion no pessimism. Society will become increasingly rationalized and scientific minded, the gross inequalities in education, opportunity, and wealth which exist within and among nations will be removed, and all wars will be outlawed. Humanity will enjoy peace and prosperity and the sun will shine only upon free men on this earth, men who recognize no other master than their reason.

In the glorious future envisaged by the new cult of progress, man will want not merely the existence of subsequent generations but their sublime happiness. His faith in science will lead him to expect extended human longevity and the progressive curtailment of the powers of death. As Condorcet himself asks, "Is it unreasonable to suppose that a period must one day arrive when death will be nothing more than the effect

---

12 For a concise summation of Condorcet's views see K. Martin, *op. cit.*, Chap. 11.

either of extraordinary accidents, or of the slow and gradual decay of the vital powers; and that the duration of the middle space, of the interval between the birth of man and his decay, will itself have no assignable limit?"[13] Even time and death are waiting to be conquered.

The ancient theory of history is cyclical in character. It regards history as an endless chain of recurrent events in which society reaches a certain stage of development and then retrogresses. Polybius furnishes a good example of this point of view. His belief in an inevitable law of growth and decay with its tendency to cause one form of government to degenerate into another is characteristic of the cyclical theory. The Christian concept of history, on the other hand (first given formal expression by St. Augustine), rejects the ancient viewpoint by looking upon historical development as linear in nature. It holds that history has a beginning and end and that it represents a direct progress toward the ultimate goal. This progress, however, is not necessary and inevitable. At times the march toward perfection receives severe setbacks as the earthly city gains predominance. During such periods, man is reminded of his wounded nature and of his need for redemption.

The new historical view advanced by the Enlightenment is also linear in nature, but the progress which it envisions is a continuing and necessary one, a steady advance from the kingdom of darkness to that of light. History is not looked upon as "something which makes us, but something which we make, which is the entirety of things which man has made, which he is making, and which he is going to — or can — make."[14] Fascinated by the belief in the infinite perfectibility of man, the prophets of the Enlightenment envision a heavenly kingdom on earth in which science and reason will reign triumphant.

Condorcet buttresses his theory of inevitable progress by the belief that acquired characteristics are inheritable. Social and political conditions in which knowledge can be freely acquired and transmitted are therefore essential to a progressive society. Many of the evils of the past can be attributed to the superior classes who kept the people ignorant in order to exploit them. The only remedy for this practice is to make truth available to all men so that none will be dependent on another. Rational

---

[13] Outlines of an Historical View of the Progress of the Human Mind (London: 1795), p. 368.

[14] Alexandre Koyre, "Condorcet," Journal of the History of Ideas, Apr., 1948, p. 131.

man must become his own master if the human race is to progress. He must cast off his servitude to political and priestly superiors. To do this, he must become educated. But this education must not consist of doctrinal views imposed by those in authority. It must be based on known facts and statistical data of high probability. In other words, it must be truth arrived at by the method of the mathematical and natural sciences.

MONTESQUIEU

The most comprehensive political theorist of the Age of Enlightenment was Baron de Montesquieu (1689–1755). Born of a well-to-do family of the *petite noblesse*, Montesquieu traveled extensively in Austria, Italy, Switzerland, Germany, Holland, and England. He began his career as a lawyer, but his interest in science and political institutions soon directed his activities into the channels of writing. Combining the happy facility for serious work with good living, he was able to win entry into the French Academy at the unusually early age of thirty-nine. He shares with the French philosophes their optimism in human progress, their faith in science, their hatred of despotism, and their inordinate anti-clericalism. He is also impressed, as they were, with British government and the intellectual outlook of the English aristocracy and middle classes. At the same time, he is more moderate in his approach, more aware of the complexities of society, and less inclined to believe in the wisdom of far-reaching social changes by human fiat.

Montesquieu's objective is to form a science of politics by discovering the rules which govern social phenomena. Standing in the tradition of Aristotle, he seeks his answers in the concrete facts of life. Observation and historical analysis are his chief instruments of research. The *Spirit of the Law*, which embodies the nexus of his social and political thinking, runs the whole gamut from analytic politics and economics to contemporary gossip and spicy anecdotes. While Montesquieu has an affinity for storytelling and is sometimes unduly fascinated with particulars, a clear and logical principle dominates his writings. He notes in the preface to his great work, "I have first of all considered mankind, and the result of my thoughts has been, that amidst such an infinite diversity of laws and manners, they were not solely conducted by the caprice of fancy. I laid down the first principles, and have found that the particular cases follow naturally from them; that the histories of all nations are only consequences of them; and that every particular law is connected with another law, or depends on some other of a more general extent."[15]

Three principles of particular significance to the development of political thought emerge from the *Spirit of the Laws*. The first pertains to the role that environment and circumstances play in the shaping of law and society; the second to the relation between norm and relativity in law and politics; and the third to the doctrine of separation of powers as a preventive against despotism.

Environment and Politics

Montesquieu is emphatic in his insistence that laws and political institutions must be adapted to the circumstances — historical, geographical, and climatic — in which a people lives. There is no exact code of laws and no set form of government that is suitable for all communities. The reconciliation of public authority and private right — the central problem of political philosophy — is not subject to a universally applicable solution. It must be achieved differently in different cultures; it depends upon the configurations of time, space, and tradition.

The spirit of the laws and of political systems is to be found in their relation to the people whom they affect and the environment in which they operate. Hence, the most appropriate form of government is one which best agrees with the disposition of the people for whom it is established. Since natural forces such as climate and soil affect human behavior, laws and social institutions should be "relative to the climate of each country, to the quality of its soil, to its situation and extent, to the principal occupation of the natives, whether husbandmen, huntsmen, or shepherds . . . to the religion of the inhabitants, to their inclinations, riches, numbers, commerce, manners and customs."[16] Cold climates foster energetic action, composure, and self-possession, while warm climates breed inertia, passion, and emotion.

In his classification of governments, Montesquieu lists three types: republican, monarchical, and despotic. The first may be either a democracy, when sovereignty is vested in the whole body of the people, or an aristocracy, when supreme power is lodged in only a select part of the

---

[15] *The Spirit of the Laws.* Excerpts from Montesquieu are taken from the Hafner edition translated by T. Nugent (New York: Hafner, 1949).

[16] *Ibid.,* I, 3.

people. Monarchy is constitutional government by a single individual while despotism is arbitrary and capricious rule by one. Monarchy also requires the existence of an aristocracy or some intermediate power standing between ruler and people and acting as a modifying influence. Despotism tolerates no such interference; the uplifted sword of the ruler regulates and curbs everything. Unlimited by law, the tyrant rules according to his own will and caprice.

Montesquieu notes that no form of government can be understood without a proper appreciation of its principles or moving force. Thus a republic, whether governed by the few or the many, depends on the civic virtue and the public spirit of its people — a genuine love of country, a willingness to sublimate individual self-interests when the common good so demands, a sense of patriotism, honesty, frugality, and equality. The spirit of equality, however, must not become excessive. Democracy is endangered when each man desires to be the equal of those whom he has chosen to rule over him.

Monarchy rests on the motivating factor of honor or a rivalry for distinction among the social hierarchy, each class being anxious to guard its rank and privileges. Although this may be a "false honor which moves all parts of the government," nonetheless, by this useful motive men can be induced "to perform the most difficult actions, such as require an extraordinary exertion of fortitude and resolution, without other recompense than that of glory and applause."[17] France had constitutional government as long as the king retained the parliaments and consulted with the aristocracy. When he failed to call the assemblies and to seek the advice of the nobility, absolutism set in. In contrast to the motivating forces of the other forms, despotism is dependent upon fear; it survives only as long as its subjects are intimidated. It is, in short, a government over slaves and not free men.

Social Relativism

Montesquieu is sometimes criticized for trying to combine an immutable natural law with a sociological and moral relativism. Such criticism, however, is not entirely warranted since it is extremely doubtful that he deviates materially from the traditional view of the relation between an objective moral law and its application in given historical circumstances. At the outset of the *Spirit of the Laws*, he defines law as "human

---

[17] *Ibid.*, III, 6.

reason, inasmuch as it governs all the inhabitants of the earth: the political and civil laws of each nation ought to be only the particular cases in which human reason is applied . . . and should be adapted . . . to the people for whom they are framed."[18] At no time does he deny the existence of a moral norm or standard to be found in the nature of man and the universe. He expressly admits the existence of first principles and at least implicitly, if not directly, denies that the sociological factors of time and circumstances take the place of these immutable laws. It would seem, although admittedly he is difficult to interpret in this regard, that his spirit of the laws refers simply to the different kinds of customs and practices of a people, which are in effect the specific determinations of first principles by that people.

This interpretation is supported by Montesquieu's view that man is not completely at the mercy of nature. As a free creature, he can help to mold his own destiny and bring about his proper end. Unfavorable climatic conditions may encourage moral degeneracy, but man can counteract these disadvantages by spiritual forces. "The more the physical causes incline mankind to inaction, the more the moral causes should estrange them from it."[19] The laws of a country must be realistic, but they must not run counter to the basic principles of nature. If the customs of a people violate such principles, it is the duty of the government to modify them through appropriate legislation. Certainly the predispositions of a people whether brought on by climate, soil, or historical circumstances, and whether violative of the natural law or not, are important factors that must always be taken into account when making laws. The inbred habits of a people, Montesquieu observes, cannot be changed overnight, and any attempt to do so might precipitate a social revolution.

As a true son of the Enlightenment, Montesquieu feels that the moral order will become more perfect as the human race advances in knowledge. He is confident that a painstaking investigation of empirical details will eventually lead man to a deep insight and understanding of nature. Aware of the complexity of the social organism, he realizes that an enormous amount of investigation and research will be necessary before intelligent reforms can be prescribed and meaningful knowledge of society obtained. Once the needed facts are accumulated and analyzed, man will be in a position to separate the constant forces of nature from the

---

[18] *Ibid.*, I, 3.   [19] *Ibid.*, XIV, 15.

variable tendencies of the human will, and thus effectively to control the future.

Separation of Powers

Montesquieu is best known today for his doctrine of the separation of powers. Previous political thinkers from Polybius to Locke had stressed the value of a "balanced" constitution or a division of powers as a make-weight against despotism. Prior to the seventeenth century, however, no writer had given expression to the idea of separating powers solely on a functional basis. The balanced constitution which earlier thinkers had sought to achieve had been founded, either on the idea of preventing any single social or economic class from becoming too predominant in government, or on the simple principle that political power should be divided among several agencies of the state so that each might act as a check on the other. In this latter scheme, no clear-cut division had been made between the nature of the functions to be entrusted to each agency. The objective had been to maintain political equilibrium by giving a portion of the sum total of governmental power, regardless of its functional nature, to different agencies. Thus the king might exercise certain legislative and judicial as well as administrative duties, while the power of the senate or parliament would not necessarily be confined to lawmaking.

It is doubtful that earlier theorists would have thought it feasible or even possible to make a complete separation between policy-formulation and policy-execution. Locke was one of the first to suggest the advisability of such a division, but his views in this respect lacked preciseness and failed to take account of the judiciary as a distinct and independent branch.[20] The task of developing and giving rational justification to the threefold division of power which is so familiar to modern day political science fell to the competent hands of the French baron.

Montesquieu is well aware that it is easier to condemn despotism than to provide against it. To form a moderate government, it is necessary to regulate political power, temper it, and give as it were a ballast to one power to enable it to withstand another. This task requires a master-piece of legislation, which chance produces rarely and prudence seldom. Montesquieu feels that the abuse of power can only be avoided by constitutional arrangements in which each element of the government is

---

[20] See ante, p. 262.

subject to the limitations of a balancing and opposing power. Such a system is necessary since "constant experience shows us that every man invested with power is apt to abuse it, and to carry his authority as far as it will go."[21]

Political functions are commonly classified as legislative, executive, and judicial. By vesting power over each functional category in different branches of government, a monopoly of public authority by a single individual or group is avoided and the conditions of political freedom better assured. For

> when the legislative and executive powers are united in the same person, or in the same body of magistrates, there can be no liberty; because apprehensions may rise lest the same monarch or senate should enact tyrannical laws, to execute them in a tyrannical manner. Again there is no liberty, if the judiciary power be not separated from the legislative and executive. Were it joined with the legislative, the life and liberty of the subject would be exposed to arbitrary control; for the judge would be then the legislator. Were it joined to the executive power, the judge might behave with violence and oppression.[22]

This principle was echoed by Madison when he wrote in the *Federalist Papers*: "the accumulation of all powers, legislative, executive, and judiciary in the same hands, whether of one, a few, or many, and whether hereditary, self-appointed, or elective, may justly be pronounced the very definition of tyranny."[23]

But how effective is it to divide formal political power among three departments of government when all three are actually under the control of one social or economic group in the community? Montesquieu recognizes the sociological implications of this question by endeavoring to supplement the legal and organizational division of powers by a balancing of social forces. To him, the monarch or executive represents social interests different from the legislature, while the judiciary represents everybody and hence nobody in particular. Where does legal sovereignty rest in such a system of divided authority? In the composite of the three powers, is Montesquieu's answer. And if they do not agree? They must agree, he replies, for political change can come about only by a "move in concert." The need for action must be subordinated to the need for consensus.

Montesquieu purports to have discovered the separation of powers

---

[21] *The Spirit of the Laws*, XI, 4.   [22] *Ibid.*, XI, 6.   [23] No. 47.

principle in the British constitution. But the constitution that he refers to is the constitution of 1689 and not its eighteenth-century development. At the very time that he was lauding British government for its separation of powers, England was actually establishing unified authority in the House of Commons. Montesquieu failed to perceive that the development of the cabinet system was destroying the very division of political power which he felt was so essential to human liberty.

Montesquieu would not have been perturbed to learn that he had misinterpreted British constitutional development. His primary concern was the preservation of human liberty under law, and he felt that the attainment of this objective depends more on the appropriateness of the political structure to its environment than on any precise arrangement of office. The important factor in ensuring moderate rule is the maintenance of a balance of political power in the community. It is immaterial whether this balance is achieved by structural and organizational devices or by other means. Montesquieu was convinced that the institutional separation of powers is the best method of guarding against the abuse of authority. He would be the first to point out, however, that the same result has been attained in the British unitary system by traditional respect for the limitations and responsibilities of public power. The English experience shows that tradition, public opinion, and civic alertness can be effective balancing forces in a mature society.

HUME

David Hume (1711–1776) was born at Edinburgh into a Scottish family of moderate means. He abandoned the study of law and a commercial career at an early age in order to devote his time to the study of philosophy and general learning. His masterpiece, the Treatise of Human Nature, appeared in 1739 but received little attention. The basic ideas which it contained were later set forth in a simpler and more readable style in such essays as the Enquiry into the Human Understanding and the Enquiry Concerning the Principles of Morals. These works at once attracted a wide audience and, together with his celebrated History of England, completed in 1761, brought him world-wide recognition. Following his success as a writer, he entered the British diplomatic corps. He retired from public service in 1769 as an undersecretary of state.

Hume's contribution to political theory is secondary and at most subsidiary to his work in general philosophy and epistemology. Although he deals with certain political problems in his *Essays, Moral and Political*, his significance to the history of political thought lies in the implications which his theory of knowledge has for civil society. He regards philosophy as an empirical "science of man" — a science that is to be conducted by the methods of the natural sciences: observation and generalization. "As the science of man is the only solid foundation for the other sciences, so the only solid foundation we can give to this science itself must be laid on experience and observation." Taking an extreme empiricist position, Hume insists that man cannot go beyond experience in his quest for knowledge. Any hypothesis that pretends to explain the ultimate original qualities of human nature must be rejected as presumptuous and chimerical.

The western tradition rests heavily on the premise of a natural moral law. Hume sets about to destroy this foundation by showing that no such law can exist and that consequently all human behavior is without rational justification. Like his empiricist predecessors, he maintains that the immediate objects of the mind are its own contents or perceptions,[24] but unlike them he insists that the scientific mind is incapable of giving any knowledge about material or spiritual substances. Man's knowledge is restricted to the appearances of things. The only connection or relation of objects which can lead us beyond the immediate impressions of our memory and senses "is that of cause and effect. . . . The idea of cause and effect is derived from *experience*, which informs us that such particular objects in all past instances have been constantly conjoined with each other."[25] Reason can tell us nothing about the relationships between matters of fact. When two events are found to be related as cause and effect, all that can really be known about them is that they occur together with a certain degree of regularity.

> When I examine, with the utmost accuracy, those objects which are commonly denominated causes and effects, I find, in considering a single instance, that the one object is precedent and contiguous to the other, and in enlarging my view to consider several instances, I find only that like objects are constantly placed in like relations of succession and contiguity.[26]

---

[24] To most of the contemporary empiricists, the mind resembled a container within which ideas originating somewhere in the external world are filtered and in which they circulate and form patterns as the figures in a mechanical slot machine.

[25] *Treatise of Human Nature*, I, III, 6.   [26] *Ibid.*, I, III, 14.

We have no way of knowing with certainty, Hume states, that any generalization based upon observed instances of phenomena remains true when we attempt to apply it to cover unobserved instances. We know, of course, that when the impression of one object is presented to us, we immediately form an idea of that which usually accompanies it. When we see a fire we think of heat, but it would be improper for us to say that the fire caused the heat. We merely observe the conjunction in time of fire and heat and infer a causal relation between the two, but we cannot penetrate into the reason of the conjunction. We may suppose but we can never prove that a necessary relationship exists in such cases, since it is always possible to assume the contrary of any matter of fact. In other words, it is possible for us to assume that the heat is not caused by the fire. Consequently, the relations which men observe between facts can never be objects of reasoning and can never "operate upon the mind but by means of custom, which determines the imagination to make a transition from the idea of one object to that of its usual attendant."

Such an epistemological approach forecloses any true knowledge of reality and hence any knowledge of a natural law, should such a law exist. If there is no cause-effect relation and no natural moral law, human behavior must be based on mere custom or expediency. There is no fundamental reason why men should be virtuous unless it be useful or convenient for them to be so. In advancing this theory of knowledge, Hume also abandons the Greco-medieval view of the pre-eminence of reason over passion. Reason, he states, can exert only a mediating influence over the passion by showing it the consequences which will likely follow any given course of action. To speak of the conflict between reason and passion is meaningless since only a contrary impulse can oppose a passion. "Reason is, and ought only to be the slave of the passions, and can never pretend to any office than to serve and obey them." Hume is not the first thinker to assign a subordinate role to reason. A similar view had been advanced at the close of the Middle Ages by Marsilius of Padua, and since that time Machiavelli, Hobbes, and others had taken analogous positions.

Despite his skepticism, Hume is unwilling to rest individual and social behavior solely on utilitarian grounds as his successors were soon to do. Recognizing the dangers to social and political stability inherent in a philosophy of moral relativism, he seeks to temper its effects by finding some basis for a natural morality in those factors that affect man's passions and impulses. In his essay repudiating the social contract theory, he notes that moral duties are divided into two kinds: those to which men are impelled by a natural instinct which operates on them such as love of children or pity for the unfortunate; and those which are not supported by any original instinct of nature but are performed entirely from a sense of obligation "when we consider the necessities of human society, and the impossibility of supporting it, if these duties were neglected." The second category includes a regard for the property of others and the willingness to observe promises.

> For as it is evident that every man loves himself better than any other person, he is naturally impelled to extend his acquisitions as much as possible; and nothing can restrain him in this propensity but reflection and experience, by which he learns the pernicious effects of that license, and the total dissolution of society which must ensue from it. His original inclination, therefore, or instinct, is here checked and restrained by a subsequent judgment or observation.[27]

It is on this utilitarian basis that government is made possible and that political obligation is founded. "A small degree of experience and observation suffices to teach us, that society cannot possibly be maintained without the authority of magistrates, and that this authority must soon fall into contempt where exact obedience is not paid to it. The observation of these general and obvious interests is the source of all allegiance, and of that moral obligation which we attribute to it."[28] Man owes obedience to the state not because of any natural or moral duty or even because of any compact he has entered into, but simply "because society could not otherwise subsist." Hume insists that men are united by more positive interests than an Hobbesian fear of each other. They have "a general sense of the common interest" which may be likened to the motive which induces two men to co-operate in rowing a boat.[29]

What restraints are there to deter men from seeking their own interests, even to the detriment of others, when they feel that they can get away with it? Hume maintains that there are two such restraints: habit

---

[27] *Essays Moral and Political*, "Of the Original Contract," in *Social Contract*, The World's Classics (Oxford: Oxford University Press, 1947), pp. 227–228.
[28] *Ibid.*, p. 228.
[29] See Charles Vereker, *The Development of Political Theory* (London: Hutchinson University Library, 1957), p. 133.

and the native sense of humanity or sympathy which man has for his fellow creatures. Men in practice constantly make moral judgments which generally agree with one another over a period of time. These judgments are not due to any intuitive knowledge of a moral standard but to the reactions of approval or disapproval which certain behavior evokes from society. Long experience, for example, shows the expediency of certain rules of social conduct. The beneficial effects which follow from observing these rules promote public feelings of moral approval toward their maintenance and moral condemnation of their disregard. With the passage of time, this social pressure establishes a pattern of behavior that becomes a matter of habit and custom.

Social approbation is not the only motivation at work in the cause of the common good. Although the whole system of justice and morality arises artificially from human self-interest, man is instinctively moved to an immediate, sympathetic response of approval or disapproval when he sees how certain actions and institutions affect the happiness of humanity at large. This inherent sympathy fosters a regard for the general welfare. As a result, actions and social arrangements which are conducive to the common good win approval within an established society, despite the conventional origin of the obligation of justice.

Interestingly enough, Hume not only laid the foundation for English utilitarianism, but he also foreshadowed (although on a radically different basis) the political conservatism of Edmund Burke.[30] The ultimate cause of all action is passion, not reason. Reason can only influence the course of behavior by drawing attention to the probable consequences of alternative courses of action. Hume calls those passions which are uninfluenced by reason "violent," and those upon which reason has been brought to bear "calm." On this distinction, he seeks to justify aristocratic government. Those whose reasoning powers have been developed by education and training and whose economic position is secure are less likely to be led by their violent passions into seeking immediate, at the expense of long range and lasting, advantage. Hence the general happiness is best promoted in a community where political power is vested in the hands of a wealthy, educated, and cultured class. A neat conclusion, and one entirely in accord with the general temper of British political thought of the eighteenth and nineteenth centuries.

---

[30] See *post*, Chap. XVI.

SUMMARY

The Age of Enlightenment was the high level mark of man's belief in human omniscience. To be enlightened is to understand that truth is to be found in the "great book of nature open for all mankind to read." The unprecedented progress in the physical sciences that had started in the seventeenth century had continued unabated into the eighteenth. Imbued with the spirit of the era, the philosophers of the Enlightenment sought to apply the methods and principles which had proved so successful in the investigation of physical phenomena to the study of metaphysics, ethics, politics, and even theology. By following this procedure, they felt certain that all the perplexities which confronted man in these spheres could be cleared up once and for all. They saw no limit to man's ability to ascertain the truth. The tools to be employed in this monumental task were observation, experiment, and analysis, accompanied by the application of exact methods of measurement. They confidently expected that through the use of these instruments the whole plan of the universe could be recognized and expressed by the human mind.

There is no reason, so the man of the Enlightenment said, to doubt that science could achieve as much in the realm of social and political relations as it had in the physical order. Once the laws governing human behavior are discovered and properly formulated, man's real desires can be brought to light and efficiently satisfied. Despite the scientific pretensions of their authors, such views brought an inflexible or dogmatic outlook to the problems of state and society — an outlook that tended to obscure the character of politics as a practical science. Influenced by the belief that there are universal laws applicable to all aspects of political behavior, men began to think in absolute terms about such concepts as freedom and equality. There were exceptions to this trend, such as those found in the writings of Montesquieu, but the general direction of thought tended to make ethics and politics speculative rather than practical sciences.

BIBLIOGRAPHY

Aiken, H. D. (ed.), Hume's Moral and Political Philosophy (New York: Hafner, 1948).

Buck, P. W., The Politics of Mercantilism (New York: Holt, 1942).

Coulson, Herbert H., "The Political Philosophy of Montesquieu," The American Catholic Philosophical Association Proceedings, 1931.

Crane, R. S., "Montesquieu and British Thought," Journal of Political Economy, August, 1941.

Crocker, Lester G., "Truth and Falsehood in the Enlightenment," Journal of the History of Ideas, October, 1953.

Ehrlich, E., "Montesquieu and Sociological Jurisprudence," Harvard Law Review, April, 1916.

Engel-Janosi, F., "Politics and History in the Age of Enlightenment," *Journal of Politics*, November, 1943.
Fletcher, F. T. H., *Montesquieu and English Politics* (London: Arnold and Company, 1939).
Gay, Peter, "The Enlightenment in the History of Political Theory," *Political Science Quarterly*, September, 1954.
Holdsworth, W. S., "The Conventions of the Eighteenth Century Constitution," *Iowa Law Review*, January, 1932.
Jacobson, N., "Political Realism in the Age of Reason: the anti-rationalist heritage in America," *Review of Politics*, October, 1953.
Koyre, Alexandre, "Condorcet," *Journal of the History of Ideas*, April, 1948.
Laird, John, *Hume's Philosophy of Human Nature* (London: Methuen, 1932).
Lowenthal, David, "Book I of Montesquieu's *The Spirit of the Laws*," *American Political Science Review*, June, 1959.
McRae, Robert, "Hume as a Political Philosopher," *Journal of the History of Ideas*, April, 1951.
Oake, Roger B., "Montesquieu's Analysis of Roman History," *Journal of the History of Ideas*, January, 1955.
Price, K. B., "Ernst Cassirer and the Enlightenment," *Journal of the History of Ideas*, January, 1957.
Rowe, Constance, *Voltaire and the State* (New York: Columbia University Press, 1955).
Smith, N. K., *The Philosophy of David Hume* (London: Macmillan, 1941).
Wickwar, W. H., "Helvetius and Holbach," in F. J. C. Hearnshaw, ed., *The Social and Political Ideas of Some Great French Thinkers of the Age of Reason* (New York: Barnes & Noble, 1950).
Wolin, S. S., "Hume and Conservatism," *American Political Science Review*, December, 1954.

Chapter XV

ROUSSEAU: POLITICAL ROMANTICISM

"By what inconceivable art has a means been found of making men free by making them subject" (Rousseau, A *Discourse on Political Economy*).

IN THE latter half of the eighteenth century, reaction to the rationalist culture and cold intellectuality of the Enlightenment began to set in. Known as Romanticism, the new movement took many forms, some clearly pagan, others Christian in inspiration and content. Whatever the form, all were unanimous in their opposition to the mechanistic concept of nature fostered by Newtonian physics and Cartesian philosophy. All protested against the efforts to reduce political and social phenomena to what resembled mathematical formulae. The Romantic movement turned to the past and not to the future, but its historical interest was dominated by a feeling for myth and poetry. The belief in the capacity of human reason to comprehend all truth lost its pervasive hold as passion and feeling became the divine elements in man. Although the reaction against reason did not lead to an abandonment of the search for truth, intuition, emotion, and sentiment replaced the intellect as the directive force.

The Romantic movement was essentially a revolt against accepted moral and aesthetic standards. Its supporters greatly admired what they referred to as *la sensibilité*, or a proneness to emotion. To be satisfactory, this emotion must be completely divorced from thought or reason, and it must be vigorous and passionate. The true romantic would be moved to tears at the sight of a poor and homeless waif but would be totally uninterested in a carefully worked out welfare plan for handling the problem of abandoned children. The temper of the romantics can be seen in their substitution of aesthetic for moral and utilitarian standards, in their praise of the pastoral and rural as against their contempt for the industrial and urban, and in their penchant for the strange and occult in literature.

The apostles of Romanticism, such as Fichte and Heine in Germany, Chateaubriand and Hugo in France, and Byron and Shelley in England, helped to carry the premises of the new movement into practically every branch of culture, art, and thought. Its followers included champions of authoritarian statism as well as utopian socialists; devout Protestants and sincere Catholics; moderates who sought only to rediscover old values and emphasize the importance of tradition in society to extremists who rejected all traditional authority and placed passion and emotion in stark opposition to reason. By challenging the spirit of scientific rationalism, the Romantic movement helped to uncover many of the basic fallacies engendered by the Enlightenment. However, its extremist tendencies, particularly its inclination to substitute the autonomy of feeling for that of reason, proved equally as dangerous as those it had exposed. When feeling is freed from the directive discipline of reason, it can lead man in any direction; and if the Romantic proclamation of the primacy of emotion led some to God, it led many more to the worship of the sacred Ego.[1]

Political speculation no more escaped the influence of the Romantic movement than did literature or the arts. The real apostle of the new spirit in the field of political philosophy was Jean Jacques Rousseau (1712–1778). Born of a low middle class family that had migrated to the city-state of Geneva in the sixteenth century as religious refugees, Rousseau was educated in the orthodox Calvinist religion. His mother died in childbirth; his father combined the professions of watchmaker and dancing teacher. The discipline, or rather the lack of it, which the widowed father exercised over the son was not conducive to the development of the child's personality and character. On many a night the young boy was kept awake until late hours listening to romances and adventure stories which his father read aloud.

When Jean Jacques was ten, his father fled from Geneva to avoid imprisonment for an altercation with another citizen. The boy was taken charge of by his mother's relatives who tried without success to apprentice him out in various trades. At the age of sixteen, he ran away from Geneva and began a life of wandering, dissoluteness, debauchery, and yet withal brilliant writing. He committed petty crimes of larceny, moving

---

[1] Hallowell, op. cit., pp. 165–166.

from place to place with the help of various patronesses, and living on his wits more than anything else. He callously adopted and changed religions when it seemed materially advantageous for him to do so.

Rousseau came to wide public attention in 1749 when his *Discourse on the Arts and Sciences* won the prize offered by the Academy of Dijon for the best essay on the theme: "Has the restoration of the sciences contributed to purify manners?" His two major works, the *Social Contract* and *Emile* appeared in 1762. When the latter was condemned by the parliament of Paris, Rousseau was forced to leave France to avoid arrest. At Hume's invitation, he went to England, where he was lionized by London society. After quarreling with his host whom he accused of plotting against his life, he returned to Paris in 1770, where he spent his last years suffering from delusions and hallucinations. He died in 1778 in great poverty.

The writings of Rousseau are at many points ambiguous and inconsistent, if not contradictory. This fact has led to a wide divergency of opinion among his interpreters. To some he appears as the champion of individual liberty, to others as the father of state absolutism. In *Emile* and the opening chapters of the *Social Contract*, he displays himself as an unmitigated individualist and a passionate lover of a prepolitical state of unbridled liberty. Conversely, in his *Discourse on Political Economy* and in the major portion of the *Social Contract*, he appears to advocate the total submersion of the individual in the state and to insist that only in political society can man fulfill his nature. As Professor Hearnshaw has so well stated, "The sum of the matter seems to be that Rousseau from time to time, and even at the same time, uttered opinions diametrically opposite to one another concerning toleration and persecution, concerning primitive man and civilized society, and concerning countless other matters. He was an unsystematic thinker, untrained in formal logic. He was an omnivorous reader with undeveloped powers of assimilation. He was an emotional enthusiast who spoke without due reflection. He was an irresponsible writer with a fatal gift for epigram."[2]

Those who have tried to reconcile the inconsistencies which appear in Rousseau's thought are often reduced to such phrases as "when he is true to himself," or when he fails "to be true to his own best insight." Yet in spite of the difficulties inherent in his writings, a study of the

---

[2] F. J. Hearnshaw, *The Social and Political Ideas of Some Great French Thinkers of the Age of Reason* (London: Harrap & Co., 1930), pp. 185–186.

social thought of the Genevan expatriate is rewarding not only because of its historical importance and the brilliant literary style in which it is presented, but also because of the incisive manner in which it raises some of the basic questions of political philosophy.

THE PROBLEM OF POLITICAL OBLIGATION

Like many of his predecessors and those who were to follow him, Rousseau is not concerned primarily with the actual institutions and governmental organs of existing states; his purpose is to discover the basis of political obligation and to solve the problem of state authority versus individual freedom. This objective is voiced in the familiarly known passage which opens the *Social Contract*: "Man is born free, and everywhere he is in chains. One thinks himself the master of others and still remains a greater slave than they. How did this change come about? I do not know. What can make it legitimate? That question I think I can answer."[3] How in other words, can the state with its exercise of coercive power be morally justified? On what rational or moral grounds can I as an individual be subjected to the forces of the entire community? Obviously the authority which the state exercises over me cannot be based on mere physical strength since force may do almost any other thing except create a right. "To yield to force is an act of necessity, not of will — at the most, an act of prudence."[4] Submission to physical coercion cannot in itself imply a moral obligation.

Aristotle and the traditionalists found the answer to the problem of political obligation in the natural character of the state as an institution essential to the perfection of man's being. They considered obedience to lawfully constituted authority to be as much a moral duty as the obedience a child owes to his parents. Men may be free to choose their form of government, but they are under moral compulsion to form political society and to submit to its reasonable demands. For them to do otherwise would be to act contrary to nature. This traditional solution is not open to Rousseau since he repudiates the existence of an original social instinct which drives men together and denies that the state is a natural institution. Only the family enjoys this title, and even here the natural authority of the parent continues only so long as needed for the preser-

---

[3] I, 1. Excerpts from Rousseau are taken from Everyman's Library edition. *The Social Contract and Discourses*, trans. by G. D. H. Cole (New York: Dutton, 1913).
[4] *Ibid.*, I, 3.

vation of the child. Once the need ceases, the natural bond is dissolved. The children are then released from the obedience they owe to the family, and the latter in turn is relieved of the obligation to care for the children.

If the formal relationship of parent and child continues beyond the point of need, it must be by mutual agreement among the parties. "If they remain united, they continue so no longer naturally but voluntarily; and the family itself is then maintained only by convention." Man's first law is to provide for his own preservation; as soon as he reaches maturity, he becomes the "sole judge of the proper means of preserving himself, and consequently becomes his own master."[5] No individual has a natural authority over his fellow creatures (except parent over child); similarly, no human agency or association has such right. Thus, a society which is not natural can get authority only from the individuals who create and make it up.

THE STATE OF NATURE

If "no man has a natural authority over his fellow creatures, and force creates no right, we must conclude that conventions form the basis of all legitimate authority among men."[6] We are thus back at the starting point of Hobbes and Locke. What are the reasons that lead men to form the social compact? Why is it necessary for them to establish some form of political authority? What motives prompt them to give up their natural freedom and voluntarily enter civil society? In the *Social Contract*, Rousseau avoids any description of the state of nature. He contents himself with the assumption that men at some time in their primitive condition had reached the point where the obstacles in the way of their preservation became so great that the human race would have perished had they not changed their manner of existence. His *Discourse on the Origin and Foundation of Inequality*, written seven years earlier, pictures man living in a sort of garden of Eden in a simple, happy, and carefree existence. During this stage the individual pursued in isolation his basic needs, living by instinct and not reason, his desires never going beyond his physical wants. Basic to his nature were two instincts: self-preservation and sympathy (*pitié*) or compassion for the plight of others.[7] Since these

---

[5] *Ibid.*, I, 2.   [6] *Ibid.*, I, 4.

[7] "Compassion is a natural feeling, which, by moderating the violence of love of self in each individual, contributes to the preservation of the whole species. It is this

original and primitive traits assisted more than they harmed the individual and his fellow creatures, it is proper to say that man is by nature good. In making this assertion about the inherent goodness of man, the founder of modern political romanticism shows no evidence of his religious background. His view that man is naturally good runs counter to the Calvinist doctrine of original sin.

Rousseau states that man's cares and desires increased as the human race grew and contacts among men became more frequent. As these changes took place, the individual found it necessary to engage in mutual undertakings with others in order to satisfy his growing needs. From the moment "one man began to stand in need of the help of another; from the moment it appeared advantageous to any man to have enough provisions for two, equality disappeared, property was introduced."[8] Greed, slavery, human misery, and the quest for power then became predominant in human society. The fear of his fellow men and their institutions caused the individual to become suspicious, self-seeking, and power hungry. Hobbes' condition of war again reappears, but it is no longer the state of nature; it is now the civil state. Wickedness and violence appear only after man has entered society and become subjected to all the artificial desires that it fosters. Man's motives unperverted by civilization are good; it is the corrupting influences of society and its institutions which make him what he is. His reliance on the brutal forms of social life calls into play a narrow egoism, and changes his native sympathy into seeking power and dominance over others.[9]

Despite the glowing terms in which he speaks of the peacefulness of primitive society, Rousseau envisions no return to it. To go back is impossible; the habits of civilization cannot be discarded. Man must recognize the existence of society, he must accept the institution of private property, and he must accommodate himself to the advancement of the arts and sciences. Contrary to what one might expect, Rousseau does not regard the state as a necessary evil. In what would appear to be a reversal of his earlier thinking, he turns to the Aristotelian concept of the state as an agency of human perfection. Outside of civil society

compassion that hurries us without reflection to the relief of those who are in distress: it is this which in a state of nature supplies the place of laws, morals, and virtues." (A *Discourse on the Origin and Foundation of the Inequality of Mankind*, contained in *The Social Contract and Discourses*, op. cit., p. 184).

[8] *Ibid.*, p. 199.
[9] See John A. Clark, "The Definition of the General Will," *Ethics*, Jan., 1943, pp. 79–88.

man is a stupid and unimaginative animal; in it he is an intelligent being and a man. Although in the political state man "deprives himself of some advantages which he received from nature, he gains in return others so great, his faculties are so stimulated and developed, his ideas so extended, his feelings so ennobled, and his whole soul so uplifted, that, did not the abuses of this new condition often degrade him below that which he left, he would be bound to bless continually the happy moment which took him from it forever."[10]

The task is not to destroy the state; it is to find its true basis, to solve the riddle of political obligation, and to define the proper relationship between civil society and the individual. If this undertaking can be accomplished, the path toward genuine social and political reform can be marked out with certainty and clarity. And if the political community can be stripped of the abuses which incite man to wrongdoing, the pristine integrity and goodness of the state of nature will be restored. In this sense, man will return to nature.

THE SOCIAL CONTRACT

Granted that civil society is a necessity and that consent is the only legitimate basis for political authority, the problem as Rousseau formulates it is "to find a form of association which will defend and protect with the whole common force the person and goods of each associate, and in which each, while uniting himself with all, may still obey himself alone, and remain as free as before."[11] If an association of this nature can be discovered, the problem of political obligation as it is posed in the *Social Contract* will apparently be solved. On the one hand, anarchy will be prevented by the establishment of public authority; on the other, the individual will retain his perfect liberty. Rousseau purports to see the answer to the dilemma he has raised in a contract to form civil society. By this agreement, the individual parties become a people, a community; they create a society and endow it with legitimate authority. Unanimity is required in this original agreement since no man can be forced to withdraw from his natural state without his consent.

What are the terms of the social contract? The answer rests in the motives or purposes that prompt men to make it. These are essentially twofold: the need for a corporate society that can mobilize the com-

---

[10] *Social Contract*, I, 8.   [11] *Ibid.*, I, 6.

mon power in support of each member; and the desire of the individual member to remain at liberty even though united with all others in mutual dependence. Both of these major objectives are attained by a mutual pact in which "each of us puts his person and all his power in common under the supreme direction of the general will, and, in our corporate capacity, we receive each member as an indivisible part of the whole."[12]

Once the social contract is consummated, immediately "in place of the individual personality of each contracting party, this act of association creates a moral and collective body, composed of as many members as the assembly contains voters, and receiving from this act its unity, its common identity, its life, and its will."[13] To this collective body — the political community — each individual surrenders completely and unreservedly himself and all his rights. "These clauses, properly understood, may be reduced to one — the total alienation of each associate, together with all his rights, to the whole community; for, in the first place, as each gives himself absolutely, the conditions are the same for all; and, this being so, no one has any interest in making them burdensome to others."[14]

Locke had held that the individual on entering civil society surrenders only the right of interpreting and enforcing the law of nature. Rousseau follows Hobbes in arguing that the individual surrenders his rights completely; but unlike the latter, he holds that the alienation is not made to any one person or group of persons but to the community as a whole, of which each member is an indivisible part. "Each man, in giving himself to all, gives himself to nobody; and as there is no associate over which he does not acquire the same right as he yields others over himself, he gains an equivalent for everything he loses, and an increase of force for the preservation of what he has."[15] In other words, the individual gives himself to society on terms equal for all men, acquiring over all the others the same power that he surrenders to them. Not only does he thereby recover the equivalent of what he loses, but he gains the additional strength of the whole group that comes from union. Every duty which he owes the other members is balanced by a duty they perform in part for his benefit, and meanwhile all of the members have gained the strength that comes from union.[16]

---

[12] *Ibid.*, I, 6.   [14] *Ibid.*
[13] *Ibid.*   [15] *Ibid.*
[16] See E. H. Wright, *The Meaning of Rousseau* (London: Oxford University Press, 1929), Chap. 3.

By this ingenious line of reasoning, Rousseau attempts to show that the social contract endows the individual with the power of the group and yet leaves him with absolute liberty. Self-imposed political chains have advantages similar to those of a rope that is shared by a group of mountain climbers. Rousseau's efforts to explain political obligation again demonstrate the consequences of rejecting a moral and natural duty on the individual to submit to legitimate social control. Without such obligation, man is compelled to seek some type of artificial reconciliation between freedom and authority.

THE GENERAL WILL

By the act of social union there is simultaneously created a new collective person: the state. This public person or body politic "is also a moral being possessed of a will." What this will, known as the general will, actually is and how it is discovered are questions crucial to Rousseau's political theory. Unfortunately, he nowhere satisfactorily answers them. He is primarily concerned with demonstrating that the state is similar to a physiological organism in which there can be no more conflict between the purposes of the whole and of the part than there can be between the health of a living body and one of its organs. If, therefore, the state is a common self with its own life and will, there can be no conflict between it and the natural liberty of the individual. For the true will and interest of the part must necessarily coincide with the will and interest of the whole.

Each member in adhering to the social pact agrees to identify his individual will with the general will of the community in all matters of public concern. The will which so arises from the political union has three important characteristics: it is always right and always tends to the public advantage; it is neither the will of the majority nor the sum total of individual wills; and it is sovereign and finds its expression in law.

The general will is an expression of what the common interests require. It is based on the theory that, when a group of individuals participate in a civil compact, their many wills (each itself egoist) offset and influence one another in such a way as to create a new will which is always directed toward the common good. The formation of the general will, as described by Rousseau, appears to be almost a mechanical or physical process. Through the mutual interaction and fusion of individual wills, as though they were atoms, the will of the state emerges. Although this will is always right in the sense that it desires the common good, Rousseau concedes that the people can fail to understand what this good is in concrete cases. He recognizes that they do not always act from unselfish motives. "Our will is always for our own good, but we do not always see what that is; the people is never corrupted, but it is often deceived, and on such occasions only does it seem to will what is bad."[17] To minimize the possibility of error, the people stand in need of a leader who can formulate the laws. The nature and function of this leader who is referred to as "legislator" will be discussed in a subsequent section.

How is the general will to be formulated? Rousseau is careful to state that it is not arrived at by taking the sum total of the wills of those who make up the community since individual wills tend to partiality. When men leave out of sight the public aspect of a question and are influenced by the expected consequences to themselves as private individuals, the decision which they arrive at, even though unanimous, is not founded on a genuine view of public interest. It is based merely on "a sum of particular wills." The general will results only when men sublimate their private interests and are able to answer affirmatively the question, "Is this for the public good?"

Rousseau does not deny that individuals may have vices and private interests which run counter to the general will.

> In fact, each individual, as a man, may have a particular will contrary or dissimilar to the general will which he has as a citizen. His particular interest may speak to him quite differently from the common interest: his absolute and naturally independent existence may make him look upon what he owes to the common cause as a gratuitous contribution, the loss of which will do less harm to others than the payment of it is burdensome to himself . . . he may wish to enjoy the rights of citizenship without being ready to fulfil the duties of a subject.[18]

Hence, in order that the social pact may not be a meaningless formula, it includes the agreement that "whoever refuses to obey the general will shall be compelled to do so by the whole body."[19] But if the individual is compelled by the force of political authority to act against his will, how does he remain as free as he was before entering society? Rousseau replies that when man's individual will appears at variance with the general will, he is simply deceived as to what his own true will is. In the

---

[17] *Social Contract*, II, 3.   [18] *Ibid.*, I, 7.   [19] *Ibid.*

social body, the true interests of the whole and the parts are identical, and the will of the whole being general and for the good of the totality can never err while the will of the individual being directed at particular things may sometimes be deceived. My real interests lie in the common good, and if I will the common good I am necessarily willing my own welfare. By compelling me to heed the general will, the state is merely forcing me to follow my own real will, "which is no more than to say that it may be necessary to compel a man to be free." The compulsion is not external; it is not the imposition of another will on mine. The general will is in effect no more than my own will coming back to me, even though I may not recognize it. By following this will, I am fulfilling myself and finding my true freedom.

Even if we accept Rousseau's metaphysical gymnastics, we are still confronted with the important question as to how the general will is to be determined or recognized. If it is formulated by the citizen body, as Rousseau says it must be, is it to be identified with the majority; and if so, how can it be reconciled with divergent minorities? Moreover, what assurance is there that the people will be motivated by public rather than private interests in their deliberations? The *Social Contract* implies that the true general will results automatically when men are permitted to express their own views freely and without pressure or coercion. If such is the case, the task of political science is to devise a governmental system in which this freedom is assured to all individuals. Rousseau recognizes that unanimity in popular decision-making is a virtual impossibility and that in the enactment of laws (through which the general will is expressed) the vote of the majority has to prevail as a matter of practical necessity. This means in effect that the general will is what the greater number declares it to be. However, Rousseau insists, the majority rules over the individual not by virtue of its numbers but because the individual has given his consent to its authority.

THE NATURE OF THE STATE

Some of the confusion in Rousseau's general political philosophy is probably due to his ambivalent view of the nature of the state — a view that vacillates between a mechanistic and organismic concept of civil society. At one and the same time he makes the state an artificial creation of man established by social contract and a "moral and collective body" with a will of its own separate and apart from the will of its members. The two views are patently inconsistent. The one regards the state as a mere instrument or mechanism, the other as an organism composed of human beings. The first can be created by an act of agreement among men; the second by some inner compulsion which, as in a biological specimen, forms and organizes the member parts into an integral unit. Rousseau seeks to join these two concepts in an uneasy combination. He wants the individual members of the state to be free but he also wants them to be wholly subordinate to the community. He is apparently convinced that total subordination is essential if the ends of society are to be attained.

Traditional thought emphasizes that the vital principle of the state is to be found in the unity which results from the collectivity of individual wills joined together in pursuit of a common end. Such a unity is not something superimposed on the community by an external force, as the *Leviathan* proposes, nor that of the unity of a herd bound together by an unconscious impulse. It is a feeling of common purpose and interests and of mutual objectives which amalgamates the people into a social body. Its moving principle is rational, not biological or mechanical. Rousseau feels the need for going beyond the artificiality of the social pact, but he rebels against any acceptance of the traditional organic doctrine. His body politic emerges from the *Social Contract* as some kind of metaphysical entity which he calls the "state" when passive, the "sovereign" when active, and a "power" in relation to other states.

Rousseau's state is analogous to or at least an embodiment of the general will. As such, "it is in the position of an individual who makes a contract with himself; and this makes it clear that there neither is nor can be any kind of fundamental law binding on the body of the people."[20] When individuals unite in political society, they agree to submit themselves to the direction of the general will. It is true that in this act of submission each person alienates "only such part of his powers, goods, and liberty as is important for the community to control." It is also true that "the sovereign cannot impose on its subjects any fetters that are useless." But these reservations are of little worth since the "sovereign is sole judge of what is important and useful." As nature gives each man "absolute power over all his members, the social compact gives the body politic absolute power over all its members also."[21]

---

[20] *Ibid.*, I, 7.   [21] *Ibid.*, II, 4.

Rousseau believes that the people organized as a community, when given the proper conditions, will always act in the interest of human freedom. He also believes that the general will is always right — ignoring the fact that for fallible man to create an infallible will is a contradiction in terms. In the final analysis, his political philosophy provides a very feeble obstacle to collective tyranny. The classical concept that political rule is always subject to the limitations of the natural law plays little part in Rousseau's thinking. He refers to it only briefly at points, intimating that it is based more on emotion and feeling than on reason. He recognizes no standard of justice extraneous to the general will which determines its rightness or wrongness. Natural law for him is no more than what the people as a political body decree it to be.

DIRECT DEMOCRACY

Law is the voice of the general will, which in turn is the will of the people organized as a body politic. It is not, Rousseau emphasizes, the command of an individual or group compelling us to act against our will. Such would not be law but force. Law is not made by compulsion but by agreement and consent of the people. And since the people are subject to the laws, they should "be their author: the conditions of the society ought to be regulated by those who come together to form it."[22] All the members of the political community should share equally in making the law since they all have a common interest in living together. Sovereignty, therefore, does not rest in the monarch or government but in the community in its collective and legislative capacity.

But how does a multitude carry out for itself "so great and difficult an enterprise as a system of legislation"? In modern democracies, the answer is found in representative parliaments elected by the people. Rousseau, however, will have nothing to do with representative government, calling it an "iniquitous and absurd system which degrades humanity and dishonors the name of man."[23] Law, as he continually reiterates, is the declaration of the general will in which the people must participate personally and not by proxy. To entrust the responsibility to others is to give up one's freedom. The people of England, "regards itself as free; but it is grossly mistaken; it is free only during

---

[22] Ibid., II, 6.
[23] Ibid., III, 15.

the election of members of parliament. As soon as they are elected, slavery overtakes it, and it is nothing."[24]

Rousseau feels that freedom is more secure when the people are able to assemble periodically for the expression of the general will. He realizes that any theory of primary or direct democracy is suited at most to the small city-state such as existed in Athens and was still found in the Switzerland of his day. "All things considered, I do not see that it is possible henceforth for the Sovereign to preserve among us the exercise of its rights unless the city is very small."[25] Ideally, the state should be neither too large for good government nor too small for self-preservation. If too large, the social tie among the people is weakened, popular participation in the legislative process is made difficult, and the citizens have less affection for their magistrates whom they seldom see. If too small, the state cannot sustain its population and it runs the risk of being swallowed up by its larger neighbors. The problem is to find a political arrangement that will permit primary democracy and yet enable a small state to maintain its existence in a world of larger states.

Rousseau apparently visualizes a system in which the large state would be broken up into many smaller sovereign units bound together for their mutual defense in some type of federation. If historical conditions make reductions in the size of the states impossible, Rousseau suggests an arrangement in which the seat of government would be moved periodically to different sections of the country. "Nevertheless, if the State cannot be reduced to the right limits, there remains still one resource; this is, to allow no capital, to make the seat of government move from town to town, and to assemble by turn in each the Provincial Estates of the country."[26] This idea, like his treatment of federation, is only casually suggested but never developed. Possibly he had in mind an early practice of the trade unions whereby local branches in different towns rotated as the governing organ of the whole union for a fixed period. This device, as Rousseau should have known, had proved wholly unrealistic and impractical, and had soon been abandoned.

Experience has demonstrated the need for representative institutions in any large country which seeks to adhere to the principle of true self-government. The nature of the general will obviously precludes any acceptance of the representative device. It is only, Rousseau states, when each individual is free from the influence of others and particularly of

[24] *Ibid.*, III, 15.   [25] *Ibid.*   [26] *Ibid.*, III, 13.

political parties, factions, and interest groups that he expresses his real feelings. The general will is formed when every individual feels himself spontaneously allied with every other member of the community. Only then is individual selfishness canceled out in voting and a residuum of genuine common will left.

> If, when the people, being furnished with adequate information, held its deliberations, the citizens had no communication one with another, the grand total of the small differences would always give the general will, and the decision would always be good. But when factions arise, and partial associations are formed at the expense of the great association, the will of each of these associations becomes general in relation to its members, while it remains particular in relation to the State; it may then be said that there are no longer as many votes as there are men, but only as many as there are associations. The differences become less numerous and give a less general result.[27]

Similarly, under a system of representative government there are no longer as many votes as there are citizens, but only as many as there are representatives. In such case, there can be no true expression of the general will.

It is clear from what has been said that the principle of subsidiarity is alien to Rousseau's thinking. His political philosophy permits of no voluntary groups or partial societies to supplement individual action. Such groups — trade unions, professional associations, political parties — endanger the true expression of the general will by the influence which they exert over the individual. They should be banned in any properly ordered state so that each citizen should think only his own thoughts. If for some reason voluntary associations are permitted, they should be kept small and numerous in order that they may neutralize each other. In no case should they be allowed to play an important part in society or to come between the individual and the state.

THE LEGISLATOR

Rousseau recognizes that the creation of a government requires great skill and ability and that few people have the attributes necessary for such a task. To remedy this deficiency, he introduces his notion of a "legislator," a sort of modern Lycurgus or Solon. The holder of this title must be a person of extraordinary genius, an expert who could

---
[27] *Ibid.*, II, 3.

draft a constitution suitable to the needs and requirements of the particular people involved. His proposals would then be submitted to the voters for ratification. Such a legislator would possess neither lawmaking nor executive powers; his job is to design the machinery of government and the basic principles for its operations.[28] Once this task is accomplished and the general directions for the government to follow marked out, the people presumably would be able to rule themselves. Whether the legislator would continue in existence as a pre-eminent adviser to and a formulator of laws for the popular assemblies is not clear.

The Greek city-states had frequently called in distinguished men with political experience to serve as lawgivers, and even modern parliamentary bodies find it necessary to rely heavily on expert advice in lawmaking. If this is all that Rousseau means, there is nothing that is radical in his general idea of the legislator. Such a device would resemble the modern system in which a group of able delegates draft constitutional provisions for submission to popular referendum. Unfortunately, Rousseau couches his description of the office in such rhetorical and mystical language ("the great soul of the legislator is the only miracle that can prove his mission," or "it is not anybody who can make the gods speak, or get himself believed when he proclaims himself their interpreter"[29]) that it is impossible to know exactly what he has in mind.

GOVERNMENT

Government is defined in the *Social Contract* as "an intermediate body set up between the subjects and the Sovereign, to secure their mutual correspondence, charged with the execution of the laws and the maintenance of liberty, both civil and political."[30] The term "government" is therefore limited to the executive branch; it does not, as is commonly understood, include the legislative power since that is left in the hands of the people. "I call then *government*, or supreme administration, the legitimate exercise of the executive power, and prince or magistrate the man or the body entrusted with that administration."[31] Government comes into being not by virtue of any contract between the people and its rulers but by an act of the sovereign will. "The

---

[28] "The legislator occupies in every respect an extraordinary position in the state. If he should do so by reason of his genius, he does so no less by reason of his office, which is neither magistracy, nor Sovereignty" (*ibid.*, II, 7).

[29] *Ibid.*, II, 7.   [30] *Ibid.*, III, 1.   [31] *Ibid.*

institution of government is not a contract but a law; that the depositaries of the executive power are not the people's masters but its officers; that it can set them up and pull them down when it likes; that for them there is no question of contract but of obedience and that in taking charge of the functions the State imposes on them they are doing no more than fulfilling their duty as citizens, without having the remotest right to argue about the conditions."[32] In the interest of stability the established government should not be overturned except for serious cause; but this is a matter of prudential policy and not a rule of right.

Government, in the sense used by Rousseau, is the instrumentality whereby the citizens as sovereign apply the laws which they make to themselves as subjects. Although the citizen obeys the government, he is its sovereign master because of his participation in the general will. Thus while he must comply with the law, he also creates it. As executor of the law, government must always play a strictly subordinate role and never attempt to substitute its own will for the general will from whence it derives its authority. In practice, however, governments sometimes usurp the position of sovereign authority by developing a general will of their own. Whenever they do so, they pervert their role in society and destroy the true basis on which the political community is formed.

Rousseau has no strong feeling as to which form of government is best. In fact, since government is subordinate to the sovereign will, it matters little to him in principle whether it is democratic or monarchical so long as it is suitable to the needs and circumstances of the particular people whom it serves. Influenced by Montesquieu, who had attempted to establish a relation between the size of a state and its form of government, Rousseau observes that generally democratic governments suit small communities, aristocratic governments those of middle size, and monarchies large states. His own preference leans in the direction of an elected aristocracy. As he states, "assemblies are probably more easily held, affairs better discussed and carried out with more order and diligence, and the credit of the State is better sustained abroad by venerable senators than by a multitude that is unknown or despised."[33] That the wisest men should govern the many is the best and most natural arrangement "when it is assured that they will govern for its profit and not for their own. There is no need to multiply instruments, or get twenty thousand men to do what a hundred picked men can do even better."[34]

---

[32] *Ibid.*, III, 18.   [33] *Ibid.*, III, 5.   [34] *Ibid.*

To entrust the administrative duties of government to the multitude would be an obvious impossibility even in a normal sized community.

Since Rousseau limits government to the executive function, he can argue for an aristocratic form of rule without affecting the truly democratic character of his state. The people would still retain the lawmaking power; they would merely entrust administrative responsibilities to a group of capable officials. It is clear that if lawmaking is placed in a category distinct from the government itself, any classification of governmental forms as normally understood becomes meaningless. When, for example, political thinkers speak of an aristocratic government they generally mean a system in which both policy-making and its execution are vested in a select group. This meaning cannot be attached to Rousseau's classification. Yet in spite of these differences in terminology, the modern concept of democracy bears some kinship to Rousseau's doctrine of governmental forms. What he refers to as an elective aristocracy, we call democracy. Lawmaking power in modern democratic theory remains with the people and is normally exercised by their representatives. At the same time there is general agreement, at least in the theory, that the administration of government should be placed in the hands of able men: an aristocracy of political and managerial talent.

SUMMARY

It is difficult to appraise Rousseau's political philosophy or to measure it against the standard of the western tradition since we cannot always be sure of the exact meaning that he intends to convey. Not only does he disregard the demands of consistency but he rarely bothers to define his terms, frequently using them in different senses at different times. Moreover, his flare for epigrammatic expression and his poetic tendencies compound the difficulty by precluding the reader from taking his more dramatic statements at face value. Any conclusions pertaining to his political philosophy can be based only on what appears to be its general tenor and logical implications.

Rousseau places great value on the human person but his individual is a man of emotion rather than reason; a man who prefers instinct to intellect, and beauty to a sense of objective fact. This practice of basing beliefs about reality upon the emotions of the heart rather than the conclusions of the intellect has serious drawbacks. There is no logical reason to suppose that such beliefs will be true. For even if the heart says the same thing to all men, which obviously it doesn't, this fact can offer no proof for the existence of anything outside our own emotions. Bertrand Russell, who certainly is no supporter of traditional philosophy, has this to say in commenting on Rousseau's sentimental illogicality

> The old arguments at least were honest: if valid, they proved their point; if invalid, it was open to any critic to prove them so. But the new theology of the heart dispensed with argument; it cannot be refuted, because it does not profess to prove its points. At bottom, the only reason offered for its acceptance is that it allows us to indulge in pleasant dreams. This is an unworthy reason, and if I had to choose between Thomas Aquinas and Rousseau, I should unhesitatingly choose the Saint.[35]

Whatever the deficiencies or contradictions of Rousseau's political philosophy, this ardent apostle of political romanticism occupies an influential position in the history of political thought. Eighteenth-century thinkers like Montesquieu and Voltaire belong almost exclusively to their era, but Rousseau reaches out into the succeeding generations. His influence was predominant not only in France where the *Social Contract* became the bible of the Revolution, but in Germany as well where it served as the starting point for the Hegelian state. Robespierre could shout of the Jacobins, "our will is the general will," and Marx could later insist that a society must be "forced to be free" in order for man to find his true self.

The frontispiece of the first edition of the *Social Contract* shows a picture of Hobbes "sovereign" with his head cut off. No other illustration could have better revealed the anomaly in Rousseau's thinking. Although a bitter foe of despotism, he seeks his answer to human freedom in a form of democratic absolutism that requires the individual to surrender himself completely to the community. The body politic thus becomes a headless leviathan motivated and directed by the general will — a will shared by all but actually possessed by none. This will, moreover, is not the will of any individual or group of individuals. It is an essentially empty will without specific objects. As such it is subject to manipulation by anyone who claims to have an insight into its nature. This characteristic of the general will has made it easy for modern totalitarian governments to justify in its name arbitrary acts of force with considerable plausibility.[36]

By the act of divestiture which man makes to the community, he relieves himself of the sense of moral responsibility and transfers it to the general will. Thereafter, the question whether he is acting justly or unjustly, morally or immorally, need no longer trouble him. All that is necessary for him to do is to follow the dictates of the state instead of his conscience. Rousseau starts from the premise that only the human person matters. He ends by actually dwarfing the individual in a social whole that exercises total powers.

Rousseau is a strong proponent of direct democracy in which all men, not a privileged class or a select few, participate. His idea of a community of free men associated in a small city-state, sharing the responsibility not only for their individual interests but for the collective good of the whole, is certainly

[35] *A History of Western Philosophy* (New York: Simon and Shuster, 1945), p. 694.
[36] See A. R. M. Murray, *An Introduction to Political Philosophy*, op. cit., p. 134.

within the western tradition. It is when he becomes immersed in his philosophical calisthenics that his political theory becomes hazy; and if he emerges from his metaphysical bouts more a collectivist and totalitarian than a democrat and constitutionalist, his intrepreters are not to be blamed for the doubts which they express. Had Rousseau been content to look upon democracy as a desirable form of government — one which gives man the fullest opportunity for self-growth and development — rather than a spiritual principle of some sort, and had he been willing to accept the state as a natural institution, he would not have found it necessary to go so far as to attribute infallibility to the general will.

BIBLIOGRAPHY

Babbitt, Irving, Rousseau and Romanticism (Boston: Houghton, 1919).

Cassirer, Ernst, The Question of Jean Jacque Rousseau (New York: Columbia University Press, 1957).

Chapman, J. W., Rousseau — Totalitarian or Liberal? (New York: Columbia University Press, 1956).

Clark, J. A., "The Definition of the General Will," Ethics, January, 1943.

Cobban, Alfred, Rousseau and the Modern State (London: Allen and Unwin, 1934).

——— "New Light on the Political Thought of Rousseau," Political Science Quarterly, June, 1951.

Green, F. C., Jean Jacques Rousseau: A Critical Study of His Life and Writings (Cambridge: Cambridge University Press, 1955).

Kelsen, Hans, "Foundations of Democracy: Rousseau's Doctrine of Democracy," Ethics, October, 1955.

Laski, Harold J., "A Portrait of Jean Jacques Rousseau," Yale Review, July, 1928.

Lewis, H. D., "Some Observations on Natural Rights and the General Will," Mind, January, 1938.

McNeil, Gordon H., "The Cult of Rousseau and the French Revolution," Journal of the History of Ideas, April, 1945.

——— "The Anti-Revolutionary Rousseau," American Historical Review, July, 1953.

Mitchell, E. T., "A Theory of Corporate Will," Ethics, January, 1946.

Nisbet, Robert A., "Rousseau and Totalitarianism," Journal of Politics, May, 1943.

Ogden, Henry, "The Antithesis of Nature and Art, and Rousseau's Rejection of the Theory of Natural Rights," American Political Science Review, August, 1938.

Osborne, A. M., Rousseau and Burke (New York: Oxford University Press, 1940).

Strauss, Leo, "On the Intention of Rousseau," Social Review, December, 1947.

Talmon, J. L., The Rise of Totalitarian Democracy (Boston: Beacon Press, 1952).

Williams, D., "Influence of Rousseau on Political Opinion," English Historical Review, July, 1933.

PART SIX THE SEEDBED OF
CONTEMPORARY POLITICAL
PHILOSOPHY

Chapter XVI

EDMUND BURKE: POLITICAL CONSERVATISM

"A disposition to preserve, and an ability to improve, would be my standard of a statesman. Everything else is vulgar in the conception, perilous in the execution" (Burke, *Reflections on the Revolution in France*).

THE reaction against the cold intellectualism and abstract reasoning of the Age of Enlightenment was not confined to the protestations of Rousseau and his fellow romanticists. Opposition of a more formidable and enduring character came from those who became known as conservatives. Although their philosophy contains romantic strains, it embodies features that differ radically from both the extreme romanticism of Rousseau and the exaggerated rationalism of the *philosophes*. These two latter movements, in fact, have a common tendency. Political romanticism, particularly as it finds expression in the *Social Contract*, calls for no less of a social transformation than the rationalists envision in their mathematical formulation of human rights and social arrangements. The conservatives, on the other hand, with their veneration of the past and their suspicion of any wholesale alteration of the social order, find themselves at odds with both of these "alien" doctrines.

Political conservatism had been the dominant force in British theory and practice from the Revolution of 1688 to the opening decades of the twentieth century. Eclipsed for a time by the successes of the Labour party, it has shown new vitality and vigor in recent years. Evidence of its renascence can be seen in the efforts of the Conservative party to engender a basically moderate and conservative approach to politics among its younger members. In this revival, the writings of the great English statesman, Edmund Burke, have emerged as the bible of the new conservatism. As one of the intellectual spokesmen of the Conservative party advised its members several years ago: "In him [Burke] is contained all

311

that is necessary to political salvation. 'Back to Burke' ought still to be our motto. Read and reread the Reflections on the Revolution in France: this is an exercise that should be performed at least once a year."[1] The surprising feature about the Burkean revival is that it has been so intense, articulate, and definitive in the United States, a country more noted for its action than its theory.[2]

The birth of conservatism as an articulate political philosophy can be traced to the period of Burke, and especially to the publication of his Reflections on the Revolution in France. For "almost singlehanded he turned the intellectual tide from a rationalist contempt for the past to a traditionalist reverence for it."[3] To study Burke, therefore, is to study a major facet of modern political thought.

EDMUND BURKE

Edmund Burke was born in Dublin in 1729. His father, an Anglican, was an attorney of moderate means; his mother was a Roman Catholic. Burke adopted the religion of his father and, like him, married a Catholic. He was educated at Trinity College, Dublin, where he won a classical scholarship for his literary proficiency. After receiving his degree from Trinity, he studied law at the Middle Temple in London. The practice of law did not prove to his liking and he soon abandoned it to devote his time to literary pursuits. His first published work was an essay entitled "Vindication of Natural Society" which appeared in 1756. Five years later he entered public service as an assistant to the Irish Secretary. In 1765 he became secretary to the British prime minister, and the following year he began a long career as a Whig in the House of Commons.

Burke was the leading spokesman of his party in its contest with George III, a monarch who was determined to rule as well as reign. He viewed the King's efforts to restore the pre-1688 prerogatives of the throne as a distinct threat to English constitutional development. Similarly, he opposed Britain's policy toward her American subjects, contending that the actions of the crown constituted an unconstitutional interference

---

[1] T. E. Utley, The Good Society (London: The Conservative Political Centre, 1953), p. 41.

[2] See, for example, Clinton Rossiter, Conservatism in America (New York: Knopf, 1955); Russell Kirk, The Conservative Mind (Chicago: Regnery, 1953); Peter Vierick, Conservatism Revisited (London: Lehman, 1950).

[3] Peter Viereck, Conservatism, From John Adams to Churchill (Princeton: Van Nostrand, 1956), p. 5.

with the jurisdiction that the colonies had long exercised over their internal affairs. He saw in the resistance of the colonists to the arbitrary proposals of the government another phase of his own resistance to royal encroachment. His attitude toward the French Revolution was entirely different. The violence and usurpation of the mobs and the uprooting of the old institutions and traditions of French society shocked his sense of law and order. Turning to his pen, he condemned the Revolution with an eloquence and feeling that led him at times into excesses of sentiment and extremes of disapproval. Despite these deficiencies, his *Reflections on the Revolution in France* remains to this day the classical expression of political conservatism and the source of most conservative arguments.

Burke's last years were not happy ones. He lost his only son in 1794, he was plagued by financial difficulties (as he had been most of his life), and he became increasingly concerned over the course of the French Revolution and its possible repercussions on the rest of Europe, including his beloved England. He was also deeply disappointed at his failure to attain cabinet status, a position which he felt his ability and his long career of distinguished public service warranted. His death came in 1797 at the age of sixty-eight.

Burke made no effort to compose a systematic treatise of politics. His political philosophy is found chiefly in four works: *Thoughts on the Causes of the Present Discontents* (1770), *Speech on Conciliation with America* (1775), *Reflections on the Revolution in France* (1790), and *An Appeal from the New to the Old Whigs* (1791), all written in response to a contemporary political situation. *The Reflections* is his most important and comprehensive political work. Written in the form of a letter to an imaginary French correspondent, it endeavors to distinguish between the orderly development of English institutions and the disorderly establishment of the French political system in the wake of the Revolution. In the course of this work and his other tracts, Burke had occasion to examine many of the basic principles underlying the state and political authority. His writings, considered in their entirety, constitute a fairly composite political philosophy despite the controversial eloquence which characterizes them.

View of Man

While Burke does not discuss his view of human nature in formal

or philosophical terms, he neither shares the optimism of the Enlightenment as to man's perfectibility nor accepts the unduly pessimistic outlook
of Hobbes. He feels sure that man's nature is basically good; it was injured but not vitiated by original sin. Man is subject to temptation and
often acts according to the promptings of his passions rather than his
reason. Nevertheless, under proper guidance and bolstered by religion,
he is capable of leading a reasonably good and salutary life and of striving
toward the perfection of his nature. As Burke observes in speaking out
against the popular misconception that men in public office are universally corrupt, "neither expecting to find perfection in men and not
looking for divine attributes in created beings in my commerce with
my contemporaries, I have seen not a little public spirit, a real subordination of interest to duty, and a decent and regulated sensibility to
honest fame and reputation."[4]

Burke has no illusions as to the equality of men. Equality can be
attributed to them only in their essential nature as human, rational, and
moral creatures of God. Beyond this and beyond equality of treatment
before the law, it is ridiculous to look for anything like equal talent, merit,
or virtue among the mass of people. Any attempt to reduce all individuals
to the same social, economic, and intellectual level would be improper
and unnatural. "Believe me, Sir, those who attempt to level, never
equalize. In all societies consisting of various descriptions of citizens,
some description must be uppermost. The levelers therefore only change
and pervert the natural order of things, they load the edifice of society
by setting up in the air what the solidity of the structure requires to be
on the ground."[5]

Man is a complex being, a creature of will, emotion, and habit as
well as reason. It is not possible, Burke insists, to arrive at a knowledge
of human nature merely by abstract speculation divorced from the totality
of experience. We can obtain a reasonable understanding of it only by
observation and study, by empirical investigation together with rational
reflection, and by placing heavy reliance on the accumulated experience
of the past through which man's nature manifests itself. It is useless to
believe that we can construct a science of human affairs in the same
way that we formulate a discipline involving the physical aspects of
nature.

---

[4] The Works of Edmund Burke (Boston: Little Brown & Co., 1865), II, 240.
[5] Ibid., III, 295.

Burke points out that this distinction is of prime importance to the field of politics. The student or statesman should remember that in approaching the subject of governmental reform he is dealing primarily with human beings and not the laws of physics or mathematics. If he keeps this distinction uppermost in mind, he will bring to his task a caution, an unwillingness to disturb the existing order without grave cause, and an awareness that politics ought to be adjusted to human nature, of which reason is but a part but by no means the greatest part.

Nature of the State

In discussing the nature of the state, Burke flatly rejects the argument that society is a contract to be dissolved at the pleasure of any generation. Men are not tied to one another by papers and seals. The state is not a man-made machine but a social or moral organism that has evolved and developed in accordance with forces that no individual can fully comprehend. As a social body it is bound together by ties of common interests, loyalties, traditions, sentiments, and habits. In an eloquent passage Burke asserts that

> the state ought not to be considered as nothing better than a partnership agreement in a trade of pepper and coffee, calico or tobacco, or some other such low concern, to be taken up for a little temporary interest, and to be dissolved by the fancy of the parties. It is to be looked on with other reverence; because it is not a partnership in things subservient only to the gross animal existence of a temporary and perishable nature. It is a partnership in all science; a partnership in all art; a partnership in every virtue, and in all perfection. As the ends of such a partnership cannot be obtained in many generations, it becomes a partnership not only between those who are living, but between those who are living, those who are dead, and those who are to be born.[6]

Burke admits that the constitution of an individual state is in the nature of a contract by which men set up a particular form and type of government. But it is not men who create civil society any more so than they create marriage. The nuptial agreement is made by two specific parties, but the institution of marriage is a product of nature. The same may be said of the state.

Man is a social creature not because of any mere gregarious animal instinct or historical accident but because he is intrinsically determined

---

[6] *Ibid.*, III, 361.

to a social and political life by the very depths of his intellectual and moral nature. Although he plays a major part in shaping the state and its institutions, he cannot wholly understand the intricate organism that has assumed such an important role in his life. He does know that without civil society he could not possibly arrive at the perfection of which his nature is capable. He also knows that "He who gave our nature to be perfected by our virtue, willed also the necessary means of its perfection — He willed therefore the state." In these views as in much of his political thought, Burke is essentially Aristotelian: an upholder of the organic and corporate nature of the state as against the mechanistic concept of the social contract theorists.

Burke's discussion of the nature of political society demonstrates a strain that runs throughout his writings. He believes that human institutions are ultimately the work of the divine intellect and hence are not fully intelligible to human reason. There is an aura of mystery surrounding life which is beyond the capability of the human intellect to penetrate. History is in a sense the unfolding of Divine Providence, a revelation of God's will in the order of time and space. Man therefore does well to heed the experience of the past and to respect the spirit of historical continuity.

Human institutions are not matters of concern to man alone; they are as it were a part of the divine order whereby God governs the world. To tamper with them unwarrantedly and without sufficient reason is like an amateur foolishly meddling with a highly complicated and expensive piece of machinery. Burke's feeling for divine immanence in the social order and its historical development is not, however, Hegelian.[7] He has no intention of substituting the "rational and necessary unfolding" of the Absolute in history for the natural law or of making the state the external manifestation of the Universal Idea at any given period in history.

The Conservative Approach to Politics

Since society and government are not fully intelligible to man, political reformers should be extremely cautious. When changes become necessary in the social and political order, they should be made with moderation and restraint, for such alterations may interfere with the natural course of the state's constitutional development and hence may adversely affect

---

[7] See post, p. 369.

the fundamental interests of the community as a corporate whole. Burke points out this danger in arguing that while parliamentary government in England has developed from obscure origins, the fact that it has evolved so successfully is evidence of its validity.

> Our constitution stands on a nice equipoise with steep precipices and deep waters upon all sides of it. In removing it from a dangerous leaning toward one side there may be a risk of over-setting it on the other. Every project of a material change in a Government so complicated as ours is a matter full of difficulties, in which a considerate man will not be too ready to decide, a prudent man too ready to undertake, or an honest man too ready to promise.[8]

The essence of social conservatism, as seen through the eyes of Burke, is the preservation of the ancient moral traditions of humanity. He views society as a spiritual reality possessing an eternal life but a delicate and involved constitution. It cannot be torn apart and reconstructed as though it were a machine. Change is, of course, necessary since society is not a static institution, and a state without the means of some change is without the means of its conservation. The wise statesman does not attempt to resist change blindly; he endeavors to render it as gradual as possible so that it can be accomplished without violence or injustice to the people.

Burke would have been in complete agreement with the statement later made by Disraeli that in a progressive country change is constant; and the great question is, not whether you should resist change which is inevitable, but whether that change should be carried out in deference to the manners, laws, and traditions of the people, or in deference to abstract principles and arbitrary and general doctrines. Burke notes that the principles of conservation and change operated at two critical periods of English history, the Restoration and the Revolution of 1688. In both instances, although the bond of union had been weakened, the political fabric was not cast aside in its entirety by the people. Instead, in each case "they regenerated the deficient part of the old constitution through the parts which were not impaired. They kept these old parts exactly as they were, that the part recovered might be suited to them."[9]

All reformation should proceed upon the principle of reverence to antiquity. The Divine purpose is revealed to man through the unfolding of history. It is foolhardy to disregard the collective wisdom of mankind,

---

[8] *Works*, III, 361.   [9] *Ibid.*

a wisdom that has been acquired through thousands of years of experience and meditation, and that finds expression in the customs and traditions of a people. Any attempt to transform radically the social and political structure, such as occurred in the French Revolution, is to do violence to the orderly growth and development of society. Burke insists that any social planner who believes that he can draft a blueprint of a new society as the engineer maps out a new construction project is a fraud. It is inconceivable to him how any man can be so presumptuous as to consider his country a tablet upon which he may scribble whatever he pleases.

A good statesman always considers how he shall make the most of the existing materials of his country. Certainly the French government prior to the Revolution was not such "as to be incapable or undeserving of reform, so that it was of absolute necessity that the whole fabric should be at once torn down, and the area cleared for the erection of a theoretic, experimental edifice in its place."[10] If a great alteration in the social or political order is really necessary, nature will fit the minds of men for it. In such case "every fear, every hope will forward it; and they who persist in opposing this mighty current in human affairs will appear rather to resist the decrees of Providence itself than the mere designs of men."[11]

Burke places the burden of proof upon those who advocate modification of the old order. True change must grow organically out of the concrete historical environment and fabric of a people and its institutions. If an attempted reform disregards the continuity of tradition and indiscriminately uproots the past, it leaves a legacy of uncertainty and instability. Peter Viereck, a perceptive proponent of the "new conservatism," contends that the failure of the Third and Fourth French Republics to gain sufficient respect and support from the people can be attributed largely to the destruction of the unifying monarchical tradition that had played such a large role in the national history of France. "For respect, in countries with old traditions, depends on an aura of legitimacy and historic continuity."[12]

The Prescriptive Constitution

Much of Burke's conservative political philosophy centers about what he refers to as "prescriptive" rights. He defines prescription as

---

[10] *Ibid.*, III, 399.   [11] *Ibid.*
[12] "Politics and Change," *Commonweal*, Mar. 4, 1955, p. 577.

a presumption in favor of any settled scheme of government against any untried project, that a nation has long existed and flourished under it. It is a better presumption even of the choice of a nation, far better than any sudden and temporary arrangement by annual election. Because a nation is not an idea only of local extent, and individual momentary aggregation; but it is an idea of continuity, which extends in time as well as in numbers and space. And this is a choice not of one day or one set of people, not a tumultuary and giddy choice; it is a deliberate election of the ages and of generations.[13]

Prescriptive rights grow out of the practices and experiences of many successive generations since these form the repository of the collective intelligence of the human race.

Burke declares that there are only two qualifications necessary for those who exercise political rule: virtue and wisdom. These characteristics can be present either actually, when the individual in fact possesses them, or presumptively, when the individual is assumed to have such qualities because of his wealth or good birth. Ownership of land is the clearest indication of virtue and wisdom; hence the man of property has a prescriptive right to play a major role in the governance of society. The possession of family wealth and the distinction which attends hereditary possessions are the surest guarantees for the protection and transmission of the great traditions of a people. They are, even at their worst, "the ballast in the vessel of the commonwealth." Civilized society requires orders and classes and a veneration of social distinctions of duty and privilege. For in the last analysis, it is the men of wealth and good birth who provide the community with the leadership necessary for its well-being. They are the "great oaks" who introduce moderate reforms from above; they make power gentle and obedience liberal. So long as they remain within the limits of the state constitution, no better form of rule could be asked.

To discover the rights which arise by prescription, man need only turn to the record of the past. For the human species is wise and "when time is given to it, as a species it always acts right." Burke argues that it was the failure of the French to respect prescriptive rights and to retain their ancient institutions that brought violence and chaos to the nation. So long as the revolutionaries insisted on speaking only of the abstract rights of men and on repudiating the past, it was vain to talk to them of the practice of their ancestors and the fundamental laws of their country.

---

[13] Works, VII, 94–95.

Burke notes that the English people have acted quite differently from the French. Working after the pattern of nature they hold and transmit their government and their privileges in the same manner that they enjoy and transmit their property. Should abuses creep into the British political system as they did in France, they would be eradicated in an orderly and constitutional fashion with due regard for the preservation of the established institutions and traditional spirit of the nation. The French, in seeking to rectify the abuses of their government, began poorly because they started by despising everything that belonged to them.

Natural Law and Natural Rights

Burke makes no attempt to define natural law in philosophical terms, but he leaves little doubt that he accepts the existence of a transcendent moral order to which human acts and human laws should conform. Even the people themselves "have no right to make a law prejudicial to the whole community . . . because it would be made against the principle of a superior law, which it is not in the power of any community, or of the whole race of man to alter."[14] It would be hard, Burke notes in his *Tract on the Popery Laws*, "to point out any error more truly subversive of all the order and beauty, of all the peace and happiness of human society, than the notion that any body of men have the right to make what laws they please." The first obligation of man is to obey the laws of God. Similarly, the primary business of the legislator or statesman is to ascertain, obey, and promote obedience to these laws as they are discerned in the natural order.

Burke reacts sharply against the rationalist doctrine that the natural law and its applications can be arrived at simply by a process of abstract reasoning. In Aristotelian fashion he distinguishes between the speculative and practical functions of the human mind:

> I never govern myself, no rational man ever did govern himself, by abstractions and universals. I do not put abstract ideas wholly out of any question, because I well know that under that name I should dismiss principles; and that without the guide and light of sound, well-understood principles, all reasonings in politics, as in everything else, would be only a confused jumble of particular facts and details, without the means of drawing out any sort of theoretical or practical conclusion.[15]

---

[14] *Ibid.*, VII, 41.   [15] *Ibid.*

By accepting the natural law, Burke also affirms man's possession of natural rights. However, he vehemently opposes the Jacobin appeal to rights derived from a mythical state of nature that antedated civil society. Man's true rights are based on human nature and Divine sanction. Since the state exists for the sake of man, it must faithfully observe the basic rights which he possesses as a creature of God. Since the conservation and secure enjoyment of natural rights is the great and ultimate purpose of civil society, all forms of government are only good in so far as they are subservient to this purpose.

In stressing the primary importance of the practical reason in human behavior, Burke notes that morals and politics cannot be dealt with as speculative sciences. The lines of morality are not like the ideal lines of mathematics. They are broad and deep, as well as long. When it comes to dealing with issues in the concrete order of reality, prudence instead of logic chopping is essential. Freedom, for example, is a basic human right but it can be made meaningful only within the context of a given situation. It is idle to discuss the relation of freedom to law as an abstract problem. Is it, Burke asks with his usual eloquence, "because liberty in the abstract may be classed amongst the blessings of mankind that I am seriously to felicitate a madman who has escaped from the protecting restraint and wholesome darkness of his cell, on his restoration to the enjoyment of light and liberty? Am I to congratulate a highwayman and murderer, who has broke prison, upon the recovery of his natural right?"[16]

Burke points out that the extent of the right of liberty, as that of other natural rights, must vary with time and circumstances. What is permissible for the individual to do under one set of circumstances might be disastrous to society under different conditions. A proper balancing between freedom and authority must constantly occur in the political community. To give liberty is easy; it only requires that the reins be released. But to strike a proper balance between freedom and authority requires sound judgment and prudence.

Burke is not a moral relativist as some of his commentators have sought to show. The whole tenor of his thinking indicates otherwise. While he often praises utility and expediency as correct principles of political action, he always does so on the condition that they be directed toward proper ends. His strictures against abstract reason simply stress the fact that the basic precepts of the natural law must find application in his-

16 *Ibid.*, III, 241.

torical reality. The classical distinction between the practical and speculative sciences involves a subordination of the former to the latter; that is to say, the practical science directs action toward an end known by the speculative intelligence.[17] Burke notes this relationship in stating that the business of the speculative philosopher is to mark out the proper ends of government while that of the politician is to find the proper means toward these ends and to employ them with effect.

Theory of Government

Consistent with his emphasis on the practical reason, Burke holds that there is no ideal form of government that is appropriate for all peoples and circumstances. Questions pertaining to the type of government, the franchise, and the qualifications for office should be settled by practical considerations and not by metaphysical abstractions — always, of course, giving due regard to the experiences of the past. He feels that in general, the most satisfactory arrangement is a mixed type of government standing midway between an absolute monarchy and a democracy with widespread popular participation. He sees the most desirable form in a constitutional monarchy modeled after the English example. Such a type is conducive to maintaining the balance and equilibrium essential to a stable social and political order. Its character is that of a "monarchy directed by laws, controlled and balanced by the great hereditary wealth and hereditary dignity of a nation; and both again controlled by a judicious check from the reason and feeling of the people at large, acting by a suitable and permanent organ."[18]

Burke's mixed government consists of a constitutionally limited monarchy, an hereditary body such as the House of Lords to represent the wealth and aristocracy of the nation, and a popularly elected assembly. Lawmaking is accomplished in accordance with the wishes of the majority, but this majority is not to be taken indiscriminately from the whole population. It is to be a "proper" majority drawn only from a body of electors qualified by tradition, education, wealth, and birth to participate in the political function. The "common man" is excluded from exercising the franchise or holding public office because he has neither the wisdom nor the time to exercise political power intelligently. "The occupation of a hair-dresser, or of a working tallow-chandler, cannot be a matter of

---

[17] See ante, pp. 66–67.
[18] Works, III, 395.

honour to any person — to say nothing of a number of other more servile employments. Such descriptions of men ought not to suffer oppression from the state; but the state suffers oppression, if such as they, either individually or collectively, are permitted to rule."[19] In support of this position, Burke quotes Ecclesiasticus: "the wisdom of a learned man cometh by opportunity of leisure. . . . How can he get wisdom that holdeth the plough, and that glorieth in the goad; that driveth oxen; and is occupied in their labours; and whose talk is of bullocks?"[20]

While Burke is a firm believer in constitutional and parliamentary government, he is not an advocate of democracy, as the term is understood today. Some of his most ardent admirers contend, and perhaps rightfully so, that Burke would have dreaded the modern democratic state. His lack of confidence in the ability of the common man and his almost inordinate esteem for the landed aristocracy caused his political beliefs to be cast within an oligarchical framework.

Whatever the form of government, Burke takes it for granted that the domination of the political community by mediocrity is contrary to nature. The good ruler is one who employs the service of able men in the governance of the state. These men are to be drawn from the ranks of the wiser, the more expert, and the more opulent members of the community; and they are to furnish guidance and protection to the weaker, the less intelligent, and the poorer groups. Despite his talk of the "natural aristocrat," it is evident that Burke actually regards wealth and good birth as the true marks of political virtue. This strong bias blinded him to the fact that the England of his day was ruled by a narrow oligarchy which, even though it may have been beneficent in many respects, actually stifled the discovery and recognition of natural talent.

The Role of the Representative

One of the problems that has intrigued political thinkers for several centuries is the proper role of the representative. One view is that he shall be a mere delegate for the people of his district to exercise their will and carry out their instructions. Opposed to this is the theory that the representative should be free to exercise full independence of judgment regardless of the desires of his constituents. Burke gives classic expression

[19] *Ibid.*, III, 296.
[20] *Ibid.*

to this latter position. Speaking to a group of voters in the city of Bristol, he concedes that a representative should keep in touch with his constituents at all times. "Their wishes ought to have great weight with him; their opinions high respect; their business unremitted attention. It is his duty to sacrifice his repose, his pleasure, his satisfactions to theirs — and above all, ever and in all cases, to prefer their interest to his own."[21] But, Burke continues, a member of parliament is responsible for the well-being of the whole nation and empire. As a representative he must be free to exercise his best judgment in the common interest whether it agrees with the wishes of his constituents or not.

In Burke's time, the practice of sending instructions to members of parliament from the constituencies was fairly common. Expressly repudiating this practice, Burke points out that parliament is not a congress of ambassadors from different states but a deliberative assembly of one nation with one interest, that of the whole. Answering the contention that the will of the representative ought to be subservient to that of the voters, he points out that "government and legislation are matters of reason and judgment and not of inclination; and what sort of reason is that in which the determination precedes the discussion, in which one set of men deliberate and another decides, and where those who form the conclusions are perhaps three hundred miles distant from those who hear the argument."[22]

The tendency in the conservative creed to look with suspicion on the common judgment is present in Burke, as we have already had occasion to observe. He feels that by proper restrictions on candidacy, membership in parliament can be limited to men of experience and wisdom. Representatives of this caliber can guide the state toward its proper objectives and help to promote the true interests of society regardless of whether these interests are so recognized by the people. As the following passage illustrates, Burke holds a sort of divine rights concept of the representative's position

> His unbiased opinion, his mature judgment, his enlightened conscience, he ought not to sacrifice to you, to any man, or to any set of men living. These he does not derive from your pleasure — no, nor from the law and the constitution. They are a trust from Providence, for the abuse of which he is deeply answerable. Your representative owes you, not his industry only, but his judgment; and he betrays, instead of serving you, if he sacrifices it to your opinion.[23]

[21] Ibid., II, 85.   [22] Ibid., II, 87.   [23] Ibid., II, 88.

The Significance of Burke

Edmund Burke stands as a stalwart champion of the conservative spirit in political thought. An advocate of cautious reform and a vigorous opponent of sweeping schemes for social improvement, he left a legacy of ideas which continue to exert great influence in the sphere of political philosophy and in turn on political action. He teaches that politics is the art of the possible. The prudent statesman always acts temperately and cautiously; he is not a doctrinaire planner nor a fanatical ideologist. Prudence in statesmanship means action informed by principles and guided by circumstances.

Burke stresses the belief that society is not founded on a social contract which the parties are free to modify or cancel at will, but on a sense of inner compulsion and a pattern of traditions and practices that are the products of a natural and organic growth. He does not object to change, but to the heritage of eighteenth-century French liberalism with its insistence on radically reshaping the political order in total disregard of history and with no other basis than rootless abstractions.

Burke detests extremes whether of the right or left. He does not consider himself a crusading force against the powers of darkness. Recognizing the relativity of political issues and conflicts, he tries to strike up an acceptable balance between divergent interests by compromise, adjustment, and accommodation. Political virtue in his eyes is primarily a matter of prudence. He believes that the solution of social and political problems can best be accomplished by a reasonable and moderate approach. His ideal is a political order entrusted to a responsible and public-spirited aristocracy.

Conservatives of many colors have gone to the Burkean shrine for support. Some of them have displayed demogogic tendencies; others have demonstrated a deep interest in the social betterment of man and a genuine concern for the principles of democratic government. Some who claim allegiance to Burke stress the weakness of man; others seek to combine constitutional procedures with social humaneness. Some emphasize orders and classes and deny social equality; others insist that conservatism is betrayed when it becomes the exclusive property of a single social or economic minority. Some are inclined to regard poverty and misfortune as part of the natural order of things and religion as the consolation for all such ills; others maintain that the moderate and evolutionary forces of the center must strike a workable balance between the urgent need for social reform and the equally urgent need for personal freedom. In this process of assimilation, the true meaning of Burke's political philosophy is often lost sight of or distorted.

THE CONSERVATIVE REACTION IN FRANCE

The reaction to the French Revolution and the "liberal" philosophy which it represented took a more pronounced or extreme form among certain continental writers. This is particularly true of such Catholic émigrés as Joseph de Maistre (1753–1821), a sympathizer of the French royalists, and Vicomte de Bonald (1754–1840), a French nobleman who fled from his native land when the monarchy collapsed in 1791. Both of these men employ the language of conservatism in support of their basically antidemocratic or authoritarian philosophies. Going beyond Burke, they call for a return to the tradition of those medieval churchmen who viewed the problem of human government solely in terms of subordination to the will of God and who regarded politics as a branch of theology.

De Maistre in his *Essay on the Generative Principles of Political Constitutions* (1810) follows Burke's central theme that constitutions and political institutions are the products of slow organic growth. He maintains that one of the great errors of the eighteenth century was the belief that a political constitution could be written down and created *a priori*. Both reason and experience demonstrate that a constitution is a divine creation, and that precisely what is most fundamental in the laws of a state cannot be written down. De Maistre sees an incredible presumption in the belief that man's intellect and judgment without divine guidance are sufficient for the attainment of human perfection. The doctrine of popular sovereignty and popular consent is pernicious to good order; the sanction for laws and government must rest in an authority superior to man. Like Bonald and the other French conservatives, he looked upon Divine Providence as the only acceptable explanation of history. Man is essentially unfit to create anything or to alter the course of history. Instead of trying to establish new social and political worlds, he should accept the order of creation.

In attacking the notion that constitutions or universal rights can be concocted by the use of pure reason, De Maistre lists four propositions which he holds to be "uncontestably true":

(1) The fundamental principles of political constitutions exist before all written law.
(2) Constitutional law is only the sanction of an unwritten pre-existing right.
(3) That which is most essential and truly fundamental is never written.
(4) The weakness of a constitution is actually in direct proportion to the number of its written articles.

De Maistre insists that it is difficult to alter things for the better. Society is too complex and reason too feeble to risk social innovation. Even if faults exist, it is better to leave the community alone than to tamper with it. The word reform will always be suspected by wisdom.

Bonald maintains that the state is similar to a house of correction and that its prime purpose is to tame man's wicked instincts.[24] Contrary to Rousseau who held that man is naturally good and that it is civilization which corrupts him, Bonald declares "Nous sommes mauvais par nature, bons par la societe" (We are evil by nature, good by society). It is the task of the state and the church to regulate the conduct of man and to save him from his evil tendencies. He agrees with De Maistre that the prelates, the noblemen, and the high dignitaries of the state are the true repositories and guardians of truth. It falls to them to teach the people truth and falsehood in the moral and spiritual order. Others have no right to reason about these things.

In Bonald, as well as De Maistre, the long discredited view that civil society is but a remedy for sin reappears once again. Bonald and his intellectual colleagues look to the monarchy, under the spiritual guidance of the church, as the stabilizing and directing element in the state. They have little regard for the efficacy of institutional checks on government, such as those proposed by Montesquieu and others. The only safeguard against the abuse of power, according to Bonald, is the ethical limitations set by the religious conscience.

The French conservatives are on sound ground in several respects.

---

[24] Bonald's political writings are contained in his *Essay on the Natural Laws of the Social Order* and in *Primitive Legislation*.

They stand in the spirit of the Greco-Christian tradition when they declare that the human intellect is not the creator and source of truth, that society cannot be refashioned as a sculptor shapes his clay, that a civil society devoid of religion contains the seeds of its own destruction, and that authority as well as freedom is essential to the well-being of a people. At the same time, they depart from this tradition when they imply that man is not fit for self-rule because of sin; when they refuse to give recognition to the necessity for change in social and political institutions; and when they tend to discredit the natural and autonomous character of the state by viewing it as a church society. Their conservatism is static, rigid, reactionary, and authoritarian. A true Burkean conservative will oppose tyranny from above — from the monarchy and privileged classes — as well as from below — from Jacobins and the sheer force of numbers. De Maistre and Bonald are too eager to support the former in their legitimate reaction to the latter.

SUMMARY

There are certain basic canons that have been commonly recognized by intellectual conservatives from the days of Burke to the present time. These can be summarized as: (1) man is a blend of good and evil; he is neither perfect nor is he perfectible; (2) society is the product of slow historical growth; (3) existing institutions embody the wisdom of prior generations; there is a presumption in favor of that which has survived the test of time; (4) religion is the foundation of civil society; (5) prudence, experience, and habit are often better guides than reason and logic; (6) society requires classes and orders — the superior classes must be allowed to have a hand in the direction of the state in such a way as to balance the numerical preponderance of the inferior classes; and (7) duties are superior to rights.[25] Although the meaning of these principles has changed from generation to generation and even from thinker to thinker, there is a substantial area of agreement among genuine conservatives in respect to their ultimate assumptions.

The tide of conservative-liberal debate still runs strong. It will doubtlessly continue on marked as it has been more by rhetoric than clarity of thought, more by looseness of definition than conciseness of meaning, more by emotion than reason. The labels, liberal and conservative, will remain disconcertingly vague and confusing. And through it all, Burke will probably continue to be an important center of theoretical attention — at least until the fad changes.

---

[25] See S. P. Huntington, "Conservatism as an Ideology," *American Political Science Review*, June, 1957; and Herbert McClosky, "Conservatism and Personality," *ibid.*, Mar., 1958.

BIBLIOGRAPHY

Brown, Stuart G., "Democracy, the New Conservatism, and the Liberal Tradition in America," *Ethics*, October, 1955.

Cobban, Alfred, *Edmund Burke and the Revolt Against the 18th Century* (London: Allen and Unwin, 1929).

Coker, Francis W., "Some Present-Day Critics of Liberalism," *American Political Science Review*, March, 1953.

Crick, Bernard, "The Strange Quest for an American Conservatism," *Review of Politics*, July, 1955.

Crowley, P. J., "Burke and Scholasticism," *New Scholasticism*, April, 1954.

Griffith, E. S., "Cultural Prerequisites to a Successfully Functioning Democracy," *American Political Science Review*, March, 1956.

Hallowell, John H., *The Moral Foundation of Democracy* (Chicago: University of Chicago Press, 1954).

Hutchins, Robert M., "The Theory of the State; Edmund Burke," *Review of Politics*, April, 1943.

Jones, Aubrey, *Pendulum of Politics* (London: Faber and Faber, 1946).

Kirk, Russell, "Burke and Natural Rights," *Review of Politics*, October, 1951.

Koyre, Alexandre, "Louis de Bonald," *Journal of the History of Ideas*, January, 1946.

MacDonald, H. M., "The Revival of Conservative Thought," *Journal of Politics*, February, 1957.

Mazlish, B., "Conservative Revolution of Edmund Burke," *Review of Politics*, January, 1958.

McClosky, R. G., *American Conservatism in the Age of Enterprise* (Cambridge: Harvard University Press, 1951).

Murray, John C., "The Political Thought of Joseph de Maistre," *Review of Politics*, January, 1949.

Nisbet, Robert A., "De Bonald and the Concept of the Social Group," *Journal of the History of Ideas*, June, 1944.

Parkin, Charles, *The Moral Basis of Burke's Political Thought* (London: Cambridge University Press, 1956).

Powers, R. H., "Degradation of Aristocratic Dogma (Burke's social and political program)," *Partisan Review*, Winter, 1957.

Rogow, A. A., "Edmund Burke and the American Liberal Tradition," *Antioch Review*, Summer, 1957.

Rothbard, M. N., "Note on Burke's Vindication of Natural Society," *Journal of the History of Ideas*, January, 1958.

Stanlis, P. J., "Edmund Burke and the Natural Law" (Ann Arbor: University of Michigan Press, 1958).

White, H. B., "Edmund Burke on Political Theory and Practice," *Social Research*, March, 1950.

Wilson, Francis G., *The Case for Conservatism* (Seattle: University of Washington Press, 1951).

Chapter XVII

THE UTILITARIANS

"Nature has placed mankind under the governance of two sovereign masters, pain and pleasure. It is for them alone to point out what we ought to do, as well as to determine what we shall do" (Bentham, *Introduction to the Principles of Morals and Legislation*).

WITH the rejection of natural law, the nineteenth century turned to other standards for determining the moral propriety of human acts and the ethical validity of human institutions. In England the movement away from the doctrine of natural law found expression in the philosophy of utilitarianism which dominated British political thought during the first seventy-five years of the nineteenth century. David Hume, together with the French philosopher, Helvetius, and the Italian thinker, Beccaria, were the principal architects of the new doctrine, but it was Jeremy Bentham who molded it into a formal theory of social reform. Its proponents were distinctly middle class in character and its program essentially a defense of middle class interests.

The Utilitarians are sometimes referred to as Philosophical Radicals because of their efforts to give a theoretical underpinning to representative democracy and universal suffrage. Actually they were cast more in the role of pamphleteers than profound thinkers. As one commentator has observed, their function was more that of the Socratic gadfly than it was the sober architect of a democratic constitution. Certainly the utilitarians could not be accused of being abstract philosophers, standing outside the stream of daily life. They were active in public affairs, serving as effective lobbyists for legal, penal, and political reforms and for the improvement of working conditions in British factories and mines.

The nature of utilitarianism and its relevancy to political thought can best be observed in the work of its two most noted representatives, Jeremy Bentham and John Stuart Mill.

BENTHAM

Jeremy Bentham (1748–1832), like his predecessor Hobbes, was an infant prodigy who read Latin before he was four and conversed in French at the age of six. His father was a wealthy lawyer who looked forward to seeing his son upon the Woolsack. After graduation from Oxford, Bentham took up the study of law and was admitted to the bar in 1769. His career as a practicing lawyer was short. Instead of devoting his energies toward establishing a law practice, he spent his time studying the defects of the existing legal system. Convinced from his reading that the well-being and happiness of a society depended upon wise legislation, young Jeremy decided that his particular job in life was to labor at the reform of law. The substantial inheritance which he received from his father enabled him to live independently and to pursue the life he desired. He was an unsuccessful candidate for Parliament in 1790, and thereafter he made no further attempts to become an active participant in the political arena.

Bentham was a prolific writer, but he seldom completed what he began. His mind seemed to jump from one subject to another and his attention from one project to others that captured his immediate interest. Because of this lack of sustained effort, much of his work appears as fragments or introductions. Thus the title to his work on political science is "Fragments on Government," and to his most widely known book on utilitarian theory is "Introduction to the Principles of Morals and Legislation." A Tory until he was sixty, Bentham became a proponent of expanded democratic government when his proposals for legal reform failed to win parliamentary support. Earlier, he had assumed that those holding political power wanted only to know what was good in order to embrace it. As he grew older, he became convinced that the ruling oligarchy in England was against reform and indifferent to the public interest because it was not truly representative of the people.

Shortly after Bentham published his *Principles of Morals and Legislation* in 1780, he devised an elaborate plan for prison reform. He proposed the construction of a model prison (the Panopticon), a circular building so designed that the warden could watch the movements of every inmate from his office in the center of the structure. For over fifteen years he gave a large part of his time and fortune in urging the British government to adopt his plan for this goldfish bowl prison. Parliament did pass a bill in 1794 authorizing the establishment of such a prison but the project was never carried out. Bentham's efforts at penal and legal reform, however, brought him international fame. When he visited Paris in 1825 he was accorded a triumphal reception, and the governments of Spain and Portugal authorized his works to be printed at national expense.

Bentham was heir to the new scientific and secular spirit that had emerged during the eighteenth century. When he came across the magic phrase "the greatest happiness of the greatest number" in Joseph Priestley's pamphlet, *An Essay on the First Principles of Government* (1766), he is said to have cried "Eureka," believing that he had discovered the determining principle of public and private morality. (Priestley had borrowed the phrase from Beccaria's short treatise on *Crimes and Punishment*.) What remained to be done was to formulate a scientific basis for measuring happiness. Once this was accomplished, man would have a precise standard of social behavior that would no longer be dependent upon the abstract principles of natural law or the uncertainties of individual conscience. Bentham's importance to political philosophy rests in his efforts to achieve this objective.

The Principle of Utility

In the opening chapter of the *Principles of Morals and Legislation*, Bentham informs his readers that the doctrine of utility "is the foundation of the present work." He then proceeds to define utility as the "principle which approves or disapproves of every action whatsoever, according to the tendency which it appears to have to augment or diminish the happiness of the party whose interest is in question."[1] Happiness which is described as "enjoyment of pleasures, security from pains," is equated with goodness, and unhappiness or pain with evil. A right action is one which increases happiness while a wrong action is one which diminishes it. Moral approbation is therefore attached to the former and moral condemnation to the latter. Like Hobbes, who defined good as the object of desire and evil as the object of aversion, Bentham fixes a nonmoral stamp on human actions.

Of an action that is conformable to the principle of utility, one may always say either that it is one that ought to be done, or at least that

---

[1] *Principles of Morals and Legislation*, I, 2. Excerpts are taken from Blackwell edition (Oxford: Blackwell, 1948).

it is not one that ought not to be done. One may say also that it is right it should be done — at least that it is not wrong it should be done; that it is a right action — at least that it is not a wrong action. When thus interpreted, the words *ought*, and *right* and *wrong*, and others of that stamp, have a meaning: when otherwise, they have none.[2]

As conceived by Bentham, the doctrine of utility is purely quantitative in nature, recognizing no distinction among the quality or kinds of pleasure. The sole test of differentiation is the *quantum* of pleasure that various acts bring. When we say that good music or poetry is better than cheap movies, we can only mean that it gives more pleasure, not that it gives a different and a higher kind of pleasure. As Bentham puts it, quantity of pleasure being equal, pushpin is as good as poetry. He realizes that the moment one introduces the element of quality in the utilitarian formula, he is appealing to a different standard of goodness. An individual may experience more satisfaction in eating his favorite dish than in reading a Shakespearian sonnet. According to Bentham's scale, the act of sensual gratification would be the better of the two for such a person since it gives him a greater quantity of happiness.

When Bentham is pressed to give some empirical proof of the validity of his doctrine, he asserts that its truth is self-evident. Is the principle of utility, he asks rhetorically, susceptible of any direct proof? No, he replies, "for that which is used to prove everything else, cannot itself be proved: a chain of proofs must have their commencement somewhere. To give such proof is as impossible as it is needless."[3] Aristotle and his successors had insisted that first principles are self-evident and their validity not susceptible to empirical verification or demonstration. It is rather strange to hear similar words uttered by one who insists on the strictly scientific approach to moral and social problems.

The Calculus of Pleasure

In order to place utilitarianism on a purely scientific basis, Bentham had to devise an empirical standard of measurement to determine the quantity of pleasure or pain which results from a particular act. His famous "felicific calculus" was formulated in answer to this need. Basic to this test is the assumption that pleasure and pain, although subject to no linear or weight measurement, can nevertheless be mathematically

---

[2] *Ibid.*, I, 10.
[3] *Ibid.*, I, 11.

calculated. If this premise is correct, the decision as to utility, and hence rightness, can be reduced to a problem of simple arithmetic.

There is little sophisticated theory in Bentham's test. It attempts to measure the quantity of pleasure by the coarsest and most mechanical criteria. Seven factors must be taken into account in determining the utility of an act: (1) its intensity, (2) its duration, (3) its certainty or uncertainty, (4) its propinquity or remoteness, (5) its fertility or "the chance which it has of being followed by sensations of the same kind," (6) its purity or "the chance it has of *not* being followed by sensations of the *opposite* kind," and (7) its extent or the number of persons to whom it extends or who are affected by it.[4] Once these determinations are made, the values of all the pleasures are totaled up on one side of the ledger and those of all the pains on the other. The extent to which the sum of one exceeds the other will give the degree of utility or dis-utility of the particular act.

Bentham does not maintain that this elaborate calculation should be made before every human act. "It is not to be expected that this process should be strictly pursued previously to every moral judgment, or to every legislative or judicial operation. It may, however, be always kept in view; and as near as the process actually pursued on these occasions approaches to it, so near will such process approach to the character of an exact one."[5] The rightness or wrongness of many acts is generally accepted in terms of their known consequences of pleasure and pain, and it is only when the propriety of an act is in dispute that it is necessary to resort to the calculus. With adequate time and all the facts at his disposal, man can make completely accurate calculations.

As a scientific instrument, Bentham's "objective" test for measuring the quantity of pleasure is sheer nonsense. Not even an omniscient God, remarks a modern commentator on utilitarianism, could make such calculations "for the very notion of them is impossible."[6] Nowhere does

---

[4] Bentham wrote the following verse to lodge "more effectually in the memory these points on which the whole fabric of morals and legislation may be seen to rest":

> Intense, long, certain, speedy, fruitful, pure —
> Such marks in pleasures and in pains endure.
> Such pleasures seek, if private be thy end;
> If it be public, wide let them extend.
> Such pains avoid, whichever be thy view;
> If pains must come, let them extend to few
> (ibid., I, 4).

[5] Ibid., IV, 6.
[6] John Plamenatz, The English Utilitarians (Oxford: Blackwell, 1949), p. 73.

Bentham attempt to define pleasure and pain or to formulate a scale of values for determining the relative importance of the factors he lists. Whether more consideration should be given to the intensity of a pleasure or pain than to its duration, or whether the certainty of pleasure should be more heavily weighted than its fertility are but a few of the unanswered questions. How, moreover, can a numerical value be attached to the intensity of a pleasure? Can the degree of pleasure that an individual derives from an act be measured by some device in much the same way that blood pressure is determined, or must the subjective judgment of the individual be accepted? Bentham conveniently disregards these questions, just as he does those pertaining to qualitative differences.

It is true that men compare the consequences of alternative actions but in doing so they do not add, subtract, divide, or multiply. In making their choice, they may take into consideration the dimensions of pleasure that Bentham refers to, but this process does not involve a mathematical calculation of quantities of pleasure and pain. If utility is to stand as an objective test of morality, recourse must obviously be had to other means of measurement than the felicific calculus.

Utilitarianism as a Standard of Good and Evil

Bentham sees clearly the need for some standard external to the individual for judging human conduct. Previous systems "consist all of them in so many contrivances for avoiding the obligation of appealing to any external standard, and for prevailing upon the reader to accept the author's sentiment or opinion as a reason for itself."[7] If an individual is inclined to think that his own approbation or disapproval of an act is a sufficient foundation for him to judge of its validity, he should ask himself whether his view is to be the standard of right and wrong with respect to every one else, or whether every other individual's view has the same privilege of being a standard for his own actions. If the former, the principle would be despotic; if the latter, it would be anarchical.

Natural law has no part in utilitarian thinking. Bentham discards it as just a name for irrational prejudice and as "simple nonsense . . . nonsense upon stilts." He speaks contemptuously of those who believe in right reason or natural justice. Whether an act is right or wrong never depends upon a knowledge of goodness or evil as such, but only upon the tendency of that act to increase or diminish the sum total of

---

[7] *Principles of Morals and Legislation, op. cit.,* I, 14.

the happiness of the person whose interest is in question. Bentham holds that by applying this utilitarian test, morality becomes grounded on objective norms and not on the whim and caprice of individual men.

The "Common Good"

On its face, utilitarianism appears to be a strictly egoistic doctrine. Why talk of the interests of the community, Bentham asks, unless we know what is the interest of the individual. "A thing is said to promote the interest or to be for the interest of an individual when it tends to add to the sum total of his pleasures; or, what comes to the same thing, to diminish the sum total of his pains."[8] The community is merely a fictitious body composed of the individual persons who are its members. The interest of society is therefore nothing more than the sum of the interests of the several members who compose it. Yet the utilitarian formula of the greatest happiness of the greatest number implies that it is as much an individual's duty to give pleasure to others as to seek it for himself. Or to express it in less positive terms, that which gives pleasure to one person is good so long as it does not diminish the happiness of other persons more. Bentham's ethical hedonism means in reality that no man can attain his own greatest happiness unless all other men do the same. We do well to further the interests of others in the hope that they in turn will advance ours. Hence an individual must seek other men's pleasures as a means to his own. This philosophical "logrolling" is often exemplified in the activities of legislative bodies.

Bentham contends that the greatest happiness principle can be achieved in practice by totaling up individual pleasures and pains according to the felicific calculus formula.

> Take an account of the number of persons whose interests appear to be concerned; and repeat the above process with respect to each. Sum up the numbers expressive of the degrees of *good* tendency which the act has with respect to each individual, in regard to whom the tendency of it is good upon the whole. Do this again with respect to each individual in regard to whom the tendency of it is *bad* upon the whole. Take the balance; which, if on the side of pleasure will give the general *good tendency* of the act with respect to the total number or community of individuals concerned; if on the side of pain, the general *evil tendency* with respect to the same community.[9]

---

[8] *Ibid.,* I, 5.
[9] *Ibid.,* IV, 6.

An action may then be said to conform to the principle of utility when the tendency it has to augment the happiness of the community is greater than any it has to diminish it. The balance sheet of pleasure and pain can serve as a policy-making guide to those charged with the governance of the community.

Bentham's version of the common good leaves at least one important question unanswered. Upon which side of the equation is the heavier stress to be placed: on happiness or number? Is an act of government which brings a high degree of pleasure to a few and some discomfort to the many to be preferred to an act which brings a modest degree of happiness to many but great pain to a few? A formula which merely adds up pleasures and pains can furnish no answer to this dilemma. The greatest happiness principle may be highly commendable as an expression of aspiration and hope, but as an operative social formula it has little to offer.

The Quality of Benevolence

Bentham apparently realizes the dangers inherent in any theory of unmitigated individualism since he trys to temper the doctrine of self-interest with something akin to a social conscience. After reiterating that the only interests which guide men are their own, he introduces with a touch of his magical wand the sentiment of "benevolence." An individual has the purely social motive of sympathy or benevolence for consulting the happiness of other men. In some vague way this sentiment constitutes a restraining guide on individual action and induces men to consult not only their own happiness but that of the general good.

Bentham is in difficulty here since benevolence or sentiment is obviously alien to any exact science of ethics and morals. Hobbes had balanced his theory of extreme individualism by a total concentration of power in the sovereign. Helvetius, while acknowledging that men necessarily pursue their own happiness, had sought to solve the problem of social stability by linking individual interest to the general advantage. The virtuous man is not one who sacrifices his personal pleasure to the common good, but one whose individual desires and passions conform so closely to the public interest that he may be said to be virtuous by necessity. Bentham rejects the Hobbesian solution, but at the same time he is unwilling to rely entirely on the equating of private and public good through the process of natural harmonization or even by means of law. As a result, he deviates from his insistence that morals must be dealt with scientifically by the admission that there is an unmeasurable factor which influences human conduct. His element of benevolence implies that government can rely on a certain amount of socially advantageous behavior that is prompted by other than self-seeking motives.

The Nature and Role of the State

The utilitarians are not concerned with the moral legitimacy of government; they are primarily interested in it as a social fact. They regard the state as an association of individuals — a fictitious body — organized for the promotion of happiness. The basis of government is not contract, but human needs. States originally came into being as a matter of convenience with no one fully understanding what had happened. Later, they were taken for granted because everyone felt that they were indispensable.

According to Bentham, the state is a political society in which there exists a habit of obedience to a governor or governors whose commands are laws. Men obey the laws not because they are ordinances of right reason, but because "the probable mischiefs of obedience are less than the probable mischiefs of resistance." They comply with the edicts of government, in other words, because it is useful for them to do so and not because there is an element of intrinsic justice embodied in the laws. "That is my duty to do which I am liable to be punished according to law if I do not do."

Bentham eschews any theory of the ideal state. His major interest in politics is to bring about improvements in existing societies by the intelligent use of government. The business of the state, as he describes it, is to promote the happiness of society by punishing and rewarding. To forbid any act is a restriction on individual liberty, and all punishment per se is an evil since it inflicts pain. One of the chief tasks of government, if not its only duty, is to reconcile conflicting claims "so to regulate the motive of self-interest that it shall operate, even against its will, towards the production of the greatest happiness." Since punishment, however, is an evil, "upon the principle of utility, if it ought at all to be admitted, it ought only to be admitted in as far as it promises to exclude some greater evil." By a judicious application of artificial pains to particular acts which are disturbing to the peace and good order of society, the state can make it unprofitable in terms of utility for an individual to perform such an act. Hence, by using the felicific calculus test, the proportion to be established between crime and punishment can be worked out with geometrical precision. In this way lawmakers and judges can provide a degree of punishment sufficient to cause a somewhat higher quantity of pain to the wrongdoer than the quantum of pleasure that he would experience in committing the wrong. The value of the punishment must not be less in any case than what is sufficient to outweigh that of the profit of the offense.

Bentham's conception of the role of government is essentially that of his *laissez-faire* contemporaries. All government is a necessary evil; its only justification is that its coercive action creates less pain than it prevents. Men are not to be interfered with in their quest for pleasure so long as their acts do not tend to diminish the total happiness of the community. There is no feeling in Bentham for civil society as a positive instrument of human perfection. He sees no relationship between the state and the moral life of its members. An individual should be left free to pursue his own pleasure as he himself determines so long as he does not unduly infringe on the happiness of others. "With few exceptions, and those not very considerable ones, the attainment of the maximum enjoyment will be most effectually secured by leaving each individual to pursue his own maximum of enjoyment, in proportion as he is in possession of the means."

In practice, Bentham and his fellow utilitarians are strongly committed to the principle of constitutional government. Philosophically, however, they depart from the traditional pattern by viewing law as the product of will rather than reason. Law is nothing more than the expression of the sovereign will of the state. When government commands, men must obey; they can never raise the defense of natural law or natural rights against the sovereign. Legally also, the powers of the state are unlimited and absolute. The extent to which the commonwealth should exercise its authority is to be determined simply by the principle of utility.

Bentham goes on to say that although there are no assignable bounds to the supreme political power, there are some practical limitations on it. People are habitually disposed to comply with the law, but there is a point beyond which "the subject is no more prepared to obey the governing body of his own state than that of any other." If government persists in enforcing an unpopular law, common resistance may arise. When this occurs the dispute should be rationally and scientifically resolved by reference to the principle of utility. The objectors should base their decision to resist or submit

> according to what should appear to them worth their while — according to what should appear to them the importance of the matter in dispute — according to what should appear to them the probability or improbability of success — according, in short, as the mischiefs of submission should appear to be a less, or a greater ratio to the mischiefs of resistance.[10]

Thus the boundaries of state authority are marked out solely by utilitarian and not by moral considerations.

When his reform plans failed to win the support of parliament, Bentham came to believe that the fundamental problem of government is to make it advantageous for the rulers to promote the greatest happiness of the greatest number. He feels that this objective can best be attained through the device of democracy, since in such a system it is to the rulers' self-interest to satisfy the desires of the community. He therefore favors the adoption of every means that will increase the dependency of the representatives on the people. These include annual sessions of parliament, universal suffrage, the secret ballot, and abolition of the monarchy and House of Lords.

JOHN STUART MILL

Among the ardent disciples that Bentham gathered about him was James Mill (1773–1836), an English journalist and economist. Mill became Bentham's most intimate friend and his stanch propagandist. The prominence of the name Mill in political theory is not due to James, however, but to his eldest son, John Stuart (1806–1873). Educated exclusively by his father under a rigorous and strict discipline, the young Mill was taught Greek at the age of three, Latin at eight, and political economy and logic (including Aristotle's logical treatises in the original) at twelve. As someone has remarked, his knowledge had such a head start that his understanding was never able to catch up with it. When he was seventeen, he entered the services of the India Company, where he remained for thirty-five years until its dissolution in 1853. He was elected to Parliament in 1865, but was defeated in the general election three years later.

---

[10] *A Fragment on Government,* IV, 39, Blackwell edition (Oxford: Blackwell, 1948).

Cradled and nurtured on utilitarianism, John Stuart Mill adopted his father's views with willing enthusiasm. Since his position with the India Service gave him ample time for intellectual pursuits, he spread the Benthamite gospel through newspaper and journal articles. By the time he was twenty, he had become the acknowledged leader of the utilitarian movement. Impaired health and an acute mental depression brought a temporary end to his intellectual activities. He emerged from his illness with the conviction that utilitarianism as conceived by his father and Bentham was too narrow and unsatisfactory. In seeking to restate the doctrine so as to remove its "insufficiencies," Mill went far toward repudiating the position of his utilitarian predecessors.

Utilitarianism Revised

Mill's treatise on utilitarianism opens by pointing out that in the practical sciences, such as ethics or politics, all action is for the sake of some end. Rules of conduct must consequently be dependent upon the end to which they are subservient. "When we engage in a pursuit, a clear and precise conception of what we are pursuing would seem to be the first thing we need, instead of the last we are to look forward to."[11] If there is a determinable end, then the test of right or wrong in individual cases is the conformity or nonconformity of the act to the end. Rejecting the classical concept of natural law as Bentham had done, Mill states that whatever consistency moral beliefs have attained in the past has been due principally to the tacit influence of an unrecognized standard — the effect of actions on man's happiness.

Aware of the objection that utilitarianism is a completely hedonistic doctrine, Mill seeks to show that the happiness it refers to is of a qualitative as well as a quantitative character. He maintains that there is no incompatibility with the principle of utility in acknowledging the fact that some kinds of pleasures are of a higher quality than others. A person may prefer one pleasure over another even though it is attended with a greater amount of discontent. The highly endowed individual requires more than sensual pleasure to make him happy. To such a person, dissatisfaction under some conditions is better than satisfaction. "It is better to be a human being dissatisfied than a pig satisfied; better to be Socrates dissatisfied than a fool satisfied."

---

[11] *Utilitarianism* (London: Parkerson, and Bourn, 1863), p. 2.

In contrast to Bentham's denial of qualitative differences in pleasure, Mill's position presents utilitarianism in a more attractive light. Yet at the same time, it constitutes a virtual rejection of utility as a scientific criterion of right and wrong. For once the element of quality is introduced, it is no longer possible to measure pleasure as one weighs potatoes. How is one able to determine which of two pleasures has the more intrinsic value? Mill can only state that the judgment of those who have experienced both must be relied on. Comparisons between qualities of pleasure are not different in principle from comparisons between quantities, and even the latter must be referred to the verdict of those most competent to judge. For "what means are there of determining which is the acutest of two pains, or the intensest of two pleasurable sensations, except the general suffrage of those who are familiar with both? Neither pains nor pleasures are homogeneous, and pain is always heterogeneous with pleasure."[12] And if the appraisals of the judges differ, the decision of the majority must be accepted as final.

The moment a utilitarian admits that pleasures can be graded as superior or inferior in quality, he is put in the illogical position, as Sabine points out, of demanding a standard for the measurement of a standard.[13] He is also ignoring the fact that if pains and pleasures are not homogeneous, the calculation and comparison of their quantities is impossible. All that can be determined is the frequency and order of men's preferences. The fact that individuals prefer some pleasure over others is no proof that those they prefer are superior in quality to the others unless it is first assumed that individuals normally prefer what is superior to what is inferior.[14]

Mill also diverges from the utilitarian school in a second and perhaps more significant aspect. While he accepts the principle of the greatest happiness for the greatest number, he rejects Bentham's method of applying this principle by means of the "felicific calculus." His reluctance to look upon pleasure solely in quantitative terms is prompted in part by his intense belief in the dignity and character of the individual. He emphasizes on several occasions that although utility is the ultimate criterion for all ethical questions, it must be a utility that is grounded on the permanent interests of man as a progressive being. In order for

---

[12] *Ibid.*, pp. 15–16.
[13] *A History of Political Theory, op. cit.*, p. 708.
[14] See John Plamenatz, *The English Utilitarians, op. cit.*, pp. 136–137.

men to be truly happy, they must "have their minds fixed on some object other than their own happiness"; they must fix them "on the happiness of others, on the improvement of mankind, even on some art or pursuit, followed not as a means, but as itself an ideal end."[15]

In place of Bentham's felicity, Mill substitutes the development of individual character. He insists that man's primary end is self-perfection, not the attainment of pleasure. A life devoted to personal pleasure-seeking is as frustrating as any other pattern of conduct which disregards the whole nature of man. For man is a social as well as a rational being, and a good portion of his happiness depends upon the satisfaction of his social impulses.

Mill is more moderate than Bentham in his criticism of natural law, but he makes it quite clear that he accepts no transcendent moral standard as the basis of human conduct. The ultimate sanction for utilitarian morality is the subjective feeling in the mind of the individual. This sanction has its roots within and not outside the mind; the restraining conscience is only a feeling in the mind, a set of acquired habits. The test of utility provides an empirical device for determining what action an individual should take. If he fails to follow the indicated course, he may be punished by the state or incur the contempt of his fellow creatures, or he may be disturbed by pangs of remorse. Moral responsibility in the traditional sense is in no way involved.

Human Freedom

The essay On Liberty, written in 1859, presents a fervent and at times eloquent defense of human freedom. Its chief objective is to point out democracy's attendant dangers and to show how they can be guarded against. The essay is clearly related to Mill's utilitarian philosophy with its psychological premise that men invariably seek the fulfillment of their individual desires. In his version of utilitarianism, men would seek higher forms of pleasure, their moral purpose would be more certain, and their social consciousness more acute if only they adequately understood themselves. He feels that the institutions and practices of organized society too often hamper the enlightenment and intellectual progress of the individual, and, consequently, the pleasures which men seek are frequently of a low order.

---

[15] Autobiography, 5th ed. (London: 1875), p. 142.

Tracing the history of individual rights and state authority, the essay notes that in the past, with the exception of ancient Greece, the relationship between ruler and subject was viewed as necessarily antagonistic. The belief that government represents an interest opposite to that of the people led in time to the establishment of various constitutional checks on the ruler. As further developments occurred, men began to feel that the state should not be an independent power opposed to the people, but should be identified with them. Once this identification was made, the interest and will of the government were looked upon as the interest and will of the nation as a whole. Carrying this belief to the extreme, Rousseau contended that there is no need to place restrictions on government since the people have no need to limit their own power over themselves.

Mill reacts strongly against the idea that the evolution of government from a position of hostility toward the popular will to one of identification with it necessarily solved the problem of liberty. When we talk of self-government or the will of the people, what we really mean is the will of the most numerous or the most active part of the people — the majority, or those who succeed in making themselves accepted as the majority. There is no assurance that this majority will not be despotic in its treatment of minorities. In addition, quite apart from political oppression, there is the danger of tyranny through social control or collective public opinion — by the attempt of society to impose, by means other than civil penalties, its own ideas and practices on those who dissent from them. Mill sees grave danger to personal development in the noticeable tendency of society to enforce conformity in customs, beliefs, and morals on all its members.

Mill maintains that there is one very simple test for determining the validity of social or governmental control over individual actions. The sole purpose for which the power of the state can rightfully be exercised over any member of a civilized community against his will is to prevent harm to others. The only part of the individual's conduct, for which he is amenable to society, is that which concerns others. His own good, either physical or moral, is not sufficient justification for the state to intervene. Yet even on this basis the range of governmental activity is broad, since in a complex society actions that affect only a single person are likely to be few and inconsequential. Mill endeavors to reduce this sphere somewhat by permitting conduct which occasions no evident harm to any particular individual even though it may not be conducive to the common good. The fact, for instance, that a person may be impairing his capacity to render service to society in general is not sufficient reason for public interference.

> But with regard to the merely contingent, or, as it may be called, constructive injury which a person causes to society, by conduct which neither violates any specific duty to the public, nor occasions perceptible hurt to any assignable individual except himself, the inconvenience is one which society can afford to bear for the sake of the greater good of human freedom.[16]

An individual is free to get drunk or not as he sees fit. If by virtue of his drinking he becomes a less productive member of society, the state has no right to punish him. If, however, his drunkenness leads to violence or to failure to support his family, public intervention is permissible.

In demarcating the area of human freedom, Mill lists three major categories: freedom of speech, freedom of vocation, and freedom of association. No society in which these liberties are not respected is free, whatever may be its form of government. In justifying these freedoms, he uses a purely utilitarian or pragmatic argument. It is important that man be free to express his views because (1) his opinion may possibly be true; (2) while it may be in error, it may contain a portion of truth; and (3) whether true or untrue, it will stimulate thought and response. "The peculiar evil of silencing the expression of an opinion is in robbing the human race: those who dissent from the opinion still more than those who hold it. If the opinion is right, they are deprived of the opportunity of exchanging error for truth; if wrong, they lose what is almost as great a benefit, the clearer perception and livelier impression of truth, produced by its collision with error."[17] If all men, therefore, were of one opinion and there was only one dissentient, "mankind would be no more justified in silencing that one person, than he, if he had the power, would be justified in silencing mankind."[18] There is no intimation here of any inalienable or natural rights possessed by man. Human freedoms are to be protected simply because they are useful to society.

Limitations on Individual Freedom

Mill's concept of individualism appears to be typical of nineteenth-

---

[16] *On Liberty*, Gateway edition (Chicago: Regnery, 1949), p. 103.
[17] *Ibid.*, p. 21. [18] *Ibid.*, p. 22.

century liberalism. He is not, however, as extreme an individualist as might appear at first sight. While the self-fulfillment of the human person is stressed throughout his works, this fulfillment must always take place within the context of the common good. Individuality is to be cultivated but within the limits set out by the rights and interests of others. Restrictions on personal freedom should be imposed only to the extent that they are essential to the self-development of others. As soon as any part of a person's conduct affects prejudicially the interests of others, society has jurisdiction over it. By developing his individuality, each person not only becomes more valuable to himself but is capable of being more valuable to others. Individual freedom, in other words, contains a substantial measure of social content.

The essay On Liberty is not the plea of a visionary divorced from reality. It fully recognizes the need for restraint, even in the exercise of basic human rights. It speaks eloquently in behalf of freedom of speech and opinion; yet at the same time it cautions that the right is not valid at all times and under all circumstances. Actions are not as free as opinions and "even opinions lose their immunity when the circumstances in which they are expressed are such as to constitute their expression a positive instigation to some mischievous act." An opinion that corn dealers are starvers of the poor "may justly incur punishment when delivered orally to an excited mob assembled before the house of a corn dealer."[19] Nearly sixty years later, the United States Supreme Court, speaking through Justice Holmes, gave judicial sanction to this same view in the well known "clear and present danger" doctrine. The question is, the Court said, "whether the words used are used in such circumstances and are of such a nature as to create a clear and present danger that they will bring about the substantive evils that Congress has a right to prevent."[20]

There are further limitations which Mill places on the liberty of the individual. Freedom to act and speak as one sees fit applies only to mature human beings. Children do not enjoy this liberty since they are still in a stage where they must be protected both against injury from others and against their own actions. A backward people is in a similar position; it does not have the capacity of being guided to its own improvement by conviction or persuasion. Liberty as a principle "has no application to

---

[19] Ibid., p. 76.
[20] Schenck v. United States, 249 U.S. 52 (1918).

any state of things anterior to the time when mankind have become capable of being improved by free and equal discussion."[21] Compulsion may properly be used to enforce compliance with the pattern of behavior prescribed by the parent or ruler, provided the purpose always be the good of the child or subject.

Mill parts company with many of his contemporaries in rejecting the classical theory of economics. Contrary to Ricardo and others, he does not believe that wages, profits, and rents are determined by immutable laws of nature. He sees no reason why man should not change the economic order if he finds it useful to do so. It may be unwise or impractical for government to interfere with wages or profits, but such action would not be a violation of individual liberty. Mill views trade as a social act which comes under governmental jurisdiction since it affects the interests of society in general. In his early years he upheld the doctrine of free trade, not on the basis of individual freedom but on purely pragmatic grounds. He argued that while economic restraints affect only that part of human conduct which society has the authority to regulate, they are wrong solely because they do not really produce the desired results.

Mill is unable to shake himself completely free from the suspicion of government. He feels that there is more likelihood of an activity being poorly performed by public authorities than by private means. He is convinced that private enterprise in a free competitive position results in greater benefits to society than a controlled economy. However, he does not believe that the pursuit of individual interest automatically results in the good of society. He is willing to have the state intervene in economic affairs to prevent injustices and to remove obstacles in the way of bettering the happiness of the general public. For this reason he supports the right of government to restrict inheritances, regulate child labor, control natural monopolies, limit working hours, and even abolish the wage system in favor of a co-operative association of producers.

Mill's writings give evidence of an awareness of subsidiarity as an operative principle applicable to all aspects of social living. Although he prefers private initiative to public action, he urges governmental intervention in cases where private means prove unable to meet the needs of society. His position in this respect is strikingly similar to that found in the modern formulation of subsidiarity. He notes three objections to governmental interference in the social and economic order. First, the

---

[21] On Liberty, op. cit., p. 13.

ordinary processes of business, industry, and education are likely to be accomplished better by individual than governmental initiative. "Speaking generally, there is no one so fit to conduct any business, or to determine how or by whom it shall be conducted, as those who are personally interested in it." Such individuals or groups are closer to the problem, they are more aware of its many implications, and they have a more vital concern in its solution. Second, when government assumes the responsibility for a particular function, the opportunity for individual growth and development through direct participation in its execution is diminished. "In many cases, though individuals may not do the particular thing so well on the average as the officers of government, it is nevertheless desirable that it should be done by them rather than by the government, as a means to their own mental education — a mode of strengthening their active faculties, exercising their judgment, and giving them a familiar knowledge of the subjects with which they are thus left to deal."[22] Third, when the state takes over a task that can be performed adequately by private means, it increases the burden on government and adds unnecessarily to its power.

Ideas on Government

Mill refutes the social contract theory saying that no good purpose is answered by inventing a contract in order to deduce social obligations from it. The fact that society is indispensable to man's well-being and development imposes an obligation on him to contribute to its maintenance. "The social state is at once so natural, so necessary, and so habitual to man, that, except in some unusual circumstances or by an effort of voluntary abstraction, he never conceives himself otherwise than as a member of a body."[23] Man as the recipient of society's benefits is under a distinct obligation to bear his share of maintaining the social entity. Taxation, military service, and compulsory education are among the legitimate duties that government may impose on him without in any way violating his freedom.

Mill is by no means a doctrinaire or even enthusiastic democrat. He favors universal suffrage, not because he considers it an abstract natural right but because he feels that it is the most practical way of securing good government while preserving individual freedom. Like his father

[22] *Ibid.*, p. 127.
[23] *Utilitarianism, op. cit.*, p. 45.

and Bentham, he has no great love for the masses or the rule of the numerical majority; yet he sees no other way of avoiding oppressive government. Bentham originally preferred a strong monarch who could accomplish the reforms that the philosophical radicals considered necessary. He turned to democracy largely out of impatience at the failure of the ruling oligarchy in England to support his proposals. Mill's father likewise accepted democratic government with less than full enthusiasm. He viewed it primarily as a device to eliminate the dangers that result when political power is vested in one or a small number of individuals.

While sharing his father's distrust of human nature, John Stuart takes a more constructive attitude toward democracy. He believes that the freedom to participate in political decisions engenders a sense of responsibility and contributes to man's development. The average person has little ability to reason — his opinions can be no more than mediocre at the best — but he has the desire to listen to reason and the capacity to respond to wise leadership. Democracy to the younger Mill means essentially rule by an educated elite selected by the people. Democracy as represented by the Jacksonian doctrine would have appalled him.

In his *Considerations on Representative Government*, Mill gives classic expression to the doctrine of representative democracy. Answering the argument that an absolute monarchy would be the best form of government if a superior and eminent ruler could be found, he describes the situation that would exist under such a person. "One man of superhuman mental activity managing the entire affairs of a mentally passive people. Their passivity is implied in the very idea of absolute power. The nation as a whole, and every individual composing it, are without any potential voice in their own destiny. They exercise no will in respect to their collective interests." What sort of human beings, he asks, can be found under such an arrangement? "What development can either their thinking or their active faculties attain under it?"[24]

The ideally best form of government is that in which sovereignty is vested in the whole community, "every citizen not only having a voice in the exercise of that ultimate sovereignty but being, at least occasionally, called upon to take an actual part in the government by the personal discharge of some public function, local or general."[25] This participation is important for two reasons: the rights and interests of an individual are

---

[24] *Considerations on Representative Government* (New York: Harper & Brothers, 1867), pp. 56–57. [25] *Ibid.*, p. 64.

only secure when he himself is able and habitually disposed to stand up for them; and the general prosperity and well-being of the people are better promoted in proportion to the amount and variety of personal energies enlisted in furthering them. Participation in the actual governance of the modern state, however, must be largely vicarious. The whole citizen body cannot take part personally in any but some very minor portions of the public business. It therefore follows that "the ideal type of a perfect government must be representative."[26]

Although Mill believes that government by the majority is the most practical way of ruling society, he is acutely aware of the need for safeguarding the rights of minorities. To provide what he considers the necessary checks against the possibility of tyranny by the majority, he advocates proportional representation, reconstitution of the House of Lords, plural voting, and the open ballot. He supports the first because of his belief that the method of electing by majority vote in single member districts gives insufficient representation to minorities. He urges that a "Chamber of Statesmen" composed of high government officials, university professors, and representatives of the nobility replace the hereditary House of Lords. Because of the ability and experience of its members, this chamber could be entrusted with the power to draft the bills that come before Commons.

Evidencing his confidence in an intellectual elite, Mill proposes a system of weighted or plural voting whereby university graduates and members of the legal profession would be given two votes. Such a system would tend to leaven the vote of the masses and reduce the dangers of class legislation. Finally, he maintains that voting is a civic responsibility which should be exercised openly under the eye and criticism of the public. He believes that the selfishness and personal interests of the voter constitute a greater source of evil than the possibility of coercion by others. When an individual is forced to declare his vote openly, he is more likely to consider the public welfare than his own selfish interests.

LIBERALISM

Utilitarianism is but another form of liberalism, a doctrine that had its beginnings during the Renaissance and that reached its fullest expression during the nineteenth century. Like conservatism, there is semantic

---
[26] *Ibid.*, p. 80.

confusion in the use of the term. The modern liberal is as different from his eighteenth- and nineteenth-century predecessor as the democratic socialist from the Marxist. The earlier brand of liberalism is often characterized as integral or classical to distinguish it from its present-day counterpart. The discussion here will be limited to a brief description of classical liberalism and an example of how it found extreme expression in the writings of Herbert Spencer.

Classical Liberalism

The predominant characteristic of liberalism is its accent on the individual. From the beginning, it has sought to vindicate the right of each person to work out his own destiny free from all but a minimum of social control. In pursuing this objective it has endeavored to limit the ambit of political authority and to discover a system of rights which the state is not entitled to invade. It was under liberal principles that the new middle class rose to a position of political dominance. Largely because of this close association, liberalism developed policies and ideas which harmonized with the class interests of the bourgeoisie. Among these was the theory that natural laws infallibly regulate economics, and hence the state should not intervene in this field except as the guardian of a free market.

The chief attributes of classical liberalism can be summed up in this way:

1. Reason, not faith or emotion, is the only true guide to man's actions.
2. Man is essentially good and perfectible.
3. There are certain natural laws in human affairs — social, political, and economic — that can be discovered by scientific investigation.
4. There are certain inalienable rights peculiar to man by virtue of his humanity, and the sole purpose of the state is to preserve and protect these rights.
5. History is a record of continual progress in which mankind, through its own efforts, is steadily improving. Change in the social and political order should therefore be welcomed and encouraged, not feared and impeded.
6. Revealed and organized religion is not necessary to man's moral progress.
7. Individual freedom is best assured by constitutional government.

Not all of these characteristics are, of course, peculiar to liberalism; some of them had long been embedded in the thought of western civilization.

Spencer

Herbert Spencer (1820–1903), a British sociologist, exemplifies the most extreme form of classical liberalism. Applying the theory of biological evolution to human society, Spencer holds that only the fittest can survive and progress in the competitive societal struggle. (It was he, not Darwin, who coined the well-known phrase "survival of the fittest.") He warns that the state should not attempt to interfere in the social and economic order, since such intervention is both futile and harmful. It impedes the law of natural selection and consequently lowers the standards of society as a whole.

Spencer notes that "a stern discipline which is a little cruel that it may be kind" pervades all nature. Man should not be led by a feeling of pity for others to follow a course of action that would impede the purifying process of nature. It may seem harsh, for example, "that widows and orphans should be left to struggle for life or death. Nevertheless, when regarded not separately, but in connection with the interests of universal humanity, these harsh fatalities are seen to be full of the highest beneficence — the same beneficence which brings to early graves the children of diseased parents and singles out the low-spirited, the intemperate, and the debilitated as the victims of an epidemic."[27]

In his best known work, *Man versus the State* (1884), Spencer notes that the function of liberalism in the past was to limit the powers of kings; in the future its function will be to restrict the powers of parliament. He urges that the state leave man alone so that the process of evolution may go on without hindrance, and the laws of nature operate freely. He believes that government will become less and less needed as the individual becomes more perfectly adapted to society. Only for the time being is a limited amount of government necessary since men still have some of the predatory instincts of their ancestors. "Only by the process of adaptation itself, can be produced that character which makes social equilibrium spontaneous. And hence, while this process is going on, an instrumentality must be employed, first, to bind man into the social state, and second to check all conduct endangering the existence of that state."[28]

---

[27] *Social Statics* (New York: D. Appleton, 1865), p. 354.
[28] *Ibid.*, p. 74.

This is the role that government is designed to play in the liberal *weltanschauung*.

Spencer's political philosophy is based on the view that society is a mere collection of human atoms, that man is by nature a solitary animal, and that the state is mere coercion. The state is a necessary evil, one that must exist for the time being while man is passing from social immaturity to civilization. It is, in brief, a transitory institution that will vanish away in the society of the future where some kind of amiable anarchism will prevail. In the introduction to his *Social Statics*, Spencer declares that to the bad, government is essential; to the good, it is not. "It is the check which national wickedness makes to itself, and exists only to the same degree. Its continuance is proof of still-existing barbarism. What a cage is to the wild beast, law is to the selfish man." There is a close parallel here between Spencer's belief that social progress will eventually make political government useless and the Marxian claim that the state is destined to wither away.

Spencer's social and political philosophy marked the swan song of *laissez-faire* liberalism. His rabid individualism could not withstand the pressures for reform that even his liberal contemporaries were beginning to advocate. As the evils of unregulated capitalism grew in intensity and scope, all hopes of salvaging classical liberalism as the social philosophy of modern society vanished. Only the most stubborn and reactionary proponents of the old school continued to preach its doctrine in undiluted form. The others realized that capitalism and perhaps even democracy were doomed unless widespread reforms were instituted in the social and economic orders.

SUMMARY

Utilitarianism was a passing phenomenon in English political thought. Its apparent simplicity had great appeal to those who were seeking practical reform, but this same simplicity also served for a time to conceal the weaknesses inherent in the doctrine. Mill realized the inadequacies of utilitarianism as originally formulated and sought to remold it along more humane lines while preserving the "greatest happiness" principle. As Lord Lindsay has pointed out, utilitarian ethics and psychology are indefensible when undiluted by the common sense and human sympathy which Mill allowed to taint the rigid doctrine of his elders.[29]

Utilitarianism has little to offer to the development of political philosophy

---

[29] *The Modern Democratic State* (New York: Oxford University Press, 1947), p. 139.

beyond that which Hobbes and others have contributed. What theoretical significance it possesses lies in its attempt to establish a precise test of social and political morality based entirely on man's desires. This effort, like that of Hobbes, sought to explain all reality in purely mechanical terms. Although utilitarian theory was closely associated with a laissez-faire concept of government, it could be made readily applicable to a socialized or even totalitarian state. Based on a natural law standard, which the utilitarians rejected, the greatest happiness principle might be interpreted as analogous to the traditional view of the common good; but based solely on man's desires, the doctrine freed political power from all philosophical restraints.

In practice, utilitarianism has much in common with the western tradition, despite the philosophical differences between the two. The social and legal reforms which it sponsored were salutary and generally progressive. But even in the practical sphere utilitarianism could contribute little in the way of a positive approach to the changes that technological developments were precipitating in the structure of modern society. Its negative theory of the state and its lack of any dynamic conception of the social good gave little political guidance at a time when circumstances were forcing government to assume a larger responsibility for the general welfare.

BIBLIOGRAPHY

Adams, K. M., "How the Benthamites Became Democrats," Journal of Social Philosophy, January, 1942.

Barker, Ernest, Political Thought in England, 1848–1914 (London: Home University Library, 1932).

Baumgardt, David, "Bentham's Censorial Method," Journal of the History of Ideas, October, 1954.

Brebner, J. B., "Laissez Faire and State Intervention in 19th Century Britain," Journal of Economic History, 1948.

Brinton, Crane, English Political Thought in the 19th Century (Cambridge: Harvard University Press, 1949).

Burns, J. H., "J. S. Mill and Democracy," Political Studies, June and October, 1957.

Coates, W. H., "Benthamism, Laissez Faire and Collectivism," Journal of the History of Ideas, June, 1950.

Davidson, William L., Political Thought in England: The Utilitarians from Bentham to J. S. Mill (London: Home University Library, 1935).

Ewing, A. C., "Utilitarianism," Ethics, January, 1948.

Halévy, Elie, The Growth of Philosophical Radicalism, trans. by Mary Morris (Boston: Beacon Press, 1955).

Hall, Everett W., "The 'Proof' of Utility in Bentham and Mill," Ethics, October, 1949.

Harris, A. L., "J. S. Mill's Theory of Progress," Ethics, April, 1956.

Harsanyi, J. C., "Cardinal Welfare, Individualistic Ethics and Interpersonal Comparisons of Utility," Journal of Political Economy, August, 1955.

Hofstadter, Richard, *Social Darwinism in American Thought*, 1860–1915 (Philadelphia: University of Pennsylvania Press, 1945).

Irvine, William, "Shaw, the Fabians, and Utilitarians," *Journal of the History of Ideas*, April, 1947.

Johnson, A., "Liberalism Old and New," *American Journal of Economics and Sociology*, April, 1948.

Larrabee, H. A., "Bentham's Handbook of Political Fallacies," *Thought*, Summer, 1953.

Letwin, S. R., "Utilitarianism: A System of Political Tolerance," *Cambridge Journal*, March, 1953.

Mack, M. P., "Fabians and Utilitarianism," *Journal of the History of Ideas*, January, 1955.

Magid, Henry M., "Mill and the Problem of Freedom of Thought," *Social Research*, Spring, 1954.

McGreal, Ian, "A Naturalistic Utilitarianism," *Journal of Philosophy*, August 31, 1950.

Mitchell, Wesley C., "Bentham's Felicific Calculus," *Political Science Quarterly*, June, 1918.

Neill, Thomas P., *The Rise and Decline of Liberalism* (Milwaukee: Bruce, 1954).

Palmer, Paul A., "Benthamism in England and America," *American Political Science Review*, October, 1941.

Peardon, T. P., "Bentham's Ideal Republic," *Canadian Journal of Economics and Political Science*, May, 1951.

Pratt, R. C., "Benthamite Theory of Democracy," *Canadian Journal of Economics and Political Science*, February, 1955.

Ruggiero, Guido de, *The History of European Liberalism* (London: Oxford University Press, 1927).

Rumney, H., *Herbert Spencer's Sociology* (London: Williams and Norgale, 1934).

Schapiro, J. S., "John Stuart Mill, Pioneer of Democratic Liberalism in England," *Journal of the History of Ideas*, April, 1943.

Swabey, William C., "Non-Normative Utilitarianism," *Journal of Philosophy*, July 8, 1943.

Viner, Jacob, "Bentham and J. S. Mill: The Utilitarian Background," *American Economic Review*, March, 1949.

Wallas, Graham, *Men and Ideas* (London: Norton, 1940).

Chapter XVIII

THE IDEALIST THEORY OF THE STATE

"For Truth is the Unity of the universal and subjective Will; and the Universal is to be found in the State, in its laws, its universal and rational arrangements. The State is the Divine Idea as it exists on Earth" (Hegel, *Philosophy of History*).

BEFORE the close of the eighteenth century, empiricism as a theory of knowledge and individualism as a theory of politics had gained wide recognition. The former had come into being as a protest against the rationalism of the Enlightenment; the latter was merely a continuance of the atomistic tendencies that had made their appearance with the Renaissance and Reformation. Hume represented the epitome of the new empiricism with his attack on natural law and his insistence that there can be no certain knowledge about anything except that which is observable. Locke and Bentham were typical of the social individualists who denied completely the organic character of the state and who sought to explain political obligation by showing that obedience to government is in the private interests of the individual.

Neither empiricism nor individualism has stood unchallenged. Both have evoked strong counterattacks, the most far reaching of which came from the German "idealists." The focus of political and social philosophy during the seventeenth century was in England and during the following one hundred years in France, but the nineteenth century belongs to Germany. The fermentation in political thought which took place there was in part due to Germany's long delayed transformation from feudalism to the modern national state. As the character of the nation's political and social arrangements changed, the need for theoretical articulation of the new course of events became more pressing. The period between the outbreak of the French Revolution and the middle of the next century proved to be productive years in German political thought as its thinkers sought to redefine the relation between the state and the individual. The dialectical idealism of Hegel and the dialectical materialism of Marx are products of this era.

Political idealism, foreshadowed in part by Kant, reached the zenith of its expression in Hegel. Later it enjoyed considerable vogue in England through the writings of such political theorists as T. H. Green and Bernard Bosanquet. Idealism cannot be simply defined; it represents different things to different thinkers. Basically, it places the emphasis on mind as in some way prior to matter, holding that the underlying reality of the universe resides in ideas, ideal forms, or an absolute. Common to all members of the idealist school is the notion that pure or abstract reason is supreme over sensation or experience. In its extreme form, idealism holds that all reality exists only in personal consciousness — only mind is real and matter has no existence independent of a mind that perceives it.

Political idealism is the application of an idealistic philosophy to the interpretation of the state and its operations. It seeks an understanding of civil society and its institutions in purely rationalistic terms with little or no reference to experience. In all of its forms, political idealism rejects the mechanistic and utilitarian concepts of the state because of their materialistic connotations. Professor Hallowell, in describing the idealism of the period here concerned, states that it was: philosophically, an attempt to rescue knowledge from Hume's skepticism and its consequent destruction of science; ethically, an endeavor to save man's moral consciousness from a diet of utilitarian self-interest; and politically, a reaction to the extreme individualism of the times.[1]

IMMANUEL KANT

It will be recalled that Hume looked upon causation as nothing but a set of happenings or connections in which one event follows another.[2] The fact that things occur in a certain order forms in the human mind the habit of expecting them to happen in the future as they have in the past. No necessary association, no cause and effect relationship, exists between these events or ideas. Consequently, neither the principles of natural science nor the laws of morality have any universal necessity. Hume's empirical theory of knowledge places in sharp perspective the

---

[1] *Main Currents in Modern Political Thought*, op. cit., p. 235.
[2] See *ante*, p. 282.

problem of the relation of the mind to external objects. His position, moreover, precludes any true knowledge of an object. Objects as such are simply a set of impressions and ideas, and there is no way of getting from the latter over to the objects which lie outside of them. If this is true, the human mind cannot possibly know reality.

The German idealists saw the dangers implicit in a skepticism which rejects the existence of both natural science and a science of morals. Immanuel Kant (1724–1804) was one of the first modern thinkers to endeavor to answer the epistemological problem basic to Hume's theory. Born in Koenigsberg, an old Prussian town on the northeastern frontier of Germany, Kant's long life was devoted almost exclusively to academic pursuits. In describing him, the German poet Heine observes that the history of his life is hard to write inasmuch as he had neither life nor history, for he lived a mechanically ordered and abstract old bachelor life in a quiet retired street in Koenigsberg. Heine goes on to say that it is doubtful whether the great clock of the cathedral there did its daily work more dispassionately and regularly than Kant. Legend has it that his fellow townspeople set their watches by him as he passed their doors on his daily walk.

After attending the University of Koenigsberg and serving as tutor in several aristocratic families, Kant was appointed an instructor, and later professor, of logic and metaphysics at the university. His intellectual development was slow and it was not until after he had reached middle age that he demonstrated his profound capacity for creative thinking. He was fifty-seven when he wrote the *Critique of Pure Reason*, the most important of his many significant works. His political ideas are contained largely in his *Metaphysical Foundations of the Philosophy of Law*, *Principles of Politics*, and *Perpetual Peace*.

Kant's contribution to the field of political theory is neither original nor substantial. Although his essay, *Perpetual Peace*, is a penetrating study of the problem of modern nationalism and world peace, his treatment of the state is largely a mixture of the political thinking of Montesquieu and Rousseau. Kant's importance to politics lies in his general philosophical formulations which so deeply influenced German intellectual life. His attempt to bridge the gap between mind and reality and to restore ethics to the status of a practical science is vitally relevant to political philosophy, which must deal with human actions and social institutions in a time and space context. He is also of particular importance to the historical development of political philosophy because of the influence that he had on Hegel and later "idealist" writers.

The intricate philosophy formulated by Kant defies any brief summation. The most that can be done here is to point out those features of his thinking that are important to political philosophy. His theory of knowledge and his theory of morals are particularly relevant in this respect.

The Kantian Theory of Knowledge

Kant sees the weakness in the rationalist claim that true knowledge can only be based upon the insights of reason unpolluted by the senses. At the same time he is aware of the grave danger to science and morals in the Humean analysis of knowledge, with its relegation of reason to the role of handmaiden for the senses. To overcome the deficiencies inherent in both of these positions, he endeavors to combine the two approaches, rationalistic and empirical, by demonstrating that knowledge is a joint product of mind and matter. His analysis of this process differs radically from the traditional theory of knowledge, which also stresses the interdependency of mind and the senses.

Kant first makes the distinction between a *priori* knowledge which exists altogether independent of experience, and a *posteriori* knowledge which arises only through the senses. The former gives rise to analytical judgments in which the predicate is contained within the subject; the latter results in synthetic propositions in which the predicate lies completely outside the subject and adds something to it. Thus all propositions which are known only through experience are synthetic. To illustrate the difference between the two types of knowledge, Kant refers to two statements: "all bodies are extended" (they occupy space) and "all bodies are heavy." He cites the first as an example of an analytic judgment and the second as a synthetic judgment. The concept of the predicate "extended" is a necessary part of the subject body and really adds nothing to it "for I need not go beyond the conception of body in order to find extension connected with it, but merely analyze the conception, that is, become conscious of the manifold properties which I think is that conception, in order to discover this predicate in it."[3] Extension, in other words, is an integral part of the definition of body. The same observation cannot be made of weight since this is a quality which a body acquires when placed in a gravitational field, and hence it can be discovered by

---

[3] *Critique of Pure Reason*, trans. by J. Meiklejohn (New York: Willey, 1900), p. 7.

experience alone. According to these definitions, rationalism abounds in purely analytic judgments while empiricism makes use of wholly synthetic propositions.

It is evident to Kant that analytic judgments cannot contribute to the advance of science through new discoveries since the mind must have recourse to the objects of sense experience in order to acquire new materials. Conversely, synthetic judgments based on sense experience alone can have no scientific validity because the senses deal with the singular and contingent. The problem, as he conceives it, is to determine whether judgments that are both a priori and synthetic are possible. Only such judgments can satisfy the scientific requirement of a knowledge that is empirically founded as well as necessary and universal.

Kant's proof of the possibility of synthetic a priori judgments begins in rationalistic fashion by affirming the supremacy of thought over being. The intellect of man is endowed with the forms of space and time and with certain categories such as substance, quality, quantity, and cause and effect. Since these intellectual forms are a priori (that is, they exist in the mind independent of any sense experience), they possess the attributes of universality and necessity. The function of these forms of sensibility is to organize sensory matter into definite structured patterns so that the human mind may attain a knowledge of external objects in their temporal and spatial aspects. Kant explains that any experience we have must always take on these forms given by our own mind. And since the structure of consciousness in general is the same for all individuals, the human mind is able to make certain universal judgments for all possible sensory experiences.

The crucial question in this whole process is whether it is possible to know reality. Hume warned that we are on firm ground only so long as we confine our speculation to the appearance of objects and do not attempt to probe their substantial essences. Kant sees no necessity to refute this premise in order to demonstrate the possibility of science. He points out that we must distinguish between the things of our experience (phenomena) and the things-in-themselves (noumena). The latter are not objects of knowledge. The human mind is capable of knowing things as they appear in conformity with the intellectual forms, but it cannot reach to a knowledge of these objects as they are in themselves. While we know that our experience must always take on the forms of time and space and of the various categories, we cannot possibly know anything beyond this except that a noumenal realm must exist. Kant insists that it is not necessary for knowledge to go beyond these experiences since the appearance of sensory matter constitutes an objective realm that will sustain scientific judgments. By imposing an order on the external world through the intellectual forms, man is able to obtain an accurate description of objects as they appear to exist and to make facts intelligible. In this way, the natural scientist is able to establish empirical laws to explain past and predict future events even though he cannot actually know reality.

Kant's attempt to overcome Humean skepticism results in a theory of knowledge quite different from traditional epistemology. By denying that the human intellect can penetrate to the real essence of things through abstraction, he rejects metaphysics as a science. To sustain logically his theory of a priori synthetic judgments, he is forced to pay the price of restricting their application to the world of experienced phenomena. He could not extend the application of such notions as cause and substance. Contrary to Kant's approach, realistic metaphysics does not hold that the mind imposes intellectual forms on external objects. Instead, it maintains that there is a real foundation for universal necessity in the objects of experience themselves, and that intellectual concepts as well as sense perceptions are derived in some fashion from external reality. The traits of universality and necessity are based on the essential structure which the intellect, in close co-operation with the senses, abstracts from the real existents.[4]

Kantian Ethics

The empirical theory of knowledge implies that there can be no ultimate demonstration of the truth or falsity of a moral proposition. Human actions can be observed and their logical consequences noted, but no judgment can be made that they are morally good or evil. Kant is not satisfied with this position since he feels the distinct need for a rational foundation of moral obligation. He can accept neither the moral relativism of the empiricists nor the moral dogmatism of the rationalists. Nor will his critical view of metaphysics permit him to accept the concept of natural law as the basis of human conduct. He does not deny the existence of an independent order of being to which man ought to

---

[4] See in this connection, J. Collins, A History of Modern European Philosophy, op. cit., p. 471.

conform in his behavior; he simply maintains that such an order belongs to the world of noumena and therefore cannot be demonstrated by the speculative reason. On this basis, as he admits, there can be no intellectual proof of the existence of God.

Despite his epistemological hesitations, Kant is convinced that there is a supreme principle that controls all moral judgments. Man feels obliged to subject himself to law; he feels a sense of oughtness and of duty. Individuals may differ in their views as to the propriety of specific acts, but each one cannot help assuming that he is morally responsible for his conduct. There are certain postulates of the practical reason which are fundamental to this assumption of moral conduct: man is a moral being with a free will and an immortal soul, and he lives in an ordered world directed by an ordering intelligence. These postulates are given to him by his reason. Their truth or falsity cannot be proved; they must be taken on faith. Man is impelled to accept them if the world is to have any meaning for him at all. This approach is somewhat analogous to saying: we need a God; our moral sense of duty demands a God; hence there must surely be one.

By reflecting on the rational concept of law and duty, man is made to feel that he should act solely for duty's sake even though such action conflicts with his inclinations and desires. Since moral consciousness functions in terms of duty, Kant formulates his standard for ethical conduct in the form of a command or imperative. There are two types of imperatives: the hypothetical, which tells us what we must do if we wish to achieve a certain end; and the categorical, which tells us what we ought to do as moral beings. It is the latter which demands that we behave in a certain way regardless of our personal desires or inclinations. Kant verbalizes this supreme principle of morality in a dictum that is similar to the Golden Rule: "Act as if the maxim of your action were to become by your will a Universal Law of Nature."[5] An act is morally good if the agent is willing that the maxim or principle behind it be universalized as law for all men. Kant uses the following example to illustrate his point:

An individual finds himself forced by necessity to borrow money. He knows that he will not be able to repay it, but sees also that nothing will be lent to him unless he promises stoutly to repay it in a definite

[5] *Fundamental Principles of the Metaphysics of Morals*, trans. by T. K. Abbott (New York: Liberal Arts Press, 1949), p. 38.

time. . . . Suppose, however, that he resolves to do so, then the maxim of his action would be expressed thus: When I think myself in want of money, I will borrow money and promise to repay it, although I know that I never can do so. . . . How would it be if my maxim were a universal law?[6]

The categorical imperative is completely a priori. It does not give particular directives for human conduct nor even proximate guidance in individual circumstances. It merely expresses the fact that man has an obligation toward society without determining or specifying just what he is obliged to perform. So long as he adopts as his rule of conduct in a practical situation what he is willing for everyone else to do, his action is morally proper. Although this does not seem to be a very satisfactory criterion for virtue, the imperative is of importance to political philosophy since its objective is to ensure a maximum of free action for all members of the community through self-regulation.

The Kantian Antinomies

According to Kant's epistemology, the human intellect can get beyond sense experience only by postulation and not by knowledge. When the mind attempts to acquire a knowledge of the noumena, it is troubled by antinomies or mutually contradictory propositions, each of which can apparently be proved. Two of these major contradictions involve the dichotomy between transcendental ideas and science, and between free will and causal determination of human conduct. These antinomies are of importance to the subsequent development of political philosophy since they constitute in large measure the starting point of Hegel's thinking.

As an example of the first antinomy, Kant points out that in the arena of experience, there is an antecedent cause for every effect. No matter how far back this line of causation is carried, we are always justified in assuming a prior cause. This process can go on ad infinitum. We maintain, as our reason must lead us to maintain, that there is some primal cause which is the cause of the phenomenon we experience but which lies outside of it. When we follow this procedure, however, we are by the same logic forced to look for another cause antecedent to the first cause, since we have brought the noumenal system within the field of causality. When the intellect becomes involved in an apparent contradiction of this

---

[6] Ibid., pp. 39–40.

kind, it is trying to know something that obviously lies outside the limits of its possible knowledge. Man must then turn to faith, in the sense of accepting the postulates, rather than to knowledge.

The second contradiction raised by Kant concerns the apparent dichotomy between man as necessarily determined by the physical laws of nature and man as a self-conscious ego with a free will. As a physical being in the field of experience, the phenomenal world, man is subject to the law of cause and effect. This subjection implies that human actions are completely determined by preceding events. On the other side of the coin, man is conscious of a sense of responsibility for his conduct — a recognition which infers that human acts are not automatically caused by preceding events but through the volition of a free being. Kant explains this antinomy by noting that man as a physical creature belongs to the phenomenal world and as such is subject to its empirical laws, but as a rational being he transcends the phenomenal order. It is this latter aspect of man that is free and that brings him into contact with the noumenal world to which morality belongs. Again, it is by postulation and not through knowledge that Kant establishes the moral nature of man.

The Political Theory of Kant

The political problem for Kant is the realization of the categorical imperative, a self-operating lawfulness, in practice. If all men would act in complete conformity to universal law, the perennial problem of reconciling the moral freedom of the individual with the like freedom of his fellow creatures would be solved. But there is a certain depravity or selfishness rooted in the nature of man that causes him at times to act contrary to his sense of duty. Because of this weakness, man is in need of a master to break his self-will and compel him to obey a will that is universally valid. If society is to exist, its members must be compelled to act according to law. Kant holds that the state must be founded on the freedom of every member as a man, on his equality as a subject, and on his self-dependency as an individual. All laws passed by the state should be informed by these principles.

The free moral will can function effectively only when men are protected from the evil acts of their fellow creatures. It is here that the role of the state as the enforcer of order becomes evident. In a certain sense, the political community personifies the categorical imperative, for it is through the instrumentality of its laws that the voluntary actions of individual persons are harmonized in accordance with the universal law of freedom. The imperative, in short, provides the moral basis or test for effecting this reconciliation. The state through its laws and institutions endeavors to enforce the observance of the Golden Rule in the social and political order.

Kant's political philosophy is partially in the liberal tradition since it posits an essentially negative role for the state, that of ensuring an ordered coexistence of individuals. He feels that the state in performing this function is actually contributing to the moral development of its citizens.

> For working against the tendency every citizen has to commit acts of violence against his neighbor, there is the much stronger force of the government which not only gives an appearance of morality to the whole state (causae non causae), but, by checking the outbreak of lawless propensities, actually aids the moral qualities of men considerably, in their development of a direct respect for the law. For every individual thinks that he himself would hold the idea of right sacred and follow faithfully what it prescribes, if only he could expect that everyone else would do the same. This guarantee is in part given to him by the government; and a great advance is made by this step which is not deliberately moral, towards the ideal of fidelity to the concept of duty for its own sake without thought of return.[7]

Kant is convinced that a satisfactory political order, national or international, cannot be attained until the principle of disinterested obedience to the moral law is accepted by mankind as the ethical basis of legal obligation. Man must realize that freedom does not mean the ability to do what he desires; it means acting in accordance with the dictates of his rational will, the source of universal law. The individual who follows his appetites and passions is not free; he is a slave to his lower nature. Man must pursue his individual ends within a legal constitution which embodies the universal will and which assures freedom to each through the laws applicable to all. The maintenance of this constitution is the chief duty of the state.

HEGEL

Georg Wilhelm Friedrich Hegel (1770–1831) was born at Stuttgart, Germany, the son of a minor customs official. His personal life, like that of Kant, was relatively uninteresting. One writer has remarked that he

---

[7] Perpetual Peace, trans. by M. C. Smith (New York: Liberal Arts Press, 1948), p. 39.

lived apparently for no other purpose than to play secretary to the Absolute.[8] After receiving his doctorate in theology at the University of Tubingen, Hegel served for a time as tutor at Berne and Frankfurt and later as headmaster of a high school in Nuremberg. In 1816, he accepted a professorship at the University of Berlin where he remained until his death in 1831 during the cholera epidemic. His brilliant tenure at Berlin was climaxed by his appointment as rector of the university in 1829. Because of his teachings and writings he became in effect the official philosopher of the Prussian state. Shortly before his death, he was decorated by Frederick William III in recognition of his outstanding contributions to German intellectual life.

There are few thinkers whose ideas have had greater influence on the future course of events than this German schoolman. His most important works are the monumental three volume study entitled *Science of Logic* (1816), the *Philosophy of Right* (1821), and the *Philosophy of History* (1837), the last named having profound effect on subsequent political theory. Not one to regard his accomplishments lightly, Hegel believed that he had reached the pinnacle in philosophical thinking. As he modestly exclaims, "It is clear that no method can be accepted as scientific that is not modelled on mine." Hegel's influence on the development of political thought has been roundly denounced. Ernst Cassirer, for example, remarks

> But it was the tragic fate of Hegel that he unconsciously unchained the most irrational powers that ever appeared in man's social and political life. No other philosophical system has done so much for the preparation of fascism and imperialism as Hegel's doctrine of the state — this divine idea as it exists on earth.[9]

And Hobhouse, writing while German bombs were falling on London during World War I, exclaimed that he was witnessing the visible and tangible outcome of a false and wicked doctrine — the foundations of which lay in the works of Hegel.[10]

Hegel's interest in political theory was secondary to his metaphysical interpretation of the universal order. His philosophy is difficult to comprehend and equally difficult to summarize. Bertrand Russell says that

---

[8] H. D. Aiken, *The Age of Ideology* (New York: New American Library, 1957), p. 71.

[9] *The Myth of the State, op. cit.*, pp. 343–344.

[10] *Metaphysical Theory of the State* (London: Allen & Unwin, 1918), p. 6.

it is the hardest to understand of all the great thinkers. Yet a knowledge of some of its more basic premises is essential to an analysis of nineteenth- and twentieth-century political thought. If Hegel had done nothing else but provide a metaphysical framework for Marxian thought, this accomplishment alone would rank him high among the influential thinkers of the world.

Hegel's Idealism

Although he greatly admires Kant, Hegel feels that his predecessor failed to answer definitively the questions which were raised by Hume's ruthless empiricism. He believes that a much stronger case can be made against the empirical position which denies the possibility of establishing a rational basis for morality. To his way of thinking, the dualism of thought and being, or mind and object, is the weak point in the Kantian answer to Hume. This aspect of Kant's philosophy had forced him to hold that reason is incapable of attaining knowledge of things-in-themselves and had led to his so-called antinomies. Hegel reasons that if this dualism can be effectively bridged, the problem of knowledge and truth will be solved. His attempt to accomplish the task results in absolute idealism: the theory that the underlying reality of the universe resides in the divine or absolute idea.

According to Hegel, nature is a coherent whole, an external manifestation of an absolute or divine reason which is progressively revealed in time and space. The absolute is spirit (geist).[11] This spirit is all enveloping although completely spiritual. It embraces the material world and the whole range of human experience. It is based upon every judgment included in total experience. It "unfolds its own nature in the phenomena of the world's existence." The finite is real only in the sense that it is a phase in the self-development of the absolute spirit. The world, in brief, is the expression of the thought of the absolute. Individual minds and actions are all parts or phases of the divine mind. They constitute steps in the development or self-actualization of the geist. The logical world in this way is made identical with the real world.

---

[11] The absolute or spirit is God in the Hegelian conception. His God, however, is organic with the world and has no reality outside that relation. If the world would cease to exist, He would cease to exist with it. God does not, as in the Christian conception, transcend the world; He is immanent in it. He starts from absolute non-being and evolves in and through the world of time and space to His consummation in absolute being.

Thought and being, subject and object, matter and form are all ultimately encompassed within the unity of an absolute mind. By this act of legerdemain, the duality which so troubled Kant is benignly eliminated.

The Dialectic

Hegel asserts that the spirit or reason has not yet achieved its full nature; it is still in the process of becoming — "a potentiality striving to realize itself." It must progressively actualize itself until it reaches perfect knowledge. This actualization takes place in a spatio-temporal context. Hegel calls the process by which the idea is developed "dialectical." The term is from the Greek *dialego*, meaning to debate or discuss. It originally referred to a process of discussion in which the Sophists would try to entrap their opponents in contradictions. The Socratic dialogues illustrate this approach, although Plato and the Greek classicists looked upon the dialectic, not as a sophistic sport, but as a means for critically examining into the truth of an opinion. Hegel uses the term in a completely different sense than the ancients; to him it means a substantive process of logical development rather than a mere method of logical procedure.

In working out his philosophy, Hegel seizes upon the classical idea of opposites or contradictions. The Greeks had observed that every event or force, if pushed too far, will tend to produce its opposite. Thus if monarchy degenerates into despotism, it will lead to democracy; similarly democracy carried to the extreme of mob rule and license will result in dictatorship. Hegel purports to see the key to all development in the interplay between extremes. He maintains that the absolute spirit finds expression in nature according to a process of contradiction. Every concept contains its own contradiction or opposite hidden away within itself. These contradictions are not obstacles to truth (as they were for Kant), but the very measures for attaining truth. But what about the traditional law of contradiction which holds that a proposition cannot be both true and false at the same time? This law poses no difficulty to Hegel since the principle of contradiction is merely a rule of formal thought operating at the empirical or finite level. Contradictions exist for the human mind only in its state of incomplete reflection on the truth of being. Nothing is wholly false and nothing that we can know is wholly true. Both the assertion and negation of a statement may be regarded as true if they are understood as imperfect expressions of a higher proposition which contains all that is significant in both of them.

In the dialectical process, truth unfolds itself in progressive changes through the interplay or conflict between opposites. Every event or idea (thesis) tends to generate an opposing or contrary event or idea (antithesis). In the conflict which ensues between these opposites, a new development (synthesis) results. This synthesis is different from the pre-existing contradictories but it is not a compromise. It contains what is vital in both thesis and antithesis and embodies it in a richer and more comprehensive entity. The new creation then proceeds to raise its own apparent contradictory or negation; and again the dialectical drama repeats itself, with each new synthesis marking a further step in the self-development of the absolute.

The Hegelian Philosophy of History

Hegel regards history as the revealing of Spirit "in the process of working out the knowledge of that which it is potentially." It is the temporal march of the absolute in its road toward perfect fulfillment. The history of the world "begins with its general aim — the realization of the Idea of Spirit — only in an implicit form." The actions of individuals and nations by which they seek to satisfy their own purposes are, at the same time, "the means and instruments of a higher and broader purpose," the media through which the world spirit attains its objectives. History is exclusively occupied with showing how "Spirit comes to a recognition and adoption of the Truth, the dawn of knowledge appears, it begins to discover salient principles, and at last it arrives at full consciousness."[12] Spirit is self-determined; it assumes progressive forms which it successively transcends. By a proper study of history, man can acquire a knowledge of this evolutionary pattern or general plan of divine reason and thereby arrive at an historically objective standard of values. Hegel intends that such a standard shall fill the place left vacant by the "collapse" of natural law.

The status quo in history represents the thesis of the dialectical triad while the revolutionary movements, the process of "becoming," constitute the antithetical principle. Fixed customs, laws, and rights clash

---

[12] Hegel, The Philosophy of History, trans. by J. Sibree (New York: Wiley Book Company, 1944), pp. 25, 53.

with contingencies that are adverse to the established system. These conflicts are essential phases in the development of truth as it strives toward consciousness of itself. To carry through the antithetical principle, the divine idea uses great leaders, "world historical individuals," as its instrumentalities. These leaders have no consciousness of the general idea that they are helping to unfold — they may act for purely selfish reasons — but they have insight into the requirements of the time and what is ripe for development. "They are great men, because they willed and accomplished something great; not a mere fancy, a mere intention, but that which met the case and fell in with the needs of the age." These men are able to arouse others to action and to win their support since people "feel the irresistible power of their own inner Spirit thus embodied" in these leaders.

The fate of the world historical individuals is not a happy one. Reason stirs them to further the temporal actualization of the spirit, but then discards them once their work has been accomplished.

> If we go on to cast a look at the fate of these World-Historical persons, whose vocation it was to be the agents of the World-Spirit — we shall find it to have been no happy one. They attained no calm enjoyment; their whole life was labor and trouble; their whole nature was nought else but their master-passion. When their object is attained they fall off like empty hulls from the kernel. They die early, like Alexander; they are murdered, like Caesar; transported to St. Helene, like Napoleon.[13]

It is the cunning of Reason "that it sets the passions to work for itself while that which develops its existence through such impulsion pays the penalty and suffers loss."[14]

Theory of the State

The Hegelian concept of the state must be examined against the backdrop of his doctrine of spirit becoming actualized through the dialectic. The state plays the same role for him that classes do for Marx: the medium whereby the ultimate goal of the world and society is to be achieved. Hegel maintains that spirit seeks the attainment of its objective not only through individuals but also the state. This institution is, in fact, the very core of historical life. It is the highest embodiment of the divine idea on earth and the chief instrumentality used by the

---

[13] Ibid., p. 31.   [14] Ibid., p. 33.

absolute in manifesting itself as it proceeds toward perfect fulfillment. "The state is mind on earth and consciously realizing itself there. . . . In considering the idea of the state, we must not have our eyes on particular states or on particular institutions. Instead we must consider the Idea, this actual God, by itself."[15] All the worth and spiritual reality which a human being has, "he possesses only through the state."

In formulating his theory of the state, Hegel rejects the social contract doctrine as wholly untenable. He criticizes Rousseau for reducing the union of individuals in a civil society to a contract and therefore to something based on their arbitrary wills, their opinion, and their capriciously given consent. Political obligation must be anchored on something more substantial than the mere acquiescence of individuals. The state is not an artificial mechanism created by man to preserve order and satisfy his needs; it is far different from that. It is an organic whole composed of individuals grouped into classes, voluntary associations, and local communities. These parts have no meaning except in relation to and as parts of the whole. It is only as a member of the body politic that the person has objectivity, genuine individuality, and an ethical life.

Idealist political thought generally views the state as an organism which is self-differentiating in such a way that the life of the whole appears in all of the parts. Hence the true life of the latter — the individuals and their social groupings — is found in and is identical with the life of the whole. As the embodiment of the absolute, the state is not a means for securing the welfare of the individual; it is an end in itself. And since it has a higher end than its parts, it can demand that these be sacrificed to its interests. Hegel and his followers insist that this sacrifice can legitimately be demanded only for the true rational and universal end of the state, and that the doctrine is not to be twisted into a justification of the arbitrary acts of rulers working for their own ends. Yet what despot or dictator has failed to proclaim that his actions were in the true interests of the people?

Consistent with his metaphysics, Hegel views the state as the product of a long and unconscious, but nevertheless predetermined, development. The absolute mind first found external expression in the family, where a substantial unity based on love existed. But as the children came of

---

[15] *Philosophy of Right*, trans. by T. M. Knox (London: Oxford University Press, 1942), p. 279.

age, they married and established new families, which were independent of the households from which their members had been drawn. In this way the original family disintegrated into a plurality of families. With this development people began to find themselves dependent on others for various necessities. In order to satisfy their private and particular needs and to further their individual interests, they formed associations and created institutions for enforcing order and protecting property. Hegel refers to this level of development as "civil society."

The unity of civil society was no more than that of a partnership, the sort of unity that might result from a social contract. While each member was free to pursue his own end, he realized that he could not fully attain his objectives without the co-operation of others. Consequently he was willing to enter into arrangements with his fellow creatures for mutual support and assistance. The relationship thereby created was one based on the self-interest of each participant and not on the unity of mutual love as in the family. Even though the family remained, its role was distinctly inferior to that of civil society. "To be sure, the family has to provide bread for its members, but in civil society the family is something subordinate and only lays the foundations; its effective range is no longer so comprehensive."[16] At this stage, the private purposes of the individual began to come in conflict with the common ends of the community. The dialectic between the universal as represented in the unity of the family and the particular as found in the competitiveness of civil society was then resolved by the emergence of the political state.

In the interplay between the universal and particular, the original unity of the family was restored but on a much higher plane. The necessity of co-operation caused man to recognize himself as a member of a social body. At first he looked upon such co-operation as merely an expedient; later he came to view it as a moral and ethical mandate. In this evolutionary process, man's particularity was mediated as the universal gradually reasserted itself. Finally in the state, universal and particular were completely reconciled as the end of the individual became identical with the universal end of the state. This conclusion raises the danger that the individual will be completely swallowed up in the universal whole. Hegel attempts to allay any such fear by insisting that the universal is bound up with the complete freedom of its particular members and with private well-being. This compatibility of interest is to be achieved

---

[16] *Ibid.*, p. 276.

in Rousseauean fashion by equating the true will of the individual with that of the whole.[17]

The State and Human Freedom

Hegel formulates his ethical theory through the dialectical contrast between right and morality. Right, as the thesis, represents the objective demands of the individual on society. Morality, as the antithesis, represents the subjective duty of the individual in his relations with others. The synthesis is found in concrete ethical life with the state as the supreme actuality of the ethical idea. "The determinations of the individual will are given an objective embodiment through the state and thereby they attain the truth and their actualization for the first time. The state is the one and only prerequisite of the attainment of particular ends and welfare."[18]

The freedom of the individual is directly related to the actualization of the universal. Freedom for man does not consist in satisfying his individual desires without reference to the universal will. True liberty consists in acting in harmony with universal reason as it progressively develops. Man acts in conformity with his real will and not according to his selfish or brutish impulses only when he seeks to identify himself with the spirit. Freedom can never be the unlimited power of choice, but only the right to act rationally. As the external embodiment of the ethical idea of reason, the state expresses the universal will and therefore the true will of every individual contained within it. Hence the individual is really obeying the laws of his own true rational self by serving and obeying the state. In this way, he is able to find genuine freedom. Professor Collins succinctly sums up this phase of Hegel's political philosophy in the following passage:

> In the state, men have borne home forcefully to them that they are free, personal subjects only within an encompassing whole, which is itself a self-conscious subject or social individual. The universal actuality, which began to display itself in family and civil society, is made manifest as the self-determining rational concept, in the state. Individuals and intermediate social groups are teleologically regulated by the concept of *rational freedom*, which is given its plenary incarnation in the state. Hence the state has absolute right over its

---

[17] See ante, p. 297.
[18] Philosophy of Right, op. cit., p. 280.

component members, both as individuals and as groups, precisely in order to achieve maximal freedom.[19]

In Hegelian thought, the individual possesses no value independent of the political society of which he is a member. His freedom consists in conformity with objective mind as actualized in the laws and customs of the state to which he belongs. The complex of social institutions and habits of any society reflect the real will of its members, and hence embody "rational" freedom. The free person is one who is able to identify himself totally with the duties and obligations imposed on him by the political community. Or to express it in another way, since the state constitutes the entire social fabric and totality of human life, it becomes the true self in which the individual is absorbed.

Political idealism is theoretically incompatible with constitutional government. Hegel declares that "the development of the state to constitutional monarchy is the achievement of the modern world," but his idea of limited rule is contradicted by his general metaphysics. Man achieves his perfection only in so far as he conforms to the universal will. Since the state is the most perfect expression of this will, it has the "highest right against the individuals." Hegel's exalted metaphysical conception of the state completely negates all philosophical foundations for human rights and lends ethical justification to totalitarianism. Even from a practical standpoint, his constitutionalism is a curious blend of limited rule and absolutism. The Prussian state which he greatly admired was certainly far from a constitutional monarchy of the British type. His concept of the state reminds one of a remark that Napoleon purportedly made to a delegation of envoys from the German states, "Je ne suis pas votre prince, je suis votre maître" (I am not your prince, I am your master).

By the same token, Hegel's political idealism is essentially anti-democratic in character. Sovereignty is vested not in the people, but in the state as a metaphysical organism. Hegel has little confidence in the ability of the people for self-rule. Commenting on the role of the legislative branch, he flatly denies that the people or their representatives are in the best position to know what is in their true interests. Such knowledge can result only from profound comprehension and insight, and it is precisely this ability that is lacking in the vast majority of

---

[19] A History of Modern European Philosophy, op. cit., p. 647.

people. Reason dictates that the government of the state be entrusted to a trained and professional bureaucracy. This elite corps should participate in lawmaking as well as administration. The elected members of the legislature should serve more in the nature of watchdogs over the bureaucracy than as lawmakers. Not all of them, moreover, should be popularly elected. Representatives of the landed aristocracy should hold their offices by virtue of inheritance. The remaining members should be selected on a functional basis by classes and associations. Hegel reminds us that man is not free when he is forced to obey the command of a majority that does not embody the universal and rational will. Every state therefore must devise institutional machinery to guarantee as far as possible that political power be exercised by a class that has the ability, character, and merit to know what the universal reason wills.

Hegel's preoccupation with the universal would seem to call for a subordination of the nation state to a larger and more comprehensive unit. His preference for a strong state to an anarchic collection of individuals should also have led him to prefer a world political organization of some sort to an anarchic group of autonomous national entities. Such, however, is not the case. The development of the absolute, he declares, requires a multiplicity of states since no single one is capable of bearing the whole idea. Each is a participant in the divine process and each has its own individual mission and its own distinct contribution. It is true that at a particular period in history, one state may become the preferred vehicle of the absolute. This favored state may be recognized by its dominant position on the world scene. Its role as the chosen arm of destiny gives it a distinct superiority over other nations; but the position is not of a permanent character. Once the chosen state has served its purpose, it loses the interest of the absolute and recedes into the background in much the same way that "world historical individuals" do. The idea then marks out a new nation for prominence on the international scene.

Hegel argues that conflict between states is as healthy as it is inevitable. There should be wars from time to time since the more perfect revelation or unfolding of the universal can come only through struggle. He regards Kant's vision of world peace as a mere illusion. Even if states were to join together in a close alliance or were to submerge their identity in a world organization, the new political arrangement would of necessity engender an opposite tendency and create a new danger. For there is no way to avoid the dialectical process in the march of world history.

SUMMARY

Idealism in one form or another has permeated political thinking since the days of Plato. It has usually empasized the unity of the state and the predominant position of the common good over the good of the individual. The philosophical premises on which it rests have forced it into extreme positions. As a result, it has not been able to effect a satisfactory reconciliation, either in theory or practice, between the state and the individual or between authority and freedom. The common objective of the political idealists has been to combat individualistic theories which view the state merely as the product of man's will.

The idealist tendency to sublimate human individuality to the political entity converts the idea of the common good into an all-encompassing sphere that leaves little room for individual discretion. In this process, human freedom is assured by a curious metaphysical device that equates the true will of the individual with that of the totality. This solution neatly avoids the problem of the one and the many, or of individual freedom and state authority. There is also a strong reliance on intuition among the political idealists. Hegel, in distinguishing between creative and reflective reason, defines the former as unconscious and instinctive — reason unaware of itself, which is manifested in the artistic or active instincts of the mind. Reflective reason, on the other hand, can only analyze and comprehend what the creative reason has already blindly accomplished. This intuitionism later became an important element of the fascist creed.

Both Kant and Hegel reject the concept of natural law. To replace its function as an objective standard of ethical conduct, Kant substitutes his categorical imperative and Hegel his universal will as actualized in the political and social institutions of the state. According to the latter view, man is assured of the moral character of his actions when he conforms to the customs and laws of the particular society in which he is living, since the fabric of social life and the state system rest upon an essentially "rational" basis. In other words, "the real world is as it ought to be." Whatever exists must necessarily be true.

Nineteenth-century political idealism, particularly in the form which Hegel gave to it, had far-reaching repercussions. Totalitarianism, both of the right and left, found in it a ready source of theoretical support. The dialectical process supplied Marx with the logical device that enabled him to fashion his theory of scientific socialism. Similarly, the deification of the state gave fascism the ideological weapon that it needed for self-justification. These assertions do not imply that the doctrines of communism and fascism are Hegelian, or that Hegel is to be held responsible for them; they indicate simply that totalitarian apologists of the twentieth century were able to use Hegelian premises to rationalize their position.

BIBLIOGRAPHY

Bosanquet, Bernard, The Philosophical Theory of the State, 3rd ed. (London: Macmillan, 1920).

Buber, Martin, "The Validity and Limitation of the Political Principle," Cross Currents, Spring, 1957.

Cannon, D. J., "Comparison between Kantian Ethics and St. Thomas," Irish Ecclesiastical Review, September, 1942.

Carritt, E. F., "Hegel and Prussianism," Philosophy, April, 1940.

Cook, T. I., and Leavelle, A. B., "German Idealism and American Theories of the Democratic Community," Journal of Politics, August, 1943.

Costanzo, Joseph, "Critique of Kant's Principles of Politics," New Scholasticism, April, 1951.

Dawson, Christopher, "Politics of Hegel," Dublin Review, October, 1943.

Evans, D. O., Social Romanticism in France, 1830–1848 (New York: Oxford University Press, 1952).

Foster, M. B., The Political Philosophies of Plato and Hegel (Oxford: Oxford University Press, 1935).

Green, Thomas H., Principles of Political Obligation, new ed. (New York: Longmans, 1942).

Hancock, R., "Ethics and History in Kant and Mill," Ethics, October, 1957.

Harris, Frederick P., The Neo-idealist Political Theory; Its Continuity with the British Tradition (New York: King's Crown Press, 1944).

Heckscher, G., "Calhoun's Idea of Concurrent Majority and the Constitutional Theory of Hegel," American Political Science Review, August, 1939.

Hogan, J., "Hegelian Dialectic and Dialectical Materialism," Irish Ecclesiastical Review, April, 1949.

Kaufmann, W. A., "Hegel Myth and Its Method," Philosophical Review, October, 1951.

Kelsen, H., "Foundations of Democracy: Property and Freedom in the Philosophy of Hegel," Ethics, October, 1955.

Knox, T. M., "Hegel and Prussianism," Philosophy, January, 1940.

Liddell, A. F., "Importance of Human Personality in the Philosophy of Hegel," Journal of Philosophy, March, 1957.

Mathur, G. B., "Hume, Kant and Pragmatism," Journal of the History of Ideas, April, 1955.

Mure, G. R. G., An Introduction to Hegel (New York: Oxford University Press, 1940).

Ortega y Gasset, Jose, "Kant and the Modern German Mind," Yale Review, Autumn, 1941.

Reinhardt, C. H., "Hegel and State Totalitarianism," Dublin Review, January, 1938.

Reiss, H. S., "Kant and the Right of Rebellion," Journal of the History of Ideas, April, 1956.

———— ed., The Political Thought of the German Romantics, 1763–1815 (New York: Macmillan, 1955).

Sabine, G. H., "Hegel's Political Philosophy," *Philosophical Review*, May, 1932.
Stanford, L., "Hegelian Concept of Man," *American Catholic Philosophical Association Proceedings*, 1951.
Townsend, H. G., "Political Philosophy of Hegel in a Frontier Society," *Monist*, January, 1936.
Tucker, R. C., "Symbolism of History in Hegel and Marx," *Journal of Philosophy*, March, 1957.
Viereck, Peter, "Realpolitik, Fichte, Hegel, and Treitschke," *Journal of Social Philosophy*, July, 1941.
Wheeler, M. C., "Concept of Christianity in Hegel," *New Scholasticism*, July, 1957.

PART SEVEN | **CONTEMPORARY POLITICAL PHILOSOPHY**

Chapter XIX

"SCIENTIFIC" SOCIALISM

"The final causes of all social changes and political revolutions are to be sought, not in men's brains, not in man's better insight into eternal truth and justice, but in changes in the modes of production and exchange. They are to be sought, not in the *philosophy*, but in the *economics* of each particular epoch" (Engels, *"Scientific" versus "Utopian" Socialism*).

DURING the eighteenth century fundamental economic changes began to take place in the western world — changes so far reaching that they eventually revolutionized the whole mode of human living. The process of transformation has become known as the "industrial revolution." Sparked off by a long series of new inventions, machine power gradually substituted itself for human exertion. With the mechanization of production, people began to move from the farm to the city, the factory system replaced manufacturing in the home, and the industrialist supplanted the landed baron and even the merchant in importance. The industrial revolution did not suddenly appear full blown on the world scene. Its beginnings can be traced as far back as the period of the Reformation when capital began to be invested in land for profit. However, it was not until after 1750 that the great advances in scientific and technical processes began to be made, initially in agricultural production and later in manufacturing. The movement first became evident in England, but by the middle of the nineteenth century it had made significant gains on the Continent.

The transformation in economic practices that grew out of the industrial revolution was accompanied by a reversal of economic theory. From 1500 until well into the eighteenth century, mercantilism had prevailed in western Europe. One of the principal characteristics of this policy is state monopoly or regulation of trade and industry. Wealth is looked upon in terms of precious metals, and the test of a nation's well-being is the

381

amount of bullion in its coffers. In 1776 Adam Smith's *Wealth of Nations* struck a final blow at the theory of mercantilism. Maintaining that consumer goods, not gold or silver, are the most important forms of wealth, Smith lays primary stress on production as the key to a nation's economic well-being. He also argues that government should interfere with industry and commerce as little as possible, since external regulation interferes with the operation of natural economic laws and upsets the harmony of interests in nature. Just as the national welfare can best be promoted by giving each individual the widest possible scope to seek his own interests, so the greatest wealth accrues to a country that lets nature take its course in the free competition of the market. Such competition keeps prices low, yields a fair return to the producer, and secures the greatest good of the greatest number.

Smith is the founder of the classical school of economics, so called because it was the first to attempt the formulation of laws universally applicable to man's economic life. The classical economists who followed Smith, such as Thomas Malthus (1776–1834) and David Ricardo (1772–1823), cast doubt on his picture of a freewheeling capitalism in which all would prosper. Whereas Smith believes that a policy of *laissez faire* will result in the good of the many, Malthus and Ricardo hold no such sanguine view. Malthus contends that poverty is unavoidable because population grows by geometrical proportions while the supply of food increases by an arithmetical ratio. With population tending to outstrip the means of subsistence, poverty, starvation, and misery are always around the corner for the great mass of people. Ricardo supplies the answer to this threat in his iron law of wages. According to this "natural" economic law, wages of the worker inevitably sink to the lowest level necessary for his subsistence. The natural price of labor is that necessary to enable the laborers to exist and perpetuate the race, without either increase or diminution. Any improvement in this level is reflected in a rising birth rate. This in turn results in a labor surplus and a decline in the wage scale which, like goods and commodities, is governed by the law of supply and demand. All social legislation designed to ameliorate the lot of the worker is not only futile but dangerous to the welfare of the state. Men should not tamper with the natural functioning of economic laws.

The industrial revolution complicated the process of government. The massing of people in large urban areas, the concentration of capital, the spread of markets throughout the world, and the increase in the number of wage earners altered political as well as social and economic relations. With the vast changes that were taking place in the modes of production and distribution, and their consequent effects on society, the necessity for a reformulation of social and political theory became painfully evident. The utilitarians and other liberal thinkers, such as Herbert Spencer, endeavored to recast political philosophy in terms of crass individualism. Hegel saw the fatal weakness in this approach, but the metaphysical subtleties of his own works offered little to a world steeped in industrial growth. The first efforts to be directed primarily at redefining political theory in the light of the new economic environment were undertaken by the socialists.

"UTOPIAN" SOCIALISM

The term socialism came into use during the early nineteenth century. It embraces a wide variety of social and economic theories, ranging from those that call only for public ownership of certain natural monopolies to those that are completely Marxist. The many types of socialism are alike in that they advocate the common ownership and control of at least some of the basic means of production. They differ considerably among themselves in several fundamental respects: (1) the extent and degree to which common ownership and control of property are advocated; (2) the ideological or philosophical doctrines which underlie their programs; and (3) the means that are used to attain their objectives.

Dissatisfied with social conditions that had been aggravated by the industrial revolution, a number of nineteenth-century French and English writers began to question the justice and validity of the capitalistic system. French socialism goes back to the revolution of 1781 and to Francois Babeuf (1760–1797) who argued that all men have an equal right to the good things of this earth. The idea that political equality is not sufficient — that there must be at least some degree of economic equality — became more prevalent in French thought as the impact of technology was felt on the Continent. Henri Saint Simon (1760–1825), an old line aristocrat who had fought with Lafayette in America, advocated that inheritance rights should be abolished, that everyone should work, and that the formula for distributing the fruits of production should be "from each according to his capacity, to each according to his deserts."

Charles Fourier (1772–1837), another French reformer, called for a major remodeling of the social order. As a child, he had witnessed the dumping of surplus rice from ships in order to keep the price of the grain up. Convinced of the unsoundness of the competitive system, Fourier proposed the reorganization of society into small self-sufficient units (phalanxes of 1620 persons) in which the members would pool their capital for the common good. The doctrine of Fourierism spread to the United States where some thirty phalanxes were founded, all of them short-lived.[1]

Louis Blanc (1811–1882), the son of a minor French official, represents still another approach to social reform. In his chief work, *Organization of Labor*, he proposes the establishment of national workshops financed by the state but owned and operated by co-operative groups of working-men. After paying interest to the government on the money advanced and after setting aside sufficient funds for paying old age pensions and replacing machinery and equipment, the balance of the earnings are to be distributed to the workers on the principle, "from each according to his abilities, to each according to his needs." This formula was later adopted by Marx.

In England, the socialist movement was pioneered by Robert Owen (1771–1837), a successful cotton manufacturer who had started his career as a shopboy and had amassed a fortune by the age of forty. Like the French socialists, Owen's approach to the problems of his day is essentially romantic. Firmly convinced that man's character is shaped by his environment — "it is formed for and not by him" — he believes that if only this point could be made clear to the world, people would take steps to ameliorate the lot of the poor instead of blaming them for their condition.

Owen proposes that the government establish co-operative villages for the poor rather than pay out doles. These villages would be self-sufficient units similar to the phalanxes of Fourier. They would raise the produce needed for their own consumption and exchange their surplus goods of different kinds with each other. Their aim would be not only to relieve the necessities of the poor, but also to train good citizens. Co-operative and noncompeting units of this type would gradually replace the capitalistic

---

[1] The most famous of the American phalanxes was Brook Farm founded at West Roxbury, Massachusetts, by George Ripley, transcendentalist and literary figure. Among others connected with the enterprise were Hawthorne, Emerson, Bronson Alcott, and W. H. Channing. The most successful Fourieristic community was established by Albert Brisbane at Red Bank, New Jersey.

system as people became acquainted with their great value. The *New View of Society* represents Owen's first efforts to propagandize these convictions. In 1825 he founded a co-operative settlement known as New Harmony on a 30,000 acre tract in Indiana. Two years later the project came to an inglorious end as the settlers fell out among themselves.

Although these various theories and experiments are of little importance in themselves, they provide a transition to the modern forms of socialism. All of them constituted attacks on the existing capitalistic system, and all of them proposed a way of life based on some form of collective control. The solutions they offered, however, were too divorced from reality, too utopian and romantic, to meet with any substantial measure of success. The social reform movements which they spawned generally collapsed when practical benefits for the workers were not immediately forthcoming. It was while utopian socialism was floundering that Karl Marx offered his doctrine of "scientific" socialism to the world.

KARL MARX

Karl Marx (1818–1883) was born in Treves, a small town in the German Rhineland. He was a descendant of a long line of Jewish rabbis on both sides of his family although his father, a well-to-do lawyer, was a convert to Protestantism. Marx received his educational training at the universities of Bonn, Berlin, and Jena. While a student, he became particularly interested in the Greek materialists, as evidenced by the title of his doctoral thesis, "On the Difference between the Natural Philosophy of Democritus and of Epicurus." After receiving his doctorate at Jena, Marx sought to obtain a university appointment. When his efforts proved unsuccessful, he turned to journalism, joining the staff of the *Rheinische Zeitung*, a democratic-liberal newspaper published at Cologne. In 1843 shortly before the paper was suppressed by the Prussian government, he went to Paris, where he came into close touch with many of the French socialists.

During his stay in France, Marx met Friedrich Engels, the son of a wealthy German textile manufacturer. Engels at the time was managing a factory in Manchester, England, but like Owen he was unhappy and dissatisfied with existing social conditions. Through Engels, Marx became acquainted with British labor conditions and British economics. The friendship and close collaboration of the two which began in Paris lasted until Marx's death forty years later. Most modern Marxists regard their writings as merely different books of the same testament.

Marx was expelled from France several years after he took up residence there because his articles in one of the Paris newspapers called for a German revolution. He then went to Brussels where he was instrumental in forming the communist league, an organization that sought to bring together those who were advocating a new brand of socialism. At its congress in 1847, the league authorized Marx and Engels to draft the *Communist Manifesto*. This document was published the following year and became one of the most influential political tracts of all times. When the revolution of 1848 broke out, Marx returned to his native Rhineland to take part in the movement. Upon its collapse, he fled to London, where he remained for the rest of his life.

In 1864 the International Working Men's Association, the First International, was founded in London. Its membership consisted mainly of continental exiles and a few British trade union leaders. The association's objective was to serve as a council representing the proletariat of all countries. Marx quickly became the dominant force in the new organization, but the many dissident elements within it foredoomed it to failure. The defeat of the Paris Commune, which Marx had supported against the wishes of many in the International, marked the end of the organization.[2] Marx thereafter took no active part in politics but devoted his time to studying and writing.

Constantly plagued by poverty and ill health, Marx's life was not a happy one. His personality was unattractive, his attitude toward others callous and domineering, and his methods ruthless. In 1843 he married Jenny von Westphalen, the daughter of a high government official, to whom he remained devoted throughout his life. Of the six children who were born of the marriage, three died at an early age. The family was sustained largely through the generous assistance of Engels. Although Marx took an active part in socialist movements and although his works

---

[2] The Second International was established in 1889 to act as a permanent link between the socialist parties of the various countries. It was a loose federation of individual parties that differed widely in ideology and method, each claiming to follow its own course in accord with national conditions. The Second International came to an end during World War I. The Third International, the Comintern, was organized in Moscow in 1919. It became strictly an agency of the Russian Communist party to promote the cause of communism throughout the world. The Comintern was dissolved by the Soviet Union in 1943 as a gesture of reassurance toward its World War II allies.

were soon to have world wide repercussions, few outside the circle of his immediate followers were aware of his tremendous significance when he died.

The Marxian Dialectic

Marx's theory of communism is based on certain underlying concepts: (1) historical development takes place through the synthesis of inherent tensions or contradictions — the dialectic; (2) social and political institutions are shaped and determined by economics — historical materialism; and (3) the dialectical movement of history finds expression chiefly in the conflict between economic groups — class struggle. Marx accepted in modified form the dialectic of Hegel and the political economy of the orthodox classical or Manchester school. These two strains of thought furnished the intellectual material upon which he drew heavily.

The University of Berlin was the center of Hegelianism while Marx was a student there. The followers of Hegel were divided into two camps, the right wing which concerned itself primarily with religious apologetics in an attempt to show that Hegelian philosophy and Christianity were compatible; and the left wing which viewed the development of the absolute as a materialistic rather than a logical process. Ludwig Feuerbach, one of the leftist leaders, provides the connecting bridge between Hegel and Marx. In his *Essence of Christianity* (1841) and his *Essence of Religion* (1845), he explains away God as a projection of human desires and needs and as man's supreme optical illusion. Anthropology, not theology, is the supreme science. Hegel had claimed that it is the absolute idea — God — which develops in history and which expresses itself in nature and in man as it evolves in and through the world of time and space. Feuerbach maintains that the absolute which Hegel speaks of is not God but nature unfolding itself in an endless process of dialectical development.

Marx seizes upon the Feuerbachian thesis to rationalize his own detestation of religion and to make the transition from Hegelian idealism to materialism. By proclaiming in effect that the absolute is no more than a reflection of matter, he seeks to use the dialectic as the governing force in the evolution of history. His intention is to turn it from a mere law of thought, as it is in Hegelian theory, to a true law of historical causation. For this purpose, the dialectic must first be given a concrete meaning that will serve the purposes of causal explanation and prediction in the social order. It can then be shown that social events, like biological and physical phenomena, are rooted in and determined by matter.

Marx was intensely antireligious ("I hate all gods," he once exclaimed) and his philosophy rests upon a materialistic metaphysics. However, he is never explicit in what he means by materialism. Feuerbach called himself a naturalist and humanist, to avoid the identification of his doctrine with the crude materialism of those who worshiped sensual pleasures to the exclusion of intellectual values. There is reason to believe that Marx has a similar view. Unlike the early materialists who were largely concerned with the physical world, he is primarily interested in man and society. He speaks of dynamic materialism, probably to distinguish it from the theory that matter evolves solely under the pressure of its environment. He indicates that the materialism he is referring to involves a process of development from within. In Hegelian thought, the idea moves forward by the contradictions inherent in being; so also in Marxian doctrine, the contradictions in matter evolve through inherent tensions. The seed must decay before new life emerges. Environmental factors may hinder or assist the evolutionary process but the driving force must come from within.

Historical Materialism

Engels defines historical materialism as "that view of the course of history which seeks the ultimate cause and the great moving power of all important historical events in the modes of production and exchange, in the consequent division of society into distinct classes, and in the struggles of these classes against one another."[3] Historical phenomena, in other words, are determined by economic factors. The culture, philosophy, politics, and even religion of any epoch are shaped by its method of production. As the economic structure of a society changes, so also does its social and political character.

According to the Marxian analysis, the way in which men satisfy their wants constitutes the foundation of society. Their social and political systems are the superstructure which they erect on this foundation. Human beings must have food, drink, clothing, and shelter first of all, before they can interest themselves in such matters as politics, science, art, and religion. The production of the immediately requisite means of sub-

---

[3] *Socialism, Utopian and Scientific*, ed. by E. Aveling (London: S. Sonnenschein, 1892), p. xix.

sistence, therefore, constitutes the foundation upon which social institutions and ideas are built.

At each stage of history the class which controls the means of production controls society. But the situation never remains static. The mode of production (the thesis) generates an opposing movement (the antithesis) which Marx refers to as the "productive forces" of the economy. The mode of production encompasses not only the technological processes of manufacturing and supplying goods but also the relationships (master-slave, lord-vassal, capitalist-worker) which characterize the existing organization of labor. It refers broadly to the conditions under which society produces and exchanges. The productive forces, on the other hand, represent the capacity to produce, the actual forces which stimulate production, and which are affected by scientific discoveries and the development of new techniques.

Sooner or later every society reaches a point at which the economic structure, the mode of production, hampers the full use of the productive forces which lie within it. "At a certain stage of their development, the material productive forces of society come in conflict with the existing relations of production, or — what is but a legal expression for the same thing — with the property relations within which they have been at work hitherto."[4] When this occurs, that is to say when new productive forces are developed which cannot be properly utilized by existing institutions, the time is ripe for social revolution to effect a new synthesis.

Historical materialism means that the manner of producing the requirements of life determines in the last instance the social ideas and institutions of an era. There is a close relationship between a particular level of technique and a particular kind of society. Fundamental changes in the former will bring about basic modifications in the latter. A set of social institutions must conform to a given mode of production; when it fails to do so, revolution is inevitable. The Marxian concept of history starts from the principle that production is the basis of every social order and that the division of society into classes is determined by what is produced and how it is produced and exchanged. Thus the hand mill gave us society with the feudal lord, and the steam mill society with the industrial capitalist. In the latter case, the new levels of technique necessitated changes in the social order. It became impossible for inde-

---

[4] Marx, A Contribution to the Critique of Political Economy (Chicago: Kerr and Co., 1904), p. 12.

pendent workers, each owning his separate means of production, to operate industrial plants. A collectivized method of production had to be worked out in some way — the result was the establishment of a capitalistic system.

Marx's approach to history has had considerable influence on modern thinking. Few historians would accept his thesis of dialectical development or complete economic determinism. Yet no social scientist today would examine an historical problem without considering the economic organization of the particular society, the interplay of class interests within it, and the influence that technological advances have upon its politics. Marx demonstrates that an examination of history in terms of economics can be fruitful. Yet by turning what is essentially a method of investigating historical phenomena into a dogma, he commits himself in advance to finding only that which fits his doctrine.

Class Struggle

Referring to his own time, Marx declares that the bourgeoisie — by subjecting nature's forces to man, applying chemistry to industry, and devising new machines and means of transportation and communication — have created more massive productive forces than all preceding generations together. Like the sorcerer's apprentice, this class now finds itself unable to control the powers that it has conjured. When this stage is reached, it becomes apparent that the material productive forces of society have come in serious conflict with the mode of production, or what is more appropriate to say, with the social and property relationships of the day. The need for readjustment is reflected in the growing intensity of the class struggle.

The importance of economic group conflicts to the political process and the idea of the divergence of group interests had frequently been expressed by theorists prior to Marx. No pre-Marxist writer, however, had advanced the concept of class struggle as an inherent and inevitable fact of human life. As Marx writes,

> No credit is due to me for discovering the existence of Classes in modern society nor yet the struggle between them. Long before me bourgeois historians had described the historical development of this class struggle and bourgeois economists the economic anatomy of the classes. What I did that was new was to prove:

(1) that the existence of classes is only bound up with particular historic phases in the development of production;

(2) that the class struggle necessarily leads to the dictatorship of the proletariat;

(3) that this dictatorship itself only constitutes the transition to the abolition of all classes and to a classless society.[5]

Class struggle and the classless society are necessary consequences of the contradictions inherent in a capitalistic economy. These results must happen regardless of whether certain empirical conditions are fulfilled. Marx is not saying in the language of science, "given these conditions, these results will follow." He is saying that the world is destined to evolve in this way by virtue of its own inner dialectic.

Hegel had referred to nations as the vehicles of the dialectical movement.[6] Marx now substitutes classes for nations. He states that in the course of providing a livelihood, the members of a society become divided into classes which perform different functions and occupy different positions in the social organization. Conflicts of interest constantly arise among these groups as each seeks to further its own well-being. The history of mankind is a continuous struggle of classes. The struggle, moreover, cannot be avoided or resolved, since it is inescapably a part of and essential to the dialectical development of history.

Although Marx casts his philosophy of history into a mold suggested by the Hegelian dialectic, he is actually concerned only with one triad: capital, labor, and the classless society. As presently constituted, society is characterized by a simple division between those who own the means of production and those who do not. The era of capitalism has not abated the class struggle; it has intensified and simplified it. "Society as a whole is more and more splitting up into two great hostile camps, into two great classes directly facing each other — bourgeoisie and proletariat."[7] The middle class, comprising those who stand between the exploiters and the masses, is gradually being eliminated. Wealth is becoming concentrated in fewer and fewer hands as the small tradespeople, shopkeepers, craftsmen, and peasants sink into the proletarian ranks.

---

[5] Letter of Marx to Weydemeyer in Marx and Engels, Selected Correspondence (1846–1895), trans. by Dona Torr (New York: International Publishers, 1942), p. 57.

[6] See ante, p. 370.

[7] Communist Manifesto, Crofts Classics edition (New York: Appleton-Century-Crofts, 1955), p. 10.

As this development continues, the misery of the proletariat increases and its dissatisfaction and resentment grow. The worker becomes increasingly aware of the injustice of the whole capitalistic system; he begins to organize and to prepare for the impending clash. "Along with the constantly diminishing number of the magnates of capital who usurp and monopolize all advantages of this process of transformation, grows the mass of misery, oppression, slavery, degradation, and exploitation; but with this too grows the revolt of the working class — a class always increasing in number, and disciplined, united, organized by the very mechanism of the process of capitalist production itself."[8] The revolutionary movement receives "fresh elements of enlightenment and progress" as "entire sections of the ruling class are, by the advance of industry precipitated into the proletariat." Finally, when the class struggle nears the decisive hour, a number of the remaining bourgeoisie who have come to comprehend theoretically the historical movement as a whole join the proletarians. The thesis, capitalism, has now called into existence its antithesis, organized labor, and from the conflict between the two the classless society emerges.

Marx differentiates the capitalist-worker conflict from previous class struggles. In the past, one class merely established a new class rule after overthrowing the dominant group in power. Under the modern capitalistic system, the proletariat has gradually absorbed all social groups with the exception of the small aggregation of capitalists. The victory of the proletariat, therefore, is the victory of all society and not an insignificant minority of it. Once the proletarian triumph is complete, class conflict will come to an end since all class divisions have been eliminated. The new synthesis will apparently be free from the inner tensions which tend to rip society asunder.

This abrupt ending to the dialectic is one of the glaring inconsistencies of Marxian thought. Man, who throughout all his past has engaged in economic warfare, suddenly changes his whole nature and becomes well disposed toward his fellow human beings. Does this mean that history, which manifests the class struggle and which progresses through dialectical development, has run its course. Marx is apparently aware of this inconsistency. He intimates that the dialectic is an eternal movement whose inner laws dictate that contradictions will be transmuted into higher and nonviolent forms once the class struggle ends. What these

---

[8] *Capital*, Modern Library Edition (New York: Random House, 1906), p. 836.

future forms of contradiction will be, he nowhere states. Marx, of course, holds that man is not innately aggressive and corrupt; it is the circumstances of his social environment — the predatory effect of the capitalistic system — which determines him to act as he does.

Marxian Economics

The economic theories advanced by Marx are designed to show that capitalism inevitably produces conditions which lead to its overthrow and which pave the way for socialism. As already noted, Marx attempts to bring back every fundamental social and political change to an economic cause. Several aspects of his economic doctrine that are closely related to the development of his political theory will be briefly examined here.

In his major economic work, Das Kapital, Marx discusses the question of value at great length. He points out that the worker must sell his labor like any commodity since he does not own the means of production. As a commodity, his labor has both use and exchange value. The first consists in the value of the goods which his work produces; the second in what he is paid. The difference between the two is surplus value, which Marx defines as the difference between the value of the product and the value of the elements consumed in the formation of that product. To cite a simple example: a worker produces five pairs of shoes which sell on the market at $5 each; for his day's toil, he receives $10. The material used in the manufacture of the shoes and the allocated overhead costs amount to $10. The worker has thus created a surplus value of $5 which will go to the capitalist as profit.

Following Ricardo, Marx maintains that the amount which the worker receives is determined solely by the cost of sustaining him and his family at a subsistence level. But the laborer actually works only part of the day to produce the equivalent of these wages; the remainder of the time he is producing surplus value or profit for the capitalist. Marx argues that this amount properly belongs to the worker since it is his labor which is responsible for the added value. By appropriating it, the capitalist is engaging in a form of theft.

Marx describes capital as the sum total of all privately owned means of production employed for the acquisition of surplus value. He distinguishes between two kinds of capital: constant and variable. That part which is represented by machinery and raw materials is constant since the value of it, or of its wear and tear, reappears in equal proportions in the manufactured product. Its value in the new article is no greater than in its original state; it does not undergo any qualitative alteration of worth in the process of production. The value of a piece of cloth that is converted into ten suits remains constant since the material is wholly used up in making the product. On the other hand, variable capital, or that part which is used to purchase labor power, undergoes an alteration of value in the process of production. It not only reproduces the equivalent of its own worth but also an excess or surplus value.

According to Marx, there is a tendency to cheapen the cost of production by increasing the relative proportion of constant capital invested in machinery. The lower the cost of labor can be kept in relation to that of raw materials and machinery, the greater the rate of profit to the manufacturer. The system of competition aggravates this tendency. To meet the constant threat of his industrial rivals, the capitalist is forced to expand his plant and to buy more machinery. This necessity compels him to reduce his labor overhead in order to lower the cost of production and thereby set aside sufficient profits for increasing his constant capital. For the larger the rate of surplus value, the greater is the amount of capital that can be accumulated. In this ruthless but inevitable process, the battle of competition is fought by lowering the price of the commodities. The cheapness of these depends "on the productiveness of labor and this again on the scale of production. Therefore the larger capitals beat the smaller."[9] The small entrepreneur is forced out of business as capital accumulates in fewer and fewer hands.

While the battle of industrial competition is going on, the workers derive no benefit from the increased production. They are unable to win higher wages since new machinery and better technological devices create large reservoirs of unemployed workers. In their competition for jobs, the unemployed keep wages down to a bare subsistence level. This surplus population is the lever of "capitalistic accumulation." It forms "a disposable industrial reserve army, that belongs to capital quite as absolutely as if the latter had bred it at its own cost. Independently of the limits of the actual increase of population, it creates, for the changing needs of the self-expansion of capital, a mass of human material always ready for exploitation."[10]

---

[9] *Ibid.*, p. 686.   [10] *Ibid.*, p. 693.

From Capitalism to Communism

The communist society which Marx speaks of does not immediately follow the social revolution of the workers. There are several steps which mark the transition from capitalism to true communism: the acquisition and consolidation of political supremacy by the proletariat, the socialization of the means of production, and finally the communist society. The first step is to raise the proletariat to the position of the ruling class by seizing control of the state. Government by the proletariat must be substituted for government by the bourgeoisie.

There is considerable dispute whether Marx taught that the transfer of power in the first stage can be accomplished only by violent revolution or whether it can be achieved by peaceful and democratic means. Marx is not consistent in working out this aspect of his theory. In the communist manifesto he unequivocally states that the ends of communism "can be attained only by the forcible overthrow of all existing conditions." He points out that the owners of the means of production sincerely believe that the present system is the best not only for themselves but also for the general public. Their stake in the community is too high to permit them to step aside voluntarily and let history run its course. Consequently they resist change and refuse to abdicate freely. Later his attitude in this regard seemed to soften. He indicates that it might be possible for the workers to attain their objective by peaceful means in countries like England and the United States. Since, however, he did not pursue this distinction further, the orthodox opinion of violent class warfare as an essential element of communism has prevailed.

The second or intermediate stage of transition is known as socialism. Economically, this stage is marked by the centralization of all instruments of production in the hands of the state and by a concerted effort to increase total production as rapidly as possible. Politically, it is characterized by the dictatorship of the proletariat and by the solidification of the instruments of power. "Between capitalist and communist society lies the period of the revolutionary transformation of the one into the other. There corresponds to this also a political transition period in which the state can be nothing but *the revolutionary dictatorship of the proletariat*."[11] During the intermediate stage the proletariat will use its political su-

---

[11] Marx, *Critique of the Gotha Programme* (New York: International Publishers, 1938), p. 7.

premacy to wrest all capital from the bourgeoisie and to place it under state control. The measures that will be used to accomplish this objective are listed in the *Communist Manifesto:*

(1) abolition of property in land and application of all rents to public purposes;
(2) a heavy progressive or graduated income tax;
(3) abolition of all right of inheritance;
(4) confiscation of the property of all emigrants and rebels;
(5) centralization of credit in the hands of the state by means of a national bank;
(6) centralization of the means of communication and transport in the hands of the state;
(7) extension of factories and instruments of production owned by the state; the bringing into cultivation of waste lands, and the improvement of the soil in accordance with a common plan;
(8) equal obligation of all to work and the establishment of industrial armies, especially for agriculture;
(9) combination of agriculture with manufacturing industries; gradual abolition of the distinction between town and country by a more equable distribution of the population over the country; and
(10) free education for all children in public schools and abolition of child labor in its present form.

Marx anticipates many of the social reforms that later became an established part of democratic practice. A surprisingly large number of the measures he advocated, such as a graduated income tax and public education, have been adopted in most of the democratic countries of the world by peaceful and constitutional means.

The transition stage in the march toward the communist heaven continues to retain some of the marks of a capitalist society. It is "still stamped with the birthmarks of the old society from whose womb it emerges." The political state remains in existence and the proletariat uses the organs of government to socialize completely the means of production and to stamp out the last vestiges of capitalism. During this stage also, complete justice and equality in the social and economic order cannot be expected. Human exploitation will be eliminated, but the distribution of the articles of consumption will continue to be based on the amount of labor performed by each individual. The worker will receive back from society exactly what he contributes to it in the way of labor.

The system of remuneration proposed for the interim period is not perfect since it is still based on the principle that the right of the worker to consumer goods is proportionate to the labor he supplies. Such a practice "tacitly recognizes unequal individual endowment and thus productive capacity as natural privileges. It is therefore a right of inequality in its content. . . ." It fails to recognize that people are not all endowed with equal ability and facilities. One man is strong and healthy, another is weak and sickly; one man is married and has a large family, another is unmarried with no family responsibilities; one man is superior to another in mental ability and talent. "Thus with an equal output, and hence an equal share in the social consumption fund, one will in fact receive more than another, one will be richer than another, and so on."[12]

The principle that each is to be rewarded according to his ability is a defect, Marx admits, but such practice is unavoidable in the first phases of communism. Unless one is willing to indulge in utopian speculation, he must not think that people will immediately after the overthrow of capitalism learn to work for society rather than for themselves. The spirit of individualism and selfishness has been too long inculcated by a bourgeois society to be uprooted overnight. The spirit of true communism can only be established gradually by abolishing the causes of selfishness, which are spawned by an unjust social order, and by a long process of education. The final stage of communism will be attained only after society has been properly prepared and conditioned.

The Political State

Equating the state with government, Marx views it as an instrument that is used by the dominant class to achieve its objectives. In the past, the state was employed by the minority to suppress and exploit the majority. During the intermediate state of socialism it will be used by the proletarian majority in behalf of the overwhelming mass of the people. It will be retained, in other words, to serve as an agency for destroying capitalism. With the accomplishment of this task, there will be no further need for the state or government, just as there is no need for the glass blower once the glass is shaped.

While Marx's concept of the state is essentially mechanistic, his view of the social body is wholly organismic. By accepting historical materialism as the basis of his theory, he is compelled to consider society as a substantial unity in which individual man functions as a cell within a

---

[12] *Ibid.*, pp. 9-10.

living body. Obviously, there is no place for constitutional government or subsidiarity in such a doctrine. The state exists to serve the needs of the dominant class; its role does not change when the workers seize political power. It merely becomes the tool of the proletariat instead of the bourgeoisie. In this capacity, it must extend its power to all fields of human life in order to "liberate" man from the religious, moral, and cultural prejudices of the past.

Although he has no patience with an "uneducated" majority, Marx apparently envisages a workers' democracy during the transition period in which a system of self-government will exist within the proletarian ranks. The communist manifesto proclaims that the first steps in the revolution of the working class are the raising of the proletariat to a position of power and the establishment of democracy. Later, Marx speaks approvingly of the Paris Commune of 1870 because its officers were elected by democratic suffrage and were responsible to the people.

Regardless of practice, communism is theoretically incompatible with democratic government. According to Marx, the character of political and social institutions must be sought in the material conditions of society. When the economic substructure changes, the cultural and political superstructure also undergoes modification. Man has little choice in the matter; the doctrine of dialectical materialism deprives him of any reasonable power of self-determination in either the political or the economic sphere. Since the proletarian revolution and the resultant dictatorship are inevitable, resistance is pointless. Man must accept the processes of nature; he has no freedom of choice as to either the form of political society or the objectives that it should seek.

The Communist Society

The final phase of communism will be attained when all class distinctions have disappeared and all production has been concentrated "in the hands of a vast association of the whole nation." When this point is reached, there will be no further need for political government. "As soon as there is no longer any social class to be held in subjection; as soon as class rule, and the individual struggle for existence based upon our present anarchy in production . . . are removed, nothing more remains to be repressed."[13] The state has no purpose in a classless com-

---

[13] F. Engels, "Scientific v. Utopian Socialism," *Selected Works* (Moscow: Foreign Language Publishing House, 1950), Vol. 2, p. 138.

munity since the substitution of socialism for capitalism removes the source of all human conflict.

The state will not vanish suddenly; it will gradually atrophy as its functions fall into disuse. As the transition from socialism to communism proceeds, "state interference in social relations becomes superfluous in one domain after another, and then dies out of itself; the government of persons is replaced by the administration of things and by the conduct of processes of production. The state is not abolished. It withers away."[14] This doctrine is grounded on the utopian belief that in a fully socialized society the individual will have no reason to violate the social order since this order guarantees the highest possible degree of happiness to everyone.

Neither Marx nor Engels has much to say about the new society that will come into being. At no point do they describe its duration, its organization, or its operating techniques. Neither of them makes any pretense of being a social planner, mapping out a blueprint for the ideal society. They sneer at the utopian socialists for attempting such "tomfoolery." Theirs was a scientific socialism produced by the inexorable course of history. The details of organization and operation are only supplementary to the character of the new society; little purpose would be served by spending much time on such matters.

In the communist utopia, the mode of distribution will undergo radical change. Instead of each individual being paid in accordance with what he produces, distribution will be governed by the principle "from each according to his ability, to each according to his needs."

> In a higher phase of communist society, after the enslaving subordination of individuals under division of labour, and therewith also the antithesis between mental and physical labour, has vanished; after labour, from a mere means of life, has itself become the prime necessity of life; after the productive forces have also increased with the all-round development of the individual, and all the springs of cooperative wealth flow more abundantly — only then can the narrow horizon of bourgeois right be fully left behind and society inscribe on its banners: from each according to his ability, to each according to his needs.[15]

Assuming that two individuals have the same needs, the one with exceptional talent will receive no more remuneration for his services than the unskilled laborer. Similarly, the clerk with a family to support will

---

14 *Ibid.*
15 Marx, *Critique of the Gotha Programme, op. cit.,* p. 31.

receive a greater share of the produce of society than the unmarried scientist with no family responsibilities. At the same time, each will be expected to serve the community to the best of his ability.

SUMMARY

Marx and Engels lived in an era of economic dislocation brought on by the changing mode of production. They witnessed the most inhumane phase of the industrial revolution: human misery, inequitable distribution of wealth, intolerable living conditions, exploitation of unorganized labor. Had their early impressions been formed at the turn of the present century, when the worst abuses of the new economic order were being abated, their approach to social problems might have been less rigid, less dogmatic, and less revolutionary. There were answers, other than those offered by Marx, to the nineteenth-century defenders of *laissez-faire* economics who were so loudly proclaiming the primacy of an uncontrolled and unregulated economy. Unfortunately, the non-Marxist replies received little audience in an age that was intoxicated by the spirit of scientism.

Marx believed that the course of history was on his side. He purported to see the inexorable drive toward a socialistic future as the dialectical process unfolded itself in the world of reality. Proletarian consciousness had only to be more fully awakened for the transformation to take place. The process was a slow one; it could perhaps be speeded up by revolution, but the results were inevitable. As Engels remarked on one occasion, "Man has only to know himself, to measure all conditions of life against himself, to judge them by his own character, to organize the world according to the demands of his own nature in a truly human way, and he will have solved all the riddles of our age." But how is man as a creature or victim of economic forces over which he has no control to rise to such heights?

Marxism is actually faced with certain basic incompatibilities. These inconsistencies led to the enormous gulf between reality and philosophy which developed when the doctrine went beyond the phase of theoretical formulation. On the one hand, Marx felt compelled to rest his system on a deterministic basis in order to stress its scientific character. One of the results of this emphasis is the theoretical subordination of political power to the economic forces operating in history. On the other hand, later communists found it necessary to emphasize the voluntaristic aspects of Marxism as they actively sought to shape the course of history. Marx taught that man can discover the dialectical laws governing social behavior and perhaps influence their acceleration, but he can do no more. Lenin and his successors virtually rejected the principle of determinism by maintaining that man is able to guide the direction of the dialectic. Acting under the pressure of political reality, they forced objective determinism to abdicate in favor of subjective voluntarism. Marx had attempted to hold the two in equilibrium, but the incompatibility between them could no longer be suppressed once the doctrine of communism had gone beyond the phase of a mere untried hypothesis.[16]

Communism is more than a political philosophy or an economic doctrine; it is a metaphysics translated into action. It is a philosophy that seeks to offer an integral interpretation of the whole of reality. It is a theology, a religion, with a program aimed at action and not abstract doctrinal exposition. It seeks to explain the universe by denying a transcendent God. In similar fashion, it attempts to solve all the problems of man and society in the light of its materialistic canons. Marxian man is a wholly material individual influenced by every change in his environment; he is not the man of Christianity.

Marxism is a complete negation of natural law. It regards a moral action as one that corresponds to the aims of the social order — aims that are fixed by man himself. For the Marxist, an ethical norm does not guide and mold society; on the contrary, that conduct is moral which fits into human society. Ethics does not shape the world, but the world shapes its own ethics. Truth and morality have meaning only in so far as they are useful to the construction of a socialist society. Communist ethics, therefore, becomes the ethics of the party which has assumed the task of bringing socialism to fruition.[17]

Discard its atheism, and the whole superstructure of communism must fall. Its doctrinal strength lies in the fact that it has become a religion. Like Christianity, it holds that the present is merely a preparation for the future; but unlike Christianity which seeks to bring about the kingdom of God that is not of this world, communism endeavors to create an earthly garden of Eden for mankind. While Christianity looks to the world beyond, it recognizes the present life of man, and seeks to make that life happy and fulsome. Communism, in contrast, ignores the realities of human nature and the present life of man in its quest for the apocalyptical vision of the earthly paradise. It consequently thinks nothing of sacrificing the individual to its messianic task. As Christopher Dawson describes it,

> The cause of the proletariat is the cause of social justice in the most absolute sense. It is a cause for which the communist is ready to suffer and die and to cause the suffering and death of others. All this is the fruit not of his philosophy or of his materialism but of the underlying religious impulse which finds expression in the revolutionary apocalyptic. It is a spiritual passion which has lost its theological object and has attempted to find independent justification in a purely rational theory.[18]

Redemption is not to be found in the sacrifice on the cross but in the creation of a new society in which the means of production are socially owned.

---

[16] See V. V. Aspaturian, "The Contemporary Doctrine of the Soviet State and its Philosophical Foundation," *American Political Science Review*, Dec., 1954, pp. 1031–1057.

[17] See G. Peterffy, "The Ethics of Communism," in *The Philosophy of Communism* (New York: Fordham University Press, 1952), pp. 225–240.

[18] *Religion and the Modern State* (London: Sheed and Ward, 1935), pp. 86–88.

The philosophical problem in the words of Marx is not to understand the world but to change it. In this respect, he would not have been disappointed with his efforts. The doctrine which he advanced has had startling effect on the course of world history. It has also had a dynamic impact on modern political thought and practices. So strong has his influence been that the defenders of democratic theory have been forced to re-examine their philosophical premises. The result has been a renewed interest in the basic tenets of the western social and political tradition which Marx so completely and deliberately disregards.

BIBLIOGRAPHY

Bailey, Sydney D., "The Revision of Marxism," Review of Politics, October, 1954.

Berlin, Isaiah, Karl Marx, 2nd ed. (London: Home University Library, 1948).

Bloom, Solomon F., "The Withering Away of the State," Journal of the History of Ideas, January, 1946.

Bowles, R. C., "Marxian Adaptation of the Ideology of Fourier," Southern Atlantic Quarterly, April, 1955.

Chang, S. H. M., The Marxian Theory of the State (Philadelphia: University of Pennsylvania Press, 1931).

Cole, G. D. H., The Meaning of Marxism (London: V. Gollancz, 1948).

Feuer, L. S., "J. S. Mill and Marxian Socialism," Journal of the History of Ideas, April, 1949.

Grampp, William D., "On the Politics of the Classical Economists," Quarterly Journal of Economics, November, 1948.

Guest, David, A Textbook of Dialectical Materialism (New York: International Publishers, 1939).

Halloway, Mark, Heavens on Earth: Utopian Communities in America (New York: Library Publishers, 1951).

Harris, A. L., "J. S. Mill's Theory of Progress (Comparison between him and Marx)," Ethics, April, 1956.

———— "Utopian Elements in Marx's Thought," Ethics, January, 1950.

Hook, Sydney, From Hegel to Marx: Studies in the Intellectual Development of Karl Marx (New York: Humanities Press, 1950).

Hunt, R. N. Carew, The Theory and Practice of Communism (New York: Macmillan, 1951).

Kluckhohn, C., "Politics, History, and Psychology," World Politics, October, 1955.

Krieger, L., "Marx and Engels as Historians," Journal of the History of Ideas, June, 1953.

La Farge, J., "Philosophical Basis of Communism," American Catholic Philosophical Association, Proceedings, 1933.

Lewis, J. D., "Individual and the Group in Marxist Theory," International Journal of Ethics, October, 1936.

Lindsay, A. D., Karl Marx's Capital: An Introductory Essay (London: Oxford University Press, 1925).

McCoy, C. N. R., "Logical and Real in Political Theory: Plato, Aristotle and Marx," *American Political Science Review*, December, 1954.

Miliband, Ralph, "The Politics of Robert Owen," *Journal of the History of Ideas*, April, 1954.

Negley, G., and Patrick, J. M., *The Quest for Utopia: An Anthology of Imaginary Societies* (New York: H. Schuman, 1952).

Niebuhr, Reinhold, "Marxism in Eclipse," *Speculum*, June, 1943.

Robinson, Joan, *An Essay on Marxian Economics* (London: Macmillan, 1942).

Simon, W. M., "History for Utopia: Saint Simon and the Idea of Progress," *Journal of the History of Ideas*, June, 1956.

Stocks, H. L., *Materialism in Politics* (London: Oxford University Press, 1937).

Tucker, Robert C., "The Cunning of Reason in Hegel and Marx," *Review of Politics*, July, 1956.

Venable, Vernon, *Human Nature; the Marxian View* (New York: Knopf, 1945).

Wilson, F. G., "Democracy and Marxism," *Social Order*, October, 1955.

Chapter XX

MODERN COMMUNISM

"The important thing is to retain power, to consolidate it, and to make it invincible" (J. Stalin, *Leninism*).

THE student of politics must go beyond Marx if he hopes to understand and evaluate communism as it is known and practiced today. Even before Marx's death, his followers had begun to interpret his writings in ways that usually suited their own purposes or that seemed compatible with the historical exigencies of the moment. As a result we have the Marx of the social democrats, the Marx of the revolutionary left, and the Marx of the Soviet dictators. Men of great power and influence, including Lenin, Stalin, and Mao Tse-Tung, have gone to the doctrinal fountain of Marxism to find theoretical justification for their political actions. Their efforts to fit communist theory to political reality have produced many strange results. The Procrustean bed has been shaped and reshaped to conform to the diverse needs of the new theoreticians. Only a philosophy that contained elements of ambiguity could serve in this capacity.

Marx intended that his theoretical formulations be the basis and stimulus to action, and in this he was not disappointed. By 1900 Marxist parties and groups were well established on the Continent.[1] The largest and best organized of these was the German Social Democratic party founded in 1875 at Gotha. During the following decade socialist parties were organized in Austria, Belgium, France, Holland, Italy, and the

---

[1] Most of the Marxist parties adopted the name "socialist" or "social democratic." To be a socialist in the late nineteenth century was, generally speaking, to be a Marxist. The word "communist," which had been originally used in the 1848 manifesto to distinguish Marxian socialists from the utopian socialists, returned to use with the Russian revolution. In 1918 the Bolsheviks officially adopted the name "communist." Since that time the term has been associated exclusively with the revolutionary brand of socialism.

Scandinavian countries. In Great Britain a socialist mass movement did not develop until after 1914. The trade unions which existed prior to that time confined their activities almost exclusively to economic functions. The Russian Social Democratic party, in terms of popular support, was likewise a relatively insignificant force before 1917. However, it early developed a corps of able leaders and exerted considerable influence on international socialism.

REVISIONISM VERSUS ORTHODOXY

Marx's successors may be divided into three main groups: revisionist, orthodox, and revolutionary. The first recognizes the class struggle as a factor in historical development but maintains that it is diminishing in intensity. It also questions the belief in the inevitability of catastrophic change and seeks to turn the socialist movement into democratic channels. The second school accepts the basic philosophical and economic premises of Marxism; and while it remains revolutionary in theory, it has become essentially evolutionary in practice. The third group is distinctly revolutionary both in doctrine and practice. It stresses the importance of viewing the class struggle in political terms and the necessity of using violence to achieve the ends of socialism.

During the late nineteenth and early twentieth centuries, a number of socialist writers began to suggest certain modifications in Marxist theory. They felt that a reassessment of its doctrinal position was called for in view of the failure of its major predictions to come true, and in the light of the changing social scene. Marx had assumed that the proletariat would sink into greater misery; instead, even by the time of his death, the worker's lot had considerably improved. He had stated that the middle class would gradually disappear into the ranks of the proletariat; on the contrary, the middle class had become stronger. He had foretold an impending economic crisis, but no such disaster occurred. With the changes for the better in the economic, social, and political environment, the socialist parties found themselves in something of a dilemma. They had for all practical purposes become the political representatives of the working class interests, and in this capacity had been able to achieve practical gains for the worker within the framework of the existing order. Yet as heirs of Marxist ideology, they were committed to the overthrow of this same order by revolutionary means. This dilemma found reflection in the works of the socialist theoreticians who succeeded Marx.

Eduard Bernstein

Eduard Bernstein (1850–1932), a German bank clerk, was attracted to socialism early in his career. Forced to leave Germany in 1878 after the passage of the antisocialist laws, he became the editor of the German socialist paper, *Social Democracy*, published first in Zurich and later in London. His principal work, *Evolutionary Socialism* was written in 1899; the following year he returned to Germany.

The rise of the Social Democratic party to a prominent place in German politics had brought with it a split in party ranks. One faction believed that gradual reform through parliamentary means would never destroy the capitalistic system; the other insisted that a socialist society can and should be attained by constitutional methods. During the 1890's the latter wing became increasingly critical of the party leadership for interpreting Marx too literally. Holding that the traditional dogma of scientific socialism was inadequate, it demanded that the party revise the theoretical assumptions on which it was based. It pointed out that the Social Democratic party received considerable support from the middle classes, and that it had to decide whether to accept the role of a responsible parliamentary party or run the risk of alienating many of its followers. Proponents of this point of view urged that the organization strive to achieve practical gains within the existing political framework, and that it forget about dogma in determining its day-to-day policies. The theoretical revision of Marxism along these new lines was largely the work of Eduard Bernstein. During his stay in England, Bernstein had come in close contact with the Fabian leaders. He was greatly influenced by their rejection of many phases of Marxian doctrine and by their belief in the gradual evolution of society toward state socialism.

In his early writings Bernstein claimed to be defending Marx against improper interpretation, but by the time he left England he had become firmly convinced that much of the Marxian analysis of capitalism was untrue or obsolete. To use his words, the further development and elaboration of the Marxist doctrine must begin with criticism of it. He holds that Marx miscalculated when he assumed that the lot of the proletariat would become increasingly worse until the day of revolution. On the contrary, the class struggle is actually becoming less intense with the passage of time. The development of joint stock companies has dispersed ownership of the means of production and has increased the number of capitalists. With the advance in political democracy and the resulting reversal in the state's attitude toward trade unions and social legislation, significant gains have been made by the worker in the political and economic spheres. The proletariat is no longer faced by a hostile state dominated by the capitalists. The rights of the propertied minority have ceased to be a serious obstacle to social progress.

Bernstein's revisionism is best expressed in a sentence from his *Evolutionary Socialism.* "What is generally called the goal of socialism is nothing to me, the movement everything." He explains that he does not mean to deny the ideals and ultimate goals of socialism, but to urge that its program not be undermined by its sense of historical mission. It is unimportant whether the socialist movement ever reaches its final goal of a classless society. Socialism is daily bringing new gains to the worker — this is the important fact to keep in mind. Referring to the English experience, he states that no intelligent socialist has any thought of an imminent victory for socialism by means of a violent revolution, and none dreams of quick conquest of Parliament by a revolutionary proletariat. Socialism must remain subordinate to the democratic process. Class struggle may be endemic, but the socialist movement can gain more adherents and win more benefits for the worker by adhering to democratic methods than by preaching class war.

Bernstein deviates from Marxism in another significant and fundamental aspect. Condemning historical materialism and the dialectic, he denies that socialism can be ethically justified on the basis of economic pressures or class struggle. No matter how worthy the goals of socialism may be, there are right and wrong ways of striving for them. An ethics that is founded on human personality and on the moral character of man must replace one that is based on the pressure of material forces.

Karl Kautsky

The chief defender of Marxism against the criticisms of the revisionists was Karl Kautsky (1854–1938). Born in Prague, Kautsky lived most of his life in Germany. In 1883 he founded the socialist paper, *Dei Neue Zeit,* which became the leading theoretical organ of Marxism. From 1885 to 1890 he resided in London, in close association with Engels. For many years, Kautsky was accepted by Lenin and other leading socialists as the great authority on Marx. Even after his attacks against the Russian communists, his early works were still cited in the Soviet Union as the best introduction to socialism (with the qualifying remark that he had subsequently fallen away from true Marxism on several important points).

Kautsky accepts the Marxian tenets of class struggle, historical materialism, and the inevitability of revolution. He admits that many of the predictions of Marx and Engels have not been fulfilled literally, but he contends that the founders of socialism were able to determine the direction of economic development for many decades in a degree that the course of events has impressively justified. Rejecting the statistical evidence of Bernstein which indicates that the possibility of class warfare is diminishing, Kautsky endeavors to show that the conditions leading to such a struggle are actually materializing. He argues that the joint stock company or corporation (which Bernstein regards as a means of diffusing wealth) is actually an effective instrument for concentrating capital. "Through the corporation the savings of even the poor are placed at the disposal of great capitalists, who are enabled to use those savings as if they were a part of their great capitals. As a result the centralizing of their own great fortunes is increased still more."[2]

In defending historical materialism, Kautsky emphasizes that individual phenomenon in history cannot always be explained in economic terms. Nor can the entire spiritual and cultural life of a period be similarly explained, since any given era inherits much from an earlier time. Only the new ideas are erected on the economic conditions of the particular period; the others must be traced back to their origins. Kautsky uses the case of Christianity to illustrate his point. Acknowledging that Christian ideas cannot be derived from existing economic conditions, he states that we must go back to the time when the movement first appeared in world history as a new phenomenon. In doing so,

> we must investigate its origins during the first centuries of our era when the democracy of antiquity broke down and an all powerful Caesarism arose. The economic relations of the time and their consequences, the impoverishment of the masses, the concentration of wealth in a few hands, loss of population, constant civil war . . . the cessation of all political activity among the people, for the impoverished masses became corrupted and could be bought while the rich sunk

---

[2] *Road to Power* (Chicago: Kerr & Co., 1909), p. 52.

themselves in debauchery: — this was the real basis out of which Christianity arose and makes it explicable.[3]

Thus the Marxist proposition about the relation between the economic substructure and the cultural and institutional superstructure is unconditionally valid only for the actually new appearance in history.

Unlike the revisionists, Kautsky believes in the revolutionary character of the socialist parties. But as Sidney Hook points out, he is careful to distinguish between a revolutionary and a revolution-making party.[4] Revolutions are not made or promoted; they are the inevitable product of history. They occur as spontaneous consequences of economic and social processes. We know, says Kautsky, "that our goal can be attained only through revolution. We know that it is just as little in our power to create this revolution as it is in the power of our opponents to prevent it." A social revolution is a profound transformation of the entire social structure brought about by the establishment of new methods of production. It is not a process that occurs overnight; it may be spread over decades. The less violent it is and the more peaceful the nature of the forms under which it is consummated, the more successful it will be.

Kautsky is outspoken in his opposition to the Bolsheviks. He consistently maintains that socialism without democracy is unthinkable. Democracy is the shortest, surest, and least costly road to socialism, just as it is the best instrument for the development of the political and social prerequisites for socialism. Democracy and socialism are inextricably intertwined. The Russian revolution was a deviation from Marxism not only because it tried to proceed faster than historical developments warranted but also because it represented a seizure of political power by a minority. The result was frightful tyranny. Kautsky argues that the socialist revolution should not take place until the workers represent the majority and until they are properly educated to assume responsible political power. Only in a democracy can these pre-conditions to socialism be attained. Democracy may sometimes repress its revolutionary thought, but it is the indispensable means for the proletariat to obtain the ripeness which it needs for the conquest of political power and the bringing about of the social revolution. The historical mission

---

[3] *The Materialistic Conception of History* (Berlin: J. H. W. Dietz, 1927), Vol. I, p. 819.

[4] *Marx and the Marxists* (Princeton: Van Nostrand, 1955), p. 51.

of the proletariat is a high one. Its objective is not to acquire power in order to oppress others but to abolish class rule and bring justice to all. The actions of the Bolsheviks did violence to these precepts.

Despite their doctrinal differences, both Kautsky and Bernstein helped to steer the course of the German Social Democratic party into democratic and constitutional channels. After World War I, the Social Democrats, together with the Catholic Center party, played a prominent role in founding the Weimar Republic. In the first election held under the new government, the party acquired the largest single representation in the Reichstag. Now thoroughly committed to a revisionist program, it was deserted at the outset by the more intransigent members who formed the German Communist party. In the ensuing years, the Social Democrats as a center group were caught between the crossfire of the extreme right (Nazis) and the extreme left (Communists).

<h3 style="text-align:center">REVOLUTIONARY COMMUNISM</h3>

With the triumph of the Bolshevik revolution, all the doctrinal differences among the successors of Marx became largely matters of academic or historical interest. There was now only one official Marxian doctrine, that laid down by the Russian Communist party. While democratic socialist parties with Marxian leanings continued to exist in European countries, their doctrinal foundations became secondary to their program of activities. The socialists who rejected the revisionary approach joined the ranks of the communist parties that were being organized under Soviet direction.

Prior to the Revolution, Russian socialist thought had been far from unified. Deep seated differences had divided the Russian Social Democratic party into two wings, the Bolsheviks (majority) and the Mensheviks (minority), the one led by Lenin, the other by L. Martov. The split had occurred at the party Congress in 1903. The faction headed by Lenin favored a small, undemocratic, well-disciplined organization with membership rigidly limited to professional revolutionaries. It advocated immediate steps leading toward revolution and opposed co-operation with the nonsocialist parties. The Mensheviks favored a broadly based and democratically operated party open to any sympathizer, co-operation with other liberal parties, and participation in parliamenfary government. They held that Russia must pass through an intermediary bourgeois stage like the rest of Europe, and that capitalism and industry must progress much further before the time would be ripe for socialism. The Bolsheviks had lost their narrow majority in the party long before 1917. However, their swift and incisive action in precipitating the overthrow of the provisional government in Russia placed them in the seat of power. Since the Mensheviks had co-operated with the provisional government headed by Kerensky, their doom was sealed once the revolutionaries were successful. Communism now entered a new stage in its development. Political power had been seized in the name of the working class and the dictatorship of the proletariat had been established. The first step toward the cherished socialist dream had been achieved. The principal architect and theoretical spokesman of the new order was Nicolai Lenin.

LENIN

Nicolai Lenin (1870–1924) was born as Vladimir Ilyich Ulyanov, the son of a middle class intellectual. His father was a school official, his mother a member of the lesser gentry. All five children in the family became revolutionaries, one of them being put to death at the age of seventeen for conspiring against the Czar. Lenin attended the University of Kazan but was expelled for political agitation. He then went to St. Petersburg where he studied law and was admitted to the bar. Some time later his propagation of Marxist doctrine led to his arrest and deportation to Siberia for three years. During his exile there he assumed the name of Lenin, after the River Lena located near his place of imprisonment. In 1900 he left Russia, spending much time in London, Paris, and Geneva. Five years later he returned to participate in the abortive revolution of 1905. Forced to flee in order to avoid arrest, he spent most of the following ten years in Switzerland, devoting himself to secret propaganda work. Early in April, 1917, he returned to Russia with the assistance of the German government. In November of the same year, he directed the successful uprising against the moderate Kerensky regime that had succeeded the Czarist government only ten months earlier.

Lenin was a man of unbounded energy, great self-confidence, and keen intellect. His talent was practical and political rather than theoretical and scientific. Although he was not a brilliant or original thinker, he had the capacity to turn Marxian theory in the direction he desired. Most important of all, he had an amazing facility for assessing a situation, and a remarkable sense of timing. He not only knew how to act boldly but he also knew when to act. During the confusing summer of 1917, Lenin alone of all the political leaders was completely confident that he knew the course to be followed. It was this supreme self-assurance, together with his intense determination, that finally convinced the skeptical Bolshevik hierarchy to follow his bold plan. During his exile abroad, Lenin had been coeditor of the revolutionary journal *Iskra*, the Spark. Before he died, he was able to enkindle the Marxian spark into a mighty flame.

Organization and Methods

Lenin spent twenty years in preparation for the time that the Bolsheviks would gain control of the state. He had carefully worked out the general plans for organization and the theoretical basis for the revolution long before the November, 1917, *coup d'état*. In 1902 he wrote a pamphlet entitled *What Is to Be Done*, a handbook of communist organization and strategy, and in the summer of 1917 he finished his most important work, *The State and Revolution*. Since his theoretical interests are action-oriented, the techniques and organization of revolutionary movements loom large in his thinking. All of his earlier writings are directed toward the establishment of an organized party of the working class based on a clear understanding of Marxist doctrine.

Like Hitler's *Mein Kampf*, the 1902 pamphlet proved to be an accurate blueprint of party goals, strategy, and tactics. In it Lenin declares that no movement can endure without an organization of leaders, and that the more widely the masses participate in the movement the more essential it is to have such an organization. This group must consist largely of professional revolutionaries who have been trained in the art of combating the political police. It must be a small compact core consisting of reliable, experienced, and hardened workers, operating under rules of strict secrecy. Such a party obviously cannot be organized along democratic lines as the Mensheviks insisted. "Think it over a little," Lenin told his fellow socialists, "and you will realize that broad democracy in party organization amidst the darkness of the autocracy and the domination of the gendarmes is nothing more than a useless and harmful toy." Conditions of this kind call for a highly disciplined party that is hierarchical in structure and centrally controlled.

Lenin has no patience with those who believe that the workers will spontaneously become adherents to socialism through their own efforts. The history of all countries shows that the working class, exclusively by its own efforts, is able to develop only trade union consciousness. It would be foolish for the Russian Social Democratic party to sit by and wait patiently until socialist ideas had permeated the working class. The impetus for revolution will never come from a mass organization which includes the lukewarm and timid; such a group inevitably spends much of its time in debate and compromise. Leadership must be assumed by a party that is the most advanced, class conscious, and revolutionary part of the working class. As stated in a resolution adopted by the Communist International in 1920, "the Communist party is the organized political lever by means of which the more advanced part of the working class leads all the proletarian and semi-proletarian mass in the right direction."[5] Such a party knows the true interests of the worker better than he knows it himself. If necessary, it can force him to follow the path that leads to his true destiny.

Revolutionary Character of Communism

In addition to working out an organizational pattern and plan of action, Lenin made three major contributions to the development of communist theory. He pruned out all evolutionary tendencies in Marxism; he put definite meaning into the expression "dictatorship of the proletariat"; and he adapted Marxism to the conditions of an undeveloped industrial society.

Lenin opens his *State and Revolution* with a vigorous attack on those who seek to adulterate or disregard the revolutionary aspects of Marxian teaching. Citing Engels' analysis of the state as "the product of the irreconcilability of class antagonisms," he notes that the state is an organ of class domination. The group which holds economic power is able to become politically dominant. In this position it can use the apparatus of state power — the bureaucracy, army, and police — to hold down and exploit the other classes. Lenin concludes that if the oppressed class is to gain control of the state, it can do so only by violent revolution since the exploiters will never relinquish their control peacefully. Once capital has gained control "it establishes its power so securely,

---

[5] The resolution is printed in *Blueprint for World Conquest* (Washington: Human Events, 1946), p. 73 f.

so firmly, that no change of persons or institutions or parties in the bourgeois republic can shake it." The liberation of the oppressed stratum of society "is impossible without a violent revolution."[6] The following passage from the *Theses Adopted by the Second Congress of the Third International* in 1920 is worth noting in this connection:

> Only a violent defeat of the bourgeoisie, the confiscation of its property, the annihilation of the entire bourgeois government apparatus, from top to bottom, parliamentary, juridical, military, bureaucratic, administrative, municipal, etc., up to the individual exile or internment of the most stubborn and dangerous exploiters, the establishment of a strict control over them for the repressing of all inevitable attempts at resistance and restoration of capitalist slavery — only such measures will be able to guarantee the complete submission of the whole class of exploiters.[7]

In answer to those who interpret Marx's statement about the withering away of the state as a negation of revolution, Lenin retorts that these words refer to the remains of proletarian statehood after the socialist revolution. The bourgeois state does not wither away, but is destroyed by the proletariat in the course of the revolution. What withers away after the uprising is the proletarian state which replaces the capitalist state as a matter of necessity during the period of transition to a communist society.

With respect to Marx's belief that socialism might be peacefully achieved in some of the more advanced industrial states, Lenin maintains that any such hope has been completely expelled by the rapid growth of imperialism during the late nineteenth and early twentieth centuries. During this period the capitalistic organization of society assumed imperialistic characteristics: monopoly capitalism within countries but bitter competition between nations for new markets and raw materials. As control of industry passed from the hands of the producers into those of the bankers, the era of finance capitalism arrived. Herein lies the chief cause of modern war, for the bankers with their high stakes in industrial expansion tend to push their governments into dangerous foreign adventures. Under these circumstances "which have been created in the whole world, and most of all in the most advanced, powerful, most enlightened and free capitalist countries . . . to admit

---

[6] *State and Revolution* (New York: International Publishers, 1932), p. 20.
[7] Reprinted in *Blueprint for World Conquest, op. cit.*, p. 44.

the idea of a voluntary submission of the capitalists to the will of the majority of the exploited — of a peaceful, reformist passage to socialism — is . . . a concealment of truth."[8]

Dictatorship of the Proletariat

Marx and Engels were never clear as to the meaning of the dictatorship of the proletariat. Lenin, on the other hand, is quite precise in interpreting this facet of Marxian doctrine. He points out that the transition from a capitalist to a communist society is impossible without a political transition period, and that the state in this period "can only be the revolutionary dictatorship of the proletariat." Once the workers have seized control of the state, suppression is still necessary; but this time it is "the suppression of the minority of exploiters by the majority of the wage slaves of yesterday." When there is suppression, there must also be violence and "there cannot be liberty or democracy." The proletariat needs the state "not in the interest of freedom but for the purpose of crushing its antagonists."[9] Lenin speaks of democracy for the vast majority of the people and exclusion from democracy of the exploiters and oppressors of the people; but the proletariat that he refers to does not constitute a majority of the population, nor for that matter a majority of the workers.

In the theses of the Communist International, Lenin declares that "the dictatorship of the proletariat is the most complete realization of a leadership over all workers and exploited . . . on the part of the only class prepared for such a leading role by the whole history of capitalism."[10] He makes it clear that this leadership cannot come from the proletarian class as a whole. The rank and file of workers are unable to grasp the real significance of Marxism. They have been too long exposed to bourgeois ideas and institutions to rise up spontaneously and embrace revolutionary socialism. They must undergo a period of training, indoctrination, and reorientation under the direction of the revolutionary elite. The leadership of the proletariat must be in effect the leadership of its most advanced element — the best representatives of the class, perfectly conscious and loyal communists enlightened by the experience gained in the stubborn revolutionary struggle. In the last analysis, the dictatorship

---

[8] *Ibid.*, p. 44.
[9] *State and Revolution, op. cit.*, p. 73.
[10] Reprinted in *Blueprint for World Conquest, op. cit.*, p. 50.

of the proletariat means nothing else than the dictatorship of the communist party.

Lenin seeks to justify this autocratic view by pointing out that the attainment of political power by the workers does not put an end to the class struggle. Many pitfalls remain in the way before the last remnants of capitalism can be wiped out. The resistance of the exploiting class will "increase tenfold after its overthrow and the dangers of counter-revolution will be ever present. Only by having such a closely united organization of the best part of the working class is it possible for the party to overcome all the difficulties which confront the proletarian dictatorship in the days following the victory." Therefore, until proletarian rule has been established beyond the possibility of a bourgeois restoration, the party can have but a small minority of the workers in its ranks. "Only when the final overthrow of the capitalist order will have become an evident fact — only then will all or almost all the workers enter the ranks of the communist party."[11] Until that time arrives, all individuals must submit unquestionably to the direction and control of the proletarian vanguard.

Not only does the dictatorship of the proletariat mean complete control by a minority party, but more correctly it signifies the dictatorship of a small group or even a single individual within that party. Lenin declares that in order to lead the working class during the long struggle, the Communist party must establish the strictest military discipline within its own ranks. The victory of the workers cannot be achieved without a severe discipline, a perfected centralization, and the fullest confidence of all members in the leading organ of the party. Lenin characterizes the structure of the party as one of democratic centralism: the election of the upper party units by those immediately below, the unconditional subordination of subordinate units to the decision of those above them, and a strong party central organ whose decrees are binding upon all the leaders of party life between party conventions. What he really means is that the degree of democratic activity on the part of the membership is completely determined by the central source. Trotsky described the system graphically while he was still a Menshevik, noting that the organization of the party takes the place of the party itself; the central committee takes the place of the organization; and finally the dictator takes the place of the central committee.

---

[11] *Ibid.*, p. 74.

Socialism in a Non-Industrial State

Communism achieved its first success in a country that was practically devoid of the economic characteristics listed by Marx as preconditions to its establishment. According to him socialism comes into being as a result of the contradictions inherent in a capitalistic society; hence socialist revolutions will occur first in those countries that are highly industrialized. No social order ever perishes before all the productive forces for which there is room in it have developed. Yet in 1917 Russia was a predominantly agricultural country with an industrial potential that was still in its infancy, and with an industrial proletariat that comprised only a small part of the population. There was still plenty of room for the development of the productive forces within the existing social order. How therefore could the Bolshevik revolution outrun the industrial and economic conditions which Marx had laid down as prerequisite to the socialist revolution?

Lenin himself in 1905 had maintained that a time of preparation must elapse between the bourgeois and the proletarian revolutions. Even if the overthrow of the Czarist government in March, 1917, could be construed as the former, the socialist revolution in November of that same year would still appear premature. Lenin, however, insists that the precipitation of the 1917 uprising was in conformity with orthodox Marxian doctrine. He contends that the world economy should be viewed as a whole instead of by individual states. When this is done, it becomes apparent that capitalism has reached the end of its development. The successful social revolution will in all likelihood spring up first in those regions where capitalism is weak and not firmly entrenched rather than in the highly industrialized countries. The front of capital will be pierced where the chain of imperialism is weakest.

Lenin borrowed his theoretical explanation of the Bolshevik revolution from Trotsky, who as early as 1906 had written that the transfer of power to the working class would depend more on the international situation and the fighting preparedness of the workers than it would on the level of the productive forces. It is possible, Trotsky stated "for the workers to come into power in economically backward countries sooner than in advanced countries." Prophetically, he added that the Russian revolution would create conditions in which power would pass into the hands of the workers before the bourgeoisie could develop their ability to govern.[12] The two revolutions, bourgeois and proletarian, can thus be combined in certain circumstances.

Lenin's rationalization of the Bolshevist seizure of political power constitutes a gross deviation from orthodox doctrine. His attempt to color these activities with a pseudo-Marxist gloss cannot conceal their repudiation of the deterministic aspects of communist theory. As Lenin admits, politics cannot but have precedence over economics. Give me an organization of revolutionaries and "we shall overturn the whole of Russia." Voluntaristic man here assumes supremacy over deterministic nature. The forces of the dialectic give way to the will of man.

The Classless Society

Despite the fact that the Russian communists have built up one of the most powerful and all encompassing governmental structures that the world has ever seen, Lenin and his successors have not abandoned the Marxian theory of eventual disappearance of the state. They follow Marx in holding that there are two stages to the attainment of the true communist society. During the first or socialist stage, many of the characteristics of the old society will remain. The means of production will become public property but the state will continue in existence, differences in wealth will still exist, and the individual will be paid in proportion to the amount of work he performs. "Every member of society performing a certain part of socially-necessary work receives a certificate from society to the effect that he has done such and such a quantity of work. According to this certificate he receives from the public warehouses where articles of consumption are stored, a corresponding quantity of products. Deducting that proportion of labor which goes to the public fund, every worker, therefore, receives from society as much as he has given it."[13]

It is impossible for communism to free itself entirely of all tradition and all taint of capitalism during this initial phase. Formal equality will be attained by the common ownership of the means of production, but real equality — the realization of the rule "from each according to his ability, to each according to his needs" — will take time to achieve. People must first be educated and conditioned to accept an unselfish social order of this kind. They must be cured of their egoism and purged

---

[12] A Review and Some Perspectives, Eng. trans. (Moscow: Communist International, 1921), pp. 35–38.
[13] Lenin, The State and Revolution, op. cit., p. 76.

of the vices and weaknesses that have been engendered by private ownership. Only when their character has been remolded, when men become
saints, will the higher end be reached. The state will wither away completely only

> when people have become so accustomed to observing the fundamental
> rules of social intercourse and when their labor is so productive that
> they will voluntarily work *according to their ability*. The narrow
> horizon of bourgeois right which compels one to calculate with the
> stringency of a Shylock whether he has not worked half an hour more
> than another, whether he is not getting less pay than another — this
> narrow horizon will then be left behind. There will then be no need
> for society to regulate the quantity of products to be distributed to
> each; each will take freely according to his needs.[14]

How long will this process take? Communist theoreticians furnish no
answer to this question. All that is certain is that the course will be long
and protracted. "But how rapidly this development will go forward, how
soon it will reach the point of breaking away from the division of labor,
of removing the antagonism between mental and physical labor, of transforming work into the first necessity of life — this we do not and *cannot*
know"[15] Lenin even hints that this final goal may never be reached. Replying to the charge of utopianism, he retorts that "it has never entered the
head of any Socialist to promise that the highest phase of Communism
will arrive." The great socialists "in foreseeing its arrival, presuppose not
the present productivity of labor and the present ordinary run of people."[16]

It is interesting to note that the Soviet state did attempt for a time to
enforce some equality in pay but this effort was soon abandoned. The
principle of higher pay for higher productivity and responsibility is today
accepted in the U.S.S.R. as fully as in capitalist countries. Communist
apologists now argue that those who produce more or who occupy posts
of higher responsibility have greater needs. One of them recently wrote
that Marxism is the enemy of wage leveling. All indications are that the
present wide range in compensation will continue even in a purely com-
munistic society, and that Marxian theory is gradually being reshaped
to justify such a practice.

Lenin is as vague as Marx in describing the final stage of communism.
The state will begin to wither away when capitalist resistance has been
completely destroyed and classes abolished. Political power will gradually

---

[14] *Ibid.*, p. 80.   [15] *Ibid.*, p. 79.   [16] *Ibid.*, p. 80.

become less necessary since such power is precisely the official expression of antagonisms in bourgeois society. Once the fundamental cause of social misconduct — the exploitation of the masses — has been removed, the need for the subjection of one man to another will vanish, since people will become accustomed to observing the elementary conditions of social life without force and subordination.[17]

Some antisocial behavior on the part of a few individuals will doubtlessly continue, but no special governmental machinery will be needed to handle these cases. They will be taken care of by the citizen body itself "as simply and as readily as any crowd of civilized people, even in modern society, parts a pair of combatants or does not allow a woman to be outraged."[18] Lenin also speaks of the eventual disappearance of the distinction between manual and intellectual work (work with the hands and work with the brains), and the establishment of a system in which all can take their turn at managing and working. The mechanics for putting into effect and administering the pure communist order, however, are matters for future determination.

STALIN

When Lenin died in 1924, a spectacular struggle for power took place within the Communist party. The two principal contenders for the apostolic succession were Joseph Stalin and Leon Trotsky. Stalin (1879–1953), whose real name was Dzhugashvili, was a Georgian, born in the Caucasian town of Gori. His father was a shoemaker, his mother an illiterate washerwoman. He became a Marxist while studying for the Orthodox priesthood at the theological seminary in Tiflis. After his expulsion from the school, he joined the Bolshevik wing of the Communist party. His revolutionary activities soon brought about his arrest and deportation to Siberia. When the Bolsheviks succeeded in taking over the government in 1917, he became commissar of nationalities. Five years later he was elected secretary general of the Communist party. The word "stalin" means "man of steel," a name Stalin began to use at the time he joined the revolutionary movement.

Leon Trotsky (1879–1940), whose original name was Lev Davidovich Bronstein, was an early convert to Marxism. He spent most of his youth, including a short stay in New York City, as a propagandist and agitator.

---

[17] *Ibid.*, p. 74.   [18] *Ibid.*, p. 75.

He took a major part in the Bolshevik revolution and was named commissar of war. In contrast to the taciturn and dull Stalin, Trotsky both wrote and spoke brilliantly. Lenin, during his last illness, left a "testament" in which he referred to the hatred that divided Stalin and Trotsky, and advised that the former be dismissed as party secretary because he was too rough and inclined to abuse power. The struggle between the two contenders began immediately after Lenin's death and continued without interruption until Trotsky was finally expelled from Russia in 1929. Stalin's position as secretary general had enabled him to gain control of the party machinery, and through it to oust his rival from power.

Stalin's contribution to the theory of communism is slight. His reputation as a Marxian scholar was poor, even among his colleagues. As one of them reminded him during a theoretical discussion, "Don't make a fool of yourself. Everybody knows that theory is not exactly your field."

But while Stalin's contributions to Marxian doctrine may not be intellectually profound, they are of considerable importance to the development of contemporary Russia and to world history in general. Two of the additions or alterations which he made to the Leninist version of Marxism are of particular significance: the doctrine of socialism in a single country, and the justification for the continuance of the totalitarian state even after socialism is attained.

Socialism in One Country

Lenin and Trotsky always spoke in terms of world revolution. They considered it imperative that the Russian revolution be followed by similar uprisings in other countries. Trotsky, for example, insisted that socialism in Russia must fail unless it is followed by communist victories elsewhere. In fact, one of the major justifications offered by the Bolsheviks for seizing power in an economically backward country was the expectation that their example would spark uprisings in other more highly industrialized states. These states in turn would supply Russia with the technical and economic assistance necessary for her survival and development. When these revolts failed to occur, the Bolsheviks had to reexamine their position. Should they direct their efforts toward the instigation of uprisings elsewhere and slow down socialization in their own country? Or should they temporarily discard the idea of world revolution and proceed to socialize the homeland fully? Trotsky insisted that the Bolshevik program should adopt the first course. He maintained that

CONTEMPORARY POLITICAL PHILOSOPHY

socialism in Russia must ultimately fail unless helped by international revolution. Stalin, on the other hand, seeing the unlikelihood of revolution on any notable scale in the near future, held that socialism could be successfully established in one country even though the rest of the world remained in the capitalist orbit.

Answering the question as to what is meant by the doctrine of a socialist victory in a single state, Stalin explains that it refers to the possibility of the proletariat assuming power and using that power to build a complete socialist society in one country, with the sympathy and support of the proletarians of other countries. The technical backwardness of Russia is not an insuperable obstacle to the construction of such a society. The Soviet Union does not need the aid of the capitalist states, only the support of communist sympathizers who will promote Russian interests in these countries by legal or illegal means. With the adoption of Stalin's position, the Soviet Union became the fatherland of the workers in all countries, and communists everywhere became its agents or fifth columnists. In the Stalinist version of history, Russia is destined to become the center of a new civilization, the savior of all mankind.

The State in Stalinist Theory

In 1936 Stalin proclaimed that the lower stage in the development of communism had been successfully achieved. Production had been completely socialized, the class system abolished, and Soviet society freed from exploitation. In a report to the Congress of the Soviets, Stalin stated that the new constitution of 1936 was "built on the principles of fully developed socialist democracy." In the main, "we have already achieved the first phase of communism, socialism."[19] A few years later, he declared that the Soviet Union was moving toward the higher state of full communism. These developments immediately raised the question: if socialism in Russia has progressed to the point where there is no longer any exploiting group to suppress and no class differences or antagonisms, why is the state becoming more powerful instead of disappearing? What reason is there for the continued existence of its coercive machinery? And how can its failure to show any withering at all be reconciled with communist doctrine?[20]

---

[19] Joseph Stalin, Selected Writings (New York: International Publishers, 1942), p. 386.

[20] See C. B. Hoover, "The Soviet State Fails to Wither," Foreign Affairs, Oct., 1952.

Stalin was sensitive to this obvious difference between Marxian theory and Soviet practice. Addressing the 18th Party Congress, he noted that

It is sometimes asked: We have abolished the exploiting classes; there are no longer any hostile classes in the country; there is nobody to suppress; hence there is no more need for the state; it must die away. Why then do we not help our socialist state to die away? Why do we not strive to put an end to it?[21]

Replying to these questions, he maintains that certain general propositions of the Marxian doctrine of the state were incompletely worked out and inadequate. One such deficiency is the failure to take into consideration the international situation of a state which is the only one that has established socialism. The Soviet Union finds itself in just such a position. Surrounded by hostile noncommunist nations, it has no choice; it must retain the apparatus of the state so long as the danger of attack by capitalistic countries remains.

No matter how far advanced Russia is toward true communism, the Soviet state must remain until the capitalist encirclement is liquidated and replaced by socialist encirclement. When Engels spoke of the withering away of the state, he did not have in mind a situation in which socialism was victorious in a single country. He proceeded "from the assumption that socialism had already been victorious in all countries, or in a majority of countries, more or less simultaneously."[22] Stalin goes on to say that the state's function of suppressing internal opposition to communism has ceased in the Soviet Union since the exploiting class has been abolished. But the function of defending the country from foreign attack remains; and this task demands total mobilization and full direction of the nation's resources. Stalin's addendum to communist doctrine fails, however, to explain why such a situation requires the continued existence of the secret police and a regime of terror, purges, and internal suppression. If democratic states have been able to mobilize for total war without destroying human freedom why is it not possible for a socialist state that has abolished all internal dissension to do likewise?

Stalin's attempt to rationalize the continued existence of the Russian state constitutes an open repudiation of Marxist political doctrine. Marx and his followers had looked upon the state as an instrument of exploitation and as a product of class antagonisms. Stalin transforms it into an

---

[21] *Selected Writings, op. cit.,* p. 468.
[22] *Ibid.,* p. 471.

instrument for protecting Soviet society (now admittedly devoid of class conflict), from capitalist aggression abroad. In his exegesis, he goes even further toward repudiating Marxian theory by converting the proletarian dictatorship into a more powerful system of guidance of society by the state. In doing so he changes the state "from the Marxist image of a class-cleft society into a symbol of class harmony; from an institution representing the interests of a specific ruling class to one representing the interests of society as a whole . . . and from a symbol of social immorality and oppression into one of high ethical value.[23] The fact that the Soviet state has its origin in a doctrine which tolerates political government only temporarily because of its inherent undesirability thus becomes one of the most fantastic contradictions in the history of political thought.

The failure of the state to wither away has left Marxist theoreticians with the single alternative of justifying it as the central institution of progress and freedom. Thus the Soviet state in contemporary thought "is venerated as a positive and constructive force whose creative mission it is to produce the environmental influences which will spawn and preserve the human and spiritual values of future Soviet man."[24] As the headline to a leading editorial in *Izvestia* on October 12, 1957 reads: "The Socialist State-Mighty Instrument for Building Communism." With the adoption of this new attitude toward the state, the original reasons for its abolition have disappeared. Stalin's thesis that the state will wither away once capitalistic encirclement is liquidated can no longer be taken seriously. Perhaps as the Russian lawyer and diplomat A. Y. Vyshinsky once remarked, the problem of the dying away of the state is a purely theoretical problem. Modern communism intends that it shall remain just that.

The Deification of Stalin

As Stalin consolidated his position of leadership, he completely destroyed whatever degree of freedom remained in the Soviet Union. From 1930 until his death in 1953, he ruled as an absolute and ruthless dictator. In a series of brutal purges, most of Lenin's original colleagues were liquidated. The long standing regulation that all party members should master the principles of Marxism-Leninism was changed to the require-

[23] V. V. Aspaturian, *op. cit.*, p. 1032.
[24] *Ibid.*, p. 1047.

ment that they simply accept these doctrines as laid down by the party hierarchy. Critical thinking of any kind was not to be tolerated. The will of Stalin was substituted for that of the communist party; the interpretation of Marxism became the interpretation that Stalin gave to it.

After Trotsky's expulsion from the country in 1929, Stalin began to industrialize the Soviet Union with a speed and ruthlessness that had no precedent. In one year, 25 million persons were forcibly shifted from farms to industrial centers. Incentive rewards were given to skilled workers and technicians. Any manifestations of discontent were violently crushed. In the course of a decade, Stalin succeeded in transforming Russia from one of the most backward states of the world into a great industrial power. The costs in human rights and human dignity were beyond calculation.

Soviet totalitarianism demonstrates in practice a striking resemblance to Nazism. This similarity became particularly noticeable after 1930 in the development of a Fuehrer cult that extravagantly praised and lauded Stalin. In one issue of *Pravda*, his name appeared on the front page no less than 101 times. Even the Soviet national anthem was changed to contain the words "Stalin brought us up in loyalty to the people. He inspired us to great toil and acts." And one of the leading Russian poets wrote of him:

> I would have compared him to a white mountain — but the mountain has a summit.
> I would have compared him to the depths of the sea — but the sea has a bottom.
> I would have compared him to the shining moon — but the moon shines at midnight, not at noon.
> I would have compared him to the brilliant sun, but the sun radiates at noon, not at midnight.

Other Soviet writings which appeared just prior to Stalin's death indicated that a revision of the Marxist-Leninist views on the role of the "great personality" in history were in the making.

But the dialectic moved on, and Stalin with it. After his death in 1953, no single individual emerged supreme. Control fell into the hands of a small committee; and while jockeying for power continued, there was a concerted effort on the part of the Soviet leaders to tear the halo from Stalin and to denounce one-man rule. The most significant episode in this campaign was a speech made by Nikita S. Khrushchev, the secretary general of the Communist party and now Soviet premier. Denouncing the "crimes of the Stalin era," Khrushchev declared that Stalin's disregard of the principle of collective leadership and his attempts to create a "cult of the individual" had done great harm to the Soviet Union. The time has now arrived "to eradicate the cult of the individual as alien to Marxism-Leninism and not consonant with the principles of party leadership and the norms of party life."[25] Khrushchev, however, has evidenced more and more the marks of a strong man despite his conspicuous disavowals of individual rule. Significantly in this respect, the downgrading of Stalin has apparently ceased, and it may be only a matter of time before his re-enshrinement is complete. Soviet experience raises the question whether it is possible for the collective leadership principle to work in a monolithic and totalitarian structure.

SUMMARY

Communism today reigns supreme over a substantial portion of the globe, encompassing within its orbit 900 million people or a third of the world's population. From its beginning in the center of Europe it has come to affect in one way or another every corner of this planet and every individual on it. No phase of human thought or action has been left untouched. States under communist rule control a greater range of human activities than any before in history, with the possible exception of the Nazi and Fascist governments. Statesmen everywhere are acutely conscious of communist power as they undertake to shape the foreign and domestic policies of their countries. No social or political thinker can afford to ignore communist doctrine and its achievements. The seed which Karl Marx planted over a century ago has blossomed forth into a system that poses a major threat to mankind.

The efforts of communism to make reality conform to totalitarian thought involve terror and indoctrination as well as social and institutional reorganization. Unlike the dictators of the past who sought to preserve the status quo to protect their own interests, twentieth-century totalitarianism aims to destroy all traditional institutions and to replace them with a society patterned on certain ideal blueprints. Ideology is used in the form of daily exhortation to give meaning to the unending search for the utopian tomorrow.[26] The task of governing a people is made infinitely easier if the subjects can be induced to accept the ideology of the rulers. The tremendous social upheaval that was brought about by the communist revolution meant misery, hardship, and even death for many. It is well to remember that at the same time soviet

---

[25] The text of Khrushchev's speech has been published in pamphlet form by The New Leader (New York: 1956).

[26] Z. Brzezinski, "Totalitarianism and Rationality," American Political Science Review, Sept., 1956, p. 755.

industrialization and collectivization opened up unprecedented opportunities for many others. Those who have so profited have acquired a self-interest in the new order that prompts close allegiance to it.

Communism preaches a classless society, yet in the process of building this society it has created a new and powerful class of exploiters that will defend its position with desperate tenacity. Milovan Djilas, a former communist leader in Yugoslavia, recently wrote that communism as practiced today is actually a new form of class society.[27] The communist state while pretending to abolish social differences must always increase them by acquiring the products of the nation's workshops and granting privileges to its ruling group. It must loudly proclaim the dogma that it is fulfilling the historical mission of liberating mankind from every misery and calamity while it acts in exactly the opposite way. This is a class, Djilas writes, whose power over men is the most complete known to history. It is the undemocratic control of this closely ingrown group which is the basis of the social power of the communists. The state owns the means of production, the party controls the state, the privileged few run the party. It is unlikely that the new rulers will readily relinquish their posts of great power, for they have too many vested interests to protect. The dialectic remains, but those who pay lip service to it can indefinitely prolong its next operation.

BIBLIOGRAPHY

———— "The Soviet Union Since World War II," Annals of the American Academy of Political and Social Science, May, 1949.

Anderson, C. A., "Soviet Russia and the Nature of Society," Southwestern Social Science Quarterly, September, 1952.

Arnold, G. L., "Stalinism," Political Quarterly, October–December, 1950.

Becker, F. B., "Lenin's Application of Marx's Theory of Revolutionary Tactics," American Sociological Review, June, 1937.

Black, C. E., "Marxism, Leninism and Soviet Communism," World Politics, April, 1957.

Bochenski, I. M., "On Soviet Philosophy," Review of Politics, July, 1951.

Brzezinski, Z. K., The Permanent Purge (Cambridge: Harvard University Press, 1955).

Bullock, A., "Communism in Practice," Speculum, October, 1946.

Crossman, Richard (ed.), The God That Failed (New York: Harper, 1949).

Einaudi, Mario, Communism in Western Europe (Ithaca: Cornell University Press, 1951).

Florinsky, Michael T., "Stalin and Marxian Theory," Current History, April, 1945).

Friedrich, C. J., and Brzezinski, Z. K., Totalitarian Dictatorship and Autocracy (Cambridge: Harvard University Press, 1955).

Haimson, Leopold, The Russian Marxists and the Origins of Bolshevism (Cambridge: Harvard University Press, 1955).

---

[27] The New Class (New York: F. A. Praeger, 1957).

Historicus, "Stalin on Revolution," Foreign Affairs, January, 1949.
Kelsen, Hans, The Political Theory of Bolshevism: A Critical Analysis (Berkeley: University of California Press, 1949).
Koestler, Arthur, Darkness at Noon (New York: Macmillan, 1941).
Kulski, W. W., The Soviet Regime (Syracuse: Syracuse University Press, 1957).
Leites, Nathan, A Study of Bolshevism (Glencoe: Free Press, 1954).
Moore, B. Jr., "Some Readjustments in Communist Theory: A Note on the Relation Between Ideas and Social Change," Journal of the History of Ideas, October, 1945.
Page, Stanley W., Lenin and World Revolution (New York: New York University Press, 1959).
——— "Russian Proletariat and World Revolution: Lenin's View to 1914," American Slavic Review, February, 1951.
Plamenatz, H., "Deviations from Marxism," Political Quarterly, January, 1950.
Selznick, P., The Organizational Weapon (New York: McGraw-Hill, 1952).
Smith, D. G., "Lenin's Imperialism: a Study in Unity of Theory and Practice," Journal of Politics, November, 1955.
Taborsky, Edward, "The Struggle for Stalin's Heritage," Southwestern Social Science Quarterly, September, 1955.
Ulam, Adam B., "The Historical Role of Marxism and the Soviet System," World Politics, October, 1955.
Vishniak, Mark, "Lenin's Democracy, and Stalin's," Foreign Affairs, July, 1946.
Wolfe, Bertram D., Three Who Made a Revolution (New York: Dial Press, 1948).

Chapter XXI

DEMOCRATIC SOCIALISM

"A sound, happy, moral civilization cannot be built up on a basis of evil material surroundings. Poverty, disease, ignorance and slumdom are not only inconsistent with our conviction that there is a divine spark in every man, but they are the certain forerunners of bitterness, strife and war. It is no use to either our personal or our social salvation merely to profess our Christianity and our democracy. We must employ them ruthlessly to create a physical human environment of justice and of decency, in which they themselves will be able to survive and become powerful factors for controlling the future of the world" (Sir Stafford Cripps, *Toward Christian Democracy*).

IN SEEKING to differentiate among the various types of socialism, two basic distinctions can be made: one pertaining to method; the other to philosophical premises. The first depends on whether the brand of socialism is evolutionary and democratic, or revolutionary and totalitarian. If the former, it is referred to as democratic socialism; if the latter, as communism. The second distinction rests on whether the movement is inspired by Marxian philosophy, or by traditional and less doctrinaire principles. Communism is always revolutionary, totalitarian, and Marxist. Democratic socialism is evolutionary, nontotalitarian, and either Marxist or non-Marxist. If it embraces Marxian doctrine, it is referred to as orthodox socialism; or Marxism stripped of its revolutionary aspects.

Socialism, in the democratic sense, has no consistent or uniform doctrinal basis. Whatever unity it possesses lies in its program of social reconstruction rather than in its philosophical premises. The potpourri of thought that has entered into its theoretical formulation has contributed to this result. One need glance only at the diverse elements that have helped to shape its development to realize why doctrinal consistency is impossible. These sources range from socialists who accept dialectical materialism but reject revolution to those who are inspired by ethical idealism; from atheists and rational humanists to religiously motivated individuals and groups.

Today, socialism generally stands for a modified program of gradually reforming the social and economic structure of society by legal and political means. Unlike communism which calls for total collectivism, socialism runs the gamut from a small to a high degree of public ownership. Some of its followers advocate the socialization of natural monopolies only; others insist on the complete abolishment of the capitalistic system. Modern socialism tends to determine on an empirical rather than a priori basis whether, in a particular instance, it will be in the common interest to transfer a specific industry to public ownership or control. In other words, socialism as an inevitable and automatic need has given way to the principle of extending state ownership only when it can be demonstrated that definite improvements in the social order will result. As a contemporary British socialist has observed, "the main task of socialism today is to prevent the concentration of power in the hands of either industrial management or the state bureaucracy — in brief, to distribute responsibility and so to enlarge freedom of choice."[1]

The beginnings of evolutionary socialism have already been observed in the works of the German revisionists. The present chapter is devoted to a discussion of democratic socialist theory as it found expression in Great Britain and the United States. For this purpose, several English writers and one American author, Norman Thomas, will be considered.

BRITISH SOCIALISM

There have been examples of socialism since time immemorial. Communal living and the rejection of private in behalf of group ownership have appeared among various peoples and sects throughout the course of history. Socialism as a major political force, however, did not come into being until the industrial revolution when it arose in the form of a protest movement. As a political philosophy it developed in opposition to a capitalistic economic system with its supporting credo of liberalism. Nineteenth-century capitalism was brutally exploitive and ruthlessly competitive. The social discontent and unrest that it engendered were reflected in the utopian socialist school and later in Marxism.

---

[1] R. H. S. Crossman, "Towards a Philosophy of Socialism," in *New Fabian Essays* (London: Turnstile Press, 1952), p. 27.

Great Britain was the first to precipitate the industrial revolution; it was also among the first to develop socialist ideas. As early as 1799, Robert Owen began his experiments with model communities, and there were strong socialist overtones to the Chartist movement of the early nineteenth century. From the start, British socialist ideas were couched in democratic terms as the character of English political life demanded. Orthodox Marxism, even when divested of its revolutionary tenets, found little reception. England's economic pre-eminence during most of the nineteenth century discouraged the development of socialism. Until the closing decades of the century, Great Britain enjoyed a phenomenal growth of trade and commerce and an unrivaled position as the workshop of the world. The belief in free competition as the regulator of economic relations reigned supreme. From 1875 on, the luster of liberalism gradually dimmed as American and German competition began to cut inroads into British trade and as depressions started to come with irritating regularity. Up to this time, labor and the trade unions had generally supported the Liberal party; but with heavy increases in unemployment, the workers became disenchanted with the party and its policies.

By the early 1880's the liberal-labor alliance began to show signs of disintegration. The socialists and some union leaders were now urging that labor pursue its own independent political course. In 1885 the Social Democratic Federation was founded on Marxian principles, and in 1892 the Independent Labour party was created as a predominantly working class body. The latter was designed to detach the trade unions from liberalism and to establish an independent political party on a class basis. Neither group succeeded in winning over the bulk of labor. It was not until 1906 that the various movements for labor's political independence culminated in the founding of the British Labour party.

Fabian Socialism

While the events noted above were taking place, a collateral movement of considerable importance to the theoretical development of democratic socialism was beginning to win recognition. In 1884 the Fabian society was founded by a group of young middle class intellectuals who had broken away from the Fellowship of the New Life (a small association that had stressed ethical reform and utopian community-making rather than political action). The new society adopted the name Fabian after Fabius Cunctator, the Roman general who had exhausted Hannibal by employing a series of delaying tactics. The organization attracted among its early members George Bernard Shaw and Sidney Webb. Shaw at the time was an obscure journalist and Webb a minor clerk in the colonial office. Under their guidance, the Fabians endeavored to do for British socialism what the philosophical radicals, with Bentham and Mill at their head, had previously done for British liberalism.[2]

The society became definitely committed to socialism with the adoption of its Basis or statement of policy in 1887. This document opens with the announcement, "The Fabian Society consists of socialists. It therefore aims at the reorganization of society by the emancipation of land and industrial capital from individual and class ownership and the vesting of them in the community for the general benefit." The Basis ends with the declaration that Fabians seek to achieve their objectives "by the general dissemination of knowledge as to the relation between the individual and society in its economic, ethical, and political aspects."[3] Later the Basis was replaced by a simple expression of socialist faith which states that the organization "aims at the establishment of a Society in which equality of opportunity will be assured, and the economic power and privileges of individuals and classes abolished through the collective ownership and democratic control of the economic resources of the community. It seeks to secure these ends by the methods of political democracy."[4]

There was no complete unity of thought among the early Fabians except in their opposition to capitalism and in their insistence on the use of evolutionary, peaceful, and democratic means. Some wanted full nationalization, others objected to giving the state such vast powers; some wanted the association transformed into an independent socialist party, others insisted that it was organized for thought and discussion and not for electoral action; some called for closer identification with the Labour party, others believed that such identification would destroy the society's role as an unfettered intellectual force.

For the most part, the Fabians accept the Marxian belief in the inevitability of socialism. Their interpretation of history is essentially economic, laying considerable stress on the tendency toward the concentration of economic power. Yet few of them agree with Marx's doctrine

---

[2] M. Beer, A History of British Socialism (London: G. Bell & Sons, 1921), Vol. 2, p. 276.

[3] Quoted in G. D. H. Cole, A History of Socialist Thought (London: Macmillan, 1956), Vol. III, Part 1, p. 125.

[4] Ibid., p. 127.

that social revolution will be brought about by the increasing misery of the working class. Webb holds a theory of continuity of development from capitalism to socialism but he does not believe that this development is dependent upon a progressive deterioration of the worker's position. He regards the social reforms which are improving the lot of the worker as the beginnings of socialism within the framework of capitalistic society, and he argues that these developments will ultimately lead to public ownership.

The Fabians reject entirely the Marxian concept of class warfare as the instrument of change. Socialism is destined to come into being as the culmination of an evolutionary and natural development in which capitalism will be progressively modified by democratic means. As a community comes to understand that the competitive system assures the happiness and comfort of the few at the expense of the many, it will dispense with private landlords and capitalists. It will also realize that nothing short of common ownership of the means of production can guarantee social justice in human society. The Fabians believe that if the desirability and advantages of socialism are brought home to the people, victory will be inevitable.

Neither Webb nor his colleagues have any illusions about a socialist utopia in which all strife is abolished and each worker gives according to his ability while receiving according to his need. They oppose all pretensions to hamper socialization with schemes for equal wages, equal hours of work, or equal authority. Even after socialism is fully established, the state will remain in existence and each individual will tend to be rewarded in proportion to his capacity and service.

As understood by the early Fabians, socialism does not necessarily mean the nationalization of all means of production under state control. The Webbs, for example, continually stress the need for developing municipal as against national enterprises to the fullest possible extent. They anticipate that a large number of industries will gradually fall into the hands of local and regional rather than national bodies. There are certain industries and services, such as the railroads and coal mines, which must be operated as national monopolies. The remainder can be taken over by local government units — the municipality or county — or when these are inadequate, by regional public authorities created for this purpose. Most Fabians feel that Great Britain possesses the necessary governmental machinery to carry out socialist measures and that no radical transformation in its political organization or structure is called for. The problem, as they visualize it, lies in making proper use of this machinery — from the parish council to the central government — in a manner that will be conducive to the well-being of the whole citizen body. They have no dogmatic preference for complete state socialization, but are eager to explore other avenues and to leave as large a field as possible for local public or even private co-operative enterprise.

G. D. H. Cole, a prominent British socialist and political philosopher, sums up Fabian social and political theory in the following perceptive passage:

> It involved, fundamentally, an identification of Socialism with collective control and planning under the auspices of a democratic parliamentary system. It brought together into a single doctrine the political tendency toward the control of society by a government responsible to a democratic electorate and the economic tendency towards the centralized planning of production, distribution and exchange; and it welcomed these two tendencies as flowing together towards an outcome which could be best described as Socialism.[5]

The Fabians have exerted strong influence on British political thought and practice. They were successful in building a bridge between the socialists and the trade unionists and in preparing the public mind for the acceptance of socialist reforms. As Clement Attlee in the preface to the New Fabian Essays observes, "The British Labour and Socialist movement has to a large extent lived on the thinking of the Fabian essayists and their successors."[6] Similarly, G. D. H. Cole refers to the Labour party as a "larger reincarnation of Fabianism."[7] When Labour took over the Fabian program, the raison d'être for the society's role as an activist group came to an end. The organization still remains in existence but it now functions largely as a home for intellectual discussion, not electoral action.

Guild Socialism

By 1910 some of the Fabians had become dissatisfied with the society's stand on state centralization. Fearing the creation of an industrial bureauc-

---

[5] Ibid., p. 115. The present treatment of Fabian thought draws heavily on Mr. Cole's many writings.

[6] Op. cit., p. vii.

[7] Encyclopaedia of the Social Sciences (New York: Macmillan Co., 1931), Vol. VI, p. 49.

racy, they advocated a form of socialism that emphasized economic management through worker-controlled guilds or associations. In formalizing their position they stressed the importance of two factors: industrial self-government and functional democracy. Agreeing with other socialists that the means of production should be communally owned, they favored worker control as opposed to state management. The chief theoretician of the new group was G. D. H. Cole. When his efforts to channel Fabian policy in the direction of guild socialism proved unsuccessful, he and his supporters withdrew from the society to form the National Guilds League.

Guild socialism views society as an aggregation of associations representing the various interests of the individual. Not only is man "a citizen or subject of his State and of the various local governing authorities within it; he is also related to the social order through many other voluntary or involuntary associations and institutions."[8] Social conflict is inevitable so long as these groups are organized as conflicting units, each concerned with securing as many benefits as possible for its members. To avoid this difficulty, society must be structured on the basis of self-governing organizations of mutually dependent people organized to discharge a particular function. Each guild will include in its membership all those employed in a specific industry or profession — from the directors and general manager to the porters and office boys, from the scientists and technicians to the white collar workers and the unskilled laborers.

In the guild plan of social reconstruction, each association will be completely self-governed by democratic means. Co-ordination among groups will be accomplished not by the state but by a joint council or congress of representatives from each major functional organization. For real democracy is to be found "not in a single omnipotent assembly but in a system of co-ordinated functional representative bodies." The co-ordinating body will be essentially a court of appeals. It will not normally initiate but only decide. "It is not so much a legislature as a constitutional judiciary or democratic supreme court of functional equity."[9]

Guild socialism rejects the commonly accepted dogma of state sovereignty and substitutes for it a doctrine of political pluralism based on

---

[8] G. D. H. Cole, Social Theory (London: Methuen & Co., 1921), p. 4.
[9] Ibid., p. 137.

the concept of function or occupation. Under this doctrine ultimate authority in the community is divided among a number of functional bodies. Although this approach involves a challenge to the prevalent theory of representative government, it recognizes that no man can truly represent other men. All that he can do is to act as the representative of common purposes which he shares with others. "Accordingly, all true representation must be functional; and there can be no single authority representing all the people in all their purposes."[10]

Man as an individual is never represented; only certain purposes common to groups of men can be achieved by lawmaking agencies. Any theory of representation which is based upon the idea that individuals can be represented as wholes is false. One of the major theoretical attractions of functional representation is that it makes no such claim. "It does not profess to be able to substitute the will of one man for the will of many. It merely provides a basis whereby, when the individual has made up his mind that a certain object is desirable, he can co-operate with his fellows in taking the course of action necessary for its attainment."[11]

According to guild socialism, true democracy is not found in a single omnicompetent representative assembly, such as the legislative organ of a state, but in a system of co-ordinated functional bodies. Since an individual has a variety of interests in addition to his means of livelihood, he may belong to several different groups: social, cultural, consumer, and the like. In a functional democracy he will have the opportunity of becoming a member of every association with which his personality or circumstances cause him to be concerned. It is the essence of a genuine democratic system that "a man should count as many times over as there are functions in which he is interested. To count once is to count about nothing in particular; what men want is to count on the particular issues in which they are interested. Instead of one man, one vote, we must say: one man as many votes as interests, but only one vote in relation to each interest."[12]

How does the state fit into the theory of the guild socialists? On this point there is no general agreement among members of the group. Some believe that the state can be reformed to serve as the co-ordinating instru-

---

[10] G. D. H. Cole, A History of Socialist Thought, op. cit., p. 247.
[11] G. D. H. Cole, Social Theory, op. cit., pp. 106–107.
[12] Ibid., p. 115.

ment in society. Others maintain that political government should be abolished and its place taken by a co-ordinating body of functional organizations. G. D. H. Cole at first took the latter position. He indicated that a joint council of representative groups should replace the state. This agency would have the power of coercion and control over the whole law enforcement apparatus. Cole later abandoned his belief that political authority could be dispensed with completely. He then became willing to grant policy control to the state in matters that pertain to the entire community.

The general tendency of guild socialism is to view the state as one of many functional organizations standing on a par with but not superior to any of the other associations. Yet supporters of this doctrine find it extremely difficult to get away from the need for centralized political control. When they set forth their abstract theory, they deny state sovereignty; but when they attempt to devise specific institutional arrangements for the operation of the community, they find it necessary to assign final and supreme power to some agency. They are in definite agreement, however, that under no circumstances should representation on this governing body be based on population and geography, as is the common practice in the modern democratic state. Only function — vocation, occupation, interest — should constitute the basis for selecting representatives.

Guild socialism did not enjoy the same popularity as Fabianism, probably because it remained in high intellectual altitudes with little reference to the everyday course of events. At the peak of its influence it had a membership of no more than 500. There were, moreover, differences of emphasis and doctrine among the members of the group that weakened its internal unity. The protagonists of the various points of view finally came to blows in the period following World War I, and shortly thereafter the whole movement broke up. Some of the guild socialists, including Cole, subsequently rejoined the Fabian society.

British Labour Party

The British Labour party grew out of a number of separate movements that came together at the close of the nineteenth century. In 1900 delegates representing trade unions and socialist organizations met in London for the purpose of establishing "a distinct labour group in Parliament." The conference elected a Labour Representative Committee

(L.R.C.) consisting of representatives from the various participating organizations. Although not a political party in the strict sense of the term, the committee constituted a meeting ground for delegates from autonomous groups that were willing to co-operate in promoting labor legislation. The alliance scored its first notable success in 1906 when twenty-nine of its candidates won seats in Parliament. In that same year the L.R.C. became officially known as the Labour party.

The motivating force of the new party was not so much socialist ideas as a desire for independent working class representation. For some time after its formation the party remained uncommitted to socialism, despite the efforts of its socialist members. The influential trade unions were too permeated with liberalist principles to succumb easily to a new doctrine. They were also suspicious of what seemed to them a theory of economic determinism. However, when the hopes of the Liberal party were shattered by the war, Labour's adoption of socialism became inevitable. Fabian efforts to spread their teachings within the party had been highly successful. Among other things, they paved the way for Webb to gain inclusion of the principle of common ownership in the party's new constitution of 1918. The acceptance of socialism was dictated more by circumstances than by any doctrinaire beliefs. Even though the party committed itself to public ownership of the means of production, it remained permeated with working class theories and assumptions. Lord Lindsay, a prominent British political philosopher, in explaining the development of labor as a political and social force, observes that "what has produced the Labour government is the gradual conversion of the working-class movement to the view that its ideals could not be attained without labour being in office, and without something which, without making very clear to itself what socialism meant, it called socialism."[13]

The goal of the Labour party is defined by its constitution in these terms: "to secure for the workers by hand or by brain the full fruits of their industry and the most equitable distribution thereof that may be possible, upon the basis of common ownership of the means of production, distribution, and exchange, and the best obtainable system of popular administration and control of each industry or service."[14] The

---

[13] F. S. C. Northrop, ed. *Ideological Differences and World Order* (New Haven: Yale University Press, 1949), p. 252.

[14] Quoted in R. T. McKenzie, *British Political Parties* (London: Heinemann, 1955), p. 479.

party recognizes that wide disparities of wealth must be abolished and each individual assured of a reasonable standard of living. It emphasizes that these objectives do not mean equal incomes for everyone. What is important is that those who receive the lowest salaries should have enough to enjoy with the others "the ordinary forms of social life."

Clement Attlee, British prime minister from 1945 until Labour's defeat by the Conservatives in the general elections of 1951, is representative of the large center or moderate faction of the party. His writings are of interest to those who desire an understanding both of the theoretical and activist-oriented aspects of English socialism. Coming from a well-to-do family and educated at Oxford, Attlee typifies the intellectual leadership (or the union between "egghead" and worker) that has characterized the labor movement. In his book *The Labour Party in Perspective,* written before Labour had succeeded in gaining political control, he points out that the party is an expression of the socialist movement adapted to British conditions. The dominant issue of the nineteenth century was political liberty; that of the twentieth is economic freedom and social equality. Political liberty without economic liberty has little meaning. The Liberals failed to see that the industrial revolution made it impossible for the individual to achieve the latter under a capitalistic system. Only by the collective control of the great forces released by modern science can economic freedom be assured to the individual.

Distinguishing the socialist movement in Great Britain from that on the Continent, Attlee points out that the number of English socialists who accept Marxism as a creed has always been small. He acknowledges that British socialism has recognized the conflict between classes as an historical fact, but he denies that it has adopted the theory of class warfare. It is neither Marxian nor revolutionary; it accepts neither historical materialism nor economic determinism. Unlike communism or orthodox socialism, Labour party doctrine has never been narrow and dogmatic. The movement has always comprised people of various outlooks, and the natural British tendency to heresy and discontent has prevented the formation of a code of rigid socialist orthodoxy. Similarly, the movement has always been practical. It has never consisted of a body of theorists or of revolutionaries who were so absorbed in utopian dreams that they were unwilling to deal with the actualities of everyday life.

British socialists from the first have participated whenever possible in the responsibilities of government. They have co-operated with other groups and other parties in the attainment of good government and social goals. The Labour party, Attlee reiterates, has deliberately adopted the method of constitutional action and has rejected the tactics of revolution. If it cannot obtain a majority, it must as a minority accept the will of the majority. It may seek to influence that majority and those to whom it has entrusted power by every lawful means, but to try to enforce its will on a majority by violence is contrary to its democratic faith. If socialism is to be introduced into society, this introduction must be by peaceful and constitutional methods. In Lord Lindsay's words, "the faith of the Labour party shows itself in certain quite simple ways: in its insistence on constitutional methods, its refutation of totalitarianism, its dislike of Communism and the Communist party just because of Communist disregard of constitutional and democratic procedure and of human good faith."[15]

There are strong religious overtones to British socialism. Commenting on the factors that have inspired many to enter the socialist ranks in England, Attlee maintains that first place must be given to religion. He claims that in no other socialist movement has Christian thought had such a powerful leavening effect. The same emphasis on the religious foundations of socialism is given by Sir Stafford Cripps, who served as Chancellor of the Exchequer from 1947 to 1950. Cripps declares that there are two tasks which confront us as human beings: "First, so to conduct ourselves as individual Christians that, in spite of the difficulties of our surroundings, we may work towards the establishment of God's Kingdom here on earth; and second, so to influence and change our social, economic and political environment as to encourage both ourselves and others to take the Christian way of life."[16]

Prior to World War II the Labour party had gained control of the government twice, in 1924 and 1929, but each time it had to rely on the support of the Liberals to give it a majority. In the general elections of 1945 it secured an undisputed majority (393 out of the 640 seats in the House of Commons) and hence for the first time was in a position to put its program into effect. It immediately began to bring under public ownership or direct public control about twenty per cent of the economy. The coal mines, telephones, Bank of England, electric

---

[15] *Ideological Differences and World Order*, op. cit., p. 250.
[16] *Towards Christian Democracy* (New York: Philosophical Library, 1946), p. 16.

power, gas, railroads and other transportation facilities, and some parts of the steel industry were nationalized in rapid order. Operation of these businesses was entrusted to public corporations standing outside the regular ministerial structure. Each corporation was made responsible to a supervisory board of governors appointed by the appropriate ministry.

Nationalization of the basic industries and services has been accompanied by a broad program of social security for everyone "from the cradle to the grave." The program is designed to guarantee a national minimum standard of living for every individual in Great Britain. The system provides comprehensive protection against sickness, unemployment, and old age. Approximately one half the cost of this coverage is met through direct contributions, similar to the Old Age and Survivors Insurance (social security) that American workers pay, and the other half is financed through general taxation.

The Labour party today feels that the objective of social services, to provide an essential cushion of security against hardship due to unavoidable ill-fortune, has now been reached. It also feels that the redistribution of taxable income has gone so far that any large-scale increase of social services would have to be paid for not by the rich but by the broad mass of the population.[17] There is also evidence of a growing awareness in England that the desired social order will not automatically result from nationalization and the planned manipulation of the economy. Many observers feel that socialism has cured the worst abuses of capitalistic society, but that it has not given the worker a new status or a sense of participation in a joint endeavor. While nationalization makes the management of industry responsible to the community as a whole rather than to a group of stockholders, it does not necessarily solve the problem of internal administration. A sharp distinction between the managers and the workers still remains under public ownership. The fact that strikes continue to occur in the nationalized industries of Great Britain indicates that the problem of industrial democracy has not been completely solved nor has the basic distinction between management and worker been obliterated.

AMERICAN SOCIALISM

Organized socialism has made little headway in the United States,

---

[17] See in this connection New Fabian Essays, op. cit., p. 63 ff.

perhaps far less than in any other western democracy. The reasons for this lack of enthusiasm are many. The American economic system under capitalism has been able to provide an exceptionally high standard of living. It has given rise to a strong middle class and to wide shareholding of the nation's wealth. The rapid expansion of the country and its seemingly unlimited opportunities created a kind of Horatio Alger complex among the masses during the nineteenth century. From rags to riches became a cherished dream of the struggling worker. The chance to rise out of class caused each one to look upon himself as a future capitalist or captain of industry. Even when disillusionment came in the latter part of the century, relatively few American thinkers, reformers, or workers called for the abolishment of capitalism. Instead, they demonstrated a remarkable loyalty to the traditional economic system.

The critics who have made the most impression on the American voters are those who have advocated partial reforms directed against particular abuses in the existing system. Although socialism has been rejected, great progress has been made in achieving social, economic, and political reforms. The United States of today is not a nation of unmitigated *laissez-faire*, unbridled competition, robber barons, and social insensitivity — traits that it demonstrated at times during the past.

Socialism of all types — utopian, Marxist, and democratic — has played a part in shaping the critical tradition in the United States. Its influence cannot be measured in terms of the sparse popular support that it has been able to win. By focusing attention on the ills and abuses of modern capitalism, the American socialists have helped to stimulate and fashion many of the reforms that have been incorporated into the nation's economic, social, and political system.

Early Socialist Movements

During its first phases, American socialism was a humanitarian or ethical rather than a political movement. It made no attempt to analyze the processes of production and exchange but devoted itself to formulating schemes of social organization. This type of socialism, utopian in character, deeply influenced many of the New England transcendentalists and led to such experiments as Brook Farm. Stressing the inherent goodness of human nature and the need to abolish unjust social institutions, it urged the establishment of small co-operative communities as a substitute for competitive capitalism. Utopian literature appeared sporadically in the United States throughout the nineteenth century, culminating in Edward Bellamy's literary fantasy, Looking Backward, published in 1887.

The hero of the story, Julian West of Boston, falls asleep on Decoration Day 1887 and awakens in the year 2000 to discover that his native city has been completely transformed into the millennium. Instead of poverty, crime, and selfish competition, West finds beauty, peace, and harmony existing in a co-operative system of production that ensures equality for every man. The state directs all activities of production and distribution, and each individual receives an income generous enough to provide all the needs of life. Coming as it did during a period of social unrest, Looking Backward attracted immediate attention. Over a million copies were sold and its author was hailed as the prophet of the new century. As a popular movement, however, Bellamyism was a failure; it never achieved political importance and was swallowed up by the populist crusade of the 1890's.

The first signs of scientific socialism in the United States appeared shortly after the Civil War. In 1877 the Socialist Labor party, based on Marxian principles, was organized. Daniel De Leon (1852–1914), a lecturer on international relations at Columbia University, became the party's most important leader and theoretician. An orthodox Marxist, De Leon argued that attempts to remedy the defects of capitalism are futile. He urged that the political state be replaced by an industrial commonwealth administered by worker representatives. Under his leadership, the Socialist Labor party sought to win the support of the unions and to convince them that socialist principles should be a condition of membership. For De Leon the road to power demands the organization of a single federation of unions. Once the workers are properly organized, they can compel the capitalist class to surrender power by mere threat of a general strike. The Socialist Labor party, however, had little appeal for the worker; at no time was it able to attract more than several thousand members.

While De Leon was trying unsuccessfully to woo the unions, a new socialist movement developed under the leadership of Eugene V. Debs (1855–1926) who began his career as a locomotive fireman. Influenced by his reading of Laurence Gronlund,[18] Debs was instrumental in giving

---

[18] In his The Cooperative Commonwealth published in 1884, Gronlund undertook to explain German revisionist socialism to an American audience.

a Fabian cast to American socialism. He took a leading part in forming the Socialist party in 1901, and was its presidential candidate five times. In the election of 1912 he polled almost 900,000 votes, the largest number that has ever been received by a socialist candidate in the United States. Under his leadership the party favored social legislation, the right of labor to organize, and the protection of civil liberties. While Debs accepted the need for replacing the capitalistic system, he called upon the party to support fully all efforts to better the condition of the working class. And as an evolutionary socialist, he urged the election of party members to political office in order to facilitate the transition to a socialist society.

Norman Thomas

When Debs died, the leadership of the Socialist party fell to Norman Thomas, a former Presbyterian minister and a brilliant journalist. Thomas rejects the dialectic as an interpretation of history and denies the doctrine of class struggle although he recognizes that men act to a large extent on lines determined by the economic group to which they belong. He believes that there is more hope of achieving democratic control of the state than there is for supplanting or outgrowing it. He is convinced that the free enterprise system is fatally defective and that adequate control of the economy without social ownership or a philosophy of cooperation is not possible.

In A Socialist's Faith, published in 1951, Thomas outlines his position on nationalization or public ownership.

Sound democratic socialism will seek public ownership under democratic control of the commanding heights of the modern economic order. It is neither necessary nor desirable, so long as there is unity of purpose in the main direction of our economy, that there should be a monolithic type of ownership and control. There is a wholesome stimulus in competition, or emulation, and in diversity of functional apparatus. There is large room for private ownership when the owners are serving a useful function, provided that their ownership does not give them undue control over our social life. Public ownership need not be of one type. Generally speaking, the state should be the agency of ownership, and public corporations or authorities of somewhat various types its administrators. But there will be a large place for cooperatives, especially consumers' cooperatives, in the good society.[19]

---

[19] A Socialist's Faith (New York: Norton & Co., 1951), p. 186.

Defining what he means by the "commanding heights" of the economic order, Thomas lists three categories: natural resources, the banking system, and great monopolies. Family farming and ownership of land should be transformed into agricultural collectives. Title to all mineral wealth and to large stands of forest should be vested in the government as the agent of society. The government should exercise much greater control over banks, credit, and investments. Finally, there should be direct public ownership and operation of public utilities and the basic industries such as coal and steel. The owners should be compensated for any industry or property taken over by the government. The nationalized industries would be administered by public agencies similar to the Tennessee Valley Authority.

Thomas has no illusions about the Marxian desideratum, "from each according to his ability, to each according to his needs." He cannot imagine, he states, a fully productive economy in which men may be induced to work without a definite material reward that is subject to variation in order to stimulate good work. He knows of no desirable substitute presently available for the wage system. All that is required is the imposition of certain reasonable restrictions by the state. "While men do not work solely for material gain, least of all unrestricted gain or profit, so long as there is a floor under wages, a deliberate assurance that no wages will be so low as to make a decent life impossible, and a ceiling on fantastic salaries, variations in wages even if they do not perfectly conform to some abstract standard of justice will be a legitimate and valuable element in getting the world's work done."[20]

Like Clement Attlee, Norman Thomas is representative of modern democratic socialism. He stands for a moderate program of gradually changing the existing society into a more co-operative commonwealth by legal and political means. In contrast to Marxism, his socialism is experimental rather than rigidly doctrinaire; it makes no pretense of presenting a complete philosophy of the universe. It is not an end but a tool designed to achieve the common good. Exhibiting strong ethical overtones, it demonstrates a positive regard for the individual by seeking social and economic arrangements which emphasize the paramount position of human dignity. Calling for planning but not regimentation, Thomas would permit a wide private sector of the economy to exist side by side with public ownership. His remarks in this con-

---

[20] *Ibid.*, p. 205.

nection are significant: "I have changed somewhat my opinion of the amount of social ownership that is desirable. I have to recognize that of itself it does not mechanically answer our economic problems and that democratic controls will not come automatically but must be thought out. Yet substantial social ownership in the socialist tradition is basic to a happy solution of problems of production and distribution."[21]

SUMMARY

Democratic socialism plays an important role in the national political life of many western states including Great Britain, Scandinavia, and the Low countries. The socialism that has prevailed in the West has generally been the moderate, non-Marxist, nondoctrinaire type. It has succeeded as a movement for economic and social reform rather than as a political-ideological weltanschauung. In several respects modern democratic socialism resembles a reformed capitalism. The need for economic planning and public control of some sort is universally recognized today as vast industrial and technological developments continue to generate changes in the social order. The basic dispute between democratic socialists and nonsocialists is not so much over the issue of control as it is over the extent and kind of regulation that should be exercised.

Modern democratic socialism calls for a greater degree of social planning, control over the economy, and communal ownership than traditional practices. Yet the basic principle that it employs in making its decisions in each case is analogous to that of subsidiarity. Democratic socialists support the growth and development of lesser associations. They feel that the political community will be healthier when individuals are not lost in one vast society but operate through groups to which they belong as producers and consumers. The state should not be all-inclusive; government should assume only those functions that are necessary to promote the well-being of the community and to secure an equitable and just social order. Clement Attlee warns that in the organization of the socialist state, the danger of overcentralization must be avoided. A socialist government should plan for the whole country but should leave considerable room for local application within this over-all blueprint. A healthy socialist state must have wide regional decentralization and must make a deliberate effort to allow each area to express the individuality of its people.

Socialist theory has no unified doctrine as to the nature of the civil society. While orthodox socialists hold that the state is merely a tool in the hands of the dominant class, many democratic socialists subscribe to the traditional organic view. Norman Thomas, for example, writes that the state developed "in answer to certain obvious needs of men who felt themselves bound by some consciousness of kind." The supreme necessity for successful

[21] *Ibid.*, pp. 3–4.

democracy must be loyalty to a society "which seeks consciously to function as a fellowship of free men."[22] The major elements of the classic conception of the state's nature are here present: the sociability of man, the natural character of political society, and the community of mind and will that unites individuals in a common purpose.

Some socialists regard democracy as the form of government most suitable to man's nature; others consider it the most expedient device for assuring the attainment of the general welfare. All of them maintain that socialism is the logical extension of democracy because of its insistence on the predominant status of man. As Norman Thomas asserts, for those who are concerned with the dignity of the individual, "there is only one standard by which to judge a given society and that is the degree to which it approaches the ideal of a fellowship of free men. Unless one can believe in the practicability of some sort of anarchy, or find evidence that there exists a superior and recognizable governing caste to which men should by nature cheerfully submit, there is no approach to a good society save by democracy. The alternative is tyranny."[23]

Has modern socialism lost its relevancy as a political philosophy? Democratic socialists everywhere are pondering this question as the New Fabian Essays clearly reveal. The situation that confronts socialism today is radically different from that at the turn of the century when the traditional Christian ethic had been virtually sabotaged by modern industrialism. Socialism had then sought to redeem that ethic in the practical order by championing the cause of the exploited and suppressed. While the movement has been successful in its programmatic efforts during the last several decades, its underlying theoretical premise — the incompatibility of capitalism with the general good — has become more and more suspect. Twentieth-century capitalism has demonstrated an amazing facility for reform, while socialism in practice has evidenced signs of weakness. Not only has the lot of the worker in a competitive economy steadily improved but large scale collectivism has failed to solve the management-worker problem. There is also empirical evidence that controlled capitalism can be more fruitful under certain circumstances than pure socialism. Even the socialists now speak in terms of a mixed economy, a private and public sector, rather than in terms of complete nationalization.

There are many, including some of its followers, who feel that socialism has outlived its usefulness. Whether this is true or not, democratic socialism has played an important and crucial role in modern western history. It has . helped to provide the conscience, the program, and the impetus that have changed the character of contemporary industrialism. It has rendered major assistance in holding the line against communism in many of the western European countries; and it has been a strong defender of human rights. If socialist criticism of the social and economic order no longer seems to fit well, it is perhaps because many of its criticisms have resulted in ameliorative action.

---

[22] Ibid., p. 154.   [23] Ibid., p. 146.

BIBLIOGRAPHY

Blum, Leon, For All Mankind (New York: Viking Press, 1946).

Buber, Martin, Paths in Utopia (New York: Macmillan, 1950).

Clarkson, Jesse D., "The Background of Fabian Theory," Journal of Economic History, Fall, 1953.

Cole, G. D. H., Socialism in Evolution (London: Penguin Books, 1938).

Cole, Margaret, "The Fabian Society," Political Quarterly, July–September, 1944.

Davies, Ernest, National Enterprise: The Development of the Public Corporation (London: V. Gollancz, 1946).

Durbin, Evan F. M., The Politics of Democratic Socialism (London: G. Routledge, 1940).

Epstein, Leon, "Socialism and the British Labor Party," Political Science Quarterly, December, 1951.

Gay, P., "Dilemma of Democratic Socialism," Journal of Modern History, June, 1954.

Gray, Alexander, The Socialist Tradition, Moses to Lenin (New York: Longmans, Green, 1946).

Greaves, H. R. G., "Public Boards and Corporations," Political Quarterly, January–March, 1945.

Hacker, Andrew, "Original Sin v. Utopia in British Socialism," Review of Politics, April, 1956.

Hayek, F. A. (ed.), Collectivist Economic Planning (London: G. Routledge, 1935).

Heimann, Eduard, Communism, Fascism, or Democracy? (New York: Norton, 1938).

Henderson, L. O., "Parasites: Perversion of the True Meaning of Socialism," Hibbert Journal, July, 1948.

Herberg, W., "The Christian Mythology of Socialism," Antioch Review, March, 1943.

Kelsen, H., "Foundations of Democracy, Alleged Incompatibility of Democracy with Socialism (Planned Economy)," Ethics, October, 1955.

Knight, F. H., "Socialism; the Nature of the Problem," Ethics, April, 1940.

Lewis, G. K., "Fabian Socialism; Some Aspects of Theory and Practice," Journal of Politics, August, 1952.

Lewis, William Arthur, The Principles of Economic Planning: A Study for the Fabian Society (London: D. Dobson, 1949).

Mack, Mary P., "The Fabians and Utilitarianism," Journal of the History of Ideas, January, 1955.

Rosenberg, Arthur, Democracy and Socialism: A Contribution to the Political History of the Past 150 Years (New York: Knopf, 1939).

Thomas, Norman, "Rethinking Socialism," Virginia Quarterly Review, Winter, 1958.

Ulam, Adam B., Philosophical Foundations of English Socialism (Cambridge: Harvard University Press, 1951).

Underhill, Frank H., "Fabians and Fabianism," Canadian Forum, March–April, 1946.

Chapter XXII

FASCISM

"We have created our myth. The myth is a faith, a passion. It is not necessary that it shall be a reality. . . . Our myth is the nation, our myth is the greatness of the Nation. And to this myth, to this grandeur, that we wish to translate into a complete reality, we subordinate all the rest" (Mussolini, *Fascism*).

THE first half of the current century saw the establishment of totalitarian governments over a substantial portion of the globe. The second half is witnessing a massive struggle between totalitarianism and the free way of life. The conflict is not presently being waged on the battlefield; it is in a stage known as the "cold war," a stage in which the participants are contending for advantage in the fields of armaments, science, and economics. In the 1920's and '30's the chief threat to liberty was fascism;[1] today it is communism. The theoretical foundations of the two systems are different, but the virulent character of their totalitarianism is the same. From the standpoint of political practice, there is little difference between them. Both involve total state control, personal dictatorship, complete submersion of the individual in the community, loss of individual rights, and the repudiation of constitutional government.

World War II marked the destruction of ruthlessly dictatorial governments in Italy and Germany. Non-communist dictatorships still exist in certain countries such as Spain and Portugal but their character is not totalitarian. They resemble more the traditional type of autocratic rule in which little attempt is made to interfere with the social, cultural, and intellectual life of the individual. The fact, however, that fascism has been destroyed for all intents and purposes as an active and major

---

[1] The term "fascism" is used in the broad sense to include both Italian fascism and German national socialism (nazism).

political force does not lessen its importance to the political theorist. It may have been a passing episode in history in the form that it assumed prior to the war. Yet it was an expression, even though extreme and grossly crude, of certain strains and tendencies that had previously been manifested in social thought. It reflected attitudes toward man, the state, and politics that had appeared at various stages of human existence.

Fascist traits such as elitism, charismatic leadership, anti-intellectualism, racialism, and exaggerated nationalism were not unknown prior to the twentieth century; nor have they been entirely eradicated in contemporary democratic society. Fascism of the Italian and German type may have been a caricature, but it provides a graphic example of the consequences that follow when certain tendencies in social and political life are pushed to their extreme. There is no assurance that a repetition of the same problems and conditions which gave rise to fascism in the past will not produce its analogue in the future.

Communism is based on a political philosophy that was carefully developed before action took place. In contrast, Italian fascism and German national socialism were established without any coherent political theory. Even at the height of their success they had no single authoritative statement of principles. There was no fascist manifesto that was universally accepted by the followers of the movement. Only after its founders came into, or were actively seeking, power by sheer opportunistic means and without any carefully defined goals did they endeavor to formulate a philosophical basis or framework for their actions. In view of these facts, it is tempting to say that fascism has no philosophy. What doctrine it has is opportunistic, intellectually dishonest, and lacking in coherence. It is largely a synthetic product put together in reaction to a real state of affairs. Yet it was assembled out of elements that had long been familiar in the West, and in this sense it belongs to the evolution of European political ideas and practices.

Fascism is known as a "rightist," communism as a "leftist" doctrine. The terms "right" and "left" are now stock words in the vocabulary of politics. They originate from the seating arrangements in continental European parliaments where the ultraconservative or reactionary parties sit to the far right of the speaker and the radicals to the left. The closer one approaches to the center from either side, the more moderate the parties or groups become. Fascism is a radical doctrine; but because it poses as the archenemy of communism and because some of its major tenets resemble (although in exaggerated and vulgarized form) those of the ultraconservatives, it is placed at the extreme right of the spectrum while communism is at the extreme left.

ITALIAN FASCISM

Fascism had its immediate origins in Italy during the period of economic distress and political instability that followed in the wake of World War I. Italy emerged from the struggle on the winning side but with few spoils. When the peace treaty failed to satisfy her nationalist aspirations for territorial accretion, disillusionment and resentment set in. As a relatively poor country, Italy had felt the strains of war more severely than either France or England. Her army had suffered great losses and her economy had been virtually crippled. After the war the whole situation was aggravated by a widespread belief among the Italians that their country had been cheated at the peace table. The old ruling class, already discredited by its failure to win more concessions at Versailles, sank lower in public estimation as it proved unable to cope with the explosive economic situation. Political instability, sporadic outbreaks of violence, large unemployment among ex-soldiers and others, widescale poverty, monetary inflation, growing social unrest, and a sense of national frustration, set the stage for "the man on horseback." That role was filled by Benito Mussolini, son of a blacksmith, ex-school teacher, journalist, police-baiter, admirer of Machiavelli and Sorel.

Mussolini (1883–1945) was born in central Italy of lower middle class parents. Prior to World War I, he was a left-wing revolutionary socialist and editor of one of the party's newspapers. During the war he parted company with his socialist colleagues by urging an end to Italian neutrality and intervention on the side of the allies. He argued that participation in the war afforded Italy a rich opportunity for achieving greatness. At the close of the conflict, Mussolini organized a small group consisting mostly of ex-soldiers into the *Fascio di combatimento* or fighting band (fascism receives its name from *fasces*, a bundle of sticks tied around an ax, the symbol of authority in ancient Rome). The new organization had no carefully formulated program. Its leader clearly stated that he relied on intuitive comprehension of situations as they arose and on *ad hoc* remedies to meet them. The accent was on inspired leadership rather than on program. This approach made it possible to appeal to a wide range of interests in the state.

The fascists had little initial success. Not a single candidate bearing their label was elected to the Chamber of Deputies in 1919. Up to this point, Mussolini and his followers had been directing their appeals largely to the workers, but labor for the most part continued its allegiance to the socialist party. After the defeat in the 1919 election, the fascists turned for support to the upper and middle classes. Posing as the defenders of the country against bolshevism and as protectors of the rights of private property, fascist bands began to break up communist meetings and assist in putting down strikes. This change in policy gained many new recruits. Fear of the "red menace" brought aid from industrialists, landlords, and owners of small properties. As a result, thirty-five Fascists, including Mussolini, were elected to Parliament in 1921. By this time, the original movement had been transformed into a full-blown political party. By this time also, appeals to national honor and national glory had begun to wean many workers from adherence to orthodox socialism. The lower middle class was convinced that Mussolini was conservative enough to protect them from being completely dominated by big business. The bankers and industrialists, on the other hand, saw in him a bulwark for their vested interests and a remedy for political instability.

Knowing that he had at least the tacit support of strong interests in the country, Mussolini prepared to strike. Addressing a grand congress of the Fascist party in 1922, he declared that the moment had arrived when the arrow must leave the bow, or the cord, too far stretched, will break. When his demands for a new election or the inclusion of fascists in the cabinet were ignored, he ordered the famous march of the Blackshirts on Rome.[2] In the face of this threat the king hastily summoned Mussolini and appointed him prime minister. As the fascist grip tightened, the new head of government was able to secure from a subdued parliament a vote of unlimited power for one year. Next he forced through a law which provided that the party receiving the largest number of votes in a general election should receive two thirds of the representation. This measure proved its worth in the 1924 elections when the fascists obtained a bare majority of the popular vote but with it two thirds of the parliamentary seats. Thereafter open opposition to Mussolini's

---

[2] The fascists adopted the black shirt as part of their uniform to symbolize the life and death struggle that the wearer had engaged to undertake.

rule withered away. Law after law was passed to make his position more secure. Elections became a farce since only the Fascist party was legally recognized and the voter was given no choice of candidates. Only the semblance of parliamentary government remained; its substance had given way to complete dictatorship.

The Political Philosophy of Fascism

During the period when the fascists were struggling for power, Mussolini declared that their basic need was discipline and not dogma, action and not talk. He insisted that the movement could not be tied down by abstract or formal principles but had to remain free to change its position as the needs of the moment demanded. Once, however, he attained full and undisputed control over the organs of government, he felt it necessary to establish a philosophical basis for his actions. "If Fascism does not wish to die, or worse still commit suicide, it must now provide itself with a doctrine."[3] In seeking to explain the need for a fascist philosophy, an apologist of the system points out that fascism must demonstrate its unchallenged primacy in the world of thought as well as it has shown its pre-eminence in the world of action. Only a philosophy can justify such a claim, for unless fascism "is the material expression of a system of thought, the transformation into reality of a body of ideas and a set of beliefs . . . it cannot advance any claim to a complete primacy in the world of man."[4] Man universally seeks to rationalize his actions even when they are irrationally motivated. He does so either to satisfy his own conscience or vanity, or because he considers it essential to convince others of the validity of his behavior. Mussolini realized that people who believe in a cause which transcends their immediate interests are more willing to make sacrifices. He also knew that dictatorial rule is made much easier if there is common acceptance of a body of dogma that explains and justifies its actions. Even for a dictator, fear and terror are extremely costly devices to secure popular compliance. Whatever Mussolini's motives may have been, he instituted, encouraged, and actively participated in the efforts to fashion a coherent theoretical doctrine of fascism.

The attempt to give doctrinal content to the fascist movement was

---

[3] B. Mussolini, *Fascism* (Rome: Ardita, 1935), p. 33.
[4] Mario Palmieri, *The Philosophy of Fascism* (Chicago: The Dante Alighieri Society, 1936), pp. xiv–xv.

made principally by three men: Alfredo Rocco, a jurist and professor of law who served as minister of justice under Mussolini, Giovanni Gentile, an internationally known neo-Hegelian philosopher who startled the intellectual world by joining the Fascist party, and Mussolini himself. Rocco paved the way for a fuller development of fascist doctrine by endeavoring to show that modern Italy was the spiritual heir of the Roman Empire. Gentile provided a philosophical foundation in terms of idealism for the totalitarian character of state control. Building upon these premises, Mussolini defined the major tenets of fascism in an article which appeared in the *Enciclopedia Italiana* in 1932. As revealed by these three apologists and by other sympathizers, Italian fascism may be characterized as nationalistic, totalitarian, anti-intellectual, elitist, anti-democratic, illiberal, and militaristic.

✓ *Nature of the State:* "The key-stone of the fascist doctrine," in the words of Mussolini, "is its conception of the *State*, of its essence, its functions, and its aims."[5] Fascism conceives of the state as an organism "which has an aim, a life, and means of action superior both in element of power and element of time to the aims, the life and the means of action of the individuals or groups of individuals who compose it." It is invested with the attributes of an ethical personality with an independent will that is dominant over all human activities: "everything in the state, nothing against the state, nothing outside the state."[6] Gentile describes it as an ethical being, which manifests its personality and achieves its historical growth in human society. It is gifted with an organic life of its own which transcends in meaning the life of the individual; its "development, growth and progress follow laws which man cannot ignore or modify but only discover and obey."[7]

This idealistic approach to civil society regards the state as a metaphysical entity with a mind and will of its own separate from the minds and wills of its members. The state is not the land, the people, or the government, nor a combination of these; it is an "idea" which transcends all particular expressions in time, or any contingent and materialistically defined form. The fascist state, to put it simply, is a product of political idealism in its most extreme form. It is the embodiment of an "ethical idea," the divine reason of Hegel working out its "becoming" in time and space. The Hegelian overtones are evident in the following passage written by Mussolini in 1923:

---

[5] *Fascism, op. cit.,* p. 27.   [6] *Ibid.,* p. 40.   [7] Palmieri, *op. cit.,* p. 122.

The work of fifty years of history and, above all, the war have made
finally a nation out of the Italians. The historic task that awaits us
is to make this nation into a national State. This is a MORAL IDEA
which finds embodiment in a system of responsible hierarchies, whose
members from the highest to the lowest feel the pride and the privilege
of doing this particular duty. . . . Our one aim must be the erection of
this single unified being: the Nation-State, the sole bearer of the whole
history, the whole future and the whole power of the Italian people.[8]

State Sovereignty: The fascists contend that democracy turns the
government of the state over to a mass of people who use it to further
their own selfish interests. This practice is gravely in error, they say,
since government should be entrusted to men capable of rising above
their private needs and desires and of working for the social collectivity
in relation to the future as well as the present. Rocco notes that the
great mass of citizens "is not a suitable advocate of social interests for
the reason that the capacity to ignore individual private interests in favor
of the higher demands of society and of history is a very rare gift and
the privilege of the chosen few."[9] Fascism must therefore reject the
dogma of popular sovereignty and substitute for it that of state supremacy.

According to fascist doctrine, the sovereignty of the state is both
absolute and totalitarian in character. As the embodiment of the universal ethical will, the state is actually the creator of all rights; hence
it has full control over the conduct of the people. And as a total philosophy of life, it cannot overlook any aspect of human living. Mussolini
describes the state as all-embracing. "Outside of it no human or spiritual
values can exist, much less have value. Thus understood, Fascism is
totalitarian, and the Fascist state — a synthesis and a unit inclusive of
all values — interprets, develops, and potentiates the whole life of a
people."[10]

Fascism denies that the good life can be realized without the complete supremacy of the state over the individual. A true and great spiritual
life cannot take place until the state has risen to a position of pre-
eminence in the eyes of man, and until the struggle between it and the
individual has finally been resolved in its favor. The state "is absolute,
individuals and groups relative."[11] They have meaning only insofar as

---

[8] Quoted in Palmieri, op. cit., p. 101.
[9] "The Political Doctrine of Fascism," International Conciliation Pamphlet, No.
223, 1926.
[10] Fascism, op. cit., p. 11.
[11] Ibid., p. 27.

they are part of the body politic and subject to its guidance and direction. The individual must make himself completely available to the state and be ready to sacrifice his own personal interests, even his life.

Men find their freedom in full submission to the state's will. If an individual was fully conscious of his great mission in the world and the meaning of human life, he would not need an agency external to his own conscience to dictate his course of action. But man is not so constituted; actually he knows how to use his freedom only for the satisfaction of his own instincts and desires. It is thus high time that he "be brought back to the vision of his true place in the universe; it is high time that he learns how to curb and master his self; it is high time that his freedom be taken away from him if he is to realize the greatest aim of life: the furtherance of the Spirit."[12]

Mussolini insists that the total supremacy of the state over the individual does not mean tyranny. "A state based on millions of individuals who recognize its authority, feel its action, and are ready to serve its ends is not the tyrannical state of a medieval lordling. It has nothing in common with the despotic states existing prior to or subsequent to 1789. Far from crushing the individual, the Fascist State multiplies his energies, just as in a regiment a soldier is not diminished but multiplied by the number of his fellow soldiers."[13] Personal liberty, moreover, is not an end in itself; it is simply a means to the realization of a much greater end: the liberty of the spirit. To be free, in the fascist conception, means to be no longer "a slave to one's own passions, ambitions and desires" but to have full liberty to will "what is true and good and just." It is not the individual, however, but the state that determines truth and justice; hence the individual is free only so long as he conforms to this determination. Man finds his true freedom by obeying the dictates of the state.

Nationalism

In contrast to the internationalism of the Communists, fascism is distinctly nationalistic in outlook. Its nationalism includes an indorsement of imperialism and a moral glorification of war. Some years before

---

[12] Palmieri, op. cit., p. 96.
[13] Fascism, op. cit., pp. 29–30.

fascism became a reality, Georges Sorel, a French syndicalist[14] and a violent critic of democracy, wrote that all great social movements have come about by the pursuit of a myth — an image that can incite human emotion and supply the drive for determined action. Mussolini, who had carefully read Sorel's works, declared in 1922 that the Italians had created their myth — the nation and its greatness. Modern Italy is the spiritual heir of the Roman empire.

The myth of national greatness demanded that Italy again become a great world power — an empire. To do so she had to secure colonies and build up a mighty army. The goal, Mussolini exclaims, "is always empire. To build a city, to found a colony, to establish an empire, these are the prodigies of the human spirit." Imperialism is nothing more than a means by which the spirit strives for expression in the world of man. It is the eternal and immutable law of life. At bottom, "it is but the need, the desire and the will for expansion which every living, healthy individual or people has in itself." Fascism sees in this imperialistic spirit or tendency on the part of nations to expand "a manifestation of their vitality." Conversely, it sees a symptom of decadence "in the opposite tendency which would limit their interests to the home country."[15]

A state that is contemplating imperialistic expansion in modern times must be prepared for forceful opposition. Fascist doctrine recognizes this need by exalting war. Pacifism is a cloak for cowardice, Mussolini declares. "War alone keys up all human energies to their maximum tension and sets the seal of nobility on those people who have the courage to face it. All other tests are substitutes which never place a man face to face with himself before the alternative of life or death."[16] The word man and the word fighter are in fact synonymous. When we speak of war, remarked one Italian fascist, it is the better part of our blood that speaks in us. Nations have the right to exist only if they can successfully compete with other states in the struggle for existence. Only the fit have the right to survive; and in the process they have the right to

---

[14] Syndicalism (from the French word for trade union, syndicat) originated in France during the nineteenth century. It regards the state as an instrument of oppression and calls for its abolition. It proposes that the means of production be owned directly by the workers organized in syndicates or trade unions. Sorel and his followers hold that the objectives of syndicalism can be obtained only through violence and the use of the general strike.
[15] Fascism, op. cit., pp. 30–31.
[16] Ibid., p. 19.

conquer and control the less fit if they are physically able to do so. Social Darwinism is here given expression in the field of international relations.

The Corporate State

As a political system, Italian fascism is characterized by a one-party system, dictatorship, and a set of governmentally controlled institutions known as corporations. Mussolini's socialist background makes him well aware of the close connection between politics and economics. He rejects the class struggle as the great historical force or moving power of human society, but he still believes that a conflict of interests exists between capital and labor. Contrary to Marx's teaching, he holds that this conflict is not irremediable; it is the duty of the state to see that a solution is effected.

Mussolini recognizes that economic relations, like all other aspects of society, cannot be left completely to the free interplay of a competitive system. His social Darwinism is limited largely to the relations among states; it does not extend to internal affairs. When Mussolini assumed power in 1922, he established the policy that the state must exercise a guardianship over the economic life of the people and that in the interests of production no conflicts between employers and workers were to be tolerated. This aspect of the fascist program is based on three assumptions: (1) the state must possess the ultimate authority to regulate every phase of economic activity, (2) the means of production should remain under private ownership, and (3) instead of attempting to suppress class consciousness in the interest of a classless society, the separate identity of both employer and worker groups should be preserved.

As a system that aimed at the complete subordination of the individual to the will of the state, fascism necessarily had to control all economic as well as social and political activity. Mussolini was not an economic determinist, but he realized that the productive forces of the nation must be brought under the supreme discipline of the government if he and his followers were to retain power. Since the fascists had gained control of the state as the defenders of private property against the threat of communism, they made no effort to socialize industry. The Labor Charter adopted by the Fascist Grand Council in 1927 specifically lays down the principle that "private enterprise in the sphere of production is the most effective and useful instrument in the interest of the nation."[17] Government intervention in economic production becomes necessary only when private initiative is lacking or insufficient, or when the political interests of the state are involved. The vagueness of this latter condition leaves the door open wide to public regulation or direct management of business and industry at any time the state sees fit.

To establish effective control over the economic life of the nation, the fascists devised a hierarchical system of syndicates, federations, confederations, and corporations. Through these institutions they sought to give concrete form to the general idea of corporatism. The fascist version of the corporate state provides for two parallel sets of institutions, one for employers and the other for employees. At the base of the organizational pyramid are the local syndicates (unions) of workers and of employers for each major occupational category. These district syndicates are grouped into national federations for each major industry, and the federations in turn are organized into national confederations representing several closely related industries. At the apex of the structure are the corporations (twenty-two in number) which include representatives of both employers and employees. Appointment to membership in a corporation is made by the government from among nominees selected by the various national confederations.

The principal functions of those groups below the corporation are the settlement of labor disputes and the conclusion of collective bargaining agreements. The corporations have the power to regulate production, establish standards of fair practice, and co-ordinate economic relations among the various industrial groups. The basic objective of the corporate state in theory is the establishment of a system of industrial and commercial self-regulation by employers and employees. However, as the system actually operated under fascist control, the corporations were little more than administrative agencies of the state. In fact, the government and the fascist party were so closely associated with the corporations and played such an important part in their decisions, that it became difficult to tell which policies were the result of official dictation and which were due to self-discipline.

Mussolini maintains that corporatism supersedes socialism and liberalism. It inherits from both that which is vital in each. It is opposed to

---

[17] The full text of the Charter is set out in *Fascism, op. cit.,* pp. 133–142. Its major provisions are also quoted in Michael Oakeshott, *The Social and Political Doctrines of Contemporary Europe* (Cambridge: Cambridge University Press, 1939), pp. 184–185.

individualism on the one hand and to government ownership of the means of production on the other. Three conditions are required to carry out the corporate system successfully. First, only a single political party must be permitted "so that rising above contrasting interests all may be bound together by a common faith." Second, there must be a totalitarian state "which absorbs all the energies, all the interests, all the hopes of a people in order to transform and potentiate them." And finally, the nation must "live a period of high ideal tension." Arms must be "crowned with victory; institutions renewed; the land redeemed; new cities founded."[18]

A further step in the development of the corporate state was taken in 1938 when the Italian parliament passed a bill to replace the chamber of deputies with a new body known as the fascist and corporative chamber. The old house had consisted of representatives elected on a geographical basis. The new chamber was composed of ex officio representatives of economic groups, principally members of the twenty-two corporation councils. Theoretically, the new arrangement placed political representation in the legislative branch of the government on a functional basis. The lawmakers were to represent occupations and economic interests rather than districts or localities. Since Mussolini and the party exercised rigid control over all the associations, the Italian experiment affords no basis for an appraisal of a genuinely corporate system. Yet because of the great emphasis that fascist writers placed upon the corporative idea, fascism and corporatism are frequently equated. Such an impression is erroneous since the principle of corporatism or functional representation could conceivably be employed in a genuinely democratic system. How feasible it would be to use this device is quite another question.

NATIONAL SOCIALISM

The rise of national socialism in Germany closely parallels the rise of fascism in Italy. Like the latter, nazism is a product of the demoralization that followed World War I. The loss of German territory, occupation by foreign troops, the burden of reparations, depression, fear of communism, and political instability, all combined to prepare the ground for the rise of dictatorship. The model had already been constructed, the course marked out, and the necessary lessons supplied. The new

---

[18] Fascism, op. cit., pp. 60–61.

"savior" of Germany had only to follow the example of his Italian counterpart.

Adolph Hitler, the founder of national socialism, was born in Braunau, Austria, in 1889. His father was a minor customs official, his mother was of peasant stock. Orphaned at the age of thirteen, Hitler's formal education ended with his failure to graduate from high school. Convinced that he had artistic talent, he moved to Vienna, where he sought unsuccessfully to be admitted to an art academy. Living from hand to mouth among the beggars, vagrants, and criminals of the city he developed a bitter hatred toward everyone around him, particularly Jews. In 1914 he enlisted in the German army, became a corporal, was gassed, and received the Iron Cross, presumably for bravery. After the war, he and a few malcontents formed the National Socialist German Workers' party.

Hitler soon discovered that his greatest asset was his remarkable gift of oratory. In speech after speech he drove home the theme: Germany did not lose the war; the nation was betrayed, stabbed in the back by Jews and Marxists. The Versailles treaty, he shouted, was illegitimately forced on Germany to enslave the fatherland; the German people are not bound by it. Encouraged by his success with the masses and inspired by Mussolini's march on Rome, Hitler overplayed his hand in 1923 by launching a coup d'état, the so-called "beer hall *putsch*," to seize control of the government. The plot was suppressed by the army on whose support Hitler had counted. He was arrested and sentenced to five years' imprisonment for high treason. During his incarceration (he was released after serving only a small portion of his term), he wrote *Mein Kampf*, the bible of the nazi faith.

From the time of his release until 1930, Hitler devoted his efforts to building up the framework of a strong organization on lines similar to those developed by Mussolini. The swastika or hooked cross was adopted as the party emblem and the brown shirt as the party uniform. As late as 1928 the Nazis had made little headway in their quest for power. In the election of that year they captured only twelve seats in the Reichstag. The party, nevertheless, continued to grow in numbers, appealing to the lower middle class particularly, and supported by the large industrialists, who contributed more or less impartially to all anti-Marxist factions. The world economic crisis which occurred in 1930 proved to be the breaking point of the Weimar republic. Assailed from both right and left, as it had been since its inception, the republic was no longer able to weather the storm. In the election of 1930 the nazis became the second largest party in the Reichstag. During the next three hectic years, utmost confusion reigned. Finally, in January, 1933, President Hindenburg appointed Hitler chancellor. From then on the story is a familiar one.

Unlike the Italian version, German fascism developed its political and social dogma during the years that it was struggling for power. The doctrine of national socialism, however, is not based on any rational considerations or supported by any systematic political philosophy. It is less a doctrine than a faith: mystical, emotional, irrational. Beliefs and prejudices that had long been in existence were combined to make a philosophical stew with strong emotional appeal. Condemned by its enemies as a "revolt against reason," national socialism not only accepted but emphasized this description. "We think with our blood." One energetic man is "worth more than a thousand intellectual babblers who are useless waste products of the nation."

The most important statements of Nazi doctrine are contained in two works, Hitler's *Mein Kamf* and Alfred Rosenberg's *Myth of the Twentieth Century*. Rosenberg, an intimate associate of Hitler from the early days of the party in Munich, was editor of the leading Nazi newspaper, *Volkischer Beobachter*, and later civilian administrator of the occupied parts of Russia. With Hitler's support he became the acknowledged intellectual leader of the party, supplying it with a spurious philosophical basis for its racist doctrine.[19] When nazi theory is pieced together, the finished product is similar to that of Italian fascism with two major exceptions: its emphasis on racism and the idea of the *Volk* as the basic political unit.

The Master Race

The racialist character of national socialism has its roots in the writings of such men as Heinrich von Treitschke (1834–96), the great apostle of German nationalism, Joseph Gobineau (1816–82), the French nobleman who first presented the Aryan myth with its corollary of Teutonic superiority, and Houston Chamberlain (1855–1927), an English writer who adopted the racial ideas of Gobineau. Chamberlain's *Foundations*, pub-

---

[19] Albert Chandler's study of Rosenberg notes that he belonged to that group of Baltic Germans who constituted the upper stratum in a Slavic community (Rosenberg was born in the Russian province of Estonia) and who consequently developed a strong sense of their superiority as Germans. *Rosenberg's Nazi Myth* (Ithaca: Cornell University Press, 1945), p. 4.

lished in 1899, is a long and ponderous work that seeks to establish a basis for Nordic supremacy. Hitler and Rosenberg built on these foundations to devise a political philosophy suitable to the new order. Their works and utterances set forth the basic postulates of the race doctrine, a doctrine that constitutes the core of nazi political philosophy.

According to Hitler and Rosenberg, the true foundation of progress is found in the law of nature which decrees that all crossing of species, stocks, or races results in weakness. Just as there is no equality among men, neither is there any among races. Since the strength of a race lies in its purity (it is the will of nature to preserve the distinction among races), the intermixture of two races necessarily results in the degeneration of the superior. All history must be interpreted in terms of the struggle between races rather than classes.

If civilization is to be prevented from sinking into the grave, the Aryan race must be preserved from contamination by inferior stock. All of the state's efforts in education and training "must be to burn the racial sense and racial feeling into the instinct and the intellect, and the heart and brain of the youth entrusted to it. No boy and no girl must leave school without having been led to an ultimate realization of the necessity and essence of blood purity."[20] But what proof is there that the Aryan race is superior to all others? Hitler contends that the evidence is conclusive; that the achievements of the world in art, science, and culture are almost exclusively the creative product of the Aryans. Although he does not give a precise definition as to what he means by the Aryan race, he indicates that it spread out from some northwestern homeland to create the great civilizations of Egypt, Persia, India, Greece, and Rome. He further notes that among Aryan peoples the purest stock, and hence the superior group, is to be found in Germany.

The Nazi Primer, the official handbook for German youth during the days of Hitler, avoids the use of the ambiguous term Aryan (which properly speaking does not apply to races but to a group of language families) and substitutes for it Nordic. The Primer maintains that this race "is uncommonly gifted mentally. It is outstanding for truthfulness and energy. Nordic men for the most part possess, even in regard to themselves, a great power of judgment. . . . They are persistent and stick to a purpose when once they have set themselves to it. . . . They are

---

[20] Adolph Hitler, Mein Kampf, trans. by R. Manheim (Boston: Houghton Mifflin, 1943), p. 427.

predisposed to leadership by nature."[21] While racial mixture has admittedly been going on for a long period of time, the Nordic race is most predominant in Germany and constitutes the principal ingredient of the German nation. This fact "justifies us in taking a Nordic standpoint when evaluating character and spirit, bodily structure and physical beauty. It also gives us the right to shape our legislation and to fashion our state according to the outlook on life of the Nordic man."[22] Tell us to what race a man belongs, and we will tell you what kind of man he is.

The development of the Nordic myth was accompanied by the growth of political anti-Semitism. Even in his early speeches in the beer halls of Munich, Hitler had preached that the Jews were the source of all man's evils. Later, in developing his theoretical attack against the Jews, he condemns them as parasites that feed on the creative forces of other races. The Jew has always been "a parasite in the body of other peoples. That he sometimes left his previous living space has nothing to do with his own purpose, but results from the fact that from time to time he was thrown out by the host nations he had misused. His spreading is a typical phenomenon for all parasites; he always seeks a new feeding ground for his race."[23] Hitler also charges the Jews with trying to undermine the strength of the German nation by intermarriage and conspiratorial action, the latter working through plutocratic capitalism and international communism.

Anti-Semitism, by making the Jew the common enemy of the German people, served a practical purpose for the nazis. It was an effective psychological device to unify the German people by channeling all their antagonism toward a single enemy that was weak enough to be attacked with impunity. It made it possible to transmute a variety of hatreds and fears into the fear of a single tangible foe. Fear of communism became fear of Jewish marxism; resentment against employers became hatred of Jewish capitalism; national insecurity became fear of a Jewish conspiracy to dominate the world; and economic instability was translated into hatred for Jewish control of big business.[24] The patent falsehood of these allegations was immaterial. They were effective in creating the myth of an internal enemy that was threatening the safety and well-being of the

---

[21] Translated by H. L. Childs (New York: Harper & Brothers, 1938), p. 20.
[22] Ibid., pp. 34–35.
[23] Mein Kampf, op. cit., pp. 304–305.
[24] Sabine, A History of Political Theory, op. cit., pp. 890–891.

German nation. Hitler always proceeded on the premise that people fall victim more easily to a big than a small lie.

The German Volk

The idea of the Volk is one of the central themes of nazi doctrine. Hitler in Mein Kampf repeatedly refers to national socialism as the theory of the "folkish" state. The term is not readily translated into English so as to express its full German connotations. The Volk might best be described as a group of men and women united by racial and cultural ties. It is analogous to a nation in that it does not necessarily correspond to the state organization. The German speaking Austrians, for example, were considered part of the German Volk even though they were under the political jurisdiction of the Hapsburg monarchy and later the Austrian state. The German Reich "must embrace all Germans and has the task, not only of assembling and preserving the most valuable stocks of basic racial elements in this people, but slowly and surely of raising them to a dominant position."[25]

Mussolini looks upon the state as more significant than the nation, since "it is the state which creates the nation, conferring volition and therefore real life on a people made aware of their moral unity."[26] To the nazis, the Volk is the more important of the two. Hitler remarks that he is concerned with the state "only as the living organism of a nationality."[27] He sees the betrayal of a nation as a more serious crime than treason against the state. Volk and race are the source and support of the individual and they prescribe organic limits within which he may fruitfully develop his creative powers. The state serves merely as agent of the Volk; it is the means or instrumentality for accomplishing the will of the nation.

Despite the apparent theoretical differences between the fascist and nazi concept of the state, these dissimilarities vanish in practice. The downgrading of the state by the nazis occurred during the period when they were struggling for power. Once they gained control of the government, they began to identify the Volk with the state and to eulogize the latter with almost as much fervor as the Italian fascists. They claimed that their attacks had been directed against the false or legalistic state which stood in opposition to the Volk. The pretender has now been

[25] Mein Kampf, op. cit., p. 398.
[26] Fascism, op. cit., p. 12.
[27] Mein Kampf, op. cit., p. 394.

replaced by the Volksstaat or "folkish" state, which combines nation and state in an organic union. The highest purpose of the new creation is "concern for the preservation of those original racial elements which bestow culture and create the beauty and dignity of a higher mankind."[28]

Within the folkish state, the individual qua individual counts for little. He must always be subordinated to the community and if necessary be sacrificed for it. His position vis-à-vis the Nazi state is made clear in the following statement issued by the government in 1937 to explain certain constitutional changes:

> Since the state consists here of the totality of citizens, united in a common destiny by common blood and common philosophy of life and comprised in a single organization, it is neither necessary nor possible to define a sphere of freedom for the individual citizen as against the State. Hence also it is neither necessary nor possible to protect "subjective rights" derived from such a sphere of freedom by means of constitutional law.[29]

The Cult of the Leader

Just as there are differences among races, so also are there differences among the individuals who comprise the Volk. And just as the best race should dominate the world, so should the best individuals within this race rule the others. The Volk consists of men of different values. Those who are superior in talent and ability must be placed in positions of importance in the community. How is this ruling elite to be chosen? The selection, Hitler says, is a natural process which takes place through the struggle for power, a struggle in which only the fittest survive. Those who are the best jungle fighters will emerge as leaders of the people.

The nazi state is based entirely on personal government. "From the smallest community cell to the highest leadership of the entire Reich, the state must have the personality principle anchored in its organization."[30] In nazi thought, the great body of men are capable neither of intelligence nor heroism; they are simply mediocre. Their highest desire is to find a leader. Der Fuehrer (leader) epitomizes the achievement of this desire. Standing at the head of the national socialist elite and ruling over the

---

[28] Ibid., p. 394.

[29] Quoted in Michael Oakeshott, The Social and Political Doctrines of Contemporary Europe, op. cit., p. 227.

[30] Mein Kampf, op. cit., p. 449.

masses, he represents the "true people," the people as they would be and act if they knew their own true duty and destiny.

The relation of the Fuehrer to the masses is essentially mystical and irrational. He is what Max Weber refers to as a charismatic leader, one who functions as a glorified symbol of a movement and can command the unquestioned obedience and devotion of his followers.[31] He can induce in them an identification with his particular ideology as a cause worth fighting and dying for. Herman Goering, one of the Nazi war lords, describes the deified position of the leader in the following words:

> Just as the Roman Catholic considers the Pope infallible in all matters concerning religion and morals, so do we National Socialists believe, with the same inner conviction, that for us the Leader is, in all political and other matters concerning the national and social interests of the people, simply infallible. Wherein lies the secret of this enormous influence which he has on his followers? . . . It is something mystical, inexpressible, almost incomprehensible, which this unique man possesses, and he who cannot feel it instinctively will not be able to grasp it at all. For we love Adolf Hitler because we believe deeply and unswervingly that God has sent him to us to save Germany.[32]

The leader is no organ of the state in the sense of a mere executive agent but rather the bearer of the collective will of the nation. It is in him that the will of the people is realized. At times it may even be necessary for him to act contrary to the subjective opinions and convictions of the citizens if these are not in accord with their objective destiny. The people must be brought to a realization that the leader is always right (*Hitler hat immer recht*); he can do no wrong. The people need only trust and have faith in him. Constitutional checks and balances are wholly superfluous; they only hinder the leader in working out the destiny of the nation. The nazis employed every conceivable means of propaganda to build up this myth and to indoctrinate the entire population with the new political faith.

The Economic System

Hitler and his supporters adopted the name "national socialism" to indicate that their brand of socialism (a term that had long been synonymous in Germany with social progress) is purely national, as opposed

---

[31] See *post*, p. 476.
[32] *Germany Reborn* (London: Mathews and Marrot, 1934), pp. 79–80.

to the internationalism of Marx. Actually, however, national socialism is not a compound of nationalism and socialism; it is a complete subjection of society to nationalism. This subjection includes full control over every phase of economic activity. In contrast to socialism, the economic order continues to be based on private property, the profit system, and inequality of wealth and income. The owner becomes the leader of the enterprise, the workers his followers. The latter have no right to organize into labor unions or to strike. In turn, the government dictates to the owner what wages he must pay, the number of hours his employees must work, what he must produce or sell and at what price.

No corporative system was attempted in Germany as it was in Italy. To facilitate their control over the economic life of the nation, the nazis established a number of so-called "estates" to apply and carry out governmental policy in this field. These agencies bear some resemblance to the Italian syndicates although their membership consisted of both employers and employees. The largest and most comprehensive of the estates was the Labor Front, to which practically all workers and employers in trade and industry were obliged to belong. The organization made no pretense of representing specific labor interests; it was simply a front to conceal actual nazi control.

SUMMARY

The twentieth century gave birth to totalitarian fascism; it also witnessed its demise. In less than three decades the movement had come into being, flourished, and then expired. An embodiment of naked power, it had repudiated reason, justice, mercy, and peace. It had sinned against humanity, horrified mankind by its brutality, and plunged the world into a catastrophic war. It had employed authority in all kinds of social and private relations and had sought to direct all phases of human life. "We are a state," Mussolini boasts, "which controls all forces acting in nature. We control political forces, we control moral forces, we control economic forces."

Fascism is the antithesis of democracy. Insisting that faith should be put in quality, not quantity, it denies that "numbers as such can be the determining factor in human society . . . it asserts the irremediable and fertile and beneficent inequality of man, who cannot be levelled by any such mechanical and extrinsic device as universal suffrage."[33] Expressing his distrust of the masses, Hitler asks, "must not the task of the leading statesman be seen, not in the birth of a creative idea or plan as such, but rather in the art of making the brilliance of his projects intelligible to a herd of sheep and blockheads,

---

[33] *Fascism, op. cit.,* p. 21.

and subsequently begging for their kind approval. By rejecting the authority of the individual and replacing it by some momentary mob, the parliamentary principle of majority rule sins against the basic aristocratic principle of Nature."[34]

Totalitarianism of both the right and left denies the existence of any objective moral law. To Mussolini the only absolute good is the success of the state while all talk of moral virtue is merely an effective way to sway men to serve your purposes. In a similar vein, the nazis view a moral code as nothing more than a self-disciplining weapon in the community's struggle for power. The authority to determine the contents of this code rests with the state, or to be more exact, with the leader. As one of the official maxims of the nazis reads, "right is whatever profits the German nation, wrong is whatever harms it."

Although fascism is dead, it has not been entirely exhumed. Fascism of the Hitler and Mussolini variety may be a passing episode in history, but in a less violent and more subtle form it still remains a potent factor in contemporary life. The irresponsible politician realizes that in a tension packed society the appeal to national, racial, or popular emotions may carry him farther than the appeal to reason, sanity, and ethics. The demagogue, the anti-intellectualist, the white supremacy advocate, the militarist, the exaggerated patriot, and the book burner, all demonstrate fascist tendencies in one degree or another. These individuals seek to exploit the fears and prejudices that find their way into society during periods of crisis.

BIBLIOGRAPHY

Ashton, E. B., The Fascist: His State and His Mind (New York: Morrow, 1937).

Barth, Hans, "Reality and Ideology of the Totalitarian State," Review of Politics, July, 1939.

Bernard, J., "Power of Science and the Science of Power," American Sociological Review, June, 1950.

Borgese, G. A., "The Intellectual Origins of Fascism," Social Research, November, 1934.

Bowen, Ralph H., German Theories of the Corporate State (New York: Whittlesey House, 1947).

Brady, Robert A., The Spirit and Structure of German Fascism (New York: Viking Press, 1937).

Chagnon, Louis, "Marxism and Materialist Philosophy," The Modern Schoolman, May, 1939.

Collingwood, R. G., The New Leviathan (Oxford: Clarendon Press, 1942).

De Gré, G., "Fascist: An Operational Definition," Social Forces, December, 1945.

Dutt, R. Palme, Fascism and Social Revolution (New York: International Publishers, 1935).

---

[34] Mein Kampf, op. cit., pp. 79–80.

Ebenstein, William, Fascist Italy (New York: American Book Co., 1939).
Edwards, A. L., "Signs of Incipient Fascism," Journal of Abnormal Psychology, July, 1944.
Elbow, M. H., French Corporative Theory, 1789–1949 (New York: Columbia University Press, 1953).
Elliott, William Y., The Pragmatic Revolt in Politics (New York: Macmillan, 1928).
Field, G. L., "Comparative Aspects of Fascism," Southwestern Social Science Quarterly, March, 1940.
Finer, Herman, Mussolini's Italy (London: V. Gollancz, 1935).
Florinsky, M. J., Fascism and National Socialism (New York: Macmillan, 1936).
Fromm, Erich, Escape from Freedom (New York: Farrar and Reinhart, 1941).
Gerth, H. H., "The Nazi Party," American Journal of Sociology, January, 1940.
Gooch, G. P., Dictatorship in Theory and Practice (London: Watts, 1935).
Greef, Etienne de, "Psychology of the Totalitarian Movement," Review of Politics, March, 1939.
Heberle, Rudolph, From Democracy to Nazism (Baton Rouge: Louisiana State University Press, 1945).
Kaufmann, F. W., "Fichte and National Socialism," American Political Science Review, June, 1942.
Murphy, E. F., "Philosophy of the Fascist State," Proceedings of the American Catholic Philosophical Association, 1933.
Nathan, Peter, The Psychology of Fascism (London: Faber, 1943).
Neumann, Franz, The Democratic and the Authoritarian State (Glencoe: Free Press, 1957).
Parsons, Talcott, "Some Sociological Aspects of the Fascist Movements," Social Forces, December, 1942.
Ranulf, S., "Scholarly Forerunners of Fascism," Ethics, October, 1939.
San Severino, B. (ed.), Mussolini as Revealed in His Political Speeches (New York: E. P. Dutton, 1923).
Sillani, Tomaso (ed.), What is Fascism and Why (London: Ernest Benn, Ltd., 1931).
Smith, T. V., "Ethics of Fascism," International Journal of Ethics, January, 1936.
Sturzo, Luigi, "The Totalitarian State," Social Research, May, 1936.
Vignaux, Paul, "Corporativism in Europe," Review of Politics, April and July, 1942.
Voegelin Eric, "The Growth of the Race Idea," Review of Politics, July, 1940.
Wagener, A. P., "Classical Background for Fascism," Classical Journal, June, 1928.
West, Rebecca, The Meaning of Treason (New York: Viking Press, 1947).
Williamson, R., "Fascist Concept of Representation," Journal of Politics, February, 1941.
Woolf, Leonard, "Hitler's Psychology," Political Quarterly, October–December, 1942.
Yarrow, Clarence H., "The Forging of Fascist Doctrine," Journal of the History of Ideas, April, 1942.

and charismatic. His purpose in introducing this classification is to formulate a conceptual scheme within which political power can be meaningfully examined. The classification is based on the claim to legitimacy that is made by each type of authority. The nature of this claim determines the kind of obedience that is rendered to a particular system of authority, the kind of administrative staff that is developed to guarantee its continued existence, and the mode in which it is exercised.

The three types are abstract constructs; none of them exists in pure form in concrete cases. But the fact that they are not so found, Weber points out, is "not a valid objection to attempting their conceptual formulation in the sharpest possible form. . . . Analysis in terms of sociological types has, after all, as compared with purely empirical historical investigation, certain advantages which should not be minimized. That is, it can in the particular case of a concrete form of authority determine what conforms to or approximates such types."[4]

Rational or legal authority rests on a belief in impersonal rules or norms and in the right of those who gain power under such rules to issue commands. This type is approximated in western society. Obedience is owed to those exercising authority only by virtue of the office they occupy, and only within the scope of authority of that office. Both the office and its powers are established and defined by law. The person who obeys such authority does so in his capacity as a member of the corporate group; what he obeys is the law — an impersonal order. How this or the other kinds of authority come into existence is not important. "What is important is the fact that in a given case the particular claim to legitimacy is to a significant degree and according to its type treated as valid; that this fact confirms the position of the persons claiming authority and that it helps to determine the choice of means of its exercise."[5]

In contrast to the first type, traditional authority is based on belief in the sanctity of immemorial traditions and the legitimate status of those exercising power under them. The object of obedience is not enacted laws but the person who occupies a position of authority by tradition, such as an hereditary monarch. His commands are legitimized partly in terms of traditions which determine the object and limits of his power. When resistance by the subjects occurs, the opposition is not directed against the system as such but against the person of the ruler on the grounds that he has failed to observe the traditional limits of his authority.

[4] *Ibid.*, p. 329.   [5] *Ibid.*, p. 327.

Similarly, so long as the holder of power does not act contrary to the traditional order, loyalty is due to him personally and not to the system.

Weber defines charisma (a term previously referred to in connection with dictatorship)[6] as "a certain quality of an individual personality by virtue of which he is set apart from ordinary men and treated as endowed with supernatural, superhuman, or at least specifically exceptional powers or qualities."[7] When an individual who possesses these attributes is recognized and treated as a leader by the people, charismatic authority arises. This recognition, which entails complete personal devotion to the leader, may be motivated by enthusiasm or by despair and hope. Gandhi, Mussolini, and Hitler are recent examples of charismatic leaders.

Charisma originates as a revolutionary force setting up the authority of an individual against the established order. Since the social and political relationships which it creates are strictly personal and based on devotion to an individual, this type of authority cannot become stabilized without becoming radically changed. The problem of succession inevitably arises when the original leader dies, and unless the method of choosing his successor is institutionalized, a struggle for power is certain to ensue within the movement. But once the method is institutionalized either by law or custom, charismatic authority begins to take on some of the aspects of rational or traditional authority.

EMILE DURKHEIM

Émile Durkheim (1858–1917) was born of Jewish parents in Epinal, Lorraine, on the northeastern frontier of France. In 1879, he entered the École Normale Supérieure de Paris, where he studied under the noted historian Fustel de Coulanges. After traveling in Germany, he taught social science and pedagogy in the Faculté de Lettres at Bordeaux. Later he accepted the first chair in sociology and education at the Sorbonne. In 1896, he founded and became editor of L'année sociologique, which served for many years as the leading French sociological journal. His major works include The Division of Labor in Society (1893), The Rules of Sociological Method (1897), and Suicide (1897).

Durkheim is interested primarily in problems of social structure and social control. He concentrates his attention on the general relations of the individual to the social group. His intellectual mentor is Comte,

---

[6] See ante, p. 467.
[7] The Theory of Social and Economic Organization, op. cit., p. 358.

from whom he inherits the two central tendencies which dominate his thinking: positivism, and the emphasis on the group in the determination of human conduct. So strong is this latter tendency that he constantly endeavors to develop the theme that society exists outside of and above individuals.

Methodology

The methodology employed by Durkheim has three distinct characteristics. It is completely independent of philosophy; it is dominated entirely by the idea that social facts are things and must be treated as such; and it is exclusively sociological.

Consistent with his positivistic orientation, Durkheim begins his study of society by denying the assumption that sociology must rest on philosophic premises. However, he is not content to reject the main philosophical traditions as unscientific, but he attempts to substitute a new philosophy based on the results of the new science of society. This science will not only advise us as to the best means of achieving social objectives but will also, through scientific observations of empirical data, select the ends which ought to be pursued. For this purpose Durkheim adopts the criterion of "normality," which he identifies with the average type. Deviations from what is general in society are, therefore, pathological.

Durkheim vigorously insists that social facts must be treated as observable objects of the external world. To study these facts the social scientist must put himself in the same state of mind as the physicist, chemist, or physiologist when he probes into a still unexplored region of the scientific domain. Because we have failed to follow this procedure "we really do not even know what are the principal social institutions, such as the state or the family; what is the right of property or contract, of punishment and responsibility. We are almost completely ignorant of the factors on which they depend, the functions they fulfill, the laws of their development."[8]

According to Durkheim, the substance of social life cannot be explained by psychological factors. He decries what he considers the unwarranted intrusions of psychology into the domain of sociology. If sociology is to merit the title of science, three prerequisites must be met. Social facts must be viewed as "things"; they must be considered me-

---

[8] *The Rules of Sociological Method*, ed. by G. Catlin (Glencoe: Free Press, 1938), pp. xlv–xlvi.

chanically determined; and they must be explained in terms of other social facts, and not in terms of biology or psychology. In short, human institutions and human behavior must be examined as the products of mechanical social causes.

Introducing an organic concept of society, Durkheim distinguishes the collective from the individual mind. The mentality of the group is not the same as that of its members. "The group thinks, feels and acts quite differently from the way in which its members would were they isolated."[9] The study of society, therefore, should begin with the examination of group phenomena, and not with the individual as Aristotle had done. For if we begin with the individual, "we shall be able to understand nothing of what takes place in the group." Psychology is of little use in understanding social behavior since it deals with individual consciousness. Sociology, on the other hand, is involved with collective consciousness which has a reality of its own.

Durkheim holds that the comparative method is the only one suited to social science. Only by comparing cases in which certain phenomena are simultaneously present or absent is it possible to demonstrate that one is the cause of the other. The proper mode of discovering causal relations is by a process of correlation. When two phenomena constantly accompany each other, the investigator can assume a relationship between them. He can then seek to determine by the aid of deduction how one of the two terms has produced or caused the other. Next, he can try to verify the result of this deduction, with the aid of new comparisons. As soon as he has proved in a certain number of cases that two phenomena vary with one another (for example, the more education a person has, the more likely he is to vote), he has established a tentative causal relationship which can be subjected to further testing. History is central to this process since it provides much of the data for comparative analysis.

Durkheim's study of suicide provides an excellent example of systematic empirical research in the social sciences. The work starts out by refuting previous attempts to explain variations in the rate of suicide in terms of climatic, geographic, racial, or psychological factors. This refutation is undertaken through an extensive statistical analysis of suicide rates in various segments of European populations. Durkheim then shows that different rates of suicide are the results of social factors. He identifies

---

[9] *Ibid.*, p. 104,

three principal types of suicide — egoistic, altruistic, and anomique — and shows that each is due to differences in the degree of social cohesion that exists in a society. Thus there is a higher rate of suicide among single and divorced than married people, since family life creates stronger bonds of cohesion. Also, in time of war there are fewer suicides, since a society generally draws closer together in response to an external threat.

Political Sociology

Durkheim's concern with institutions as they relate to the problem of social control leads him into the field of political theory. Here he seeks to demonstrate the importance of the group to political life and to lay the theoretical basis for functional representation. His major thesis is that the social mind exerts a strong constraining force on the individual. Its efficacy, however, depends largely on the degree of solidarity or cohesion that exists in the group. If the ties that bind the members together are weak, the group's control over individual behavior will be correspondingly ineffectual.

Durkheim distinguishes two principal types of social solidarity: mechanical and organic. The first is characteristic of primitive societies, where people are relatively homogeneous and where individual mentality and initiative are almost completely blanketed out by the common life of the group, with its rigid customs, taboos, and traditions. The second is found in civilized societies, where the division of labor has led to dissimilarities among the members by introducing different functions, specialities, and experiences. In this type of community the differences among individuals become as important as similarities were in the old society. Law remains as an instrument of control but its function now is to blend people into a differentiated but well-integrated nexus, whereas its former function was to impose similarities upon the group. Presumably, the binding force in the new society is rooted in the need which the people have for each other.

The transfer from mechanical to organic solidarity has given rise to difficulties in social control. The relationships of modern life are extremely complicated. Accustomed from time immemorial to authoritative control by the family, tribe, church, or government, the individual finds it difficult to adjust to the new conditions which give him a larger area of freedom and discretion, but yet make his security more precarious. As the influence of the old institutions has declined and the state has grown more impersonal with its increase in size, no closely knit group has remained to impose a moral discipline on the individual. Homogeneity has been lost, while organic solidarity has not developed sufficiently to furnish the individual with guidance. This lack of cohesion is reflected in growing crime rates, suicides, class struggles, and general social maladjustment.

In his *Division of Labor in Society*, Durkheim maintains that the most disturbing feature of modern society is the virtually anarchical conditions which exist in economic affairs. Although economic activities constitute an important aspect of an individual's life, there are no regulations or fixed customs to guide his behavior. Disputes between employer and employee are resolved according to the relative strength of the parties. One possible remedy for this condition is state regulation, but governmental machinery is poorly adapted to handle the highly specialized and intricate matters involved in economic activities and relations.

Durkheim believes that the solution to the problem of social control in modern society lies in enlarging the role of functional or occupational groups. He points to the effective constraint that professional organizations, such as legal and medical associations, exert over their members. Such groupings are well adapted to enforce social control. They are more agreeable to the individual than governmental regulation; they are closer to him and less impersonal; and they permit him to associate more easily and directly his own interests with those of the group. Durkheim argues for the creation of a nonpolitical regulatory body with legal power to deal with the problems of modern industrial life. This agency would be separate from the state although subject to its general supervision. It would be selected by separate syndicates of workers and employers in each industrial category and would have broad authority to regulate economic affairs. The individual syndicate would also be endowed with sufficient authority to enter actively into the regulation and direction of the personal life of its members.

The proposal to give occupational groups a major role in government is not original with Durkheim: the idea had long existed in various forms among political thinkers. The modern political scientist is not interested in Durkheim's recommendations for governmental reorganization but in the general approach or methodology which he employs in formulating them. By first devising a general theory of social control on the basis of empirical research, he establishes a conceptual framework for analyzing concrete political structures. This framework provides him with a means of discovering the strength and weakness of existing political systems from the viewpoint of social cohesion. With this knowledge, he is then able to make proposals for improving institutional arrangements in order to achieve greater social stability.

VILFREDO PARETO

Vilfredo Pareto (1848–1923) was born in Paris. His father was an Italian nobleman who had been exiled from Genoa as a supporter of Mazzini. When Pareto was eleven, his family returned to Italy and settled in Turin. He studied engineering there and followed this profession for some time after his graduation from a polytechnical institute. When he was in his early thirties, he received an inheritance which enabled him to devote his time to study and research. In 1893 he was appointed to a professorship in economics at the University of Lausanne, Switzerland, where Mussolini was one of his students. During his early years at Lausanne he did outstanding work in mathematical economics. Later he turned to sociology, feeling the need for a broader science to supplement his economics. His major work is *A General Treatise on Sociology*.[10]

Methodology

From mathematical economics, Pareto had but a short step to take to a social science in which social and political relationships are described in quantitative terms. His approach, as might be anticipated, is purely empirical. Only observation and experimentation can be taken as guides to the study of social phenomena. Anything beyond this cannot become the object of science. No speculation or moralizing, no *a priori* element or principle, can be permitted to influence the study. Progress in the social sciences calls for precision in terminology and the quantitative expression of social facts. Although Pareto admits that mechanical conceptualizations are not entirely adequate when applied to social reality, he loses sight of these limitations as he proceeds with his work.

The inductive method employed by Pareto involves the comparison of large numbers of similar data, to separate the constant from the variable

---

[10] An English translation of this work is available under the title *Mind and Society*, edited by A. Livingston, 4 vols. (New York: Harcourt Brace, 1935).

elements. He begins by distinguishing between logical and nonlogical actions. An action is logical if its end is objectively attainable, not only from the point of view of the actor but also for those who have a more extended knowledge. All other actions are nonlogical, and it is these which predominate in social life. "There are certain principles of non-logical conduct from which human beings deduce their laws. Such principles of nonlogical conduct are correlated with the conditions under which human beings live, and change with those conditions."[11]

The import of this argument is that men usually act first and then find reasons for their actions. The nonlogical elements in human behavior are the constant while the logical are the variable factors. There is in human conduct "on the one hand an instructive, nonlogical element that is constant; on the other, a deductive element that is designed to explain, justify, demonstrate, the constant element."[12]

The greater part of Pareto's treatise on sociology is devoted to a classification of the nonlogical factors that motivate men. Since these factors or drives are constant, they are the same in every society. Pareto refers to them as residues and to the logical or variable elements as derivations. The residues are "the manifestation of instinct and senti-ments as the elevation of mercury on a thermometer is the manifestation of a rise in the temperature."[13] Although he discusses some fifty different residues and divides them into six principal classes, only two classes are relevant for our purposes: combination and group persistences. These provide the two poles of his theory of social dynamics. The first results from combining certain things in our thinking, usually with no logical justification, such as always associating good with democracy or progress. The second implies that by a sort of inertia established customs or beliefs are clung to with great stubbornness and tenacity.

Derivations are the surface manifestations of residues or the under-lying forces in human life. They are ideologies, as it were, by which men seek to rationalize their conduct and beliefs; and as such they constitute the variable factors in human behavior. One of the residues, for example, involves the drive in individuals to impose their own standards of conduct and beliefs on others. This drive is the same whether in the religious or political fanatic; yet in each case, the residue is cloaked in a different

---

[11] *Mind and Society*, *op. cit.*, I, 407.
[12] *Ibid.*, II, p. 845.
[13] *Ibid.*, II, p. 875.

form or derivation. The rationale of the religious zealot is quite different
from that of the political ideologist.

Political Sociology

Pareto's analysis of residues and derivation forms the basis for his
substantive theories of social and political life. Residues of combination
and persistence are distributed unequally among individuals and social
groups. There are those with strong residues of the first class and others
with numerous residues of the second type. The character of the predominant residue greatly influences the personality and behavior of the
individual group. Associated with the residue of combinations are qualities of innovation and scheming. The tendency of those in whom this
residue is strong is to seek attainment of their ends by cleverness and
resourcefulness, and to circumvent rather than boldly face obstacles.
These individuals, whom Pareto refers to as *speculators,* are the entre-
preneurs who are always contemplating some new combination, whether
in business or politics. Persons strong in the residue of persistence, who
are called *rentiers,* are conservative, strong-willed, and decisive in action.
Suspicious of innovation, they try to preserve and maintain that which
already exists.

Based on the distinction between the two types of residues, Pareto
formulates his famous theory of the circulation of elites. He first divides
society into two classes, elite and non-elite. The elite are those who greatly
excel the masses in any particular field. They are determined by a system
of measurement in which each individual is ranked on a scale of one to
ten according to his capacity as a statesman, lawyer, author, businessman,
and so on — each person being compared with others in the same field.
The elite, in turn, are divided into the governing class, comprising those
who directly or indirectly play important roles in the manipulation of
political power; and the nongoverning elite, consisting of capable men
who are not involved to any major degree in the political process.

The character of government in a state will be determined largely
by which residue prevails among the ruling elite. If those with strong
combinations are in power, social and economic innovations can be expected. This group retains the support of the masses through various
humanitarian schemes and democratic machinations. When the *rentiers*
are in control, little change takes place, opposition is suppressed by force,
and government assumes dictatorial characteristics.

Having formulated his theory of residues and derivations, Pareto proceeds to analyze the dynamic structure of society which he calls social equilibrium. He concludes that an aristocracy of leadership is essential to an ordered society, and that change is ultimately effected in social equilibrium by changes in leaders. When new leaders with different type residues infiltrate the ruling class, modifications in the social system are inevitable. Usually the transformation takes place over a period of time, but on occasions it can be abrupt and violent.

> In virtue of class-circulation, the governing elite is always in a state of slow and continuous transformation. It flows on like a river, never being what it was yesterday. From time to time sudden violent disturbances occur. There is a flood — the river overflows its banks. Afterwards the new governing elite again resumes its slow transformation.[14]

When the *rentiers* hold the reins of government, their willingness to use force enables them to remain in power. However, this situation does not prevail indefinitely, since there is a natural and continual process of circulation of the elite. A governing class that is strong in persistence residues finds that the continued use of force to maintain power has serious disadvantages. It is costly in terms of maintaining order, and it lowers economic production by destroying the loyalty of the masses. Consequently, the tendency is for the rulers to turn more and more to combinations or ruse as a means of governing. This reorientation leads to the incorporation into the ruling class of those skilled in the art of manipulation. In this way, power gradually becomes transferred from the *rentiers* to the *speculators*. The cycle then continues since the unwillingness of the new rulers to use force permits those strong in persistence residues to organize and eventually to challenge the governing elite. On the basis of this analysis, society might be characterized as a system in imperfect equilibrium.

SUMMARY

Weber, Durkheim, and Pareto are representative of the contemporary attempt to raise the study of society to the scientific level of the other disciplines. In their thinking, social and political theory implies some conceptual scheme of relationships which can serve as a basis for interpreting social behavior and institutions. The modern theorists who attempt to explain political phenomena solely in terms of power exemplify this general approach. Today,

---

[14] *Ibid.*, III, p. 2056.

however, most of those working in the field of social science no longer attempt to present an all-inclusive systemization of political theory by constructing it around some basic or cosmic force in the total social process. Instead there are more intensive studies of various aspects of society and the formulation of a series of lesser theories — "theories of the middle range" — with the hope that these will ultimately grow into an all embracing theory.[15]

The methodology employed by modern theorists emphasizes the distinction between the scientific and the moral approach to the social sciences, insisting that these two considerations be kept separate in studying social and political relations. There is wide recognition that empirical research, with its focus on causal theory formulation, holds a rightful place in political science. As several writers pointed out in a recent symposium on the practical uses of political theory, there is no reason to object to the employment of quantitative methods or to deny the validity and significance of their results. It is only when the character of man as free moral agent is equated to the realm of physical things, and the quantitative approach to politics held out as the only scientific and promising one, that doubts begin to rise. For how can a purely descriptive theory of political behavior fulfill the normative function of setting the goals of political society?[16]

To ignore the contemporary work in political science would be shortsighted; to shun traditional political philosophy extremely foolish. Man lives in an increasingly complex political world. At no other time in human history has he held within his grasp the weapons of total annihilation. The need for sound political theory in such a milieu is great and compelling. The accumulated wisdom of the past must be joined with modern findings and techniques in efforts to adapt political theory to the demands of a global and nuclear age.

BIBLIOGRAPHY

Ascoli, Max, "Pareto's Sociology," Social Research, February, 1936.
Barnes, Harry E., An Introduction to the History of Sociology (Chicago: University of Chicago Press, 1948).
Becker, Howard, and Barnes, H. E., Social Thought from Lore to Science (Washington, D. C.: Harren Press, 1952), 2 vols.
Bendix, Reinhard, "Social Stratification and Political Power," American Political Science Review, June, 1952.
Bongiorno, Andrew, "A Study of Pareto's Treatise on General Sociology," American Journal of Sociology, November, 1930.
Cox, Oliver, "Max Weber on Social Stratification," American Sociological Review, April, 1950.
Gouldner, A. W., "Theoretical Requirements of the Applied Social Sciences," American Sociological Review, February, 1957.

---

[15] For a discussion of this question see N. S. Timascheff, "Sociological Theory Today," American Catholic Sociological Review, Mar., 1950.

[16] See Hans Jonas, "The Practical Uses of Theory," Social Research, Summer, 1959; and the accompanying comments by S. E. Asch, Erich Hula, and Adolph Lowe.

Heberle, Rudolph, *Social Movements* (New York: Appleton Century Crofts, 1950).

Henderson, L. J., *Pareto's General Sociology* (Cambridge: Harvard University Press, 1935).

Hunter, Floyd, *Community Power Structure* (Chapel Hill: University of North Carolina Press, 1953).

Hyneman, Charles S., *The Study of Politics* (Urbana: University of Illinois Press, 1959).

Laswell, Harold, and Kaplan, A., *Power and Society* (New Haven: Yale University Press, 1950).

MacIver, Robert, *The Web of Government* (New York: Macmillan, 1947).

Merton, Robert K., "Sociological Theory," *American Journal of Sociology,* May, 1945.

Michels, Roberto, *First Lectures in Political Sociology,* trans. by Alfred de Grazia (Minneapolis: University of Minnesota Press, 1949).

Parsons, Talcott, *The Structure of Social Action* (Glencoe: Free Press, 1949).

Seligman, Lester, "The Study of Political Leadership," *American Political Science Review,* December, 1950.

Schumpeter, Joseph, "Vilfredo Pareto," *The Quarterly Journal of Economics,* May, 1949.

Sorokin, Pitirim, *Contemporary Sociological Theories* (New York: Harper, 1928).

Timasheff, N. S., "Law in Pareto's Sociology," *American Journal of Sociology,* September, 1940.

————— "Sociological Theory Today," *American Catholic Sociological Review,* March, 1950.

Appendix

SUPPLEMENTARY READINGS

THE following list of selections from the original works of the major political theorists offers suggestions for supplementary reading to accompany the text. Paperbacks and other inexpensive editions are cited whenever available. The list of editions is representative but not complete.

Chapter I
Since the first chapter is introductory in character, no specific selections are suggested. The journal articles listed in the selected bibliography for the chapter deal with various aspects of the material covered therein. A more extended bibliography of pertinent articles is found in Charles S. Hyneman, *The Study of Politics* (Urbana: University of Illinois Press, 1959), pp. 211–225.

Chapter II
Thucydides, *The Peloponnesian War*, Book II, Ch. VI, 33–47; Book IV, Ch. XVII.
Modern Library Edition (New York: Random House).

Chapter III
Plato, *The Republic*, Books II; III (412–418); IV; V; VI (500–504); VII (514–512, 535–542); VIII; IX (571–584).
Modern Library Edition (New York: Random House).
Everyman's Library (New York: Dutton).
Mentor Book (New York: New American Library), paperback.
Oxford University Press (New York), paperback.

OTHER RELEVANT WORKS:

Plato, *The Statesman* (New York: Library of Liberal Arts), paperback, published by Liberal Arts Press.
Excerpts from Plato's *Seventh Letter* are contained in Hafner Library of Classics edition, *Aristotle: The Constitution of Athens and Related Texts* (New York: Hafner).
Xenophon, *Memorabilia*, Loeb Classical Library (Cambridge: Harvard University Press).

Chapter IV
Aristotle, *Politics*, Books I; II (Ch. 1–8, 10); III; IV; V (Ch. 9, 11); VI (Ch. 2–6).
Modern Library Edition (New York: Random House).
Everyman's Library (New York: Dutton).

OTHER RELEVANT WORKS:

Aristotle, *Nicomachean Ethics*, Gateway Edition (Chicago: Regnery), paperback.
Everyman's Library (New York: Dutton).
Loeb Classical Library (Cambridge: Harvard University Press).
Aristotle, *Metaphysics*.
Everyman's Library (New York: Dutton).

Chapter V

Cicero, *De Republica*, Books I (i–viii, xix–xlvii); II (ix–xvi, xxx–xxxiii).
De Legibus, Book I (v–xxviii).
Loeb Classical Library (Cambridge: Harvard University Press).

OTHER RELEVANT WORKS:

Lucretius, *De Rerum Natura* (a poetic account of Epicurus' doctrine).
Mentor Book (New York: New American Library), paperback.
Marcus Aurelius, *Meditations*.
Gateway Edition (Chicago: Regnery), paperback.
Epictetus, *Discourses*.
Loeb Classical Library (Cambridge: Harvard University Press).
Mentor Book (New York: New American Library), paperback.

Chapter VI

St. Augustine, *City of God*. Book XIX.
Modern Library Edition (New York: Random House).
Everyman's Library (New York: Dutton).
Hafner Library of Classics (New York: Hafner).

OTHER RELEVANT WORKS:

Seneca, *Epistulae Morales*.
Loeb Classical Library (Cambridge: Harvard University Press), 3 vols.

Chapter VII

No English translation of any of the works relevant to this chapter are readily available. Numerous excerpts from John of Paris' *De potestate regia et papali* are contained in John Courtney Murray's article "Contemporary Orientation of Catholic Thought on Church and State in the Light of History," *Cross Currents*, Fall, 1951.

Chapter VIII

St. Thomas Aquinas, *Treatise on Law* (Summa Theologica, I, II, Q. 90–97).
Gateway edition (Chicago: Regnery), paperback.
St. Thomas Aquinas, *On Kingship*, Book I.
(Toronto: Pontifical Institute of Medieval Studies).

Chapter IX

John Calvin, *Institutes of the Christian Religion*, Book IV, Ch. 20.
Contained in *John Calvin: On God and Political Duty* (New York: Library of Liberal Arts), paperback.

Chapter X

Machiavelli, *The Prince*, Chapters XIV–XVIII, XXV–XXVI.
    Gateway edition (Chicago: Regnery), paperback.
    Crofts Classics (New York: Appleton Century Crofts), paperback.
Machiavelli, *The Discourses*, Book I (Ch. 1–9, 20–35, 55–59).
    Modern Library Edition, *The Prince and the Discourses* (New York: Random House).

Chapter XI

Bodin, *Six Books of the Commonwealth*, Book I (Ch. 1–10).
    (Oxford: Blackwell).
Grotius, *Prolegomena*.
    (New York: Library of Liberal Arts), paperback.

Chapter XII

Hobbes, *Leviathan*, Chapters VI; XI; XIII–XV; XVII–XXVI.
    Gateway edition (Chicago: Regnery), paperback.
    (Oxford: Blackwell).
    Everyman's Library (New York: Dutton).

OTHER RELEVANT WORKS:

    Descartes, *A Discourse on Method*.
        (New York: Library of Liberal Arts), paperback.
        Everyman's Library (New York: Dutton).

Chapter XIII

Locke, *Second Treatise of Civil Government*, Chapters I–V; VII–XV; XIX.
    (New York: Library of Liberal Arts), paperback.
    (Oxford: Blackwell).
    Everyman's Library (New York: Dutton).

OTHER RELEVANT WORKS:

    Harrington, *The Commonwealth of Oceana*.
        Important sections are contained in *The Political Writings of James Harrington* (New York: Library of Liberal Arts), paperback.
    Filmer, *Patriarcha*.
        (Oxford: Blackwell).

Chapter XIV

Montesquieu, *The Spirit of the Laws*, Preface; Books I–III; XI; XII; XIV.
    Hafner Library of Classics (New York: Hafner).
Hume, *Political Essays* (New York: Library of Liberal Arts), paperback.

OTHER RELEVANT WORKS:

    Hume, *An Enquiry Concerning Human Understanding*.
        Gateway Edition (Chicago: Regnery), paperback.
        (New York: Library of Liberal Arts), paperback.
    Hume, *Essays, Moral and Political*.
        Selections are contained in *Hume's Moral and Political Philosophy* Hafner Library of Classics (New York: Hafner), paperback.

Chapter XV

Rosseau, *Social Contract*, Books I to III.
Everyman's Library (New York: Dutton).
Hafner Library of Classics (New York: Hafner), paperback.

Chapter XVI

Burke, *Reflections on the Revolution in France*, approximately first 50 pages.
Gateway edition (Chicago: Regnery), paperback.
Everyman's Library (New York: Dutton).

Chapter XVII

Bentham, *An Introduction to the Principles of Morals and Legislation*, Chapters I–VI; X; XI; XIV.
(Oxford: Blackwell).
Mill, *Considerations on Representative Government*, Chapter II.
Hafner Library of Classics (New York: Hafner), paperback.
Mill, *On Liberty*, Chapters I; II; IV.
Gateway edition (Chicago: Regnery), paperback.
Crofts Classics (New York: Appleton Century Crofts), paperback.
(New York: Library of Liberal Arts), paperback.
(Oxford: Blackwell), includes *Considerations on Representative Government*.
Everyman's Library (New York: Dutton), includes *Considerations on Representative Government*, and *Utilitarianism*.

Other Relevant Works:

Bentham, *A Fragment on Government*.
(Oxford: Blackwell), included in same edition as *An Introduction to the Principles of Morals and Legislation*.
James Mill, *An Essay on Government*.
(New York: Library of Liberal Arts), paperback.

Chapter XVIII

Kant, *Perpetual Peace*.
(New York: Library of Liberal Arts), paperback.
Hegel, *Philosophy of History*, Introduction.
(New York: Library of Liberal Arts), paperback.

Other Relevant Works:

Kant, *Critique of Pure Reason*.
Everyman's Library (New York: Dutton).
Kant, *Critique of Practical Reason*.
(New York: Library of Liberal Arts), paperback.
Kant, *Fundamental Principles of Metaphysics of Morals*.
(New York: Library of Liberal Arts), paperback.

Chapter XIX

Marx and Engel, *Communist Manifesto*.
    Crofts Classics (New York: Appleton Century Crofts), paperback.
    Gateway edition (Chicago: Regnery), paperback.

OTHER RELEVANT WORKS:

    Marx, *Das Kapital*.
    Modern Library Edition (New York: Random House).

Chapter XX

Lenin, *State and Revolution*, Chapters I; V.
    (New York: International Publishers), paperback.
Stalin, Problems of Leninism, Chapters I to VII.
    (New York: International Publishers), paperback.

Chapter XXI

Norman Thomas, *Democratic Socialism, A New Appraisal*.
    (New York: League for Industrial Democracy, 1953), pamphlet.

Chapter XXII

Alfredo Rocco, "The Political Doctrine of Fascism," *International Conciliation Pamphlet No. 233*, 1926.

Chapter XXIII

Max Weber, Chapters IV; VIII; IX in *From Max Weber: Essays in Sociology*, trans. by H. Gerth and C. Wright Mills.
    Galaxy Book (New York: Oxford University Press), paperback.

INDEX